Investment Treaty Law Current Issues

Volume V

The Regionalization of International Investment Treaty Arrangements

Edited by

N. Jansen Calamita and Mavluda Sattorova

British Institute of International and Comparative Law

Published and Distributed by
The British Institute of International and Comparative Law
Charles Clore House, 17 Russell Square, London WC1B 5JP

British Library Cataloguing in Publication Data
A Catalogue record of this book is available from the British Library

ISBN 978-1-905221-54-7

Typeset by Cambrian Typesetters
Camberley, Surrey
Printed in Great Britain by Polestar Wheatons Ltd
Cover design by Nick Clarke

Investment Treaty Law Current Issues

Volume V

The Regionalization of International Investment Treaty Arrangements

Contents

Editors' Preface

International investment treaty arrangements (IIAs) have emerged as the most dynamic and fast-evolving form of international agreements. Although IIAs—and bilateral investment treaties in particular—were signed in their thousands in the second half of the 20th century, they remained relatively obscure documents, often signed without much thought and seldom thought of again once agreed. It has only been in the 21st century that the power of these agreements has come to be appreciated more widely, and with that appreciation has come evolution and change.

This volume brings together the insights of leading scholars, practitioners and policy-makers about a particular feature of this ongoing development—regionalization. Whereas investment treaty arrangements were once the peculiar province of bilateral agreements and the *El Dorado* of multilateral negotiations, the past five years in particular have seen a rapid move towards the regionalization of investment treaty disciplines, whether as standalone investment treaties or as chapters in wider regional economic integration agreements. The papers in this volume are drawn originally from papers presented at a public meeting of the Investment Treaty Forum at the British Institute of International and Comparative Law (BIICL) held in London in September 2012. In addition to those papers, additional papers have been commissioned from leading legal, economic and political participants in the field. It is hoped that this volume will serve as a useful contribution to understanding the drivers of this move towards regionalism as well as its implications for international investment law more broadly.

This book is the fifth volume in the Investment Treaty Forum's periodic series on Current Issues in Investment Treaty Law. It is the product of a great deal of hard work, not only by the contributors, without whom it would not exist, but by a great many others as well. In particular, the editors wish to thank BIICL's Publications Editor Anna Riddell for her consistently assured management of the publications process, and her interns Natalia Spyridaki, Anna Lehane and Laura Hofmann for their assistance with collating and copyediting the contributions.

The Investment Treaty Forum will continue to explore the terrain of international investment law through its research and events. We are grateful to the Forum's members for their support and encourage new members, both corporate and individual, to join the Forum.

N Jansen Calamita and Mavluda Sattorova
London, 20 June 2014

About the Investment Treaty Forum

The Investment Treaty Forum is a special project of the British Institute of International and Comparative Law (BIICL) begun in 2004. The Forum builds upon BIICL's expertise in public international law for the purpose of carrying out applied research and analysis in the increasingly complex field of international investment law. In addition, the Forum facilitates dialogue and serious debate among lawyers, senior business managers, policy advisers, academics, and government officials. Like BIICL itself, the Forum enjoys a reputation for independence, even-handedness and academic rigour.

The Investment Treaty Forum is supported by its members, drawn from among the leading participants in the field of international investment law. Further information about membership in the Investment Treaty Forum and the Forum's work is available at: www.biicl.org.

Foreword

Anna Joubin-Bret[1]

Treaty-watchers, not unlike bird-watchers, like to put a name on the species they are patiently following and finally spotting. They look for patterns, for similarities that fit established categories. That is, until a hybrid or an entirely new species emerges that bears some similarities with its family but is yet a different creature.

For keen investment treaty-watchers, it had become difficult to identify a pattern in the complicated and atomized network of investment treaties, particularly when looking for a regional dimension and establishing regional trends. After a period of strong momentum in the 1970s when many regional organizations were established, with the purpose of fostering closer economic integration,[2] regional investment negotiations became largely overshadowed by the explosion of bilateral investment treaties (BITs) in the 1990s and early 2000s and the priority given to cementing multilateral trade rules. However, the negotiation of BITs has been slowing down significantly for several years now, and efforts to establish multilateral investment rules have stalled, and the pendulum is swinging back towards the regional level with the growth of Regional Trade and Investment Agreements (RTIAs) and Free Trade Agreements (FTAs) with investment chapters, and the emergence of a new species: the trans-regional or mega-regional treaty, which brings together not just the countries of a single region, but multiple regions of the globe.

The chapters in this volume are revised and updated versions of papers originally presented at a public meeting of the Investment Treaty Forum (ITF) convened in London in September 2012 by ITF Director, N. Jansen Calamita. The timing of that conference, and of this subsequent volume, could not have been better. Investment treaty-making practice is at a watershed moment. The chapters of this volume take stock of recent developments in regional investment treaties, identify patterns and trends, and analyse the latest generation of investment treaty negotiations—the mega-regionals—with respect to their scope, their format, and their membership.

[1] Avocat à la Cour, Paris (France).

[2] See in this volume the insightful discussion by George Burn about the 'rediscovery' of the Agreement for the Promotion, Protection and Guarantee of Investments Among Member States of the Organization of the Islamic Conference, Chapter 7.

These contributions, drawn from leading international experts in law, economics and international relations, offer readers a unique, interdisciplinary perspective about what is driving this new regionalism, how these agreements are forming the basis for the emergence of trans-regional treaties, and the implications of these developments for the investment treaty regime as a whole. The issues addressed in this book are of interest and use to anyone wishing to understand how the global regulation of international investment is developing.

* * *

The rich contributions to this volume demonstrate the complexity of the present and emerging regime for the protection and regulation of international investment. Taken as a whole, three key observations emerge from the pages which follow.

1. Free-Trade Agreements containing investment chapters are on the rise

A clear trend in investment rule-making is the replacement of BITs by FTAs. As chronicled by Hamed El-Kady in his analysis of the current state of the investment treaty regime,[3] the negotiation of broad Free Trade Agreements (FTAs) containing chapters on trade disciplines, customs treatment, rules of origin, intellectual property and public procurement etc, together with rules covering substantive investment protection and liberalization, is on a steady rise as the number of BITs under negotiation slows. The drivers of this development appear to be varied. For many countries, such as Chile for example, the cost-to-benefit ratio of negotiation time and resources is seen to be better served by pursuing broader scoped agreements than focusing on agreements solely addressed to investment. For other states, FTAs better serve the political purpose of legalizing deeper economic integration, which is what one sees in the treaty practice of the United States, Canada and a majority of Asian and Latin American countries that are following the so-called 'North American' approach. Moreover, with respect to Europe in particular, now that the European Union has competence for negotiating treaties covering foreign direct investment—where it once only had competence for matters of trade—the EU has made clear its priority to negotiate treaties of the broad FTA-style, rather than treaties simply focused on investment.

FTAs are not the same as regional agreements of course. What characterizes FTAs is the breadth of their scope and coverage, not the geographical scope of their application. Indeed, the majority of FTAs with investment

[3] Chapter 2.

chapters concluded so far are bilateral in their membership, with some notable exceptions, such as the North American Free Trade Agreement (NAFTA) and the United States-Central America-Dominican Republic FTA (DR-CAFTA).[4] As the chapters herein reveal, however, they constitute the template for the negotiation of the emerging regional and mega-regional treaties covering investment.

2. *Regional Investment Integration through Regional Trade and Investment Agreements (RTIAs) is moving at an accelerated pace*

Historically, regional economic integration has been more successful in trade than in investment. As analyzed by Stephen Woolcock,[5] while States have signed up to numerous regional trade agreements addressing trade disciplines in goods and services, the numbers of these agreements which include provisions on investment (the so-called RTIAs) has historically been low. Investment cooperation has not necessarily followed the path of other forms of regional economic integration. In some regions, there have been exceptions, of course, such as the 1994 NAFTA and the 2004 DR-CAFTA, but in general it has taken longer for states to act regionally on investment. That, however, is changing. Overwhelmingly, states in regions across the globe are negotiating and agreeing disciplines on investment by either consolidating, revising or creating new dimensions to regional commitments on economic integration.

However, as the chapters in this volume demonstrate, discerning patterns in this global push towards regionalism is difficult. States continue to surprise with the heterogeneity of their agreements and initiatives, both in terms of substance and structure. In Asia, for example, as examined by Myrna Austria,[6] the Association of Southeast Asian Nations (ASEAN)[7] is at the eve of its full economic integration in 2015 and has been actively negotiating so-called ASEAN-plus agreements with other States and regional groupings of States, including, most recently, a Regional Comprehensive Economic Partnership (RCEP). While the ASEAN approach builds upon the foundations of a long-existing organization for regional cooperation, and the treaties being negotiated by ASEAN resemble in many ways the approach to RTIAs seen in other regions, elsewhere in the world different approaches are taking

[4] The DR-CAFTA is among five Central American countries (Costa Rica, El Salvador, Guatemala, Honduras, and Nicaragua), the Dominican Republic, and the United States.

[5] Chapter 3.

[6] Chapter 4.

[7] ASEAN is comprised of Brunei, Cambodia, Indonesia, Laos Malaysia, Myanmar, the Philippines, Singapore, Thailand, and Vietnam.

shape. In Africa, for example, the COMESA[8] and SADC[9] regions are moving forward at varying paces in a part of the world where regional integration is growing but still relatively nascent when compared to regions like Asia. As analyzed by Dirk te Velde and Themba Munalula,[10] while the benefits of economic integration in COMESA appear compelling, five years on from its signature the Investment Agreement for the COMESA Common Investment Area (CCIA) is yet to come into force, while more recently, and with a more modest model bilateral investment treaty, the SADC countries have moved closer to having their own internal rules on investment and thereby a regional investment framework. What works in one region will not necessarily work in another.

Learning from past experiences and gathering political support for objectives is essential. In Central and Latin America, for example, early efforts to negotiate investment rules on a regional level bore no fruit: attempts such as the Free Trade Area of the Americas (the FTAA), the investment rules in the Andean Community,[11] investment protection within Mercosur,[12] and investment integration in SIECA[13] were inconclusive, and the conclusion of the DR-CAFTA relied upon the impetus of US involvement. But initiatives to address investment rules regionally continue in Latin America, including those examined by José Manuel García Represa[14] among the States of ALBA[15] and UNASUR[16] to establish new regional mechanisms and new regional rules to address investment protection and, potentially, replace the investment treaties of the States within those groupings (not only amongst themselves but with third States as

[8] COMESA is the Common Market for Eastern and Southern Africa, comprised of Burundi, Comoros, Democratic Republic of Congo, Djibouti, Egypt, Eritrea, Ethiopia, Kenya, Libya, Madagascar, Malawi, Mauritius, Rwanda, Seychelles, Sudan, Swaziland, Uganda, Zambia, and Zimbabwe.

[9] SADC is the Southern African Development Community, comprised of Angola, Botswana, Democratic Republic of Congo, Lesotho, Madagascar, Malawi, Mauritius, Mozambique, Namibia, Seychelles, South Africa, Swaziland, Tanzania, Zambia, and Zimbabwe.

[10] Chapter 6.

[11] Bolivia, Columbia, Ecuador and Peru.

[12] *Mercado Común del Sur*. The five full members of Mercosur are Argentina, Bolivia, Brazil, Paraguay, Uruguay, Venezuela. There are also six 'associated' members.

[13] *Secretaría de Integración Económica Centroamericana*

[14] Chapter 9.

[15] Bolivarian Alliance for the Peoples of Our America ('*Alianza Bolivariana para los Pueblos de Nuestra América*', also known as the '*Alternativa Bolivariana para las Américas*' or 'ALBA': Antigua and Barbuda, Bolivia, Cuba, Dominica, Ecuador, Nicaragua, Saint Lucia, St. Vincent and the Grenadines, and Venezuela.

[16] Union of South American Nations ('*Unión de Naciones Sudamericanas*'): Argentina, Bolivia, Brazil, Chile, Colombia, Ecuador, Guyana, Paraguay, Perú, Suriname, Uruguay, Venezuela.

well). In the Caribbean, on the other hand, as Chantal Ononaiwu explains,[17] the States of the Caribbean Community (CARICOM)[18] have taken a rather different approach through the creation of an investment code designed to harmonize the treatment of investment into the region, while continuing to negotiate with particular third States for specialized rules in preferential trade and investment agreements.

With these developments and initiatives come new challenges. In his contribution, Hi-Taek Shin goes to the roots of regionalism, attempting to give order to regional developments by identifying three distinct approaches that have emerged in recent initiatives on investment and raising the question as to whether regionalism is likely to lead to a more or less level playing field for investors of different nationalities.[19] Co-editor of this volume, Mavluda Sattorova, in her chapter addresses the role played by local and regional preferences, capacities and idiosyncrasies on the way regional agreements deal with regulatory flexibility provisions, questioning the role of universality and regional diversity in setting investment rules.[20]

3. *Regional Investment Cooperation is moving beyond geographical and geopolitical regions*

Going into the future, the pertinent dimension of international investment negotiations in the absence of multilateral rules on investment (which continue to seem far off) appears to be trans-regional or mega-regional. As discussed in insightful contributions by Julian Chaisse,[21] James Mendenhall[22] and Stephen Woolcock,[23] since 2011, a number of high-profile negotiations have been opened for trans-regional trade and investment agreements, such as the Trans-Pacific Partnership (TPP), the Transatlantic Trade and Investment Partnership (TTIP), and Regional Comprehensive Economic Partnership (RCEP) in Asia. As with the move towards regionalism more generally, the drivers for these mega-regional negotiations vary from State to State but do seem to share the central commonality of a political conclusion that in a global marketplace for investment and trade, and with the rise of China as a world leading economy, agreements based simply on physical

[17] Chapter 8.

[18] Antigua and Barbuda, the Bahamas, Barbados, Belize, Dominica, Grenada, Guyana, Haiti, Jamaica, Montserrat, Saint Lucia, St. Kitts and Nevis, St. Vincent and the Grenadines, Suriname, and Trinidad and Tobago.

[19] Chapter 1.

[20] Chapter 11.

[21] Chapter 5.

[22] Chapter 10.

[23] Chapter 3.

geography are not enough to ensure competitiveness. Looking at these proposed trans-regional treaties in the round, and their scope and detail, it is fair to suggest that if these treaties are concluded, these mega-regional agreements could become the cornerstone of the international investment framework for years, if not decades, to come.

1

The Regionalization of Investment Treaty Arrangements: Development and Implications

*Hi-Taek Shin**

I. INTRODUCTION

Major economies in the world are increasingly incorporating their international investment agreements into regional integration arrangements or preferential trade agreements, in particular, free trade agreements (FTAs). The 2012 UNCTAD World Investment Report observed that quantitatively, 'bilateral agreements still dominate international investment policy-making; however, in terms of economic significance, there has been a gradual shift towards regionalism.'[1] Strong regional initiatives are noticeable in almost all regions including Africa, Asia, Europe, and North, Central and South Americas.

International investment law lacks a multilateral framework like the World Trade Organization (WTO) and is an inherently fragmented system comprised of more than 3,000 bilateral and regional arrangements.[2] The

* Professor of Law, Seoul National University School of Law, htshin@snu.ac.kr. The theme of this paper was delivered in a keynote speech at the Nineteenth Investment Treaty Forum Public Conference: The Regionalization of Investment Treaty Arrangements: Developments and Implications, British Institute of International and Comparative Law, held on 14 September 2012 in London. Research for this article was supported by the fund from the Law Research Institute of Seoul National University. The author thanks Julie A. Kim for her invaluable assistance in preparing this paper.

[1] United Nations Conference on Trade and Development, 'World Investment Report 2012: Towards a New Generation of Investment Policies' (5 July 2012) UN Doc UNCTAD/WIR/2012 84.

[2] By the end of 2011, the overall number of international investment agreements consisted of 3,164 agreements, which included 2,833 bilateral investment treaties and 331 'other IIAs including free trade agreements or economic partnership agreements containing investment provisions,' ibid.

current trend of the regionalization of international investment arrangements, amid the intense web of existing bilateral investment treaties (BITs), will lead to a system of multi-layered international investment rules further adding to the complexity of international investment law. Views differ widely from an optimistic one seeing this trend as a stepping stone towards a more coherent harmonization which might lead to a multilateral set of investment rules to a pessimist view perceiving this trend as 'another type of noodles in the spaghetti bowl'.[3]

This paper is divided into two parts. The first part will provide an overview of the three distinctive approaches that have emerged in recent regional initiatives on international investment arrangements. The second part will discuss the implications and challenges of these approaches with respect to the level playing field of investors of different nationalities, the achievement of which has been one of the core objectives of international investment law by use of the most-favored-nation (MFN) treatment clause in BITs.

II. OVERVIEW OF RECENT REGIONAL INVESTMENT INITIATIVES

While the word 'regionalism' or 'regional investment agreement' is commonly used, it is a vague term that refers to many different agreements or arrangements made in many different contexts or frameworks. In this paper, regional investment agreements or arrangements will refer to any one of the following three phenomena discernible in recent developments. The first has been the conclusion of an investment agreement adopted by or placed within the framework of a regional integration organization. The second trend involves the apparent proliferation of investment agreements or rules negotiated and concluded as an integral part of preferential trade and investment agreements (PTIAs) as seen particularly in FTAs. Thirdly, regional integration organizations have been negotiating and concluding PTIAs or FTAs containing investment liberalization and/or protection provisions at the regional level with a non-member country. This phenomenon is intrinsically related to the second trend.

(1) Regional Investment Agreements in the Framework of Regional Economic Integration

Regional initiatives on investment rules are not new. Ever since multilateral efforts to establish the International Trade Organization failed, various

[3] A Joubin-Bret, 'Preferential Trade and Investment Agreements and Regionalism: A Stepping-stone towards a Multilateral Set of Investment Rules or Another Type of Noodles in the Spaghetti Bowl?' (forthcoming).

regional efforts have been made to define investment rules in the context of regional integration or cooperation. A prime example of successful regional integration that includes investment rules is the European Economic Community which has gradually expanded to become the European Union (EU). The success of the EU has inspired other regions to seek regional integration and cooperation, though with differing degrees of integration, institutionalization, and successes. The objectives and the depth of the regional integration differs by region to adjust for the particular needs of member countries determined by the political, social, historical, and economic factors prevalent in the region. As a consequence, the priority given to an investment agenda by such regional integration initiatives, as well as the level of commitment by member states with respect to implementation, varies significantly.

In the past several decades, there were waves of initiatives to establish a regional investment agreement in the framework of regional integration by Arab countries. For instance, the Agreement on Investment and Free Movement of Arab Capital Among Arab Countries concluded by the member states of the Agreement of Arab Economic Unity in 1970 is one of the early initiatives.[4] The Arab states concluded another regional investment agreement titled the Unified Agreement for the Investment of Arab Capital ("Unified Agreement") that entered into force on 7 September 1981.[5] It included provisions on the standard of treatment for investors, guarantee of free transfers, protection against expropriatory measures and compensation, and detailed provisions on the settlement of investment disputes, including international arbitration and recourse to the Arab Investment Court.[6] However, according to a report by the Organisation for Economic Cooperation and Development (OECD), these instruments have not been effectively implemented or are even unknown by investors.[7]

A well-known example of earlier regional initiatives in Latin America was the effort made in the framework of the Andean Pact aimed to formulate

---

[4] The League of Arab States signed the Agreement of Arab Economic Unity in 1957, which entered into force in 1964. It envisioned a framework for achieving Arab economic unity in stages from free trade area, customs union, common market, economic union, and, finally, complete economic integration. SA Sakr, 'Economic Integration and Co-operation among the Arab Countries' in *Liaison Bulletin Between Development Research and Training Institutes: Inter-Regional Cooperation in the Social Sciences for Development* (OECD Publishing, 1980) 107.

[5] Unified Agreement for the Investment of Arab Capital in the Arab States, 26 November 1980, <http://unctad.org/sections/dite/iia/docs/Compendium//en/36%20volume%202.pdf> ['Unified Agreement'].

[6] Ibid chs II & VI.

[7] Draft note from the MENA–OECD Working Group on Investment Policies and Promotion, 'Strengthening Regional Investment Frameworks in the MENA Region' (Paris 15–16 December 2010) para 10 <http://www.oecd.org/mena/investment/46581975.pdf>. The Arab Investment Court, which was instituted by the Unified Agreement, has settled only one case as of 2010, ibid para 11.

within the region a common policy on foreign investment.[8] The Commission created under the Andean Pact adopted Decision 24, or more commonly known as the Andean Investment Code, to control the negative effects of foreign investment through a common regime applicable to the member countries.[9] Another ambitious regional investment regime in Latin America was formulated by the Member States of the Common Market of the Southern Cone (Mercosur).[10] In 1994, Mercosur Member States concluded two regional investment agreements as protocols to the Treaty of Asuncion: the Protocol of Colonia for the Promotion and Reciprocal Protection of Investments in Mercosur and the Protocol of Buenos Aires for the Promotion and Reciprocal Protection of Investments Coming from Non-Mercosur State Parties. The former defines the rights enjoyed by investors from a Member State making investments in other Member States, while the latter outlines the general legal principles to be applied by a Member State to investments coming from non-Member States. However, as of the end of 2012, these two investment agreements have not entered into force due to Member States' failure to ratify the protocols. Another initiative, albeit less ambitious, is the Asia–Pacific Economic Cooperation (APEC) Non-Binding Investment Principles[11] made in the spirit of APEC's open regionalism and adopted in 1994 by the APEC member countries. While the principles are non-binding, they are commendable for taking a liberal position on issues important to the promotion of investment such as non-discrimination, national treatment, investment incentives, expropriation and compensation, repatriation and convertibility, and the settlement of disputes.

Compared to the foregoing early efforts which have not been effectively implemented or implemented at all, recent regional investment agreements concluded in the framework of the Association of Southeast Asian Nations

---

[8] The Andean Pact was created by the Cartagena Agreement and adopted on 26 May 1969 by Bolivia, Chile, Colombia, Ecuador and Peru with the purpose of the establishment of a customs union. Venezuela joined later in 1973.

[9] The Andean Investment Code took effect on 30 June 1971. Subsequent decisions of the Commission indicated that there had been a shift in perspective of the member states on investment policy over a period of time. Decision 24 of 1973 Cartagena Agreement (1977), 16 ILM 138, was later replaced by Decision 220 of 1987 of the Commission of the Andean Pact (1988), 27 ILM 974, which dismantled the uniform restrictive policy towards foreign investment and technology imposed by the supplanted Decision 24. In Decision 291 of 1991 of the Commission of the Andean Pact (1991), 30 ILM 1283, the member countries agreed to adopt a more friendly investment regime for foreign investors.

[10] Mercosur was created by the Treaty of Asuncion and signed on 26 March 1991 by the founding members, Argentina, Brazil, Paraguay, and Uruguay, with the objective to establish a common market promoting a common investment policy.

[11] APEC Non-Binding Investment Principles was adopted in November 1994, <http://www.apec.org/Press/News-Releases/2010/~/media/965E37FDA6D848B4A0350D68D2A4BE1C.ashx>.

(ASEAN)[12] and the Common Market for Eastern and Southern Africa (COMESA)[13] deserve careful attention as they might be viewed as exemplary models for creating investment rules in regional integration organizations in the developing world. Both the ASEAN and COMESA investment agreements are based on a vision of establishing a common market among Member States and a common recognition of the need to have a liberal and transparent investment regime and improved protection of investors and investments to attract higher and sustainable levels of direct investment flows into the region. Both agreements comprehensively address issues of concern to investors which are typically dealt within the BITs pursued by capital exporting developed countries. The difference between the two regional investment agreements is that while the ASEAN investment agreement is a product of evolution over a long period of time and based upon the proven record of implementation of earlier ASEAN agreements, the COMESA agreement does not share this background and the its level of implementation is not at all certain at this stage. Nonetheless, some of the salient features of these agreements are worth highlighting.

The ASEAN Member States concluded the ASEAN Agreement for the Promotion and Protection of Investments,[14] the first ASEAN regional investment agreement in 1987, and the Framework Agreement on the ASEAN Investment Area in 1998.[15] These two investment agreements reflected the recognition by ASEAN Member States of the strategic importance of foreign investment for development. ASEAN countries decided to consolidate and upgrade the two agreements into the ASEAN Comprehensive Investment Agreement (ACIA)[16] which was signed in 2009 and entered into force in

[12] ASEAN was established in 1967 with the signing of the ASEAN Declaration by five founding Member States, namely Indonesia, Malaysia, Philippines, Singapore and Thailand. Brunei Darussalam, Viet Nam, Lao PDR, Myanmar, and Cambodia have joined over the years. With the ASEAN Chapter having entered into force in 2008, it is now operating under a more institutionalized legal framework. For an overview of ASEAN: <http://www.asean.org/asean/about-asean/overview>.

[13] The treaty establishing COMESA was signed on 5 November 1993 and entered into force on 8 December 1994, with an objective to create a common market in Eastern and Southern Africa. As of the end of 2012, COMESA has 19 Member States. Treaty Establishing the Common Market for the Eastern and Southern Africa, November 5, 1993, 33 ILM 1067 (1994) <http://vi.unctad.org/files/wksp/iiawksp08/docs/wednesday/Exercise%20Materials/invagreecomesa.pdf> ['COMESA Investment Agreement'].

[14] The ASEAN Agreement for the Promotion and Protection of Investments of 1987, 27 ILM 612 (1988).

[15] Framework Agreement on the ASEAN Investment Area <http://www.asean.org/images/2012/Economic/AIA/other_document/Framework%20Agreement%20on%20the%20ASEAN%20Investment%20Area.pdf>.

[16] ASEAN Comprehensive Investment Agreement, 26 February 2009 <http://cil.nus.edu.sg/rp/pdf/2009%20ASEAN%20Comprehensive%20Investment%20Agreement-pdf.pdf> ['ACIA'].

2012. The ACIA is intended to be 'forward-looking, with improved features and provisions, comparable to international best practices in order to increase intra-ASEAN investments and to enhance ASEAN's competitiveness in attracting inward investments into ASEAN.'[17] The objective of the ACIA is 'to create a free and open investment regime in ASEAN in order to achieve the end goal of economic integration' through progressive liberalization of the investment regimes of Member States, provision of enhanced protection to investors and their investment, improvement of transparency and predictability of investment rules, regulations and procedures and cooperation to create favorable conditions for investment.[18]

The ACIA contains comprehensive investment provisions on liberalization, promotion, facilitation and protection of investments into and within ASEAN. In particular, it has provisions on national treatment, MFN treatment, fair and equitable treatment, full protection and security, expropriation and compensation, prohibition of performance requirements, and resolution of dispute between an investor and a Member State through an international arbitration.[19] At the same time, the ACIA has a number of balancing provisions in order to guard the Member States' regulatory flexibility such as measures to safeguard the balance of payments, broadly termed general exceptions, and self-judging security exceptions.[20] For instance, reflecting the experience in the Asian financial crisis, in the event of serious balance-of-payments and external financial difficulties or threat thereof, the ACIA allows a Member State to adopt or maintain restrictions on payments or transfers related to investments, subject to certain provisos, including that the restrictions be consistent with the Articles of Agreement of the International Monetary Fund (IMF). In addition to the usual exceptions on public order or safety and health related exceptions, under the general exceptions clause,[21] a Member State is allowed to adopt or enforce measures (i) necessary to secure compliance with laws or regulations including those relating to the prevention of deceptive and fraudulent practices to deal with the effects of a default on a contract and the protection of the privacy of individuals in relation to the processing and dissemination of personal data and the protection of confidentiality of individual records and accounts, and safety, (ii) aimed at ensuring the equitable or effective imposition

[17] ACIA pmbl.

[18] ACIA art 1.

[19] For instance, art 5 (National Treatment), art 6 (Most-Favored-Nation Treatment), art 7 (Prohibition of Performance Requirements), art 11 (Treatment of Investment), art 14 (Expropriation and Compensation) and Section B (Investment Dispute Between an Investor and a Member State). National treatment is accorded with respect to admission, establishment, acquisition and expansion in addition to management, conduct, operation and sale or other aspect of business activities.

[20] ACIA art 18 (Security Exceptions).

[21] ACIA art 17 (General Exceptions).

or collection of direct taxes, (iii) imposed for the protection of national treasures of artistic, historic or archaeological value, and (iv) relating to the conservation of exhaustible natural resources if such measures are made effective in conjunction with restrictions on domestic production or consumption.

In 2007, Member States of the COMESA adopted the Investment Agreement for the COMESA Common Investment Area (COMESA Investment Agreement).[22] This Agreement was entered into with recognition that foreign direct investment is an important source of finance for sustaining the pace of economic, industrial, infrastructure, and technology development and that Member States would need to attract a higher and sustainable level of investment flows in COMESA. At the same time, the COMESA Member States took into account that pressures on the balance of payments of a Member State in the process of economic development or economic transition may necessitate the use of restrictions to ensure the maintenance of a level of financial reserves adequate for the implementation of its economic development or economic transition plans.[23] Thus, the stated objectives of COMESA Investment Agreement include the desire (i) to establish a competitive COMESA Common Investment Area with a more liberal and transparent investment environment in order to substantially increase the free flow of investment into COMESA from both COMESA and non-COMESA sources, and gradually eliminate investment restrictions and conditions which may impede investment flows and the operation of investment projects in COMESA and (ii) to provide COMESA investors with certain rights in the conduct of their business within an overall balance of rights and obligations between investors and Member States.[24]

While the COMESA Investment Agreement embodies the typical standards of treatment for investors commonly seen in BITs,[25] the balance is apparently tilted in favor of the Host States. For example, Article 14(1) states that 'Member States shall accord fair and equitable treatment to COMESA investors and their investments, in accordance with customary international law.' Stating the understanding of the parties that 'different Member States have different forms of administrative, legislative and judicial systems and that Member States at different levels of development may not achieve the

---

22 COMESA Investment Agreement (n 13).

23 Ibid pmbl.

24 Ibid arts 2 & 11.

25 The protection accorded to investors includes fair and equitable treatment, transfer of assets, national treatment and MFN treatment, expropriation and compensation, and investor-State arbitration mechanism allowing various arbitration options to investors including ICSID arbitration or ad hoc arbitration under UNCITRAL Arbitration Rules. *See* COMESA Investment Agreement, n 13, art 14 (Fair and Equitable Treatment), art 15 (Transfer of Assets), art 17 (National Treatment), art 19 (Most-Favored-Nation Treatment), art 20 (Expropriation) and art 28 (Investor-State Disputes).

same standards at the same time,' Article 14(3) adds that the fair and equitable treatment in Article 14(1) does 'not establish a single international standard in this context.' As in ACIA, the COMESA Investment Agreement attempts to reserve substantial regulatory flexibility by providing for multiple exceptions including general exceptions, special treatment of tax measures, emergency safeguard measures, measures to safeguard balance of payments.[26]

As indicated earlier, ACIA and the COMESA Investment Agreement are significant. Both of these regional investment agreements among developing countries recognise the importance of foreign investment and consequently attempt to address comprehensively the usual concerns of foreign investors by providing substantive rights and dispute settlement procedures, including resort to investor-State arbitrations in an international forum. In that sense, we might view these agreements as being liberal and forward-looking with a high level of sophistication. On the other side, however, the contents of the substantive treatment standards and the scope and nature of the exceptions carved out in both of these arrangements reflect the growing desire of the developing world to preserve substantial leeway for government measures to meet the future socio-economic needs of the country and to tailor the standards to fit the current level of development. Thus, despite their generally liberal nature, in this regard these regional efforts represent an investment policy direction diverging from the standard historically pursued by the United States and European capital exporting countries in international investment agreements.

(2) Proliferation of Investment Agreements as an Integral Part of FTAs

Another prominent phenomenon is the increasing number of investment agreements that are being framed as integral parts of the FTAs creating free trade areas. Due to the lack of progress in multilateral trade negotiations in the Doha round, major economies have recently shifted their priorities towards negotiating regional or bilateral FTAs covering a broad range of objectives. Typically, the scope of FTAs has come to cover issues such as market access for trade in services, investment liberalization, investment protection, intellectual property, competition policy coordination, and sustainable development in addition to the core issues traditionally included in the preferential trade agreements. A substantial number of them are bilateral FTAs between trading partners of variable geographic proximity. Others are between regional economic integration organisations and individual trading partner countries. As the same country enters into multiple bilateral FTAs

[26] Ibid art 22 (General Exceptions), art 23 (Non-Application to Taxation Measures), art 24 (Emergency Safeguard Measures) and art 25 (Measures to Safeguard Balance of Payments).

with its trading partners, the free trade areas thus created may become linked together through the complementary functions of trade and investment and by the application of MFN treatment provisions. Those multiple and concurrent bilateral FTAs thus come to create a 'region' of free trade areas even if the parties to the FTAs are not necessarily in the same region in a geographical sense. For instance, Korea has FTAs with both the EU and the United States. An EU investor may consider locating manufacturing facilities in Korea rather than in China for products to be exported to the United States to get the benefits of the Korea-US FTA if tariff savings through the FTA and other factors overweigh the difference in the cost of production between China and Korea.

The United States has been at the forefront of pursuing regional and bilateral FTAs. The North American Free Trade Agreement between the United States, Canada, and Mexico (NAFTA) entered into force in 1994 and began an important trend in state practice by including a comprehensive investment chapter in the framework of the preferential trade agreement based upon the model BIT of the United States.[27] Earlier FTAs entered into by the US with trading partners like Israel had not addressed investment issues. Chapter 11 of the NAFTA contains detailed provisions on investment liberalization commitments by providing national treatment and MFN treatment provisions with respect to the right of establishment and acquisition of investments, a full array of investment protection and treatment standards, and a detailed investor-State arbitration mechanism.[28] Reflecting the experience of defending investors' claims brought under the NAFTA, the United States developed the 2004 model BIT in an effort to guard its sovereign right to regulate against the possibility of expansive interpretation of standards of treatment by arbitral tribunals.[29] In subsequent FTAs, the United States has pursued the practice of including an independent, full-fledged chapter on investment.[30] In addition to the NAFTA, the United States has concluded a regional FTA with five Central American countries (Costa Rica, El Salvador, Guatemala, Honduras, and Nicaragua) and the Dominican Republic in 2004 (CAFTA-DR FTA). Twelve bilateral FTAs are in force between the United States and major trading partners such as Singapore, Chile, Australia, Peru and Korea.[31]

---

[27] For a history of the BITs entered into by the United States and the development of model BIT negotiating texts, see K J Vandevelde, *US International Investment Agreements* (OUP 2009) 2.

[28] See ch11 (Investment) of NAFTA, 17 December 1992, US–Canada–Mexico, 32 ILM 605 (1993).

[29] Vandevelde (n 27) 91.

[30] As of end of 2012, the United States has 14 FTAs in force with 20 countries. For more information, see USTR, Free Trade Agreements <http://www.ustr.gov/trade-agreements/free-trade-agreements>.

[31] Ibid.

Moreover, a substantial number of recent regional or bilateral FTAs negotiated and concluded by other countries have tended to follow the NAFTA model and include comprehensive investment rules. A recent example of such FTAs is the Mexico-Central America FTA which was signed between Mexico and the Central American countries in November 2011.[32] Upon entry into force, the FTA will replace the bilateral FTAs Mexico had entered into with Costa Rica, Nicaragua, and the Northern Triangle (El Salvador, Guatemala, and Honduras). Mexico[33] is actively pursuing similarly arranged FTAs with other trading partners, as is Canada.[34]

Major emerging economies such as Korea, China, Singapore, and India also are pursuing FTAs that include investment rules to greater or lesser degree. For instance, by the end of 2012, Korea had eight FTAs in force with the United States, the EU, Singapore, ASEAN, Chile, India, Peru, and EFTA.[35] As the list shows, Korea's FTA partners are not limited to developed countries. With the exception of the FTAs with European parties, all FTAs concluded by Korea contain a full-fledged chapter on investment containing investment liberalization and protection provisions. A notable development in this regard is the conclusion of the trilateral investment agreement between Korea, China, and Japan in May 2012.[36] While it is a stand-alone tri-party investment agreement at the moment, it is intended to act as the first step towards a tripartite FTA, the negotiation of which was officially declared in November 2012. It is the very first visible outcome of the regional economic integration initiative among the three far eastern economies. When the trilateral investment agreement goes into effect after the completion of the ratification procedures by the parties, it will coexist with the existing BITs between China–Japan, Japan–Korea, and Korea–China, allowing the investor to rely upon existing BITs should the investor consider them to be more favorable than the trilateral agreement.[37]

Elsewhere in Asia, Singapore has entered into FTAs with Australia, China, Jordan, India, Japan, Korea, New Zealand, Panama, Peru, EFTA, and the

[32] OAS, Foreign Trade Information System, Background and Negotiations on the Central America Countries–Mexico <http://www.sice.oas.org/TPD/CACM_MEX/CACM_MEX_e.asp>.

[33] See M Angeles Villarreal (CRS Report for Congress), 'Mexico's Free Trade Agreements' <http://www.fas.org/sgp/crs/row/R40784.pdf>.

[34] For a current status of Canadian FTAs, see Foreign Affairs and International Trade Canada, Free Trade Agreements <http://www.international.gc.ca/trade-agreements-accords-commerciaux/agr-acc/index.aspx?lang=en&view=d>.

[35] For further details, see the Ministry of Foreign Affairs and Trade, FTA Status of ROK, <http://www.mofat.go.kr/ENG/policy/fta/status/overview/index.jsp?menu=m_20_80_10>.

[36] Agreement Among the Government of Japan, the Government of the Republic of Korea and the Government of the People's Republic of China for the Promotion, Facilitation and Protection of Investment (Japan–Korea–China) (13 May 2012) <http://www.mofa.go.jp/announce/announce/2012/5/pdfs/0513_01_01.pdf> ['Trilateral Investment Agreement'].

[37] Ibid, art 25 (Relation to Other Agreements) & note to art 25.

United States. It is negotiating FTAs with Canada, Mexico, Pakistan, Ukraine, and the EU and is also participating in the on-going negotiations of the Trans-Pacific Strategic Economic Partnership Agreement.[38] China is also very active with seven FTAs in force with Pakistan, Chile, New Zealand, Singapore, Peru, Costa Rica, and ASEAN. FTAs with the Gulf Cooperation Council, Australia, Iceland, Norway and the Southern African Customs Union (SACU) are also under negotiation.[39] India is also pursuing negotiations of the Comprehensive Economic Partnership Agreement (CEPA), which is the Indian version of FTAs.[40] Although these emerging economies pursue FTAs containing investment rules, the contents differ significantly depending upon their respective positions as sources or destinations of foreign investment. As Korea has successfully transformed into a net capital exporter, it in general seeks a high standard of protection. On the other hand, China, still being a net capital-importer, is rather cautious in accepting high standards of protection and continues not to agree to grant national treatment with respect to establishment and acquisition of investment.

Among the initiatives in pursuing investment rules as a part of a FTA, two recent developments have the potential to substantially impact the future direction of the international investment law community: the on-going negotiations of the Trans-Pacific Partnership Agreement (TPP), currently being negotiated among 12 countries in the Pacific Rim including the United States[41] and the launch of negotiations for the Transatlantic Trade and Investment Partnership (TTIP).[42]

---

[38] See the International Enterprise Singapore, Singapore FTAs <http://www.fta.gov.sg/sg_fta.asp>.

[39] See Ministry of Commerce of the People's Republic of China, China FTA Network <http://fta.mofcom.gov.cn/english/index.shtml>.

[40] For the status of India's preferential trade agreements, see Ministry of Commerce & Industry, International Trade <http://www.commerce.nic.in/trade/international_ta.asp?id=2&trade=i>.

[41] The first round of the TPP negotiation began in Melbourne, Australia in March 2010 among nine countries including Australia, Brunei Darussalam, Chile, Malaysia, New Zealand, Peru, Singapore, United States, and Vietnam. Canada and Mexico joined the TPP in October 2012. By the end of 2012, there had been 15 rounds of negotiations. In the State of the Union Address made on 12 February 2013, US President Obama stated that '[t]o boost American exports, support American jobs and level the playing field in the growing markets of Asia, we intend to complete negotiations on a Trans-Pacific Partnership.' <http://www.whitehouse.gov/sotu2013?sss_id=412da73a> ['2013 State of the Union Address'].

[42] In the 2013 State of the Union Address, President Obama said that 'we will launch talks on a comprehensive Transatlantic Trade and Investment Partnership with the European Union—because trade that is fair and free across the Atlantic supports millions of good-paying American jobs.' Ibid. See also J Jowit and E MacAskill, 'David Cameron Sets Free Trade Agreement as his G8 Priority' *Guardian* (London 1 January 2013) <http://www.guardian.co.uk/politics/2013/jan/01/david-cameron-free-trade-agreement-g8>.

In November 2011, the leaders of nine Asia Pacific countries announced the achievement of the broad outlines of 'a comprehensive, next-generation regional agreement that liberalizes trade and investment and addresses new and traditional trade issues, and 21st-century challenges.'[43] In this announcement, the leaders stated that 'this agreement will be a model for ambition for other free trade agreements in the future.' The text of the investment chapter of the TPP being negotiated is not officially disclosed to the public. The United States Trade Representative has provided the following description:

> The investment text will provide substantive legal protections for investors and investments of each TPP country in the other TPP countries, including ongoing negotiations on provisions to ensure non-discrimination, a minimum standard of treatment, rules on expropriation, and prohibitions on specified performance requirements that distort trade and investment. The investment text will include provisions for expeditious, fair, and transparent investor-State dispute settlement subject to appropriate safeguards, with discussions continuing on scope and coverage. The investment text will protect the rights of the TPP countries to regulate in the public interest.[44]

Given the proximity in time between when the TPP negotiations began and when the 2012 US BIT model was released, it is fair to assume that the United States will negotiate the investment chapter in the TPP along the lines of the 2012 US model BIT negotiating text[45] which contains high standards of investor protection backed by an investor-State arbitration mechanism cautiously balanced by provisions that seek to preserve the public policy domain in general, and the environment and labour in particular.

It is also expected that the United States and the EU will officially launch a negotiation of a FTA styled as the Transatlantic Trade and Investment Partnership (TTIP) in 2013. The United States–EU High Level Working Group on Jobs and Growth (HLWG) issued a final report on 13 February 2013 recommending that 'a comprehensive US–EU trade agreement should include investment liberalization and protection provisions based on the highest levels of liberalization and highest standards of protection that both

[43] Press Release, USTR, Trans-Pacific Partnership Leaders Statement (12 November 2011) <http://www.ustr.gov/about-us/press-office/press-releases/2011/november/trans-pacific-partnership-leaders-statement>.

[44] USTR, Outlines of the Trans-Pacific Partnership Agreement <http://www.ustr.gov/about-us/press-office/fact-sheets/2011/november/outlines-trans-pacific-partnership-agreement>.

[45] The United States released the new model BIT on 20 April 2012 <http://www.ustr.gov/sites/default/files/BIT%20text%20for%20ACIEP%20Meeting.pdf>.

sides have negotiated to date.'[46] It is noteworthy that in April 2012, the EU and the United States agreed on a Statement of Shared Principles for International Investment in the framework of the Transatlantic Economic Council.[47] Recognizing the importance of creating and maintaining open and stable investment climates and policies, the Shared Principles call for, among other things, broad market access for foreign investors on the national treatment and MFN basis, strong protection of investors and investments, and effective and binding procedures for dispute settlement. While this statement embodies very broad principles, it signifies the objective of the two most influential players in the international economy in the negotiation of the investment rules in the context of the TTIP.[48]

While closely following the basic structure of the typical investment agreements developed by capital exporting countries, the regional investment rules of ASEAN and COMESA are rules tailored to suit the situation among Member States in the developing world. On the other hand, the investment rules in the TTIP will be the rules to be negotiated by two of the world's largest sources and destinations for foreign investment, and as such will have a very significant impact on the future direction of international investment policy making. Compared to the TTIP, because the economic development status of TPP negotiating countries as well as their respective position as a source and a destination of foreign investment differs widely, the level and contents of the investment disciplines TPP could achieve might be different from those of the TTIP.

(3) Negotiation of Investment Agreements by Regional Integration Organizations at Regional Level

Lastly, another emerging trend has been the negotiation and conclusion of investment agreements by regional integration organizations at the regional

[46] USTR, Final Report of the US–EU High Level Working Group on Jobs and Growth <http://www.ustr.gov/about-us/press-office/reports-and-publications/2013/final-report-us-eu-hlwg>.

[47] The Statement of the European Union and the United States on Shared Principles for International Investment <http://trade.ec.europa.eu/doclib/docs/2012/april/tradoc_149331.pdf>. For more background, see also European Commission, EU and US Adopt Blueprint for Open and Stable Investment Climates (10 April 2012) <http://trade.ec.europa.eu/doclib/press/index.cfm?id=796>.

[48] Under the auspices of the Transatlantic Economic Council, on 12 October 2012, the US and the EU convened a meeting of the Working Group on Investment to exchange a dialogue between senior officials. The two sides reaffirmed their shared commitment to maintaining and promoting investment policies that are open, transparent, and non-discriminatory, including through the negotiation of high-standard international investment agreements. See Press Release, European Commission, The EU and the US Advance Work to Promote Open, Transparent, and Non-discriminatory Investment Policies (24 October 2012) <http://trade.ec.europa.eu/doclib/press/index.cfm?id=837&serie=551&langId=en>.

level either as an integral part of FTAs or in the form of stand-alone BITs with non-member states. Whether individual Member States maintain competence to enter into a separate investment agreement with a non-Member State depends on the depth of regional integration and the level of institutionalisation to develop and enforce regional policy-making. The EU and ASEAN illustrate two different approaches in this regard.

In the case of ASEAN, individual Member States retain the authority to enter into preferential trade agreements and investment agreements. ASEAN has concluded FTAs with countries such as Korea, China and Japan, but individual Member States of ASEAN continue to enter into FTAs or investment agreements with the same parties as have entered into FTAs with ASEAN at the regional level. For example, Korea has a FTA with Singapore[49] as well as with ASEAN[50] and is currently negotiating FTAs with Indonesia and Vietnam which are ASEAN Member States. The Korea–Singapore FTA contains a comprehensive investment chapter whereas the Korea–ASEAN FTA includes an independent agreement on investment. Thus, the regional level investment agreement in the Korea–ASEAN FTA coexists with the investment chapter of the Korea–Singapore FTA resulting in a multi-layered system of investment rules. In addition, the negotiation of the Regional Comprehensive Economic Partnership (RCEP) was officially launched in November 2012 by ASEAN and six of its FTA partners (Korea, China, Japan, Australia, New Zealand, and India).[51] RCEP will also include investment rules. With some of the ASEAN Member States also participating in the TPP negotiation, if all of those initiatives are successfully concluded, it could result in a very complicated structure of overlapping investment rules, potentially susceptible to inconsistencies and redundancies.

In the case of the EU, individual EU Member States long retained the exclusive authority to enter into investment protection agreements. Since 2009, however, now that the Treaty of Lisbon has become effective, the European Commission has been given exclusive competence to negotiate treaties addressing both liberalization and the protection of investments on

---

49 Republic of Korea–Republic of Singapore Free Trade Agreement (Korea–Singapore) (4 August 2005) <http://fta.customs.go.kr/html/kor/_down/Kor-Sing-00-ENG-Total.pdf>. Chapter 10 of the Korea–Singapore FTA is on investment.

50 The Korea–ASEAN FTA is composed of five separate agreements: Framework Agreement on Comprehensive Economic Cooperation Among the Governments of the Republic of Korea and the Member Countries of the Association of Southeast Asian Nations (signed on 13 December 2005), Agreement on Trade in Goods (signed on 24 August 2006), Agreement on Dispute Settlement Mechanism (signed on 13 December 2005), Agreement on Trade in Services (signed on 21 November 2007), and the Agreement on Investment (signed on 2 June 2009).

51 Press Release, ASEAN, ASEAN and FTA Partners Launch the World's Biggest Regional Free Trade Deal (20 November 2012) <http://www.asean.org/news/asean-secretariat-news/item/asean-and-fta-partners-launch-the-world-s-biggest-regional-free-trade-deal>.

behalf of the EU Member States. The transfer of competence on foreign direct investment from member states to the EU has raised many substantive and procedural issues as to how to deal with the existing bilateral or regional investment agreements that EU Member States have previously concluded and how the future negotiations of investment agreements at the EU level will be conducted.[52] In July 2010, the European Commission laid out the direction of the new common investment policy in a Communication titled 'Towards a comprehensive European international investment policy' (2010 Communication)[53] and an accompanying proposal for a regulation on transitional arrangements for existing bilateral investment agreements (Regulation). The EU Parliament and Council adopted the proposed regulation on transitional arrangements in December 2012.[54]

In its 2010 Communication, the European Commission stated that the EU investment policy is focused on providing EU investors and investments with 'legal certainty and a stable, predictable, fair and properly regulated environment in which to conduct their business, in line with the existing international rules that are most relevant this area' such as GATS, the Guidelines for Multinational Enterprises' and other OECD instruments. Within this framework, the EU Commission has said that it will pursue the following objectives when negotiating investment rules: (1) improving market access by providing that foreign investments both at pre- and post-establishment stages are treated like domestic ones, (2) fostering transparency by clarifying the regulatory framework, (3) ensuring that host and home States fully retain their right to regulate the domestic sectors, (4) freeing the flow of payments and investment-related capital movements, while preserving the possibility to take safeguard measures in exceptional circumstances, and (5) facilitating the movement of investment-related natural persons.[55]

With this exclusive competence on foreign direct investment, the EU is actively negotiating comprehensive FTAs with investment protection

---

[52] For example, see R Dolzer, 'Remarks at Proceedings of the Annual Meeting' (2011) 105 *Am S Intl Proc* 325, 339; see also NJ Calamita, 'The Making of Europe's International Investment Policy: Uncertain First Steps' in NJ Calamita, D Earnest & M Burgstaller (eds), *The Future of ICSID and the Place of Investment Treaties in International Law* (BIICL, 2013) and articles in M Bungenberg, J Griebel and S Hindelang (eds), 'European Law and International Investment Law' (2010) *European Ybk Intl L*.

[53] European Commission, Communication from the Commission to the Council, the European Parliament, The European Economic and Social Committee and the Committee of the Regions, Towards a comprehensive European international investment policy, COM(2010)343 <http://trade.ec.europa.eu/doclib/docs/2011/may/tradoc_147884.pdf> ['2010 Communication'].

[54] The Regulation (EU) No. 1219/2012 of the European Parliament and of the Council of 12 December 2012 establishes transitional arrangements for bilateral investment agreements between Member States and third countries. Commission Regulation 1219/2012, 2012 OJ (L351) 40 ['EU Regulation'].

[55] Ibid.

provisions as well as investment liberalization commitments in recognition of the inter-dependence and complementarity between trade and foreign investment. In September 2011, the EU Council issued the first negotiating directives to the EU Commission to conduct negotiations on investment protection in FTAs with Canada, India, and Singapore.[56] According to the EU Commission, the EU–Canada trade and investment agreement under negotiation is the first occasion for the EU-wide rules on investment to be incorporated into a broad trade agreement[57] and will replace the individual BITs that Canada has with Hungary, Poland, and Romania. Existing bilateral agreements concluded between the EU Member States and the same partner states will be replaced by the investment agreements concluded at the EU level.

The Regulation on transitional arrangements for existing bilateral investment agreements describes the EU's position on the way it will deal with existing investment agreements that contain provisions on investment protection in force between individual Member States and third States. According to the Regulation, Member States are required to notify the EU Commission of all BITs with third countries signed before 1 December 2009 (when the Lisbon Treaty entered into force) by 8 February 2013 or before the date of the Member State's accession to the EU.[58] The Regulation also allows Member States to enter into negotiations with a third country to amend an existing or to conclude a new bilateral investment agreement subject to the conditions made in the Regulation.[59] The number of BITs to be affected could amount to 1,200.[60] Many States who are parties to existing BITs with EU Member States are keenly interested in how this will further develop in the EU. For instance, Korea has 21 BITs with EU Member States. The European Commission's exercise of exclusive competence on foreign direct investment and how the counter-parties respond thereto will greatly affect not only the existing BIT network of EU Member States, but also the overall contours of the global investment law regime.

III. IMPLICATIONS FOR THE LEVEL PLAYING FIELD AMONG INVESTORS

A serious side effect of the recent state practice of including investment protection provisions in regional integration agreements or FTAs is its potential to

---

56 The EU Council adopted further negotiating directives for four countries (Tunisia, Morocco, Jordan and Egypt) and for Japan. See European Commission, Investment <http://ec.europa.eu/trade/creating-opportunities/trade-topics/investment/>.

57 Ibid.

58 EU Regulation (n 54) arts 2 and 3.

59 Ibid, art 7.

60 2010 Communication (n 53).

distort the level playing field among investors of different nationalities built upon the MFN provisions in the existing network of BITs. The MFN principle is a fundamental principle in the WTO multilateral trade regime.[61] Regionalism is a system of preferential treatment among member states, and as such, it is a system of discrimination against third parties outside the region. Regionalism in trade is recognised as an exception to the fundamental principle of non-discrimination in the multilateral trading regime.[62] With respect to investment as opposed to trade, in the absence of a multilateral treaty imposing non-discriminatory treatment on states, the MFN treatment clauses, together with the national treatment clauses, in international investment agreements are important tools that ensure competitive conditions among investors of different nationalities in a Host State. Mirroring international trade law, a substantial number of BITs nonetheless provide that the MFN treatment obligation does not apply to benefits of treatment, preference, or privilege granted by way of regional integration agreements, FTAs, or customs unions (the so-called REIO exceptions).[63] The intent behind this exception is clear: to preserve to the parties the benefits and concessions specifically negotiated in deep integration agreements and to avoid the 'free rider' issue.

Because of the REIO exceptions contained in many of the existing BITs, when investment rules are included as part of a regional integration agreement or FTA between a Host State and a third country (third party treaty), they are beyond the reach of the MFN treatment promise in the BIT between the Home State of the investor and the Host State (basic treaty) regardless of the nature, purpose, and contents of such investment rules. This results in the creation of different classes of investors in a Host State depending on the scope of REIO exception in the basic treaty and whether the third party treaty offering the more favorable treatment to investors than the basic treaty is a BIT, a regional investment agreement or FTA. In a sense, incorporation of investment rules into regional investment arrangements or FTAs effectively converts the investment rules into a part of the preferential trade regime beyond the reach of the typical MFN clause in BITs. This frustrates the basic objective of international investment law which is to ensure the level playing field among foreign investors in a Host State through the MFN treatment clause.

---

[61] See General Agreement on Tariffs and Trade, 30 October 1947, 55 UNTS 194, art 1 (General Most-Favoured-Nation Treatment).

[62] In order for a regional trade agreement to qualify as an exception to the WTO MFN obligation, it needs to meet the specific conditions stipulated in the WTO rules. GATT art 24 (Territorial Application-Frontier Traffic-Customs Unions and Free-trade Areas).

[63] For instance, examples of the REIO exceptions are seen in art 3(4) of the Korea–China BIT of 2007 and art 22(3) of the Korea–Japan BIT.

The Japan–Peru Economic Partnership Agreement (EPA) and Korea–Japan BIT illustrate this problem. In 2008, Japan and Peru entered into a stand-alone bilateral investment agreement containing legally binding investment liberalization commitments and investment protection provisions.[64] Thereafter, in 2011, Japan and Peru entered into an EPA, which is the Japanese version of a comprehensive FTA and includes a provision to the effect that the provisions of the 2008 Japan–Peru BIT would be incorporated into the Japan–Peru EPA. The Korea–Japan BIT accords MFN treatment to investors and investment of each party with respect to establishment and acquisition of investments as well as in the post-establishment phase, subject to a typical REIO exception clause in Article 22(3) stating that such MFN obligation shall not be extended to 'any preferential treatment resulting from its membership of a free trade area, customs union, an international agreement for economic integration or a similar international agreement.'[65] By operation of the MFN clause in the Korea–Japan BIT, Korean investors could claim MFN treatment in Japan if the 2008 Japan–Peru BIT provides more favorable treatment to Peruvian investors than the treatment accorded to Korean investors under the Korea–Japan BIT. An interesting question that could arise after the Japan–Peru BIT is incorporated into the Japan–Peru EPA concerns the effect of the provisions in the Japan–Peru EPA of 2011 incorporating the BIT into the EPA; that is, would Korean investors in Japan be able to claim treatment on par with Peruvian investors in Japan by invoking the application of the MFN clause under the Korea–Japan BIT? This example demonstrates what may occur should the principles developed in international trade law be indiscriminately applied to investment law.

Let us refer to the EU for another example. In its policy announcement, the European Commission assured European investors of the best available practices of protection under existing BITs in an investment agreement to be negotiated at the EU level. This policy statement could be interpreted to indicate that EU will formulate super investment protection provisions that incorporate the highest protection standards among the existing BITs entered into by EU Member States, and thus grant uniform protection to all EU investors in a Host State. Foreign investors from a treaty partner country will also get the benefit of a uniform standard of treatment throughout EU Member States. Notwithstanding the apparent benefits for European investors or foreign investors in Europe, the new investment policy of the

---

64 Agreement between Japan and the Republic of Peru for the Promotion, Protection and Liberalization of Investment, 21 November 2008 http://www.mofa.go.jp/region/latin/peru/agree0811.pdf> ['Japan–Peru BIT'].

65 Agreement between the Government of the Republic of Korea and the Government of Japan for the Liberalization, Promotion and Protection of Investment (22 March 2002) <http://unctad.org/sections/dite/iia/docs/bits/korea_japan.pdf> ['Korea–Japan BIT'].

EU, which was outlined earlier, will create complex multi-layers of different classes of investors who are accorded potentially different standards of treatment in an EU Member State, that is, (i) investors of EU Member States (some of them under existing intra-EU BITs), (ii) investors from a state party to a FTA at the EU level,(iii) investors from a State party to a stand-alone BIT concluded at the EU level, (iv) investors from a State party to an existing BIT with an EU Member State, and (v) investors from a State without any such investment arrangement. The investment protections those investors may claim by invoking MFN treatment clauses will also be different depending on the specific scope and exceptions built in such MFN treatment clauses in the basic treaty. This multi-layer will produce a very odd result should an investor invoke the MFN treatment on the basis of the existing BITs. To illustrate, if the EU concludes a FTA with Canada which replaces the existing BITs between individual EU Member States and Canada, from the perspective of investors covered by existing BITs between the EU Member States and third States, the pool of BITs which they may invoke the MFN treatment on the basis of such BITs will be reduced thereby while the investment rules contained in the EU–Canada FTA would be beyond the reach of the MFN treatment in the existing BITs. However, should the EU conclude a new EU level investment agreement with Canada in a stand-alone BIT, it will be subject to the MFN treatment clause in the existing BITs.

From a policy perspective, State parties may have a legitimate rationale to shield specific market liberalization commitments from the application of a MFN treatment clause. However, it is not very convincing to deny the application of the MFN treatment clause to investment protection provisions depending on whether such protections are offered in a stand-alone BIT or in a comprehensive regional integration agreement or a FTA. Considering the recent trend that even investment chapters of some FTAs include an MFN treatment clause that reaches out into the higher standard of protections included in the future economic integration agreements,[66] the rationale for differentiating investment protection provisions in BITs from those in FTAs in the REIO exceptions appears rather tenuous.

The main objective of capital importing countries entering into BITs is to improve their investment climate to attract foreign investment through means of an international instrument. The protections offered by typical BITs are intended to increase legal certainty for foreign investors by ensuring that the domestic regulatory framework will remain stable, transparent, and non-discriminatory. Unlike preferential trade agreements, BITs are not intended to create an exclusive preferential bloc between the parties discriminating

[66] For example, Free Trade Agreement between the Republic of Korea and the United States of America, Chapter 11 (Investment) arts 4 and 11.12(2), Annex II <http://www.ustr.gov/trade-agreements/free-trade-agreements/korus-fta/final-text> ['Korea–US FTA'].

against the investors or investments from a non-party State. In general, State parties tend to grant the MFN treatment generously in BITs and, in fact, some of the earlier BITs do not even carve out any exceptions to the MFN treatment. Thus, the universe of BITs is an 'inclusive' system in that any higher standard of protection agreed to in the third party BIT could theoretically be extended to an investor in a Host State if the basic treaty between his Home State and the Host State grants the MFN treatment.

Even with respect to investment liberalization, some states may be willing to extend MFN treatment without requiring reciprocity. The situation among China, Japan, and Korea illustrates the inclusiveness of the MFN network of BITs as it relates to the investment liberalization commitments. Japan and Korea each have a BIT with China: the Japan–China BIT of 1988[67] and the Korea–China BIT of 2007.[68] Neither of China's BITs with Japan or Korea provides for national treatment with respect to establishment and acquisition, but both provide for MFN treatment in respect of the admission of investment.[69] The intent behind this MFN provision is clear. Recognizing that China was not ready to accord national treatment with respect to establishment and acquisition at the time of the conclusion of the respective BITs, Japan and Korea decided to accept the MFN treatment standard with respect to establishment and acquisition of investment to ensure that Japanese or Korean investors could claim treatment on par with investors from a third country in China. Based upon the MFN clauses in China's BITs with Japan and Korea, Chinese investors may claim equal treatment on the establishment and acquisition of investment in Korea or in Japan to the extent that the Japanese investor enjoys in Korea or the Korean investor enjoys in Japan pursuant to the Japan–Korea BIT. Japan and Korea entered into a bilateral investment agreement in 2002 with each party agreeing to give investors of

[67] Agreement between Japan and The People's Republic of China Concerning the Encouragement and Reciprocal Protection of Investment, 27 August 1988, <http://www.bilaterals.org/IMG/pdf/china_japan.pdf> ['China–Japan BIT'].

[68] Agreement between the Government of the Republic of Korea and the Government of the People's Republic of China on the Promotion and Protection of Investments, 8 September 2007, <http://tradeinservices.mofcom.gov.cn/en/b/2007-09-07/29727.shtml> ['Korea–China BIT of 2007'].

[69] Art 3(3) of the Korea–China BIT of 2007 states, in pertinent part, that '[e]ach Contracting Party shall in its territory accord to investors of the other Contracting Party and to their investments ... treatment no less favourable than that accorded in like circumstances to the investors and investments ... by the investors of any third State (hereinafter referred to as 'most-favoured-nation treatment') with respect to investments and business activities, *including the admission of investment* [emphasis added].' Art 2(2) of the China–Japan BIT provides that '[n]ationals and companies of either Contracting Party shall within the territory of the other Contracting Party be accorded treatment no less favorable than that accorded to nationals and companies of any third country *in respect of the admission of investment and the matters in connection therewith* [emphasis added].'

the other party and their investments national treatment and the MFN treatment with respect to establishment and acquisition of investments.[70] Given that Japanese and Korean investors are accorded national treatment in the Korea–Japan BIT, Chinese investors could effectively claim national treatment with respect to establishment and acquisition to the extent Korean or Japanese investors enjoy such treatment as provided for in the Korea–Japan BIT.

As observed in a recent United Nations Conference on Trade and Development (UNCTAD) report, it is true that the MFN treatment clauses have been 'rarely invoked to challenge the actual level of treatment given to foreign investors' as a breach of the MFN clause per se.[71] Rather it has been used by claimants in investment treaty arbitrations seeking to import more favorable substantive or procedural provisions from a third party treaty into the basic treaty. Whether such practice is conducive to the sound development of international investment law remains the subject of keen debate. Furthermore, the argument that the expansive application of the MFN treatment clause beyond what was originally intended or anticipated by the parties seriously undermines the credibility and legitimacy of international investment law is legitimate considering that many of the BITs which are controversial on this point were negotiated during the early phase of BIT development when the ramifications of the MFN treatment clause were not fully appreciated. At the same time, however, we should not ignore the fact that the very purpose of the MFN treatment clause is to ensure the equality of treatment given to investors of different nationalities, and as such, the legitimate expectations of investors for a level playing field in a competitive environment in reliance upon the existing network of MFN treatment promises should be given due consideration in the treaty making process.[72]

IV. CONCLUSION

In conclusion, the regionalization of investment arrangements or the proliferation of FTAs which contain investment rules could result in a gradual conversion from the inclusive BITs regime interlinked by the MFN treatment clauses into an exclusive, preferential, and discriminatory investment regime incorporated in the overall network of regional or preferential trade arrangements. Moreover, in situations in which the existing BITs co-exist with newly negotiated investment rules in regional investment agreements or FTAs, we

---

[70] Korea–Japan BIT arts 2(1)–(2).

[71] United Nations Conference on Trade and Development, 'Most-Favoured-Nation Treatment,' UNCTAD Series on Issues in International Investment Agreements II (New York and Geneva 2010) 17 ['UNCTAD Series on MFN'].

[72] For detailed discussion of policy options, see UNCTAD Series on MFN (n 71) 102.

will face a challenging task of interpretation of further complicated multi-layers of investment rules.

Regional investment arrangements and investment disciplines integrated into comprehensive trade agreements definitely have many positive aspects and will contribute to the facilitation of investment flows, among and into, the Member States by offering investment liberalization and protection that is more tailored to the perceived regional development goals and needs. It will also provide a valuable opportunity to reassess the existing network of bilateral and regional investment law regimes, to formulate a new framework that reflects the development dimensions of the region or trading partners, and to rebalance private and public rights for the preservation of public policy flexibility for the regional development.

However, a rational decision by an individual State or regional organisation does not necessarily result in a positive outcome from the perspective of the global community. Unlike the pre-World War II trading blocs, recent regional or preferential trade arrangements are not entirely exclusive arrangements; there is strong impetus for States to pursue FTAs with multiple parties beyond their region so that the same States or integrated regions may become parties to multiple regional arrangements or FTAs. The resulting multiple and cumulative free trade areas or expanded regions thus created and linked by the MFN treatment clauses might function as a mitigating factor against the creation of exclusive regional rival blocks that would compete against each other. With the proliferation of regional integration agreements and FTAs containing investment rules, international investment law will get closely interlinked with trade law disciplines and form an integral part of a multi-layered and multi-faceted system of regional preferential trade and investment. We will face new sets of difficult questions and the resolution of such questions will require collaboration and cooperation among multi-disciplinary experts.

2

An International Investment Policy Landscape in Transition: Challenges and Opportunities

*Hamed El-Kady**

A fundamental paradox underlies international investment relations: while governments recognize the importance of foreign direct investment (FDI) in their national development strategies and acknowledge the need to regulate FDI, negotiations on a cross-sectoral multilateral investment treaty have universally failed. This has created a regulatory vacuum in the area of investment, prompting countries to map investment regulations through a bilateral approach, weaving a complex web of bilateral investment treaties (BITs). The global BIT network today comprises over 3,000 treaties, involving 182 countries. What is more, during the past decade there has been a gradual shift in international investment policy-making from the bilateral to the regional level. In 2012 alone, more than 110 countries were engaged in more than 22 regional negotiations. While this regionalization trend provides an opportunity to consolidate the International Investment Agreement (IIA) regime, it has in fact in its current conceptualization, added to the complexity of the investment policy landscape. This article sheds light on some of the major developments at the regional level and the opportunities and challenges which have arisen from the rapid swell in regional investment policy-making.

* International Investment Policy Officer at the United Nations Conference on Trade and Development (UNCTAD) in Geneva. The author may be contacted at hamed.el.kady@unctad.org. The views are those of the author and do not necessarily represent those of UNCTAD. This contribution draws on UNCTAD's World Investment Report 2013, UNCTAD's Investment Policy Framework for Sustainable Development (IPFSD) and a note prepared by UNCTAD on Regional integration and foreign direct investment for the Trade and Development Board, 28–30 January 2013, Geneva. Comments were received from Elisabeth Tuerk, Wolfgang Alschner, Thomas Turner, Mathabo le Roux and Diana Rosert.

I. THE RISE OF BITS

The period from 1990 to 2002 saw an explosive proliferation of BITs globally, averaging 154 BITs per year. In 1995 and 1996 alone, 400 BITs were signed, representing more than the total number of BITs signed between 1959[1] and 1990. BIT negotiations based on template models with a uniform set of core legally binding investment protection provisions, created the impression that BITs are the most effective and quick way to regulate and protect international investments between countries. In addition, BITs were increasingly being perceived as an effective investment promotion tool used by countries competing to attract FDI to send positive signals to potential investors that the country enjoyed a stable and predictable legal framework. Furthermore, large numbers of BITs were signed for purely political reasons without any feasibility studies or economic impact assessments. The proliferation of BITs in the 1990s was encouraged by the low number of BIT-based investor-State disputes (ISDs) with only 37 cases recorded between 1990 and 1999, compared to 408 cases recorded between 2000 and 2011. However, more influential in the rise of BITs was a dominant global economic policy discourse which emphasized the importance of deregulation, free market policies and limited government intervention in economic affairs.

In recent years, this liberal economic ideology has been challenged by a series of crises in finance, food security, and the environment, as well as other emerging social challenges especially with regard to poverty alleviation and income inequality. These crises and challenges are having profound effects on the way investment policy is shaped at the global level,[2] and have increased and accentuated the role of governments in the global economy, in both the developed and the developing world. With social and environmental concerns taking centre stage, new challenges have surfaced leading governments to reflect on an emerging investment policy paradigm that accounts for inclusive and sustainable development goals as well as investment attraction and protection.

As a result of these emerging challenges, the discourse about international investment policy-making intensified at both the domestic and international levels, leading to a period of reflection on the future orientation of the BIT regime to make it more conducive to sustainable development. At the national level, investment stakeholders—including civil society, business and parliamentarians—have begun to voice their concerns about the costs and

---

1 Year of signature of the first BIT between Germany and Pakistan.

2 UNCTAD, *Investment Policy Framework for Sustainable Development* (2012), <http://unctad.org/en/PublicationsLibrary/diaepcb2012d5_en.pdf>.

benefits of entering into BITs.[3] The call for increasing transparency and inclusiveness of BIT-related decision-making is also gaining traction.

Internationally, a similar discourse was carried forward in forums such as the UNCTAD Investment Commission, the Organisation for Economic Co-operation and Development (OECD) Investment Committee, joint meetings of OECD and UNCTAD, regional conversations co-organized by UNCTAD and regional organizations such as the Common Market for Eastern and Southern Africa (COMESA), the Islamic Development Bank, the Southern African Development Community (SADC) and the Association of South-East Asian Nations (ASEAN) in order to strengthen the development dimension of BITs. UNCTAD's World Investment Forum 2012, which involved a broad range of investment stakeholders in the Ministerial Round Table and the 2012 International Investment Agreements Conference were particularly important fora for this discourse at the international level.

II. THE DOWNFALL OF BITS: FROM RISING INVESTOR-STATE DISPUTES TO INCONCLUSIVE IMPACT ON FDI FLOWS

Since 2002 traditional investment treaty making through BITs has been losing momentum (Figure 1). In 2011 only 33 BITs were signed representing a considerable decline compared to the 200 BITs signed in 1996. This trend is expected to continue in the years to come with fewer BITs concluded annually. In quantitative terms bilateral agreements still dominate international investment policy-making; however, in terms of economic significance and number of signatory States, there has been a gradual shift towards regional investment agreements and free trade agreements with investment chapters involving more than two contracting parties.

Several reasons may explain the decline in the number of BITs signed annually:

First, countries have realized that investment protection through BITs is becoming increasingly sensitive, primarily owing to the spread of BIT-based ISDs. In contrast to the number of new BITs, the number of new ISDs has been increasing rapidly. 2012 saw the highest number of new treaty-based cases filed ever with over 60 cases initiated, bringing the total of all known cases to over 500 at year's end (Figure 2).[4] The total number of countries that

---

[3] UNCTAD, *World Investment Report 2011: Non-Equity Modes of International Production and Development* (2011) 100, <http://www.unctad-docs.org/files/UNCTAD-WIR2011-Full-en.pdf>.

[4] Most arbitration fora do not maintain a public registry of claims, so the total number of actual cases could potentially be higher.

Figure 1. Annual number of BITs, 1980–2012

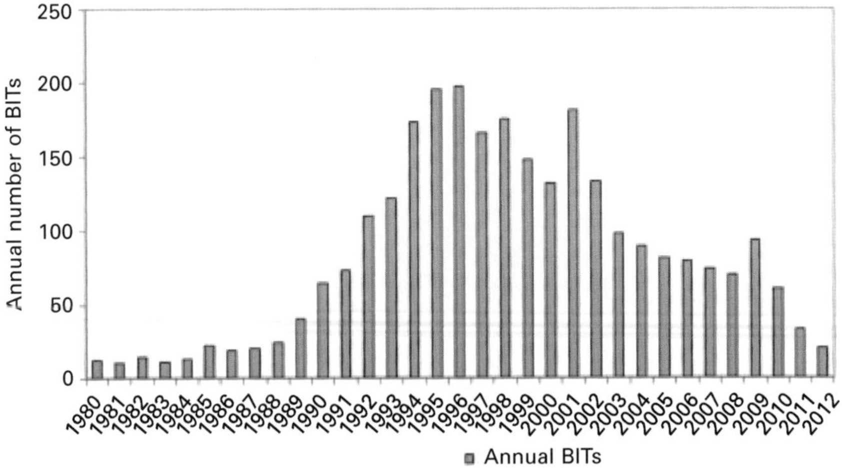

Source: UNCTAD.

Figure 2. Annual and cumulative number of known treaty-based investor-State disputes

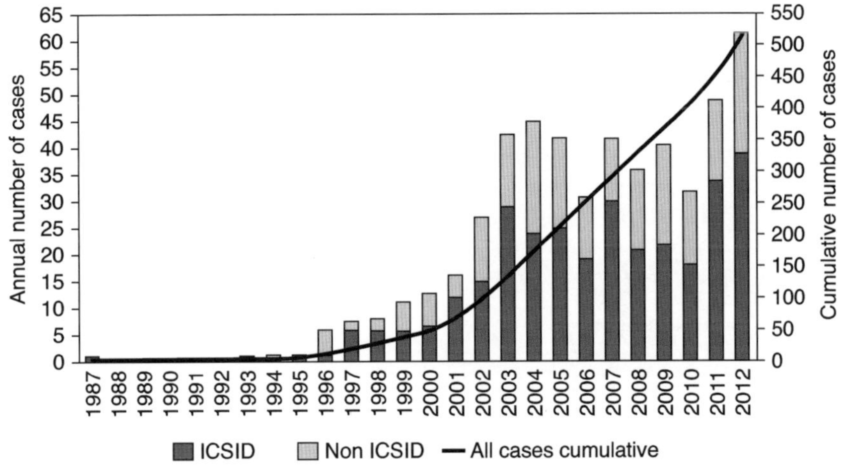

Source: UNCTAD.

have responded to at least one investment treaty claim over the years has increased to 95.[5]

In addition to the quantitative factor, recent arbitral awards demonstrate that tribunals continue to disagree on the core interpretation of BIT clauses resulting in inconsistent awards and a general lack of predictability and trust in the system. Perhaps even more important is the impact of the investor-state arbitration system on a country's right to regulate key public policies, such as health,[6] nuclear phase-out[7] or sovereign debt restructuring.[8] The loss of policy space to regulate FDI for development may hamper a country's effort to devise new investment policies and regulations to address specific development objectives emerging as a result of changes in the political landscape within the State. This may include, for example, legitimate measures aimed at combating corruption, creating jobs and addressing social imbalances.

Second, there are growing concerns about the effectiveness of BITs in attracting FDI. Various studies have analyzed the impact of BITs on FDI flows and have reached different conclusions.[9] In light of the increasing difficulties in managing large BIT networks, the increase in the number of ISDs globally and the inconclusive evidence of the impact of BITs on FDI flows, governments are increasingly emphasizing the importance of other less risky

---

5 UNCTAD, 'Recent Developments in Investor-State Dispute Settlement' (2013) 1 IIA Issues Note, <http://unctad.org/en/PublicationsLibrary/webdiaepcb2013d3_en.pdf>.

6 See for example *FTR Holdings S.A. (Switzerland) v Oriental Republic of Uruguay*. ICSID Case No: ARB/10/7.

7 See *Vattenfall AB v Federal Republic of Germany*; ICSID Case No. ARB/12/12.

8 *Abaclat v Argentine Republic*; ICSID Case No: ARB/07/5. For more information see J Beess und Chrostin, 'Sovereign Debt Restructuring and Mass Claims Arbitration before the ICSID, The Abaclat Case' (2012) 53(2) *Harvard International Law Journal* 505–517.

9 See for example, UNCTAD, *The Role of International Investment Agreements in Attracting Foreign Direct Investment to Developing Countries* (2009), <http://unctad.org/en/docs/diaeia20095_en.pdf>; P Egger and V Merlo, 'The Impact of Bilateral Investment Treaties on FDI Dynamics' (2007) 30(10) *The World Economy* 1536–1549; KP Gallagher and MBL Birch 'Do Investment Agreements Attract Investment? Evidence from Latin America' (December 2006) 7(6) *The Journal of World Investment and Trade* 961–974; M Hallward-Driemaier 'Do Bilateral Investment Treaties Attract FDI? Only a Bit and They Could Bite' (2003) *World Bank Policy Research Paper* 6/2003, WPS 3121 <http://papers.ssrn.com/sol3/papers.cfm?abstract_id=636541>; E Neumayer and L Spess 'Do bilateral investment treaties increase foreign direct investment to developing countries?' (2005) 33 (10) *World Development* 1567–1585; RJ Orr 'The impact of BITs on FDI: Do investors now ignore BITs?' (2007) 4(2) *Transnational Dispute Management Journal*; JW Salacuse and NP Sullivan 'Do BITs Really Work? An Evaluation of Bilateral Investment Treaties and Their Grand Bargain' 46 *Harvard International Law Journal* 67–130; KP Sauvant and LE Sachs (eds.) *The Effects of Treaties on Foreign Direct Investment: Bilateral Investment Treaties, Double Taxation Treaties and Investment Flows* (OUP 2009); J Tobin and S Rose-Ackerman *Bilateral Investment Treaties: Do They Stimulate Foreign Direct Investment?* (2006), <http://s3.amazonaws.com/zanran_storage/www.upf.edu/ContentPages/822485.pdf>.

policy tools, including more pro-active and targeted investment promotion policies that have proven more effective in attracting FDI. While BITs remain an important policy tool available to governments to attract FDI, they are increasingly perceived as being ineffective or unnecessary in the absence of more important FDI determinants such as market size, income levels, natural resources availability and labour cost and skills. For instance, Brazil has not ratified a single BIT as a matter of policy. Despite the absence of any BITs, Brazil attracted $66.7 billion in 2011 amounting to 54 per cent of all FDI inflows to South America.[10] Another example is the significant quantity of FDI flows between the United States and China which exist despite the absence of a BIT between the two countries. This uncertainty about the merits of BITs as FDI attraction tools has led countries to question the trade-off between restricting regulatory space and increasing exposure to ISDs with the mere expectation of increased FDI flows as a result of treaty protection.

Third, there are emerging concerns about the balance between the rights and obligations of States and investors in BITs. At the national level, countries are placing more emphasis on corporate responsibility by promoting the adoption of private codes of corporate conduct. Internationally, corporate responsibility initiatives; standards and guidelines for the behaviour of international investors are increasingly shaping the investment policy landscape. BITs do not reflect these developments as they currently do not establish any obligations on investors in return for the protection rights they are granted. Such obligations could make BITs more balanced and strengthen their development dimension, although there are concerns among developing countries that they may also act as barriers to investment.

Overall, the increasing awareness about BITs and their implications makes governments today more cautious in choosing treaty partners and entering into BITs. Governments have started conducting feasibility and impact assessment studies[11] before signing treaties and are increasingly reluctant to embark on negotiations without an appropriate and careful examination of the policy implications. Increasing awareness also means that governments are refraining from entering into legally binding BITs for purely political or other non-economic reasons. This has resulted in an increasing number of countries re-assessing their international investment policies[12] through the

---

[10] UNCTAD, *World Investment Report 2012: Towards a New Generation of Investment Policies* (2012) 171, <http://unctad.org/en/PublicationsLibrary/wir2012_embargoed_en.pdf>.

[11] See for example, EU FTAs Sustainability Impact assessments, <http://ec.europa.eu/trade/analysis/sustainability-impact-assessments/assessments/> and the Environment Assessment of the Canada–Colombia and Canada–Peru FTAs, <http://www.international.gc.ca/trade-agreements-accords-commerciaux/agr-acc/andean-andin/final-ea-colombia-peru-ee-finale-colombie-perou.aspx?view=d>.

[12] Examples include South Africa, Egypt, Philippines, Bosnia and Herzegovina, and Croatia.

revision of their model BITs and conducting major reviews of their BIT networks. The South African Government for example adopted a new investment policy framework in July 2010.[13] The new framework was the result of a comprehensive review conducted by the Government to assess investment protection policies. The review was prompted by a series of challenges and by changed circumstances in the international investment treaty environment.[14] Similar efforts are underway or are under consideration in a number of countries.[15]

Finally, there is a gradual shift from bilateral to regional investment treaty making. This may take various forms. A group of countries may decide to conclude a plurilateral investment agreement among them instead of engaging in various BITs. Alternatively, countries may conclude comprehensive agreements that cover investment among other disciplines such as trade and services, making the conclusion of separate bilateral agreements on investment unnecessary. These agreements may replace or incorporate existing BITs, further consolidating and reducing the number of BITs in existence.[16] Regional integration groups may decide to update or include investment provisions in their integration framework instead of signing BITs with each other. In addition, regional groups (instead of their individual members) may start negotiating investment treaties with third States. By comprehensively addressing trade, investment and other elements of international economic activities, such broader agreements can better respond to the needs of today's economic realities, where international trade and investment are increasingly interconnected.[17]

III. THE RISE OF REGIONAL INVESTMENT COOPERATION

Negotiations at the regional level on economic agreements with investment provisions have intensified in the recent years. In 2012 alone, at least 110 countries were involved in the negotiation of 22 regional agreements.

---

13 Similar reviews have been undertaken by a number of countries, both developed and developing, including Norway, the United States, Canada, Sweden, Brazil and more recently by a number of Latin American and Arab countries.

14 South African Department of Trade and Industry (2010), *Policy Statement: The South African Government's Approach to Future International Investment Treaties* <http://www.jadafa.co.za/LinkClick.aspx?fileticket=9A6eXZstRl0%3D&tabid=432>.

15 Bosnia and Herzegovina, Egypt, India, Philippines and Tunisia are examples of countries rethinking or considering revising their future BIT strategy to reflect a more balanced and development oriented approach.

16 They may also exist in parallel to BITs, see section on 'The way forward', infra.

17 UNCTAD, *World Investment Report 2012: Towards a New Generation of Investment Policies* (2012) 86, <http://unctad.org/en/PublicationsLibrary/wir2012_embargoed_en.pdf>.

1. Europe

Since the entry into force of the EU Lisbon Treaty in December 2009, the EU has exclusive competence on FDI policy-making, paving the way for the European Commission to negotiate agreements that not only cover the liberalization of trade and investment, but that also cover the protection of investment on behalf of all member States. This is a major development that will entail important changes in the global investment policy landscape. EU countries have signed over 1,300 BITs accounting for almost half of the world BITs. New EU-wide investment treaties will replace BITs between the EU treaty partner and individual EU member States resulting in a further decline in the number of existing BITs as they will be gradually replaced with EU comprehensive FTAs or investment agreements. From a potential EU investment treaty partner perspective, negotiating an agreement that involves the political and economic weight of 28 EU countries may result in more difficult negotiations as the bargaining power of the European bloc will certainly be difficult to balance with the interest of a single partner country.

In September 2011, the EU Council issued the first three negotiating directives to the EU Commission to conduct negotiations on investment protection chapters in Free Trade Agreements (FTAs) with Canada, India and Singapore. As addressed in the Communication of the European Commission, '*Towards a Comprehensive European International Investment Policy*'[18] and the Conclusions by the European Council,[19] the objective for future agreements containing provisions on investment protection is to preserve the high level of investment protection contained in existing Member State BITs (eg the inclusion of intellectual property rights as protected investment; provisions for the fair and equitable, most-favoured-nation and national treatment of investors; and investor-state arbitration). In December 2011, the EU Council adopted negotiating directives for deep and comprehensive FTAs with Egypt, Jordan, Morocco and Tunisia, which will also include provisions on investment protection. Taken together, these agreements can potentially replace 81 BITs signed between these Arab countries and EU member countries.

Negotiations on the EU–Canada Comprehensive Economic and Trade Agreement (CETA) are likely to include a full-fledged investment chapter. To date, Canada has signed six BITs with EU member States all of which have acceded to the EU in 2004 or 2007.[20] The EU–Canada FTA is expected to

---

[18] European Commission, *Towards a Comprehensive European International Investment Policy* (2010), <http://trade.ec.europa.eu/doclib/docs/2011/may/tradoc_147884.pdf>.

[19] Council of the European Union, *Conclusions on a Comprehensive European International Investment Policy* (2010), <http://www.consilium.europa.eu/uedocs/cms_data/docs/pressdata/EN/foraff/117328.pdf>.

[20] Czech Republic (2009), Hungary (1991), Latvia (2009), Poland (1990), Romania (2009) and Slovakia (2010).

replace these agreements. The EU Commission has officially reported substantial progress towards the conclusion of the negotiations with Canada in November 2012.[21] However, a number of important issues related to the CETA's envisioned investment chapter seem to remain open. More specifically, difficulties remain with regard to negotiations on the exclusion of specific sectors from liberalization commitments; country-specific reservations to national treatment provisions; prudential carve-out of financial services; and, most importantly, public policy exceptions in cases of indirect expropriation.

In December 2012, the EU concluded a trade agreement with Singapore and continues discussions on an investment agreement. Meanwhile, negotiations with India are still ongoing with a number of technical meetings involving senior level officials scheduled for the first quarter of 2013 to focus on core trade and investment elements.[22] At the same time, the EU adopted new legislation on BITs that aims at ensuring a smooth transition towards a new EU investment policy. The regulation clarifies the legal status of BITs concluded between individual EU member countries and third countries under EU laws and confirms that they may be maintained in force until replaced by an EU investment agreement. The regulation also allows EU member countries—under certain conditions—to negotiate BITs with countries not immediately scheduled for the EU-wide investment negotiations.[23] Ongoing negotiations between the EU and selected third parties may implicate at least 182 BITs (table 1).

Another European integration group which is active in formulating investment policies at the regional level with third parties is the European Free Trade Association (EFTA).[24] The scope and depth of investment provisions in EFTA FTAs with third countries vary greatly and does not seem to follow a specific model or template. While some FTAs with third parties include substantive investment-related provisions;[25] other treaties have only limited

---

[21] 'EU and Canada Move Towards Conclusion of Trade Negotiations' *European Commission* (Brussels 23 November 2012) <http://trade.ec.europa.eu/doclib/press/index.cfm?id=844>.

[22] For an updated and comprehensive overview of EU FTA negotiations: <http://trade.ec.europa.eu/doclib/docs/2006/december/tradoc_118238.pdf>.

[23] 'EU Takes Key Step to Provide Legal Certainty for Investors Outside Europe' *Europa* (Brussels 12 December 2012) <http://europa.eu/rapid/press-release_IP-12-1362_en.htm>. For further information 'Q&A EU Gives Greater Clarity to EU Investment Rules' *Europa* (Brussels 12 December 2012) <http://europa.eu/rapid/press-release_MEMO-12-977_en.htm>; 'Trade Topics: Investment' (Europa) <http://ec.europa.eu/trade/creating-opportunities/trade-topics/investment/>.

[24] EFTA Member States are Iceland, Liechtenstein, Norway and Switzerland.

[25] See for example chapter 4 of the EFTA FTA with Singapore which provides for pre-establishment national treatment and MFN and an investor-state dispute mechanism; EFTA FTA with Hong Kong which applies to commercial presence; articles 24 of the EFTA FTAs with Egypt and Tunisia which provide for fair and equitable treatment as well as protection and security in accordance with international law.

Table 1. Selected EU FTAs under negotiation or consideration and number of existing BITs with third party

FTAs under negotiations or consideration[26]	Number of existing BITs with EU members
China	25
Egypt	23
India	23
Morocco	20
Vietnam	20
Jordan	19
Tunisia	19
Malaysia	15
Singapore	12
Canada	6

provisions on investment cooperation and promotion.[27] The relationship between investment provisions found in EFTA agreements and existing BITs is still unclear. This will have to be clarified in order to ensure that investment obligations emanating from BITs do not overlap and create inconsistencies with EFTA FTAs.

In South-East Europe, countries have also been dealing with investment at the regional level. The Amended Central European Free Trade Agreement (CEFTA) signed in 2006[28] consolidates over 30 bilateral free trade agreements in the Southern European region into a single regional trade agreement. The Agreement contains an important investment chapter that provides fair and equitable treatment and full protection and security, national treatment, most-favoured nation treatment (MFN), but does not include an investor-state dispute settlement mechanism. An EU press release dated 19 December 2006 welcomes the signing of the CEFTA and describes it as an important contribution to economic development and a stepping stone for candidate countries towards full membership in the EU.[29]

[26] Excluding Economic Partnership Agreements (EPAs) between the EU and African regional integration bloc groups.

[27] See for example art 24 of the EFTA FTA with Montenegro and art 26 of the EFTA FTA with Lebanon which include investment promotion provisions aimed at identifying investment opportunities and information channels on investment regulations.

[28] CEFTA was signed by Albania, Moldova, Bosnia and Herzegovina, Montenegro, Bulgaria, Romania, Croatia, Serbia, Macedonia and Kosovo.

[29] EU Press Release, EU welcomes signing of new Central European Free Trade, Brussels, 19 December 2006, <http://europa.eu/rapid/press-release_IP-06-1837_en.htm?locale=EN>.

In the Eurasian context, regional investment cooperation occurs under the framework of the EuroAsian Economic Community (EurAsEC). In 2008, an agreement on the Promotion and Reciprocal Protection of Investments in the Member States of the Eurasian Economic Community was signed with investment provisions similar to those found in BITs.[30]

2. *Asia*

In Asia, the Association of Southeast Asian Nations (ASEAN)[31] has traditionally taken the lead in regional investment treaty making activity. ASEAN's efforts to establish investment rules at the regional level began in 1987 when the Agreement for the Promotion and Protection of Investments—also known as the ASEAN Investment Guarantee Agreement (IGA)—was signed with provisions granting fair and equitable treatment, protection against expropriation, free transfer of funds and an investor-state dispute settlement mechanism. The agreement was amended in 1996 to include provisions fostering transparency.[32]

In 1998, ASEAN members signed the Framework Agreement on the ASEAN Investment Area (AIA),[33] which aimed to make ASEAN a 'competitive, conducive and liberal' area for investment by undertaking various concerted measures. The agreement provides pre-establishment national treatment and MFN, explicitly excludes portfolio investments from the scope of the treaty, and establishes an ASEAN Investment Area Council. The agreement also includes various exceptions relating to the time frame for implementation, the safeguard of the balance of payments, the protection of national security and the prevention of fraud.

In 2009, the ASEAN Comprehensive Investment Agreement (ACIA) consolidated the 1998 AIA Agreement and the 1987 ASEAN IGA. In addition to building on past agreements and clarifying in greater detail the scope and content of substantive treaty protection provisions, the 2009 agreement

---

[30] The Agreement on the Promotion and Reciprocal Protection of Investments in the Member States of the Eurasian Economic Community was signed by Belarus, Kazakhstan, Kyrgyz Republic, Russia and Tajikistan.

[31] ASEAN members are Brunei, Cambodia, Indonesia, Laos, Malaysia, Myanmar, the Philippines, Singapore, Thailand and Vietnam.

[32] ASEAN Agreement among the Government of Brunei Darussalam, the Republic of Indonesia, Malaysia, the Republic of the Philippines, the Republic of Singapore and the Kingdom of Thailand for the Promotion and Protection of Investments (signed on 15 December 1987), <http://www.asean.org/communities/asean-economic-community/item/agreement-among-the-government-of-brunei-darussalam-the-republic-of-indonesia-malaysia-the-republic-of-the-philippines-the-republic-of-singapore-and-the-kingdom-of-thailand-for-the-promotion-and-protection-of-investments-manila-15-december-1987-2>.

[33] The Framework Agreement on the ASEAN Investment Area was signed by Economic Ministers at the 30th ASEAN Economic Ministers Meeting in Makati City, Philippines on 7 October 1998.

also includes innovative provisions recognizing the importance of according special and differential treatment to the newer ASEAN Member States and promoting and facilitating investment through specific and well defined activities.

Parallel to the ASEAN regional investment agreements described above, the group has also been actively pursuing negotiations on framework agreements with third parties (ASEAN+).[34] The aim of these agreements is to minimize barriers and deepen economic linkages between the third parties and ASEAN by lowering business costs; increasing intra-regional trade and investment; and creating a larger market to enhance FDI attraction. In 2008, ASEAN started deepening the framework agreements by concluding comprehensive FTAs with third parties. These agreements substantially expanded the scope of the framework agreements and included legally binding investment provisions. The first comprehensive FTA signed by ASEAN was with Japan in 2008. The FTA was complemented by the ASEAN–Republic of Korea Investment Agreement which was signed in 2009. ASEAN also concluded an important FTA with Australia and New Zealand (AANZFTA) that included a substantive investment protection chapter. In 2010, ASEAN completed an investment agreement with China and is currently negotiating one with India.[35] The conclusion of ASEAN+ agreements has not led to the termination of existing BITs between individual ASEAN members and third countries. This might be the case because the contracting parties wish to ensure the most favourable treatment to foreign investors arising from the different treaties in force. For example, the ASEAN–China Investment Agreement coexists with 10 BITs between individual ASEAN countries and China. This may eventually increase the risk of overlapping and conflicting provisions on investment between individual ASEAN members and the third party. In this context, a careful examination and review of the existing BITs between the parties and how they relate to more recent FTAs is necessary.

Another recent regional investment initiative in Asia that deserves attention is the 2012 trilateral investment agreement between China, Japan and the Republic of Korea. The three signatories, who have also agreed to start negotiating a comprehensive FTA, account for one fifth of both world population and global GDP.[36] The investment agreement includes provisions on

---

[34] Framework Agreements were signed between ASEAN and China (2002), India (2003), Japan (2003), the Republic of Korea (2003) and the United States (2006).

[35] For more information on the ASEAN–Indian cooperation, read 'Vision Statement at the ASEAN–India Commemorative Summit' (New Delhi 20 December 2012), <http://www.asean.org/images/2012/news/documents/Final%20version%20of%20ASEAN-India%20Vision%20Statement.pdf>.

[36] UNCTAD, *World Investment Report 2012: Towards a New Generation of Investment Policies* (2012) 85, <http://unctad.org/en/PublicationsLibrary/wir2012_embargoed_en.pdf>.

fair and equitable treatment, protection against direct and indirect expropriation and MFN treatment. At the same time, the agreement maintains the right of governments to exclude certain domestic investment policies including existing discriminatory measures from the scope of the treaty. It also grants regulatory space for the pursuit of certain policy objectives (eg through detailed exceptions with respect to taxation, essential security interests and prudential measures as well as temporary derogation from the free-transfer obligation). The treaty also includes some new disciplines regarding the enforcement of domestic intellectual property rights. The agreement does not terminate BITs previously signed between the parties and provides that nothing in the agreement shall be construed to prevent investors from relying on existing BITs that may be more favourable to them.[37] By including such a clause, the parties ensure that the new agreement does not lower the standards that otherwise exist under other treaties. On the other hand, this may create overlapping obligations between the treaty and the existing BITs.

More attempts at fostering regional cooperation in Asia were highlighted during the ASEAN 21st Summit in November 2012, where negotiations were officially launched between ASEAN and six other countries (Australia, China, India, South Korea, Japan and New Zealand) on a Regional Comprehensive Economic Partnership Agreement (RCEP). The six partner countries already have separate FTAs and/or Investment Agreements with ASEAN. The RCEP, which may potentially replace a large number of existing FTAs and BITs, seeks to create a liberal, facilitative, and competitive investment environment in the region. Negotiations for investment under the RCEP will cover the four pillars of promotion, protection, facilitation and liberalization based on the Guiding Principles and Objectives for Negotiating the Regional Comprehensive Economic Partnership.[38] The negotiations are expected to commence in early 2013 and to be completed by the end of 2015. The RCEP will be open for accession by any ASEAN FTA partner that did not participate in the RCEP negotiations and any other partner countries after the conclusion of the RCEP negotiations.

In addition to ASEAN-led initiatives, the South Asian Association for Regional Cooperation (SAARC), formed in 1985 by seven South Asian countries,[39] initiated trade integration in 1995 when the SAARC Preferential

[37] See Agreement Among the Government of Japan, The Government of the Republic of Korea, and The Government of the People's Republic of China for the Promotion, Facilitation and Protection of Investment (signed on 13 May 2012), art 25, <http://www.mofa.go.jp/announce/announce/2012/5/pdfs/0513_01_01.pdf>.

[38] The Guiding Principles were adopted by the Economic Ministers in Siem Reap, Cambodia in August 2012, and endorsed by the ASEAN Leaders at the 21st ASEAN Summit.

[39] The seven founding members are Sri Lanka, Bhutan, India, Maldives, Nepal, Pakistan, and Bangladesh. Afghanistan joined the organization in 2007.

Trading Agreement (SAPTA) took force. SAPTA was replaced in January 2004 by the South Asian Free Trade Area (SAFTA) that commenced trade liberalization in July 2006. In terms of investment provisions, SAARC Member States agreed to consider the adoption of measures to remove barriers to intra-SAARC investments already under the SAFTA Agreement. This was reinforced by the SAARC Agreement on Trade in Services in 2010 which extended the SAFTA Agreement to the services sector.[40]

In 2009, China, Bangladesh, India, Laos, Sri Lanka and the Republic of Korea, as members of the Asia–Pacific Trade Agreement (APTA), previously named the Bangkok Agreement, signed a Framework Agreement on the Promotion, Protection and Liberalization of Investment.[41] The framework agreement on investment does not provide for substantive obligations on investment, but includes an investment protection programme to be implemented by the participating countries. The programme requires the formulation and conclusion of an APTA agreement on the promotion and protection of investments with substantive provisions similar to those found in BITs. The agreement would, among other things, provide post-establishment national treatment and MFN, full protection and security, protection against expropriation and an investor-state dispute settlement mechanism.[42] If signed, this agreement may potentially replace 12 BITs in existence among the member States.

In Oceania, negotiations towards a comprehensive Pacific Agreement on Closer Economic Relations known as PACER plus involving 15 States are underway.[43] Negotiations for PACER plus include a substantive investment protection chapter. Once signed and entered into force, the agreement is likely to replace the South Pacific Regional Trade and Economic Cooperation Agreement (SPARTECA) that governs trade in goods between Forum Island Countries (FICs) and Australia and New Zealand.

---

[40] SAARC Agreement on Trade in Services (SATIS) <http://commerce.nic.in/trade/SAARC%20Agreement%20on%20Trade%20in%20Services%20SATS.pdf>.

[41] The UN Economic and Social Commission for Asia and the Pacific (ESCAP) functions as the secretariat for the Agreement. 'The Asia–Pacific Trade Agreement' *ESCAP* (19 June 2012), <http://www.unescap.org/tid/apta.asp>. The APTA members also concluded in 2009 the Framework Agreement on Trade Facilitation and in 2011 entered into the Framework Agreement on the Promotion and Liberalization of Trade in Services.

[42] See Framework Agreement on the Promotion, Protection and Liberalization of Investment among APTA States (signed in 2009) Schedule IV, <http://www.unescap.org/tid/apta/fa_inv.pdf>.

[43] Countries involved in PACER plus are Australia, New Zealand, Cook Islands, Federated States of Micronesia, Kiribati, Nauru, Niue, Palau, Papua New Guinea, Republic of Marshall Islands, Samoa, Solomon Islands, Tonga, Tuvalu and Vanuatu.

3. *Latin and Central America*

International investment policies in Latin and Central America have been formulated mainly through bilateral agreements rather than regional initiatives. Latin and Central American countries have been taking the lead together with the United States, Canada, Singapore and Japan in concluding comprehensive FTAs with investment chapters. For example, since 2005, Chile, Colombia, Costa Rica, Guatemala, Mexico, Panama and Peru were involved in 40 per cent of all bilateral FTAs signed worldwide.[44]

At the regional level, MERCOSUR[45] formulated investment policy frameworks dating back to the 1990s. However, the 1994 MERCOSUR agreements promoting and protecting investments (the Buenos Aires Protocol and the Colonia Protocol) have not been ratified by any of the member States. The ratification of these instruments, or alternatively, the adoption of new regulations on investment among MERCOSUR members would fill an existing regional investment regulatory gap and would foster deeper integration among the group members by complementing existing trade-related initiatives.

More recently there have been signs of stronger regional cooperation on investment issues in Latin and Central America. In 2011 for example, Mexico signed an FTA with the Central American States (Costa Rica, El Salvador, Guatemala, Honduras and Nicaragua). Together, the six countries account for almost a quarter of Latin America's GDP. This treaty establishing a free trade area, with its fully fledged investment chapter, will replace three earlier FTAs which Mexico had signed with the participating countries.

2012 saw the creation of a new regional initiative which could renew the momentum of regional investment policy making in Latin America. On 6 June 2012, Chile, Colombia, Peru and Mexico signed a framework agreement that establishes the Pacific Alliance as a deep integration area, an initiative launched in 2011.[46] Based on the existing trade and investment agreements between the Parties, the Pacific Alliance aims to establish the free movement of goods, services, capital and people; to promote investment flows among the signatory States; and to foster ties with the Asia–Pacific region.

---

[44] 38 FTAs, out of a total 93 signed since 2005, involved one or more of these seven countries. The majority of these FTAs include an investment protection chapter.

[45] Argentina, Brazil, Paraguay and Uruguay were the founding members. In 2008, Venezuela, Chile and Bolivia became associate members. Peru, Ecuador and Colombia have expressed their willingness to join the group, and Mexico has shown a growing interest. Venezuela became a full member in July 2012.

[46] 'Mandatarios suscriben Acuerdo Marco de la Alianza del Pacífico' Presidencia de la República del Perú (Anfogasta 6 June 2012) <http://www.presidencia.gob.pe/mandatarios-suscriben-acuerdo-marco-de-la-alianza-del-pacifico>.

4. *Africa*

African countries had an early start in the process of trade and investment regional integration. The first economic integration area was created in 1964 with the adoption of the Treaty Establishing the Customs and Economic Union of Central Africa (UDEAC or CEUCA), which later became the Monetary and Economic Union of Central Africa (CEMAC). In 1965, the members of UDEAC signed the Common Convention on Investments. The agreement contained only a few relatively unique protection provisions applying to all foreign investors.[47]

Since then, a large number of regional integration initiatives have been adopted. The most notable recent regional initiative dealing with investment is the COMESA[48] Common Investment Area, which is another example of the shift in treaty making momentum from the bilateral to the regional level. The treaty includes substantive investment protection provisions clarifying the meaning of certain standards such as fair and equitable treatment. At the same time, the treaty aims to strike a balance between the rights of investors and the State's right to regulate. For example, it includes a provision on investor responsibility, and allows for exceptions to national treatment through a 'Sensitive List', set out in an annex of the Agreement. It also includes a detailed general exception clause allowing the parties to take measures designed to protect national security; public morals; human, animal or plant life; and the environment. In addition, the treaty includes an investment promotion and awareness programme that provides for specific actions to stimulate and encourage investment flow among the members.

The Southern African Development Community (SADC)[49] Finance and Investment Protocol signed in 2007 is another example of African regional cooperation on investment issues. The agreement includes provisions on fair and equitable treatment; free capital movement; protection against expropriation and an ISDS mechanism. In addition, the agreement includes innovative provisions relating to the promotion of local and regional entrepreneurs, the right to regulate in public interest, special treatment for the least developed Parties, the harmonization of investment policies and laws and corporate social responsibility.

---

[47] For a historical evolution and review of substantive investment obligations found in regional integration agreements in Africa, see UNCTAD, *Investment Provisions in Economic Integration Agreements* (2006), <http://unctad.org/en/Docs/iteiit200510_en.pdf>.

[48] Members of COMESA are Burundi, Comoros, Democratic Republic of the Congo, Djibouti, Egypt, Eritrea, Ethiopia, Kenya, Libya, Madagascar, Malawi, Mauritius, Rwanda, Seychelles, Sudan, Swaziland, Uganda, Zambia and Zimbabwe.

[49] Member States of SADC are Angola, Botswana, Democratic Republic of the Congo, Lesotho, Malawi, Mauritius, Mozambique, Namibia, Seychelles, South Africa, Swaziland, Tanzania, Zambia and Zimbabwe.

African regionalism has also taken the form of agreements among two or more regional economic integration organizations. In 2011, the Heads of State and Government of the Common Market for Eastern and Southern Africa (COMESA), the East African Community (EAC) and the Southern African Development Community (SADC) signed a declaration launching negotiations for the establishment of the COMESA–EAC–SADC Free Trade Area (FTA). Negotiations for the establishment of the Tripartite FTA were launched with the establishment of the Tripartite Trade Negotiation Forum (TTNF) as a body responsible for technical negotiations and guided by the adopted Roadmap for the negotiations. A number of critical TTNF meetings were held in 2012 during which negotiators concluded the situational analyses on key thematic issues for substantive negotiations and submitted their work programmes for consideration by the TTNF. The Tripartite FTA involves 26 African countries with the strategic objective of consolidating existing regional economic communities to achieve a common market covering the African continent. The draft stipulates that members undertake to create a single investment area, develop policies and strategies which promote cross-border investment, reduce the cost of doing business in the region, and create a conducive environment for private sector development.[50] If a substantive investment chapter is included in the COMESA–EAC–SADC Tripartite Free Trade Area, this may replace 47 BITs between the members of the three organizations.

At the same time, there is recognition that multiple memberships in regional blocs in Africa may create overlapping trade and investment commitments that can hamper the potential gains from regional integration:

> Following on the aspiration expressed in the Abuja Treaty to create a pan-African bloc, the African Union decided in 2006 to suspend, until further notice, the recognition of new REIOs with the exception of eight (African Maghreb Union, The Community of Sahel–Saharan States, COMESA, EAC, The Economic Community of Central African States, The Economic Community Of West African States, Intergovernmental Authority on Development and SADC).[51]

African groups are also engaged in negotiations on comprehensive Economic Partnership Agreements (EPAs) with the EU. The Cotonou Agreement

---

[50] COMESA–EAC–SADC Tripartite Framework: State of Play, Report by the Chair of the Tripartite Task Force, (February 2011) <http://www.eac.int/index.php?option=com_content&view=article&id=581&Itemid=201&showall=1>. See also UNCTAD, 'Regional Development and Foreign Direct Investment in Developing and Transition Economies' (3 December 2012) TD/BC.II/MEM.4/2.

[51] UNCTAD, 'Regional Development and Foreign Direct Investment in Developing and Transition Economies' (3 December 2012) TD/BC.II/MEM.4/2.

signed in June 2000, established the legal basis for a new trade and investment regime between the EU and African countries and paves the way for the conclusion of EPAs. While negotiations have been slower than expected between the EU and the various sub-regional African groups, some progress has been made. The EU concluded an EPA with the Ivory Coast in November 2008, while negotiations are ongoing with the Economic Community of West African States (ECOWAS).[52] Interim Agreements were reached with SADC (2007);[53] the Eastern and Southern Africa (ESA) States (2009);[54] and the EAC (2009). The scope and depth of the investment provisions has been an important element in ongoing negotiations. The new EU mandate may allow for the inclusion of substantive investment protection chapters. In combination, these agreements may potentially supersede 224 BITs between EU member States and individual African countries.

In 2012, work on a SADC model BIT template continued to embody a harmonized approach to investment rulemaking. The model BIT is designed to assist SADC member States in formulating balanced provisions in future international investment agreements with third countries.[55] 'The draft template represents a distinct effort to enhance the sustainable development dimension of future international investment agreements, by including provisions on environmental and social impact assessments; measures against corruption; standards for human rights, environment and labour; corporate governance; and the right of States to regulate and pursue their development goals'.[56]

---

52 ECOWAS members: Benin, Burkina Faso, Cape Verde, Gambia, Ghana, Guinea, Guinea-Bissau, Ivory Coast, Liberia, Mali, Niger, Nigeria, Senegal, Sierra Leone and Togo.

53 The EU is currently in negotiations for an EPA with Angola, Botswana, Lesotho, Mozambique, Namibia, Swaziland and South Africa, as the SADC Economic Partnership Agreement group. The other six members of SADC—the Democratic Republic of the Congo, Madagascar, Malawi, Mauritius, Zambia and Zimbabwe—are negotiating Economic Partnership Agreements with the EU as part of other regional groups, namely Central Africa or Eastern and Southern Africa. For more information see, <http://ec.europa.eu/trade/creating-opportunities/bilateral-relations/regions/sadc/>.

54 Eastern and Southern Africa countries: Comoros, Djibouti, Eritrea, Ethiopia, Madagascar, Malawi, Mauritius, Seychelles, Somalia, Sudan, Zambia, Zimbabwe.

55 The preparation of the SADC Model BIT Template has been undertaken in an interactive process by a drafting committee consisting of representatives form Malawi, Mauritius, Namibia, South Africa and Zimbabwe, with technical support provided by the International Institute for Sustainable Development (IISD) <http://www.iisd.org/itn/wp-content/uploads/2012/10/SADC-Model-BIT-Template-Final.pdf>.

56 UNCTAD, *World Investment Report 2012: Towards a New Generation of Investment Policies* (2012) 89, <http://unctad.org/en/PublicationsLibrary/wir2012_embargoed_en.pdf>.

5. *Middle East*

Some of the first initiatives to promote intra-regional trade and investment through regional agreements took place in the Arab world. As early as the 1960s and 1970s, Arab States had already concluded agreements aimed at encouraging intra-Arab FDI flows.[57] In 1980, the Unified Agreement for the Investment of Arab Capital in the Arab States was signed with provisions granting the free transfer of funds and providing protection to Arab investors investing in Arab States.[58] Since then there has been a loss of momentum in regional investment treaty making in the Arab world, with countries increasingly relying on BITs to govern international investment relations. There are currently over 550 BITs concluded by Arab countries, with over 100 between Arab countries.

More recently, after a wave of popular uprisings demanding social justice swept through the region, many Arab governments began reconsidering investment policies in the context of an inclusive development agenda that emphasizes the importance of FDI in creating sustainable jobs and fostering equitable economic growth. This process of investment policy reconsideration has also been prompted by a decline in FDI inflows to Arab countries from $68.7 billion in 2010 to $43 billion in 2011.[59] As a result, many Arab governments are reassessing their investment protection policies or are working on new model BITs that reflect a balance between the rights and obligations of States and investors and that address public policy concerns. Debates and discussions have also emerged on the need for a modern regional Arab investment agreement that reflects the new realities of international investment law and its implications for national development strategies.[60]

Arab countries adopted, on 22 January 2013, a draft inter-Arab investment agreement during the third Arab economic summit held in Riyadh,

---

[57] The Agreement on Arab Economic Unity was concluded in 1957 with the aim of fully liberalizing the movement of persons, capital and goods among the Arab League States. The Agreement on Investment and Free Movement of Arab Capital among Arab Countries was concluded in 1970 to promote preferential investment treatment between Arab countries. The Convention Establishing the Inter-Arab Investment Guarantee Corporation signed in 1971 to create an enabling framework for investment flows within the region and the Agreement on Promotion, Protection and Guarantee of Investments among Member States of the Organization of the Islamic Conference (1981).

[58] The agreement also prohibits the nationalization of Arab investments unless it is for the public benefit, in a non-discriminatory manner and accompanied by fair compensation. Moreover, the agreement entitles Arab investors to unimpeded entry and residence within the territory of the Arab State in which the investment is made and provides for an Arab Investment Court to settle disputes arising from the application of the agreement.

[59] UNCTAD, *World Investment Report 2012: Towards a New Generation of Investment Policies* (2012) 89, <http://unctad.org/en/PublicationsLibrary/wir2012_embargoed_en.pdf>.

[60] H El-Kady, 'Towards Harmonizing and Strengthening the Framework for Intra-Arab Investment (2009) 1 *Transnational Dispute Management Journal*.

Saudi Arabia.[61] The agreement which was expected by many observers to reflect changing political, social and economic conditions in the Arab world through the insertion of pro-active provisions aimed at encouraging FDI that creates jobs, transfers technology, and respects corporate social responsibility, has in fact been drafted in way that maximizes protection to Arab investors investing in other Arab States and that minimizes the space available to host Arab countries to regulate FDI for development and inclusive growth. These issues will need to be addressed in future negotiating rounds to ensure a balanced regional agreement that reflects not only the interests of capital exporting Arab states, but that also takes into account the aspirations and interests of capital importing Arab countries.

6. *Cross-regional*

Initiatives also exist to conclude agreements dealing with investment covering more than one region. Perhaps the most important recent initiative is the Trans-Pacific Partnership Agreement (TPP). The fifteenth round of negotiation was concluded in December 2012 with the next round scheduled for December 2013. Currently, 11 countries[62] are participating in the negotiations. In October 2012, Canada and Mexico formally joined the negotiations. Japan and Thailand have also expressed interest in joining the negotiations. Meanwhile, civil society groups continue voicing concerns about the negotiations. A draft investment chapter of the agreement which leaked to the press in 2012 seeks to establish a free trade area and includes a fully-fledged investment chapter with high standards of investment liberalization and protection—including ISDS.[63] If all of the countries sign the deal, the treaty could potentially replace over 20 BITs. The draft investment chapter of the TPP includes all core elements found in modern BITs. It offers a detailed set of substantive and procedural obligations protecting investments at the pre and post-establishment phases; it clarifies in greater detail the meaning of certain provisions such as fair and equitable treatment (FET) and indirect expropriation; provides ISDS for a broad category of disputes, including not only disputes arising out of the chapter but also disputes arising out of the breach of investment authorizations and investment contracts (ie State contracts); and seeks to establish a balance between the rights and obligations of investors and States by including good corporate governance

---

[61] 'Third Arab Economic Summit Brings Arab Free Trade Zone Closer' *ahramonline* (22 January 2013), <http://english.ahram.org.eg/NewsContent/3/12/63045/Business/Economy/Third-Arab-economic-summit-brings-Arab-free-trade-.aspx>.

[62] Australia, Brunei Darussalam, Canada, Chile, Malaysia, Mexico, New Zealand, Peru, Singapore, the United States and Vietnam.

[63] Citizens Trade Campaign, <http://www.citizenstrade.org/ctc/blog/2012/06/13/newly-leaked-tpp-investment-chapter-contains-special-rights-for-corporations/>.

clauses (eg CSR, and transparency). The TPP draft investment chapter also includes an innovative provision dealing with public debts, clarifying that the purchase of debt issued by a party by foreign investors entails commercial risks. The clarification aims to avoid the use by investors of the agreement to challenge sovereign debts and sovereign debt restructuring.

IV. AN INTERNATIONAL POLICY LANDSCAPE IN TRANSITION: THE WAY FORWARD

1. Unsustainable bilateralism

The network of more than 3,000 BITs may have in part filled the international investment regulatory vacuum created by the absence of a multilateral investment agreement. But the fragmented, uncoordinated and asymmetrical nature of these bilateral investment deals has created problems of its own, especially for developing countries with large BIT networks. These countries face the risk of overlapping and sometimes contradictory obligations arising from different treaties, which may result in policy incoherence. This incoherence not only affects the international investment policy regime but also has implications for the way investment policy interacts with other national policy areas, including industrial development policy, private sector development, and policies in support of technological advancement, international trade and job creation. BITs perpetuate and accentuate the lack of systemic coordination on international investment issues. The spaghetti bowl is growing larger and more unwieldy in the absence of a global organisation steering international investment policy-making. Perhaps more disconcertingly, bilateral investment negotiations capture smaller developing countries in asymmetrical bargaining relations, often yielding BITs that do not reflect their interests, but rather those of their more powerful negotiating partners.

The bilateral nature of international investment policy-making creates a barrier to the effective participation of developing countries in the evolution of the international investment regime. Most developing countries are investment rule-takers rather than rule-makers, and passively bear witness to a rapidly evolving system, effectively unable to make any substantive contributions that would safeguard their own national interests and priorities. It is weaker countries that will benefit most from a measured recalibration of the system. Paradoxically, however, the lack of capacity, so often endemic to these countries, precludes their input to effect changes to the system that would be meaningful for them. Thus they are ensnarled in a system whose increasing burden of complexity weighs even more heavily on them, precisely because of their lack of capacity.

The fragmented BIT system poses other systemic risks, notably by exposing countries to treaty-based ISDS in international tribunals, which itself has not stood up under scrutiny. The vulnerability of developing countries is accentuated by persistent shortcomings of the ISDS system on matters of substance. These include the broad interpretation of BIT provisions beyond the parties' original intent; contradictory interpretations of key BIT provisions by ad hoc tribunals leading to uncertainty about their meaning; and inconsistent awards and decisions resulting in a general sense of legal unpredictability.[64]

2. *Rethinking regionalism to achieve consolidation*

The prognosis described above is not encouraging. In addition, rising regionalism in international investment policy-making, in its current conceptualisation is effectively leading to a multiplication of treaty layers, making the network of international investment obligations even more complex and prone to overlap and inconsistency. Where regional investment agreements do not entail the replacement of older BITs[65], the result is the multiplication of treaty layers, making the network of international investment obligations even more complex and prone to overlap and inconsistency. A review of selected regional investment agreements reveals that most regional treaties maintain the existence of BITs in parallel to the regional treaty (table 2). In contrast, replacing, suspending or incorporating existing BITs has been more common in bilateral FTAs. Some agreements have included provisions suspending existing BITs on the date of entry into force of the FTA, and replacing them—in whole or in part—with the investment chapter of the trade agreement.[66] Other FTAs have incorporated existing BITs and made them part of the FTA *mutatis mutandis*.[67]

The parallel existence of prior BITs and more recent regional agreements with investment provisions poses a number of legal and policy challenges. The first challenge is how to deal with possible inconsistencies between the treaties. Some regional agreements include specific provisions clarifying which agreement prevails in the case of an inconsistency.[68] However, other

---

64 For more details on growing discontent with the ISDS system, see UNCTAD, *World Investment Report 2012: Towards a New Generation of Investment Policies* (2012) 86 <http://unctad.org/en/PublicationsLibrary/wir2012_embargoed_en.pdf>.

65 See for example art 25 of the trilateral investment agreement between China, Japan and the Republic of Korea.

66 See for example art 1.2 of the United States–Morocco FTA.

67 See for example art 2 of the Japan–Peru FTA and art 9 of the Japan–Vietnam FTA.

68 The COMESA CCIA, for example, in art 32.3 states 'In the event of inconsistency between this Agreement and such other agreements between Member States mentioned in paragraph 2 of this Article, this agreement shall prevail to the extent of the inconsistency, except as otherwise provided in this Agreement'. Similarly, art 2.3 of the ASEAN–Australia–New Zealand FTA states that 'In the event of any inconsistency between this Agreement and any other agreement

Table 2. Relationship between selected regional agreements and bilateral treaties with investment provisions

Regional Agreement	Affected bilateral treaties	Relationship*	Relevant article
Association of Southeast Asian Nations Comprehensive Investment Agreement	26	Parallel	Article 44
Association of Southeast Asian Nations-China Investment Agreement	10	Parallel	Article 23
Association of Southeast Asian Nations-Korea Investment Agreement	8	Parallel	Article 1.4
Consolidated Central European Free Trade Agreement (CEFTA)	11	Parallel	Article 30
Common Market for Eastern and Southern Africa Common Investment Area	24	Parallel	Article 32
Eurasian Investment Agreement	9	Silent	NA
Central America–Mexico FTA	4	Replace	Article 21.7
Energy Charter Treaty	654	Parallel	Part III, Article 16
Central American Free Trade Agreement (US–DR–CAFTA)	4	Parallel	Article 1.3
Association of Southeast Asian Nations-Australia–New Zealand Free Trade Agreement	2	Parallel	Article 2
China–Korea–Japan IPPA	3	Parallel	Article 25
Economic Community of West African States Energy Protocol	14	Parallel	Article 16
Southern African Development Community Protocol on Finance and Investment	16	Silent	N.A.

Source: UNCTAD, World Investment Report 2013.

Note: The above regional agreements include substantive investment provisions.

* *Parallel*: Nothing in the Agreement affects the rights and obligations of a Party under any bilateral investment agreement.
Replace: Upon entry into force of the agreement, pre-existing agreements between the parties will be terminated.
Silent: No provisions on relationship with bilateral agreements.

agreements are silent on the issue. In the absence of such a conflict rule, customary international law rules on interpretation, such as those found in the Vienna Convention on the Law of Treaties would apply. Second, there is a challenge in the context of ISDS. Parallel IIAs may create situations where a single government measure could be challenged by the investor (the shareholder, the enterprise, the investment) under different IIAs. In practice, it is

to which two or more Parties are party, such Parties shall immediately consult with a view to finding a mutually satisfactory solution'.

often the case that the investor and the investment will claim the breach of different instruments. This creates a situation that multiplies the risks for host countries in facing investment disputes while increasing possibilities available to foreign investors to sue governments. In this context, parallelism is becoming a source of uncertainty in international investment relations, fostering even further the already multi-faceted, multi-layered IIA regime.

For regionalism to rationalize the IIA regime and tailor a more coherent, manageable and development-oriented set of investment policies, the relationship between regional investment agreements and previous BITs has to be reconsidered. Instead of adding an additional layer of international obligations on Host States by maintaining the rights and obligations of the parties under previous BITs, regional agreements with investment provisions should effectively replace BITs. The standards of protection granted under newer regional agreements are often higher or equal to those found under previous BITs and therefore do not entail a degradation of investor protection standards. In addition, newer regional agreements often reflect the latest trends in international investment treaty-making, including with regards to clarifying in greater detail the meaning of certain standards and ensuring the protection of public policy concerns. Despite this, some regional agreements such as the tripartite investment agreement between China, Japan and Korea (2012) explicitly confirms in Article 25 the continued existence of BITs between the parties. One may assume that such a provision is included because the tripartite agreement offers low investment protection standards, setting a legal floor whereas the BITs provide for extra provisions not found in the BITs. This is not the case as the BIT between China and Japan (1988) limits ISDS to compensation over expropriation and does not contain a performance requirements clause. Hence it provides less instead of more substantive protection. In such a situation, the continued existence of older BITs raises a number of questions related to the purpose and intent of the parties to maintain BITs in parallel to the regional agreement. Furthermore, even in a typical North–South context, the replacement argument appears to be logical from the point of view of both capital exporting countries (wishing to maximize investor protection through newer treaties) and capital importing countries (wishing to streamline international investment obligations).

Despite the present formulation of the relationship between BITs and regional agreements, treaties with investment provisions currently under negotiations still present important windows of opportunity to consolidate the BITs regime. Twelve selected major regional negotiations currently on-going, may potentially overlap (if a full investment protection chapter is included) with 370 BITs, constituting more than 13 per cent of the global BITs network (table 3). To the extent that parties incorporate their prior BITs into the new regional IIA, or terminate/abrogate them, and possibly/eventually replace them with

Table 3. Selected regional initiatives under negotiations and existing number of concluded BITs between the parties

Regional initiative	BITs between the parties
Inter-Arab investment draft agreement	96
Regional Comprehensive Economic Partnership Agreement (RCEP) between ASEAN and Australia, China, India, Japan, New Zealand and the Republic of Korea	68
EU–MERCOSUR FTA	55
Tripartite Free Trade Area between COMESA–EAC–SADC	47
EU–India FTA	23
Trans-Pacific Partnership Agreement (TPP)	21
EU–Morocco Deep and Comprehensive Free Trade Area (DCFTA)	20
EU–Singapore FTA	12
EU–Thailand FTA	12
EU–US Transatlantic Trade and Investment Partnership (TTIP)	8
Canada–EU Comprehensive Economic and Trade Agreement (CETA)	6
PACER-Plus	2
Total:	370

investment chapters in these agreements, this would help move towards a more consolidated network of IIAs.

Rethinking regionalism from this point of view provides a number of important opportunities:

First, in quantitative terms, regional investment agreements have the potential to supersede a substantial number of older BITs, thereby creating a less convoluted set of international investment obligations that becomes easier to manage. This in the long term would disentangle the web and help countries, especially those in the developing world, move towards a set of more coherent, manageable and development-oriented investment policies.

Second, the negotiating process of regional investment agreements differs substantially from bilateral negotiations. It typically involves multiple parties at different levels of economic development, which may create a conducive environment for countries to express specific concerns and developmental challenges that may be easier to address at the regional, rather than the bilateral, level. In terms of substantive negotiations, the emergence of regional investment agreements provides an opportunity for countries to reach more balanced agreements that move away from the investment protection-oriented model that goes beyond investment protection to also address emerging social, economic, environmental and developmental challenges.

Third, regional investment agreements can build on and foster economic integration among a group of countries, including in a south–south regional integration context. The importance of inter-regional FDI to economic integration has been noted in a number of research papers.[69]

> FDI has become more important than trade for delivering goods and services to foreign markets. In addition to integrating markets, FDI also integrates production activities internationally through the corporate production systems established by transnational corporations (TNCs). Such deep integration constitutes, in many ways, the productive core of the globalizing world economy.[70]

Creating regional legal frameworks governing FDI flows among members belonging to the same economic bloc will certainly constitute a step forward towards deeper integration.

Fourth, regional cooperation on investment can establish useful precedents and build consensus among countries on core elements of investment protection and sustainable development. This may, in turn, spur a more constructive dialogue on international investment policy, representing a crucial step towards multilateralism.

Against the backdrop of a shifting international investment policy landscape, UNCTAD has developed a new Investment Policy Framework for Sustainable Development (IPFSD).[71] The framework consists of a set of core principles for investment policy-making, guidelines for national investment policies, and guidance for policy-makers on how to engage in the international investment policy regime, in the form of options for the design and use of international investment agreements. The IPFSD identifies a *'new generation'* of investment policies that aim to operationalize sustainable development through concrete measures and mechanisms at the national and

---

[69] See for example, P Brenton, F Di Mauro and M Lücke 'Economic Integration and FDI: An Empirical Analysis of Foreign Investment in the EU and in Central and Eastern Europe' (1998) Kiel Working Paper 890 <http://papers.ssrn.com/sol3/papers.cfm?abstract_id=139908>; JH Dunning and P Robson *Transnational Corporations and Regional Economic Integration, The United Nations Library on Transnational Corporations* (1988) vol 9; C Daude, E Levy Yeyati, and EH Stein, 'Regional Integration and the Location of FDI' (2003) IDB Working Paper 4343 <http://www.iadb.org/en/research-and-data/publication-details,3169.html?pub_id=wp-492>; MG Plummer and D Cheong 'FDI Effects of ASEAN Integration' (2008) MPRA Paper 26004 <http://mpra.ub.uni-muenchen.de/26004/>; DW te Velde and D Bezemer, *Regional Integration and Foreign Direct Investment in Developing Countries* (2004), <http://unctad.org/en/docs/iteiit20062a3_en.pdf>

[70] KP Sauvant, 'New Sources of FDI: The BRICS: Outward FDI from Brazil, Russia, India and China' (2005) 6(5) *Journal of World Investment & Trade* 639.

[71] UNCTAD, *Investment Policy Framework for Sustainable Development* (2012), <http://unctad.org/en/PublicationsLibrary/diaepcb2012d5_en.pdf>.

international levels in policy-making and implementation. Broadly, 'new generation' investment policies strive to create synergies with wider economic development goals or industrial policies, to achieve seamless integration with development strategies, and to foster responsible investor behaviour through incorporating principles of corporate social responsibility.

Rising tides lift most boats. The shifting trend from bilateral to regional investment treaty-making and the quest for a more balanced and manageable set of international investment obligations may be expected to prompt more developing countries to strengthen cooperation on investment policies at the regional level. In this context, UNCTAD's IPFSD can be a useful tool for countries seeking guidance when approaching the negotiation table to forge a regional investment pact.

3

The Role of Preferential Trade Agreements in International Investment Policy

*Stephen Woolcock**

ABSTRACT

Preferential trade agreements have played an important role in the evolution of international investment policy. Indeed, the emergence of international investment policies over the last half century or more can be best described as a multilevel process. Policies and rules have been shaped by initiatives at all levels starting from top-down multilateral efforts and ranging through, plurilateral, regional and bilateral initiatives to unilateral actions. Bilateral investment treaties and more recently bilateral comprehensive trade and investment agreements have had a major impact, but these must still be seen in the context of broader plurilateral and regional initiatives. The current debate is shaped by a renewed belief that preferential initiatives will further international, meaning global, investment rules. There are regional (such as the Trans-Pacific Partnership), plurilateral (such as the International Services Agreement) and bilateral initiatives (such as the shape of the Transatlantic Trade and Investment Partnership). But such recent policy developments really confirm the multilevel nature of investment policy and the fact that the choice of level is largely shaped by the strategic interests of key agents.

1. INTRODUCTION

This article provides a broad historical background to the current debate on investment in free trade agreements. It covers the period from the late 1940s to the present day and therefore does not reach into the detail of how the content of investment agreements and rules have evolved, although it points

* Associate Professor, London School of Economics, s.b.woolcock@lse.ac.uk.

to differences between the predominant 'models' as these continue to shape policy and international agreements. The article also identifies a number of different phases in the evolution of this multilevel process that suggest shifts in the relative importance of the different levels over time.

2. EARLY MULTILATERAL EFFORTS: THE LEAGUE OF NATIONS TO THE OECD

The origins of efforts to introduce international investment rules date, as is well documented, from the 1920s and 1930s with the draft investment provisions of the League of Nations.[1] These were based on the so-called Hull formula of 'prompt, adequate and effective' compensation in cases of expropriation, which in turn dated from US concerns about Mexican expropriations in the 1920s. The central tension at that time was between capital importing countries that subscribed to the Calvo doctrine that investment should be regulated according to Host State law and capital exporting countries that sought protection for investment undertaken by their nationals in independent but developing countries that did not provide, in the view of the investors, adequate protection under their national laws.

The next major multilateral effort to establish multilateral investment rules came with the negotiation of the 1948 Havana Charter of the International Trade Organisation (ITO). Just as in the 1930s there was a tension between the US on the one side and capital importing countries on the other over the scope for national laws and national governments to determine inward investment and investment policy. The US led because it was the capital exporting country *par excellence* of the day with the European economies destroyed or indebted. The US was keen to establish a strong multilateral order in the post-World War II period. This combined with the fact that the State Department led the negotiations and put foreign policy or systemic issues high on its agenda, meant that the US agreed to provisions in the ITO (in Articles 11 and 12 in particular) that ceded to Host States powers to screen and restrict investment and impose 'reasonable requirements' on established investors. These provisions were seen to be too much of a concession to capital importing countries by US business interests and a major reason why the US private sector opposed the ratification of the ITO in the US Congress.[2] With no ITO all that remained was the General Agreement on Tariffs and Trade (GATT) negotiated in 1947, which had no specific provisions on investment. As will be shown below some GATT principles such as national treatment in Article III and the Article XI provisions on restrictions to trade

---

[1] K Vandevelde, *Bilateral Investment Treaties: History, Policy and Interpretation*, (Oxford University Press 2010).

[2] W Diebold, *The End of the ITO* (Princeton University 1952).

could have been applied to limit performance requirements imposed on investment by host governments. But the focus of the GATT was on the reduction of tariff barriers and there was no support for such an expansive interpretation of the GATT. As a result the post 1945 economic order contained no significant provisions on international investment.

The next effort to agree on genuine international investment rules came in the Organisation for Economic Cooperation and Development (OECD) or in reality in its fore runner the OEEC. Again following a US initiative discussions were held on an investment instrument. Once more the divide between capital exporters and capital importers created difficulties. A draft text, building on the so-called Abs-Shawcross text,[3] was produced in an effort to bridge the divide,[4] but this was again seen as too weak by US investor interests that were not ready to accept an agreed text that condoned what they saw as low standards. In the 1960s European governments also wished to retain policy autonomy over foreign investment and so tended to favour investment rules that reflected this. This lack of support for liberal investment policies in Europe was reflected in the Spaak Report[5] and then in the Treaty of Rome establishing the European Economic Community (EEC). Although the Treaty of Rome is presented as providing for the 'four freedoms'—namely for goods, services, capital and labour—it stopped short of full capital liberalization. The freedom of capital anchored in Article 56 was limited to that required for the establishment of a common market. Thus there was provision for free capital movement but EEC Member States continued to screen and restrict foreign direct investment.

The Abs-Shawcross draft, although not accepted as the basis for an international instrument, did provide the basis for European model bilateral investment treaties (BITs). This model covered investment protection only. It included post-establishment national treatment and classic expropriation provisions (ie no de facto expropriation). Standards of protection were at that time broadly defined with no attempt at refinements on national treatment and fair and equitable treatment. The first such European BIT was negotiated between the Federal Republic of Germany and Pakistan in 1959. Germany was possibly more interested in ensuring investment protection for its investors because compared to Britain, France or even the Netherlands it did not have a concentration of investment in colonies or former colonies.

---

[3] H Abs and H Shawcross 'Draft Convention on Investments Abroad' in 'The proposed convention to protect private foreign investment: a round table', 1 *Journal of Public Law* (1960) 115–118.

[4] OECD, Draft Convention on the Protection of Foreign Property, No. 15637 (1962).

[5] 'The Brussels Report on the General Common Market' Information Service, High Authority of the European Community for Coal and Steel (1956).

3. PLURILATERAL LIBERALIZATION AND BILATERAL PROTECTION: 1960 TO 1980

The period roughly between 1960 and 1980 could be said to have been characterized by a bilateral approach in terms of investment protection and a plurilateral approach to liberalization. The bilateral initiatives came mostly from the European capital exporting States with agreements negotiated with developing countries, using the European model BIT based on the Abs-Shawcross text. Between 1959 and 1980 there were 250 BITs negotiated, mostly by European governments.[6] Note that these were agreements negotiated by individual countries not the EEC or EC. The EC had no competence in investment, except arguably that resulting from implied competence resulting from Article 56 EEC.[7]

The plurilateral liberalisation initiatives came through continued work in the OECD among like-minded OECD countries and took the form of the OECD Codes of Liberalisation of Capital Movements and of Current Invisible Operations of 1964.[8] These codes began a long period in which work within the OECD shaped the evolution of investment norms and investment policy.[9] During the initial years of the codes they mostly contributed to removing restrictions on capital movements and enhancing the transparency of controls on investment, without any significant liberalization of controls on foreign direct investment or enhanced access.

The gap between north and south, capital exporting and capital importing countries was if anything accentuated during this period. The south in the shape of the G77 group of developing countries effectively pushed for a reaffirmation of the Calvo doctrine as part of their demands for a New International Economic Order (NIEO) from about 1973 until the late 1970s. This initiative from the G77 led to the 1974 UN Charter on the Economic Rights and Duties of States that was adopted in the General Assembly of the UN and clearly reflected the interests of the developing countries.[10] A motivating factor behind the UN initiative was the desire on the part of developing country governments to reaffirm their ability to control the activities of multinational companies (MNCs). During the 1970s investment by MNCs was seen as potentially undermining the development strategies of developing countries that were based on the promotion of

[6] UNCTAD, *World Investment Report* 2000, UNCTAD Geneva, 2000.

[7] Implied competence in the context of European law is when competence for an external policy is 'implied' as a result of there being EC competence internally within the European Community or now European Union.

[8] E Snyder 'Foreign Investment Protection: a Reasoned Approach' 61 *Michigan Law Review* 6 (1963) 1087–1124.

[9] For a general description of the OECD instruments see OECD, 1987.

[10] General Assembly resolution 3082 (XXVIII) of 6 December 1973 (Charter of Economic Rights and Duties of States)

indigenous infant industries as a means of countering dependence on the developed economies. This multilateral or global initiative by the G77 was opposed by OECD countries as a retrograde step back from the policy of progressive liberalization followed by the OECD. The OECD countries proposed a plurilateral alternative that then took the form of the 1976 OECD Declaration and Decisions on International Investment and Multinational Enterprises. This provided a non-binding set of Guidelines for Multinational Enterprises[11] and an equally non-binding provision on national treatment.[12]

Perhaps the most significant initiative in the field of investment policy during the period was the shift in national policies to liberalise investment. These unilateral initiatives came right at the end of the period, led by the United States and followed by the United Kingdom. The US had always pursued a liberal investment policy, but before the 1980s many European countries retained policies of screening and controlling inward investment as part of their national-champion-based industrial policies. This was explicit in the case of countries such as France, but rather more implicit in the case of West Germany which maintained a nominally liberal policy. These unilateral initiatives both reflected a shift in thinking away from investment policies shaped by national ownership considerations and contributed to policy change by establishing competition between States in attracting FDI. This competition has been subsequently seen as one of the main vectors of policy diffusion of liberal investment policies and agreements.[13]

The period from around 1960 to the end of the 1970s therefore illustrates the multilevel nature of investment policy. It started with renewed efforts to establish liberal investment rules at an international level. When these again failed, largely because of ideological differences between capital exporting and capital importing countries, the former opted for plurilateral liberalization initiatives and bilateral treaties to protect investment. Capital importers sought to use their numerical advantage in the UN to push through a resolution that they hoped would help strengthen the collective action of the developing countries in resisting liberal investment pressure. But it was the unilateral decisions to move to significant liberalization among some leading OECD countries that were to have the greatest impact. The various international instruments, such as the OECD codes

[11] <http://www.oecd.org/daf/inv/mne/oecdguidelinesformultinationalenterprises.htm>.

[12] OECD *Foreign Direct Investment: Policies and Trends in the OECD Area during the 1980s* (Paris 1993).

[13] Z Elkins, AT Guzman and B Simmons 'Competing for Capital: The Diffusion of Bilateral Investment Treaties 1960–2000', Berkeley Law: Berkeley Law Scholarship Repository: 1-1-2008 (2008) <http://scholarship.law.berkeley.edu/facpubs>.

and BITs, became the means by which liberal policies were codified and made irreversible.[14]

4. 1980–1994 POSITIVE SYNERGY?

The period 1980 to 1994 was one of increasing activity at all levels of policy. Initially this activity created a positive synergy in terms of regional initiatives promoting wider international agreement. By the end of the period, however, it became clear that the alternative of bilateral approaches to investment liberalization and rules was undermining efforts to create comprehensive multilateral rules for investment.

In the early 1980s the United States took a number of initiatives in the field of investment. At the multilateral level the US administration pressed for investment, as well as services and high technology trade, to be included in the GATT agenda. The apparent intention of the US was to include a fully-fledged investment agreement in the GATT as part of a new round of trade negotiations. This followed an earlier proposal in the 1970s for a GATT for investment.[15] The proposals put forward by the US administration in 1981 did not find support among developing countries and the European Community was also generally negative on the idea of starting a new round of trade negotiations. At that time economic growth was slow so many EC Member State governments were not ready to move on a liberalization agenda and some were concerned that the US would attack the EC on agricultural protection. The GATT Ministerial meeting in 1982 at which the US made the case for a trade round to include, among other things investment, was therefore inconclusive and the US Trade Representative at the time (William Brock) announced that the US would seek alternative routes to liberalise trade and investment in the shape of free trade agreements with Israel and Canada.[16]

---

[14] While governments can use their sovereign rights to repudiate treaties and agreements this is not without costs in terms of reputation and lost investment. The OECD instruments provided for an explicit ratchet mechanism. OECD governments were not obliged to liberalize a certain sector or category of investment, but once they did the ratchet was there to stop the reintroduction of controls. Bilateral investment treaties can be repudiated and are from time to time, but under international law protection provided by BITs tends to continue for a decade after the repudiation of a treaty by any party. In other words the various investment instruments are there to provide predictability and security for investors.

[15] CP Kindleberger and P Goldberg 'Towards a GATT for Investment: A Proposal for Supervision of International Corporations' *Law and Policy in International Business* 2 (1970) 295–323.

[16] J Croome *Reshaping the World Trading System: The History of the Uruguay Round* (DIANE 1996).

The case of Canada is interesting because the US challenged Canadian policy on inward investment under GATT. The dispute concerned the application of performance requirements by Canada and specifically under the Foreign Investment Review Act (FIRA). The FIRA case went through GATT dispute settlement and the GATT panel found that local content requirements were inconsistent with GATT Article III:4, but not export requirements. The case therefore highlighted the limited scope for use of the GATT 1948 to challenge national investment policies and specifically the use of performance requirements. The US response was to seek to negotiate stronger international disciplines at the multilateral level in the GATT or alternatively at the bilateral level in the Canada–US Free Trade Agreement.

At the same time the US developed a comprehensive policy on investment in the shape of the 1982 US model bilateral investment treaty (BIT). Up to this time the US had not engaged in many bilateral investment negotiations and it had been the Europeans using the Abs-Shawcross format that had shaped the nature of investment agreements. The 1982 US model BIT was far more comprehensive. It covered investment liberalization (pre-establishment national treatment) as well as investment protection (post-establishment national treatment). The 1982 US model BIT also set out to prohibit a large number of performance requirements, reaching far beyond those that could be challenged under existing GATT rules. In terms of investment protection the US model included provisions on both classic and de facto expropriation, or 'regulatory takings' as it became known, in other words protection against regulation by host governments that effectively reduces the value of assets. This was all to be backed-up by investor-State dispute settlement.[17] Here, then, was a statement of the high standards the US was seeking in investment agreements and a model that was to be used by the US in subsequent negotiations, whether with Canada and Mexico in the subsequent North American Free Trade Agreement) or in bilateral negotiations for subsequent comprehensive trade and investment agreements. It also established a high standard and thus high expectations for any plurilateral or multilateral negotiation. Anything that fell short of these standards was certain to be criticized by US investors and the US Congress as sub-standard.

At the multilateral level negotiations on what was to become the Uruguay Round of the GATT began to gather pace during the 1980s. The European Community in particular moved to adopt a more positive position on a new round including on the topics of services and to a lesser degree investment. The services issue relates to investment because one of the four modes by which services can be delivered is establishment. Commitments

---

[17] US Senate, US–Panama Bilateral Investment Treaty, Senate Treaty Document 99–14, 99th Congress, 2nd Session, 27 October (1987).

on establishment in services were to take the form of national treatment and thus liberalization. The Uruguay Round also included what came to be called Trade Related Investment Measures or TRIMs. This term covered all those investment measures adopted by host governments seeking to ensure that foreign investment contributes to the local value added. These are referred to as performance requirements on inward investors. Developing countries, led by India and Brazil, were opposed to the inclusion of investment per se in the Uruguay Round so the compromise was to look at investment measures that could be seen as restricting trade. This concerned the negotiation of increased GATT disciplines governing performance requirements. Ambitions varied between the US, which was seeking GATT disciplines of 14 TRIMs and developing countries and the Newly Industrialising Countries that favoured merely a clearer definition of which TRIMs were covered by the existing GATT. The European Community's position and that of Japan took up an intermediate position favouring a ban on a limited number of six core TRIMs.

During the course of negotiations the US used unilateral measures to strengthen its leverage. This took the form of the threat to use US trade legislation in the shape of section 301 of the US Trade Act of 1974 to act against countries that were seen to be 'unfairly' restricting investment. The domestic political economy of US trade policy and the interaction between the US Administration, which was seeking agreement on the round, and the US Congress, which had rather more aggressive aims of opening up large developing country markets for US investors, meant that support for a new round of trade liberalization could only be obtained from Congress in return for a strengthening of US trade legislation. This took the form of the Omnibus Trade and Competitiveness Act of 1988, which provided the US with powers to act against countries that pursued what were defined as unfair measures, including some restrictions on investment and a lack of respect of intellectual property rights. For developing countries this then increased the costs of rejecting any discussion of investment in the Uruguay Round.

The Omnibus Trade and Competitiveness Act also granted formal negotiating authority to the executive branch to negotiate a free trade agreement with Canada. The negotiations with Canada had begun in 1986 and were finalized in 1988. The Canada–US FTA effectively incorporated the comprehensive provisions of the US model BIT. It was presented by US negotiators as 'showing how it can be done', in other words as a model for a wider trade and investment agreement. Discussions on a regional agreement to include Mexico also began in 1990. These were to lead to the NAFTA agreement, which was signed in December 1992 but first implemented in 1994 after the Clinton Administration had negotiated a number of side agreements to obtain congressional approval. The NAFTA again embodied the US model BIT provisions. It covered pre-establishment national treatment and thus liberalization, based on a negative list system. Twelve performance requirements were prohibited. There was protection against classic and de facto expropriation and unrestricted freedom for funds transfer. Finally, the NAFTA included detailed provisions on investor-state dispute settlement including the use of international arbitration procedures.

There was another important regional initiative in investment policy taking place in the European Union. By the mid to late 1980s many national policies had shifted to a more liberal stance. This can be seen to have been in part due to the effects of competition leading to unilateral liberalisation of investment policies. The general move to create a Single European Market and thus end the fragmentation of the European market due to the pursuit of national champion strategies by many European governments also facilitated a shift towards more liberal investment policies. In 1988 the European Community adopted an Investment Directive that finally implemented the treaty aim set out in Article 56 EEC of free movement of capital within the single market.[18] This meant full liberalization of capital flows, but with the safeguard that capital controls could be reintroduced in exceptional circumstances when flows disrupt monetary policy objectives.

During the negotiations on multilateral rules on investment in the Uruguay Round of the GATT, which covered both TRIMs and the establishment provisions in the General Agreement on Trade in Services (GATS), based on a positive list approach to coverage, there were therefore parallel bilateral and regional initiatives. Whether these bilateral and regional initiatives facilitated multilateral negotiations or detracted from them has not been definitively resolved.[19] At the time regional initiatives were certainly presented as models for wider multilateral agreements, but the NAFTA approach failed to gain much traction in the GATT negotiations. The draft final text of the Uruguay Round that emerged in December 1991 was closer to the EC/Japanese position and prohibited only six TRIMs. By at least as early as 1991 it was clear that the GATT was not going to deliver high standard rules on investment liberalization, let alone investment protection.

At about the same time that the scope of the Uruguay Round provisions on investment were becoming clear there were renewed efforts to strengthen the OECD's investment instruments. These took the form of the OECD review of the National Treatment instrument of 1991. This encompassed the section on national treatment of the 1976 Declaration on International Investment and Multinational Enterprises (the 'Declaration') and the procedures adopted to implement the Declaration, such as the requirement to

---

[18] See the Capital Liberalisation Directive, Council Directive 88/361/EEC June 24th for the implementation of art 56 of the Treaty.

[19] S Woolcock, (ed) *Trade and Investment Rule-making: The Role of Regional and Bilateral Agreements* (United Nations University Press 2006).

notify exceptions to national treatment, the obligation not to reintroduce a restriction on investment once it had been removed (the ratchet mechanism) and peer review procedure. The aim of the 1991 review was to make the instrument binding. But differences emerged within the OECD membership. For example, should the instrument cover sub-federal level government? This was a demand of the European Community because EU legislation reached down to the level of states and provinces, whereas federal states and provinces in the US and Canada were not covered. Another sensitive issue was whether investment controls could be imposed on the grounds of national security, such as when a foreign company invests or gains control of a company that is seen to have strategic importance for the host state. The problem here was (and remains) how to define what was necessary for national security in order to prevent such an exception being abused as a means of restricting foreign investment. There was also a question concerning the treatment of preferential (trade) agreements under the OECD instrument. These differences prevented an agreement at the plurilateral level of the OECD on a strengthening of the investment instruments. The negotiations were concluded with an agreement to continue discussing the scope for a wider investment instrument within the OECD.[20] This was to later emerge as the proposal for a 'Multilateral Agreement on Investment' (MAI). The issues raised in the negotiations on the National Treatment instrument continue to shape the debate today and remain to be addressed in the current negotiations on a Transatlantic Trade and Investment Partnership (TTIP).[21]

As noted above the nature of the Uruguay Round outcome on TRIMs was more or less clear by 1991. This was not the case for the negotiations on establishment under the auspices of the GATS. A framework agreement and commitments on some sectors were agreed as part of the Uruguay Round in 1993 and ratified in 1994, but negotiations continued until 1997 on sector agreements in financial services and telecommunications. These latter sector agreements were in effect plurilateral agreements and took binding rules further than for the GATS as a whole.

5. 1995–2000: COMPETITIVE LIBERALIZATION

The Uruguay Round resulted in rather modest advances in two areas of investment rules, those on performance requirements and on establishment in the service sector, where commitments were disappointing with most being limited to the OECD countries that were already engaged in liberalization. In

[20] OECD, C (91)147/FINA (12 December 1991).

[21] See for example, the Resolution of the European Parliament on European Union trade and investment negotiations with the United States of America 2013/2558(RSP)

retrospect the GATS has come to be seen as a means of codifying or binding unilateral moves towards liberalization. In the immediate post Uruguay Round period there was a general consensus among policy-makers in the established developed economies that investment represented an area in which liberalization was lagging compared to trade, but there was no consensus on the level at which new initiatives should be taken. In terms of policy statements the European Union came out in favour of a multilateral approach to investment and pushed for the inclusion of investment in the WTO. In 1994 the European Commission produced a communication arguing for a level playing field for investment.[22] This favoured negotiations at a multilateral level on investment, because most of the barriers to investment were in developing countries and not in the OECD where considerable progress had been made in liberalization. The Commission also argued that developing countries would not accept a 'fait accomplit' from the OECD and could therefore not be expected to sign up to a wider investment instrument emanating from the OECD process. There were also internal EU issues and interests at stake. The Commission argued that the growing number of EU Member State BITs was distorting investment flows within the EU as some Member States had far more bilateral BITs with third countries than others. A negotiation in the WTO would also have furthered the Commission's aim of extending de facto EU competence, as it was the norm that only the Commission spoke in the WTO whereas the Member States negotiated in the OECD.[23] The fact that the Commission had right of initiative in matters of trade and in effect in the WTO, meant that it was able to include investment as one of the so-called Singapore issues pushed by the European Union at the time of the first WTO Ministerial meeting in Singapore in 1996.

The US government's position favoured a plurilateral route in order to ensure that any agreement that was reached would set high standards. The poor record of negotiations at the multilateral level stretching back over decades and confirmed by the experience of the Uruguay Round efforts to strengthen multilateral disciplines on investment, had convinced US interests in the private sector and government, that any WTO agreement would not fit the bill in terms of a high standard agreement. The idea with what became the Multilateral Agreement on Investment (MAI) negotiations that were launched in May 1995, was that international rules for investment would be negotiated that would in time replace the patchwork of different bilateral

---

[22] European Commission 'Towards a Level Playing Field for International Investment' (1994).

[23] The European Commission also participated in OECD discussions and there was an effort to coordinate Member State positions, but the fact that Member State governments negotiated and spoke in OECD meetings meant it was easier for national governments to hold off any slippage of competence to the EU.

agreements that had emerged. Negotiating an agreement among likeminded states would facilitate agreement on high standard rules that would then attract new signatories.

In the event both the plurilateral and the multilateral approaches failed. The OECD initially made more rapid progress and draft agreements were developed by 1998. But the negotiators were not able to resolve some of the underlying differences between OECD countries that had already been present at the time of the debate on the binding National Treatment instrument in the early 1990s. To these persistent differences between OECD members came the now well known concerted civil society campaign against the MAI as the latest embodiment of a form of globalization that was seen to be counter to the interests of developing countries, the environment and organized labour.[24] Negotiators began to modify the draft agreement to address the concerns of civil society, which then undermined business support. Governments then saw little to gain from supporting the MAI but a potential to lose votes and, led by France, they withdrew from the negotiations in 1998.

The failure of the MAI undermined the probably already remote prospect of including investment in the planned millennium trade round that was to be launched in Seattle in late 1999. Although a WTO working group had been established[25] to look at trade and investment after the Singapore ministerial meeting, work on investment was opposed by developing countries and the developed economies gave a clear preference to the OECD work. The collapse of the MAI was seen as a victory for global civil society, which went on to campaign against the launch of a new round of the WTO in Seattle. In the Seattle meeting the Singapore issues, including investment, were supported only by the EU, Japan, Korea, Hungary and Switzerland. Although the EU in particular continued to press for the inclusion of the Singapore issues in the WTO agenda, the prospects after the MAI were slim and investment along with government procurement and competition were finally dropped from the WTO's Doha Development Agenda at the Cancun Ministerial meeting in September 2003.[26]

In the background of these plurilateral and multilateral efforts there was a burgeoning of bilateral initiatives in the shape of comprehensive trade and investment agreements. From the mid-1990s there was also a shift in opinion in the United States away from seeing preferential agreements as a means of furthering wider multilateral approaches, as had been the position up to then, to a policy of competitive liberalization, which saw preferential approaches as an alternative to multilateral or wider international approaches

---

24 D Henderson *The MAI Affair: a story and its lessons* (RIIA, 1999).

25 <http://www.wto.org/english/thewto_e/whatis_e/tif_e/bey3_e.htm>

26 <http://www.wto.org/english/thewto_e/minist_e/min03_e/draft_decl_e.htm>

provided they brought about liberalization.[27] Initially held up by the lack of formal negotiating authority, the policy of competitive liberalization was applied actively from 2001 when the Bush Administration gained Trade Promotion Authority. There followed a series of comprehensive FTA negotiations that applied the US model BIT with regard to investment.[28] The US BIT model was also updated in 2004 and again in 2012.[29] With rare exceptions, the investment provisions in these agreements were based on the NAFTA and thus the US model BIT. This strategy of opting for the alternative of bilateral agreements meant that the US was able to extend its influence over international investment policy. It did so in order to seek high standards and not accept weaker rules in any plurilateral or multilateral agreement.

The fact that the US was able to influence international investment policy right through to the current period was in part because there was no single comprehensive common EU investment policy. In the Uruguay Round there had been a common EU position on GATS and TRIMs because the Member States had effectively ceded de facto, if not de jure, competence to the EU. But formal competence remained divided between the EU where the Commission played a strategic role in trade negotiations and the Member States which retained competence to negotiate and conclude BITs. The European approach to investment protection was still essentially based on the old Abs-Shawcross text and applied through separate Member States BITs. The Member State BITs generally do not include any liberalization of investment. The standards of protection, moreover, continue to be couched in general principles of national treatment and fair and equitable treatment that are not more closely defined. This has been seen as providing a significant scope for interpretative discretion in arbitration proceedings such that national policy could well be shaped by arbitral bodies outside the political process. This concern is exacerbated by the fact that the transparency provisions in the Member State BITs are not well developed either. With shifts in the flow of investment it has been argued that the EU Member States may find themselves on the receiving end of expensive damages claims, as has been the case for some of the new Member States. With more investment flowing into the EU from emerging markets there may be more claims. But this position has been countered by a majority of Member States that argue that they have not yet lost a case. In 2010 the adoption of the Treaty on Functioning of the European Union (the Lisbon treaty) resulted in foreign

---

27 S Evenett and M Meier 'An Interim Assessment of the US Trade Policy of Competitive Liberalization *The World Economy*, Vol 31 Issue 1 pp 31–66.

28 Agreements with Jordan 2001, Singapore and Chile 2004, Australia 2005, Morocco and Bahrain 2006 and agreements were signed with CAFTA-DR in 2005–6, Colombia and Peru 2004 and Korea 2007 that were only ratified with a delay.

29 The US Model BIT had already been revised as a result of experience with NAFTA.

direct investment becoming the exclusive competence of the EU. This means that Member States have lost the ability to negotiate bilateral investment agreements without EU authorization, but in the transition period from Member State to EU BITs the Member State governments have continued to resist any change in the established policies and have sought to stick to the existing European style of BIT in negotiations with third countries.[30]

The shared competence between the EU and Member States prior to the Treaty of Lisbon meant that the EU was not able to negotiate comprehensive trade and investment agreements as the US did during the 2000s. The EU did, however, negotiate some bilateral FTAs, such as EU–Chile in 2001, which included liberalization of investment. In July 2006 the Commission, which had long sought to enhance the EU's role in investment policy, developed a so-called agreed platform for establishment, trade in services and ecommerce for future FTA negotiations. This came at a time when the EU shifted (back) to a more active strategy of negotiating bilateral FTAs with growth markets in the Global Europe policy statement of 2006 (Evenett, 2006). The platform then shaped the liberalization elements of subsequent EU FTAs.[31]

The inability to conclude comprehensive trade and investment agreements on a par with the US reduced the EU's influence on international investment policy over the past 20 years. After the adoption of the Lisbon treaty the question now becomes whether the EU can develop an EU model BIT and whether it can use this to shape international policy. The early discussions on EU investment policy suggest, as noted above, that the Member States are fighting a rear guard action to retain the existing approach and the Commission has ruled out the formal development of model treaty language.[32] European business is concerned that investment policy will become politicised, as the MAI was in the 1990s, and would therefore prefer to avoid a broad public debate. Following the Treaty of Lisbon any formal EU model investment agreement would need to get the consent of the European Parliament, which is sometimes seen as a source of politicizing EU external trade and investment policy. The shift in the EU to an active policy of negotiating comprehensive trade and investment agreements therefore

---

[30] 'The EU Approach to International Investment Policy after the Lisbon Treaty', Directorate General for External Policies, Policy Department, the European Parliament, EXPO/B/INTA/FWC/2009-01/Lot7/07-08-09 (2010).

[31] See for example the EU's agreements with Colombia and Peru, the Comprehensive Economic Partnership Agreement with CARIFORUM and the FTA with Korea. The Interim EPAs with developing countries in the ACPs have not included these provisions on establishment, cross border supply of services and ecommerce.

[32] NJ Calamita, 'The Making of Europe's International Investment Policy: Uncertain First Steps' in NJ Calamita et al (eds) *The Future of ICSID and the Place of Investment Treaties in International Law* (BIICL 2013).

provides further impetus to 'competitive liberalization' as the EU seeks to match what the US does and others seek to match what such major WTO Members do.[33]

Apart from the US and the EU a number of other countries are concluding comprehensive trade and investment agreements. Many of these follow the NAFTA model, thus agreements negotiated by Mexico, Chile and Singapore with third countries following their agreements with the US, also adopted the NAFTA model, as has Canada.[34] China has negotiated some FTAs that include investment, for example the bilateral agreement with Peru includes both investment liberalization and investment protection, and even include investor-State dispute settlement although with a less detailed set of enforcement mechanisms. The one notable absence is anything on labour or environmental standards. There is a trend among capital importing developing countries to reassess their BITs. In the 1990s developing countries were falling over themselves to conclude BITs in the belief that this would lead to more FDI and facilitate their access to the international economy and global supply chains. With limited evidence that BITs have made such a contribution there has been a reassessment in a growing number of countries such as South Africa and a number of Latin American States.

6. CURRENT CHALLENGES

The current period is dominated by preferential trade and investment negotiations rather than initiatives at the multilateral or plurilateral level. In the services sector there is an initiative, led by the United States, to negotiate an International Services Agreement. This was initially presented as a plurilateral initiative in which only like-minded countries ready to make real commitments would participate. Given the WTO rules on plurilateral agreements, however, which require the endorsement of the Ministerial Conference by consensus, it soon became clear that a plurilateral agreement within the WTO would be improbable. This would require developing countries that had previously opposed the inclusion of investment as one of the Singapore issues in the Doha Development negotiations to accept an agreement that could shape the de facto policy environment, but which they had had no say in shaping. The promoters of a services agreement will therefore probably use

---

33 Another policy consideration here is that if the EU were to manage to develop a clear comprehensive model for investment agreements it may set the bar at a specific level in terms of standards just as the US NAFTA model has. This would reduce the EU's flexibility in negotiating preferential agreements. To date the EU has shown more flexibility than the US in such negotiations (K Heydon and S Woolcock *The Rise of Bilateralism* (Ashgate 2009).

34 J Reiter 'Investment' in Woolcock (n 19).

Article V of the GATS, which provides for preferential agreements in the services sector, if they wish to ensure the agreement comes within the WTO.

A theoretical case might be made that the time is now ripe for negotiation of a genuine multilateral investment agreement. The case for this is based on the view that the emerging markets will become progressively more important as capital exporters and the established OECD countries will become increasing importers of capital, thus redressing the structural imbalance of investment flows that has been at the root of many differences in previous negotiations. It may also be argued that the emergence of globalized production and value chains has meant that all governments have an interest in ensuring that investment is liberalized and protected. The emergence of the EU as a stronger actor in investment policy could also be seen as strengthening the chances of a multilateral agreement as EU policy since the 1990s has supported multialteralism. The historical record should, however, be enough to warn against undue optimism on this front.

The US does not appear to have changed its strategy of competitive liberalization, which includes the aim of seeking to shape international rules and standards by means of preferential agreements. For a period in the second half of the 1990s and the beginning of the 2010s US policy on trade and investment was quiescent due to a lack of domestic support for active policies. In the last two years however the US has re-emerged with an active strategy and it remains one of competitive liberalisation through the promotion of the Trans-Pacific Partnership (TPP), the International Services Agreement and more recently the Transatlantic Trade and Investment Partnership (TTIP). The belief is that agreements covering such important economies will establish *de facto* international standards for trade and investment. Since 2006 the EU has also pursued an active FTA strategy. Thus whilst appearing more supportive of multilateral solutions than the US the EU has begun to follow a similar approach. Recent trends therefore seem to confirm that bilateral or other preferential initiatives will undermine the prospect of international agreement on investment.

7. CONCLUSIONS

International investment policy has always been multilevel. For much of the post-war period the United States as the major capital exporter has been the driving force behind international investment policy. It has sought multilateral approaches and repeatedly promoted plurilateral initiatives but without success. In the recent past it has adopted a competitive liberalization strategy that seeks to both open investment markets and shape international investment standards through bilateral or preferential agreements. As a result the dominant norm for investment agreements has become the NAFTA model.

Europe has offered something of an alternative approach based on bilateral agreements of EU Member States and EU efforts at liberalization, but the fragmented nature of the EU has meant this has had less influence in shaping policy, at least to date.

A case can be made that there is a chance to develop multilateral investment policies. The major shifts in the world economy brought about by emerging markets means that there are changes in the balance of capital flows. The EU now has an opportunity to develop a coherent investment policy following the extension of exclusive competence to foreign direct investment. And developing economies are reassessing their positions on FDI. But the analysis above suggests that preferential agreements will remain the main factor shaping investment policy.

4

Towards a Free Flow of Investment: Is ASEAN Making Progress?

*Myrna S Austria**

1. INTRODUCTION

Foreign direct investment (FDI) has been an essential factor influencing economic development and growth of the individual member economies of the Association of Southeast Asian Nations (ASEAN).[1] The common benefits associated with FDI to a host country's economic development include access to world markets, employment generation, high wages and benefits to workers, technology transfers, high levels of research and development, sophisticated managerial and marketing techniques, and spillover to the rest of the economy.[2] However, to the ASEAN economies, FDI has been much more than these. As host to the global production network (GPN) of multinational companies (MNCs) since the 1990s, FDI has been central to the economic integration of the region.[3] The falling barriers to trade, investment and improvement in information and communication technology enabled MNCs to locate various stages of their highly complex production processes in the most cost-efficient markets among the ASEAN economies. The production model led to the expansion of intra-ASEAN trade through the

* Full Professor and Vice Chancellor for Academics, De La Salle University, myrna.austria@dlsu.edu.ph. The author would like to thank Gio Punsalang for the excellent research assistance provided.

[1] See eg S Urata and M Ando, Investment Climate Study on ASEAN Member Countries, ERIA Research Project Report 2008, No 1 Economic Research Institute for ASEAN and East Asia, 2009; R Aldaba and J Yap, 'Investment and Capital Flows: Implications of the ASEAN Economic Community', *PIDS Discussion Paper Series*, No. 2009-01, 2009.

[2] T Moran, *Foreign Direct Investment and Development: The New Policy Agenda for Developing Countries and Economies in Transition* (Washington DC, Institute for International Economies, 1999).

[3] M Austria 'Moving Towards an ASEAN Economic Community' (2012) 29 *East Asia: An International Quarterly* 141–156.

regionalization of the manufacture, assembly and export phases of the production cycle. This FDI-trade nexus propelled the ASEAN-5 economies to high economic growth as well as increasing economic integration with other East Asian economies.[4]

Sustaining FDI inflows to the region over the past two decades, however, has always been a continuing challenge to the ASEAN economies. The Asian financial crises of 2007–08 and the US/EU financial crisis of 2008–09 demonstrated the vulnerability of FDI inflows to the ASEAN region. As will be discussed later, the share of the region to FDI inflows and stock to developing countries has not increased beyond the levels achieved prior to the Asian financial crisis. Likewise, China has overtaken ASEAN in attracting FDI inflows due to its rise as an economic power. Similarly, the proliferation of bilateral as well as regional free trade agreements almost everywhere around the globe has created many new competitors for the ASEAN economies, both for their exports as well as sources of FDI.[5]

The constant pressure to stay competitive created momentum for ASEAN leaders to establish in 2003 the ASEAN Economic Community (AEC) with the goal of deepening and broadening regional economic integration. The AEC is characterized by four pillars: single market and production base, highly competitive economic region, a region of equitable economic development, and a region fully integrated into the global economy.[6] While the original timeline for AEC was 2020, it was subsequently accelerated to 2015 in response to the confluence of regional as well as global challenges that confronted the region. As a single market and production base, the AEC is envisioned to have five core elements: (i) free flow of goods; (ii) free flow of services; (iii) free flow of investment; (iv) more free flow of capital; and (v) free flow of skilled labour.[7]

As one of the core elements of AEC, a free and open investment regime is the key to enhancing the region's competitiveness in attracting FDI. However, the region's investment climate has evolved as a product of bilateral as well as regional investment treaties between member economies or with economies outside of the region, giving rise to the infamous 'spaghetti-bowl effect'.[8] Instead of attracting FDI, the diverse investment treaties may divert FDI away from the region.

---

[4] ASEAN-5 includes Indonesia, Malaysia, Philippines, Singapore and Thailand.

[5] Austria (n 3).

[6] ASEAN Blueprint, 2009; ERIA, *Mid-term Review of the Implementation of AEC Blueprint: Executive Summary* (ERIA, Jakarta, October 2012).

[7] *Roadmap for an ASEAN Community 2009–2015*, (ASEAN Secretariat, Jakarta, 2009).

[8] The 'spaghetti-bowl effect' was first associated with free trade agreements (FTAs), whereby countries belonging to different FTAs are connected to each other by spaghetti-like strands of preferential trade agreements that are very different from each other. Such differences give rise to overlaps and inconsistencies among the FTAs.

The primary objective of this paper is to analyze the ASEAN's investment regime and its effect on attracting FDI into the region. Is the ASEAN making progress towards achieving the goal of a free flow of investment? The remainder of this paper is organized as follows: Section 2 discusses the ASEAN Comprehensive Investment Agreement (ACIA), the ASEAN's framework for a free and open investment regime. Section 3 discusses ACIA vis-à-vis other international investment agreements to which the ASEAN or the individual member economies are party. Section 4 analyses FDI trends and performance drawing implications from the investment environment. Section 5 discusses the need to address FDI-policy related issues in order to achieve the goal of free flow of investment. Finally, Section 6 presents the summary and the way forward.

2. ACIA: ASEAN'S FRAMEWORK TOWARDS A FREE AND OPEN INVESTMENT REGIME

The ASEAN's investment regime has evolved gradually since the late 1980s. Originally, separate frameworks governed investment protection and investment liberalization. Investment protection was guided by the ASEAN Agreement for the Promotion and Protection of Investment or what is commonly referred to as the ASEAN Investment Guarantee Agreement (IGA), signed in 1987. On the other hand, investment liberalization was driven by the Framework Agreement on the ASEAN Investment Area (AIA), signed in October 1998 and amended in 2001. In response to the emerging competitive global environment for FDI and hence, the need to enhance the region's competitiveness as an investment destination, the AIA and IGA were revised and merged into a single comprehensive investment agreement, the ASEAN Comprehensive Investment Agreement (ACIA). The agreement was signed in February 2009 and took effect three years later on 29 March 2012.[9]

Through ACIA, the ASEAN reaffirmed its commitment to establish a free and open investment regime in the region in order to achieve the end goal of economic integration under the AEC. In accordance with the AEC Blueprint, the ACIA encompasses all four major aspects of investments namely, liberalization, facilitation, protection and promotion.[10] Article 1 of the agreement clearly states this:

---

[9] ACIA is the third of a set of agreements—the other two being the ASEAN Trade in Goods Agreement (ATIGA) and the ASEAN Framework Agreement on Services (AFAS)—that serve as the framework towards achieving AEC by 2015. Collectively, they represent a comprehensive set of rules that will govern the conduct of business within ASEAN and with ASEAN.

[10] The AEC Blueprint provides the road map and the schedule for its implementation towards achieving the AEC by 2015.

(a) progressive liberalization of the investment regimes of the Member States; (b) provision of enhanced protection to investors of all Member States and their investments; (c) improvement of transparency and predictability of investment rules, regulations and procedures conducive to increased investment among the Member States; (d) joint promotion of the region as an integrated investment area; and (d) cooperation to create favorable conditions for investment by investors of a Member State in the territory of the other Member States.

The ACIA provides higher standards for investment agreements than its predecessors. It has a shorter deadline (2015) for a free and open investment than AIA (2020). As a single investment agreement, it provides clearer interaction between liberalization and protection, unlike AIA and IGA which are two separate agreements. Also, the benefits under ACIA apply to both ASEAN investors and foreign investors based in ASEAN. In contrast, AIA provided different timelines depending upon investors' nationality: 2003–2010 for ASEAN investors and 2020 for non-ASEAN investors. Whereas the AIA required the approval in writing of the local national government before making the investment, the ACIA requires approval in writing only where applicable. And where specific approval in writing is required, Annex 1 of ACIA provides clear and transparent procedures for obtaining approval.

While the ACIA effectively terminated AIA and IGA, the agreement requires that there should be 'no back-tracking of commitments made under the AIA and IGA'.[11] Investors under the ambit of the AIA and IGA may choose to apply the provisions of these agreements, but only in their entirety, for a period of three years after the termination.

Investment Protection. The provisions on national treatment (Article 5) and most-favoured-nation (MFN) treatment (Article 6) accorded to investors and investment 'with respect to the admission, establishment, acquisition, expansion, management, conduct, operation and sale' leave no room for discrimination against foreign investors either in the pre- or post-establishment stages of investment. By providing protection, the risks to investors decrease. National treatment, in particular, is a remarkable evidence of investment protection, as it touches on economic and politically sensitive domestic issues.[12]

Building upon the relevant elements of the precursor agreements, the ACIA reaffirms the other core investor protections introduced under AIA

---

[11] ACIA, art 2e.

[12] J Xiao, 'The ASEAN–China Investment Agreement: A Regionalization of Chinese New BITs', Working Paper No.2010/09 (Society of International Economic Law, 2009).

and IGA such as, fair and equitable treatment (Article 11), full protection and security (Article 11), transfers (Article 13), and compensation in the event of expropriation (Article 14). Furthermore under Article 3(5), these investment protection measures also apply to trade in services with respect to the commercial presence mode of service supply but only to the extent that they relate to an investment under the ACIA, regardless of whether or not such service sector is included in the commitments of a member economy under the ASEAN Framework Agreement on Services (AFAS). The inclusion of services, albeit with the limitation provided for by Article 3(5), is a substantial improvement from the AIA.

However, the reservations list (Article 9), which provides exceptions to the provisions on national treatment (Article 5) and senior management and board of directors' composition (Article 8) raises a concern. Every ASEAN member entered a reservation list. The reservation list approach tries to preserve national autonomy over investment policy.[13] But the long lists covering various sectors and industries erode the provision on national treatment. Nonetheless, Article 9 provides for the reduction or the elimination of the reservations in accordance with the schedule specified in the AEC Blueprint.

Investment Liberalization. ACIA provides for progressive liberalization of the following sectors: (i) manufacturing; (ii) agriculture; (iii) fishery; (iv) forestry; (v) mining and quarrying; (vi) services incidental to manufacturing, agriculture, fishery, forestry, mining and quarrying; and (vii) any other sectors, as may be agreed upon by all the members (Article 3). The same sectors are covered by AIA, except for item (vii). Furthermore, whereas ACIA covers portfolio investment (Article 4c), AIA did not.

ACIA also includes other liberalization measures which were not covered by the AIA/IGA, such as: (i) prohibition of performance requirements under WTO-TRIMs (Article 7); and (ii) an article on senior management and board of directors' composition to encourage inflow of foreign managerial and senior management personnel (Article 8). Nonetheless, ACIA does not include TRIMs-plus commitments such as prohibition of export requirements, value-added requirements, local hiring requirements and technology transfer requirements.

Liberalization is expected to progress steadily towards 2015, as Member States gradually phase out their reservation lists regarding investment in certain industries.

---

[13] D Jarvis, *Foreign Direct Investment and Investment Liberalization in Asia: Assessing ASEAN's Initiatives*, (National University of Singapore, Singapore, 2009).

Promotion of Investment. The ACIA promotes the region as an integrated investment area in order to increase FDI into the region, including intra-ASEAN FDI. Promotion will be done through the following (Article 24): (i) encouraging the growth and development of ASEAN small and medium enterprises and multi-national enterprises; (ii) enhancing industrial complementation and production networks among multi-national enterprises in ASEAN; (iii) organizing investment missions that focus on developing regional clusters and production networks; (iv) organizing and supporting the organization of various briefings and seminars on investment opportunities and on investment laws, regulations and policies; and (v) conducting exchanges on other issues of mutual concern relating to investment promotion.

Facilitation of Investment. This will be carried out through the following (Article 25): (i) creating the necessary environment for all forms of investments; (ii) streamlining and simplifying procedures for investment application and approvals; (iii) promoting dissemination of investment information, including investment rules, regulations, policies and procedures; (iv) establishing one-stop investment centres; (v) strengthening databases on all forms of investment for policy formulation to improve ASEAN's investment environment; (vi) undertaking consultation with the business community on investment matters; and (vii) providing advisory services to the business community of the member economies.

Facilitation of investment will also be carried out by observing transparency (Article 21) by informing the AIA Council of any new investment-related agreements, or the introduction of new laws or of changes to existing laws and by making publicly available all relevant laws and regulations.

3. ACIA: A COMPARISON WITH OTHER INTERNATIONAL INVESTMENT AGREEMENTS

Apart from ACIA, the ASEAN members have entered into investment treaties, either bilaterally between themselves or with other economies outside of the region, or regionally as ASEAN. This sub-section of the paper discusses those investment treaties vis-à-vis the ACIA.

ASEAN–China Investment Agreement. Signed in August 2009, the ASEAN–China Investment Agreement formed part of the ASEAN–China Free Trade Area (ACFTA). The agreement provides high standards of investment protection in comparison with the existing bilateral investment treaties between China and individual ASEAN member economies.[14] This comes in

[14] Xiao (n 12).

the form of national treatment, MFN treatment, expropriation, and investor-state dispute resolution, etc. However, the investment agreement does not include investment liberalization, despite that the Framework Agreement of ASEAN–China FTA provided for creating a liberal investment regime and that the ASEAN member economies had insisted on provisions of investment liberalization in the negotiations of the investment agreement. Likewise, the agreement contains provisions that recognize the host country's policy discretion as to its compliance with the agreement. In other words, it is limited to investment made in accordance with relevant domestic law, policies and regulations of the host country.

China has bilateral investment treaties (BITs) with individual ASEAN members. These BITs differ significantly in rules on some key issues.[15] What the ASEAN–China Investment Agreement accomplished was to address such differences; in effect, regionalizing the BITs with ASEAN members.

ASEAN–Australia–New Zealand Investment Agreement. The investment agreement formed part of the ASEAN–Australia–New Zealand Free Trade Area (AANZFTA) that entered into force on 1 January 2010. Chapter 11 of the AANZFTA provides substantial investment protection as found in most investment protection treaties. This includes national treatment, fair and equitable treatment, full protection and security, transfer payments and compensation for expropriation. However, the agreement does not provide for an MFN clause.

The ASEAN economies have BITs with either Australia or New Zealand, creating the possibility of overlaps and inconsistencies among the BITs. The AANZFTA specifies that its provisions will not apply to agreements among ASEAN economies or any ASEAN economy and Australia or New Zealand. With this, the AANZFTA left open the resolutions of overlaps and inconsistencies among the BITs, leading to further complications. When there are overlaps and inconsistencies, it remains an open question as to which of the investment treaties will apply to a given investment project.

Bilateral investment treaties (BITs). The ASEAN economies are signatories to 411 BITs, 52 of which were signed between members (Table 1). Viet Nam has the most BITs with other ASEAN member economies. Brunei has no BITs with any other ASEAN member.

An analysis of the BITs shows that commitments vary. For example, national treatment is not included in the Thailand–Indonesia, Thailand–Cambodia or Singapore–China BITs. The latter also covers investment but not investors.

---

[15] Ibid.

Table 1. Number of Bilateral Investment Treaties, ASEAN Economies

Country	Number of BITs	Number of BITs with ASEAN Members	% of BITs with ASEAN Members
Brunei Darussalam	6	0	0.00
Cambodia	22	7	31.82
Indonesia*	63	7	11.11
Lao PDR	23	7	29.17
Malaysia*	57	4	7.02
Myanmar	67	4	5.97
Philippines*	35	5	14.29
Singapore*	41	4	9.76
Thailand*	39	6	15.38
Viet Nam*	58	8	13.79
Total	411	52	12.65

* Belgium and Luxembourg are in one BIT

Source: UNCTAD

Likewise, there are no MFN or NT clauses in the Thailand–Philippines and Singapore–Indonesia BITs.

To summarize this section of the paper, the ACIA provides for internationally accepted standards for investment protection, liberalization, promotion and facilitation, compared to its predecessors as well as the other investment treaties that the ASEAN has entered into, either bilaterally between themselves or regionally with other economies or regional groupings. ACIA has significant implications for investment strategies and production activities in the ASEAN region. By promoting the region as an integrated investment area, investors (both local and foreign) are encouraged to think in regional terms and adopt regional investment strategies.

It has been a year since ACIA took effect. The challenge now is to ensure implementation by each member economy in order to realize the goal of a free flow of investment. This is especially so since the AEC Blueprint does not provide for penalties for member economies that fail to implement ACIA.

4. FDI TRENDS AND PATTERN: ASSESSMENT TOWARDS THE GOAL

The ASEAN region was a leading investment destination among developing countries in the early 1990s. However, its share of FDI flows during the past

Figure 1. Share of ASEAN and China to FDI flows in Developing Countries, 1990–2011 (%).

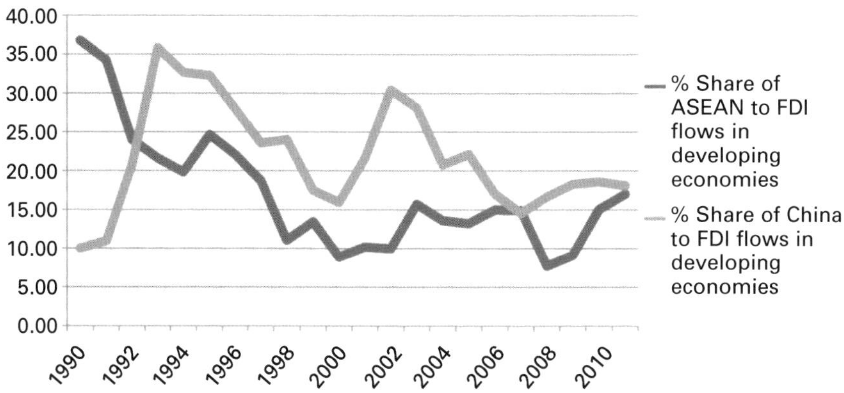

Source: Author's calculation using UNCTADStat Database

decade was below its performance in the 1990s (Figure 1). The average annual share during the period 1990–2000 was 21.4 percent. It dropped to 11.1 per cent during the period 2000–11. Figure 1 shows that the ASEAN has been successful in attracting FDI after the 2007/2008 financial crisis; but the region is losing attractiveness of FDI. The share has been consistently increasing over the past 3 years but the 17 per cent share in 2011 was way below the region's share prior to the Asian financial crisis in 1997–98. This means that the ASEAN has been losing from competition for FDI from other developing countries, even discounting the 1997–98 and 2008–09 financial crises. China, for example, has overtaken the ASEAN since 1993 (Figure 1). Since then, China's share has been consistently higher than the ASEANs. China has emerged as a global export powerhouse and the massive economies of scale offered by its huge and rapidly growing consumer markets have driven FDI towards the country.[16]

On the other hand, ASEAN's share of FDI stock in developing countries has been consistently higher than China's share since 1990 (Figure 2). Nevertheless, the share has hardly increased over the past decade. As a percentage of GDP, FDI has remained small, less than four per cent every year, on the average, over the last two decades (Figure 3).

Inward FDI to the region went up from US$21,808 million in 2000 to US$92,278 million in 2010 (Figure 4). The amount registered a sharp fall in

[16] P Intal, HH Narjoko and M Simorangkir 'ERIA Study to Further Improve AEC Scorecard and Trade Facilitation', Powerpoint presentation at ASEAN Trade Facilitation Forum, Manado, Indonesia, 2012.

Figure 2. Share of ASEAN and China to FDI stocks in developing countries, 1990–2011 (%)

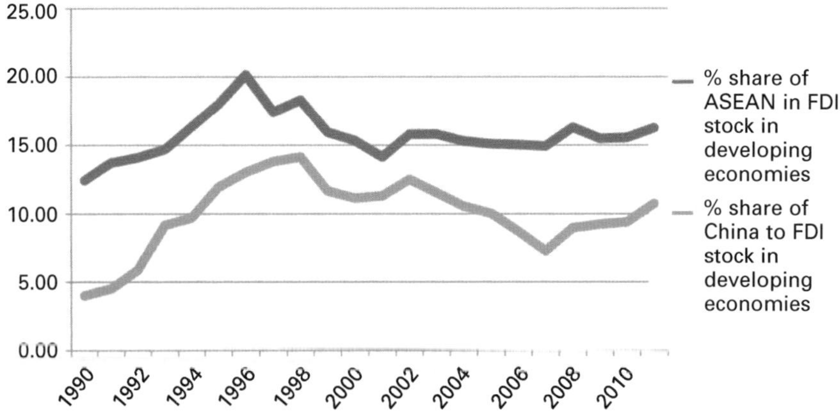

Source: Author's calculation using UNCTADStat Database.

Figure 3. FDI Flows as Percentage of GDP, ASEAN, 1990–2011 (%)

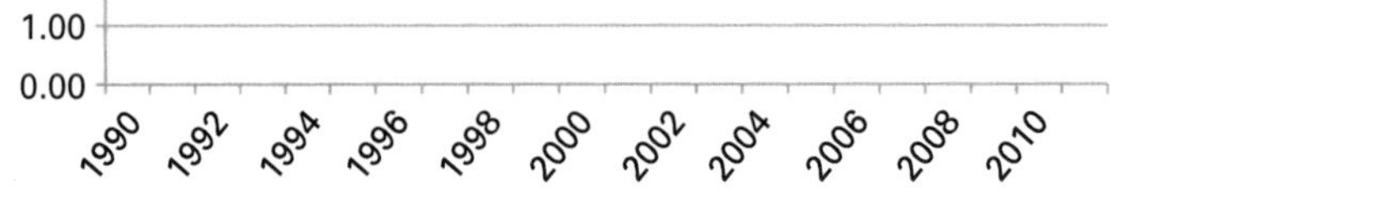

Source: Author's calculations using UNCTADStat Database

2008 and 2009 due to the EU/US financial crisis but bounced back in 2010 and 2011 with the resumption of global capital flows, exceeding the pre-crisis level. Performance of individual member economies varies, with Singapore accounting for more than 50 per cent of total FDI (Figure 5). This signifies the country's superior attractiveness to FDI over all the other member economies.

Intra-ASEAN FDI. While FDI inflows from outside ASEAN have been variable, it is interesting to note that intra-ASEAN FDI has been increasing. The share of total FDI inflows in the region went up from less than four per cent in 2000 to 23 per cent in 2011 (Table 2). Likewise, there was a significant

Figure 4. Inward Intra and Extra-ASEAN FDI, 2000–2011

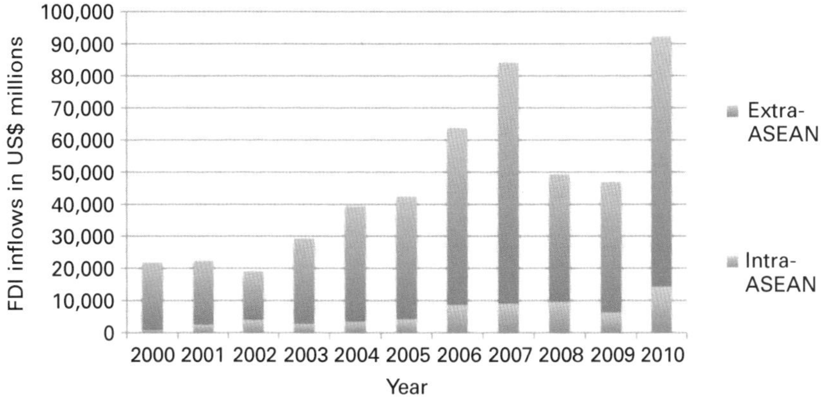

Note: See Appendix Table 1 for FDI by country.

Source: ASEAN Secretariat—ASEAN FDI Database.

Figure 5. Distribution of Inward FDI, by ASEAN Member Economy, 2000–2011 (%)

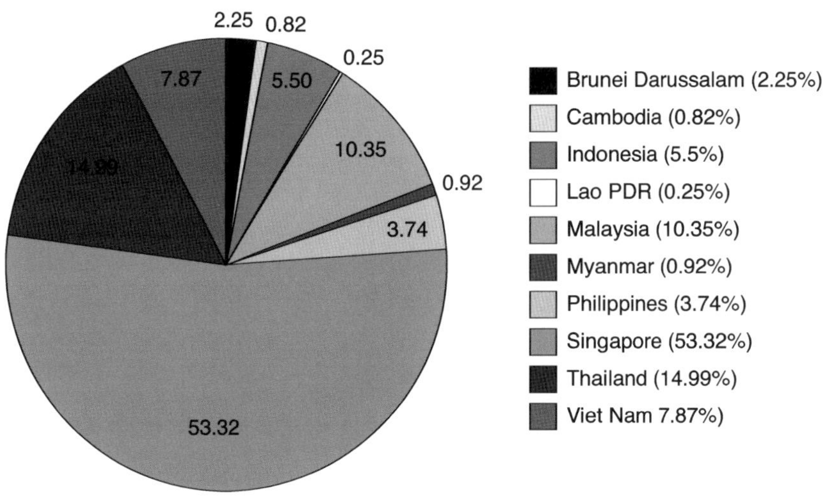

Source: Author's calculations using ASEAN Secretariat Database.

Table 2. **ASEAN Inward FDI, 2000–2010**

Year	Amount (US$ million)			% Distribution		% Change		
	Intra-ASEAN	Extra-ASEAN	Total	Intra-ASEAN	Extra-ASEAN	Intra-ASEAN	Extra-ASEAN	Total
2000	853.05	20955.48	21808.53	3.91	96.09	–	–	–
2001	2541.39	19783.82	22325.21	11.38	88.62	197.92	–5.59	2.37
2002	4084.88	15000.00	19084.88	21.40	78.60	60.73	–24.18	–14.51
2003	2830.77	26446.73	29277.49	9.67	90.33	–30.70	76.31	53.41
2004	3516.63	35869.80	39386.43	8.93	91.07	24.23	35.63	34.53
2005	4210.64	38345.80	42556.44	9.89	90.11	19.73	6.90	8.05
2006	8641.87	55047.35	63689.23	13.57	86.43	105.24	43.56	49.66
2007	9113.02	75039.33	84152.35	10.83	89.17	5.45	36.32	32.13
2008	9728.86	39560.88	49289.74	19.74	80.26	6.76	–47.28	–41.43
2009	6300.19	40596.55	46896.74	13.43	86.57	–35.24	2.62	–4.85
2010	14322.70	77955.94	92278.64	15.52	84.48	127.34	92.03	96.77
2011	26270.61	87839.98	114110.59	23.02	76.98	83.42	12.68	23.66

Note: Refer to Appendix Table 1 for FDI by member economies.

Source: ASEAN Secretariat.

Table 3. Percentage Distribution of Inward Intra- and Extra-ASEAN FDI, by Country, 2000–2010 (%)

Country	Ave. 2000–2005		Ave. 2006–2010	
	Intra-ASEAN	Extra-ASEAN	Intra-ASEAN	Extra-ASEAN
Brunei Darussalam	3.85	96.15	8.31	91.69
Cambodia	18.77	81.23	33.98	66.02
Indonesia	144.08	–44.08	30.24	69.76
Lao PDR	24.97	75.03	23.26	76.74
Malaysia	11.72	88.28	15.21	84.79
Myanmar (1)	18.68	81.32	17.09	82.91
Philippines	26.59	73.41	4.55	95.45
Singapore (2)	5.26	94.74	6.83	93.17
Thailand	22.22	77.78	24.11	75.89
Viet Nam	13.52	86.48	13.17	86.83
Total ASEAN	10.87	89.13	14.62	85.38

Source: Author's calculations using ASEAN FDI Database.

rise in intra-ASEAN FDI, consistent with the improved investment climate. Intra-ASEAN FDI registered higher percentage increases almost every year compared to extra-ASEAN FDI. In nominal terms, intra-ASEAN FDI grew by an average of 51.4 per cent per year during the period 2000–11 while extra-ASEAN FDI grew only by an average 20.82 per cent per year during the same period. Among the member economies, intra-FDI has become an important source of FDI to Cambodia, Indonesia, Laos and Thailand (Table 3).

However, despite the ease of access and investment protection accorded to ASEAN investors by the investment agreements, there has been an uneven distribution of intra-ASEAN FDI among the member economies. Over the past decade, the bulk of intra-ASEAN FDI went to Indonesia, Malaysia, Singapore and Thailand. In other words, these economies absorbed the greater part of intra-FDI; together, they accounted for 81.2 per cent for the period 2000–05 and 84.3 per cent for the period 2006–10 (Table 4). A similar pattern was registered for the sources of intra-ASEAN FDI. A large percentage originated from Singapore and Malaysia, with both economies accounting for 87.3 per cent and 80.8 per cent for the period 2000–05 and 2006–10, respectively (Table 5).

In terms of sectoral distribution, manufacturing accounted for the bulk of intra-ASEAN FDI (Table 6). Despite the liberalization and protection of investment for agriculture, fishery, forestry, mining and quarrying, again as

Table 4. Percentage Distribution of Inward Intra-ASEAN Flows, by Host Country, 2000–2010 (%)

Country	2000	2001	2002	2003	2004	2005	2006	2007	2008	2009	2010	Average Share (2000–2005)	Average Share (2006–2010)
Brunei Darussalam	1.24	0.42	0.52	1.27	0.54	0.47	0.11	0.68	0.01	0.05	0.63	0.74	0.30
Cambodia	0.00	1.46	0.21	0.70	0.91	3.07	1.80	2.98	2.48	2.76	2.44	1.06	2.49
Indonesia	–27.26	–8.71	31.74	13.54	5.81	20.98	15.67	12.16	34.93	21.91	41.22	6.02	25.18
Lao PDR	1.61	0.12	0.07	0.11	0.22	0.16	0.12	1.10	0.49	0.91	0.95	0.38	0.71
Malaysia	30.26	3.15	0.00	8.87	27.87	17.12	5.34	41.48	16.91	–0.96	3.67	14.55	13.29
Myanmar	8.68	2.65	0.61	0.86	0.26	0.91	0.82	1.03	1.06	1.08	1.20	2.33	1.04
Philippines	14.70	7.83	2.14	6.19	2.02	0.08	8.16	–7.74	3.16	–0.08	0.28	5.49	0.76
Singapore	1.44	16.26	25.32	27.46	35.87	27.15	12.33	15.00	7.93	44.30	31.90	22.25	22.29
Thailand	45.60	67.31	34.48	37.46	19.58	26.16	53.54	27.32	5.23	23.22	8.64	38.43	23.59
Viet Nam	23.73	9.50	4.91	3.55	6.91	3.91	2.11	5.99	27.80	6.80	9.08	8.75	10.36
Total	100	100	100	100	100	100	100	100	100	100	100	100	100

Source: Author's Computations based on data from ASEAN Secretariat – ASEAN FDI Database.

Table 5. Percentage Distribution of Outward Intra-ASEAN Flows by Country of Origin 2000–2010 (%)

Country	2000	2001	2002	2003	2004	2005	2006	2007	2008	2009	2010	Average Share (2000–2005)	Average Share (2006–2010)
Brunei Darussalam	3.90	1.64	0.49	–9.39	0.52	0.67	–0.43	–0.03	0.90	2.00	0.21	–0.36	0.53
Cambodia	0.27	0.04	0.03	0.20	0.10	0.00	0.00	0.01	0.13	–0.10	0.26	0.10	0.06
Indonesia	12.55	12.73	9.92	11.25	9.90	3.71	6.88	2.65	8.91	15.37	10.19	10.01	8.80
Lao PDR	1.15	0.01	0.00	0.00	0.00	0.00	0.48	0.11	–0.74	0.01	0.24	0.19	0.02
Malaysia	20.49	8.17	29.34	30.17	33.75	32.18	10.38	10.76	35.18	41.78	19.97	25.69	23.61
Myanmar	0.67	0.13	0.44	0.30	0.20	0.35	0.57	0.69	0.66	1.13	0.48	0.35	0.71
Philippines	11.45	1.34	0.53	–0.50	4.37	1.65	1.81	3.67	–2.27	–6.51	1.71	3.14	–0.32
Singapore	75.11	78.58	50.07	59.46	45.31	60.98	77.11	70.46	47.40	35.21	55.79	61.59	57.19
Thailand	–26.35	–2.73	7.59	8.30	5.64	0.24	3.11	9.71	8.40	9.38	8.41	–1.22	7.80
Viet Nam	0.75	0.09	1.59	0.22	0.20	0.22	0.08	1.97	1.43	1.74	2.74	0.51	1.59
Total	100	100	100	100	100	100	100	100	100	100	100	100	100

Source: Author's Computations based on data from ASEAN Secretariat – ASEAN FDI Database.

Table 6 Percentage Distribution of Intra-ASEAN FDI flows by Economic Sector 2000–2010 (%)

Country	2000	2001	2002	2003	2004	2005	2006	2007	2008	2009	2010	Average Share (2000–2005)	Average Share (2006–2010)
Agriculture, Fishery and Forestry	2.61	0.99	4.28	2.81	2.99	0.70	0.73	23.08	3.06	1.61	2.61	2.40	6.22
Mining and Quarrying	–14.19	37.39	3.54	6.82	1.25	0.89	–0.81	7.88	7.90	4.83	4.25	5.95	4.81
Manufacturing	43.75	17.86	12.74	–1.18	15.89	36.75	18.08	24.61	33.85	13.84	19.56	20.97	21.99
Construction	–1.10	1.55	–0.54	4.27	0.24	1.21	2.15	4.87	8.52	2.16	0.40	0.94	3.62
Trade/Commerce	1.26	8.48	21.28	28.96	12.78	1.73	2.04	–2.55	9.65	–3.24	11.43	12.41	3.47
Financial Intermediation (incl. Insurance)	–3.27	–5.77	29.08	13.46	–4.17	15.56	32.71	26.63	24.14	24.54	20.17	7.48	25.64
Real Estate	–18.68	17.74	20.72	28.10	39.76	14.91	11.09	8.96	15.54	48.98	26.18	17.09	22.15
Services	16.98	11.57	6.45	5.73	5.66	25.55	5.69	9.51	–6.48	4.68	15.38	11.99	5.75
Other Activities	33.88	0.13	0.66	1.34	6.78	–1.28	17.86	1.94	2.12	3.07	0.14	6.92	5.02
Unspecified	38.77	10.05	1.80	9.69	18.82	3.98	10.46	–4.92	1.72	–0.47	–0.11	13.85	1.34
ASEAN TOTAL	100	100	100	100	100	100	100	100	100	100	100	100	100

Note: Refer to Appendix Table 2 for the amount of FDI, by sector.

Source: Author's Computations based on data from ASEAN Secretariat – ASEAN FDI Database.

provided for by the investment agreements, these sectors remained unattractive to intra-ASEAN FDI. Together, they accounted for only 8.3 per cent of the total in 2000–05 and 11.0 per cent in 2006–2010. It is interesting to note, however, that the share of financial intermediation and real estate has been on the rise in recent years (Table 6).

Sources of FDI. During the past decade, the European Union, Japan and the USA accounted for the bulk of FDI to the ASEAN (Table 7). The share of these countries, however, has been declining. In contrast, the share of non-traditional suppliers such as China, South Korea, intra-ASEAN, and of recent years, India, has been increasing. From an average of less than one per cent per year during the period 2000–05, the share increased to three per cent for China and South Korea and two per cent for India during the period 2006–2010. On the other hand, intra-ASEAN FDI went up from almost 11 per cent to 14.6 per cent during the same periods.

Trade and FDI. The above pattern of FDI is closely associated with the intra-industry trade in the ASEAN-5 and East Asia and the establishment of vertically integrated production networks. With inputs sourced from developed countries, these are further processed and assembled in developing economies where wages are low and the final product is exported back to developed economies. Economic integration in the region is driven by this form of international trade. Intra-ASEAN trade accounted for about a quarter of ASEAN's total trade (Figure 6) and highly concentrated on machinery and transport equipment products.

As shown in Figure 7, these products accounted for an average of 69.8 per cent and 65.3 per cent of intra-ASEAN and total ASEAN's exports of manufactured products, respectively, during the period 1995–2010. Specific products include (i) electrical machinery, apparatus and appliances, (ii) office machines and automatic data processing, and (iii) telecommunication and sound recording apparatus. These products together accounted for an average of 84.3 per cent of ASEAN's total exports of machinery and transport equipment products (Figure 8) and 77.5 per cent of intra-ASEAN exports of same products (Figure 9). The same pattern can be observed with ASEAN's imports of these products (Figures 10, 11, and 12).

The supply chain process is also reflected in ASEAN's trade with Japan, South Korea, China and recently India (Figure 13). Exports to and imports from these countries are steadily on the rise and together, they accounted for an average of 30 per cent and 35 per cent, respectively, of ASEAN's trade. As discussed earlier, the shares of intra-ASEAN, South Korea, China and India to ASEAN's total FDI have been steadily increasing over the past decade. Because of ASEAN's role in the supply chain, these countries have become new sources of FDI in the region.

Table 7. Percentage Distribution of Inward FDI flows to ASEAN by Dialogue Partner, 2000–2010 (%)

Country	2000	2001	2002	2003	2004	2005	2006	2007	2008	2009	2010	Average Share (2000–2005)	Average Share (2006–2010)
Intra-ASEAN	3.91	11.38	21.40	9.67	8.93	9.89	13.57	10.83	19.74	13.43	15.52	10.87	14.62
Australia	-1.67	-0.67	0.47	0.71	1.49	0.60	0.89	2.58	2.11	2.12	2.80	0.16	2.10
Canada	-3.56	-0.29	1.42	-1.64	2.52	1.60	0.57	0.49	1.29	1.54	1.51	0.01	1.08
China	-0.65	0.63	-0.50	2.25	1.89	1.45	3.04	2.46	2.45	3.95	3.02	0.84	2.98
European Union 27	59.63	32.26	22.23	32.79	29.03	27.55	24.82	26.03	18.00	17.19	18.44	33.91	20.90
India	0.37	0.13	0.70	0.41	0.20	1.11	-0.15	3.11	2.84	1.31	3.63	0.49	2.15
Japan	2.53	10.73	19.74	10.33	14.64	15.47	16.89	10.37	8.80	8.08	11.66	12.24	11.16
New Zealand	0.20	0.07	0.43	-0.26	-0.06	1.40	-0.23	0.14	-0.22	0.21	0.00	0.30	-0.02
Pakistan	0.02	0.04	-0.01	0.01	0.01	0.01	0.01	0.02	0.01	0.03	0.03	0.01	0.02
Republic of Korea (ROK)	-0.23	-1.01	1.11	1.98	2.25	1.24	2.03	2.91	3.15	3.83	4.08	0.89	3.20
Russian Federation	0.00	0.00	0.00	0.00	0.00	0.00	0.00	0.04	0.16	0.30	0.07	0.00	0.11
USA	34.34	23.92	1.25	4.14	11.03	7.67	4.67	12.35	6.61	12.16	13.84	13.72	9.93
Total from dialogue members	94.88	77.19	68.25	60.38	71.93	67.98	66.12	71.30	64.96	64.16	74.59	73.44	68.23
Non Dialogue Partners	5.12	22.81	31.75	39.62	28.07	32.02	33.88	28.70	35.04	35.84	25.41	26.56	31.77
ASEAN TOTAL	100	100	100	100	100	100	100	100	100	100	100	100	100

Note: Refer to Appendix Table 3 for the amount of FDI by source.

Source: Author's Computations based on data from ASEAN Secretariat – ASEAN FDI Database.

Figure 6. Intra-ASEAN trade, 2000–2011

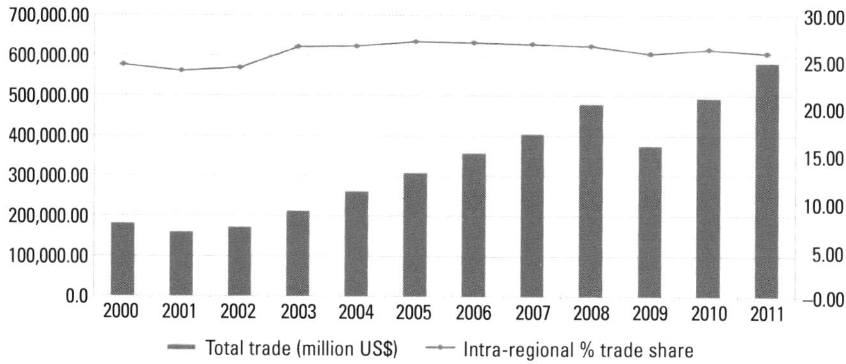

Source: ADB-ARIC Database (Downloaded 22 December 2012)

Figure 7. Share of Machinery and Transport Equipment to ASEAN's Total Exports of Manufactured Goods, 1995–2010 (%)

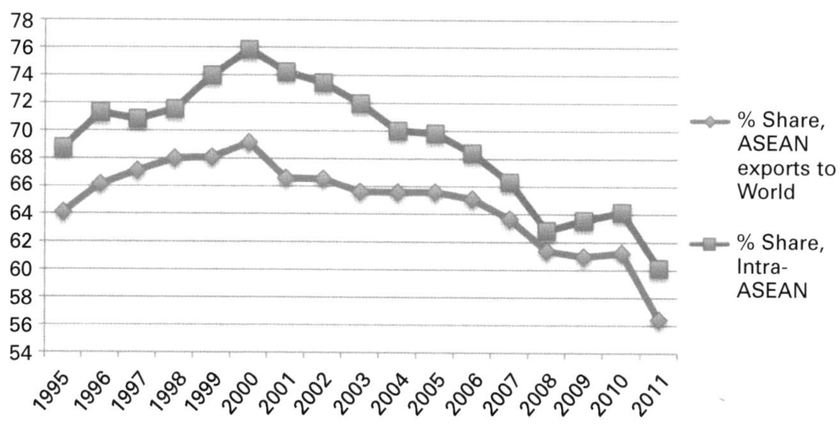

Source: Author's Computations based on data from UNCTADStat

5. THE NEED TO ADDRESS FDI-POLICY RELATED ISSUES

The preceding sections point to some modest achievement of increasing inflows of FDI and intra-ASEAN FDI with an improved investment climate through AIA, IGA and ACIA. However, the series of studies done by Urata and Ando[17]

[17] S Urata and M Ando, 'Investment Climate Study on ASEAN Member Countries', 2009 *ERIA Research Project Report* No.3 (Economic Research Institute for ASEAN and East Asia, 2010).

Figure 8. Percentage Distribution of ASEAN's Total Exports of Machinery and Transport Equipment, by Product, 1995–2010 (%)

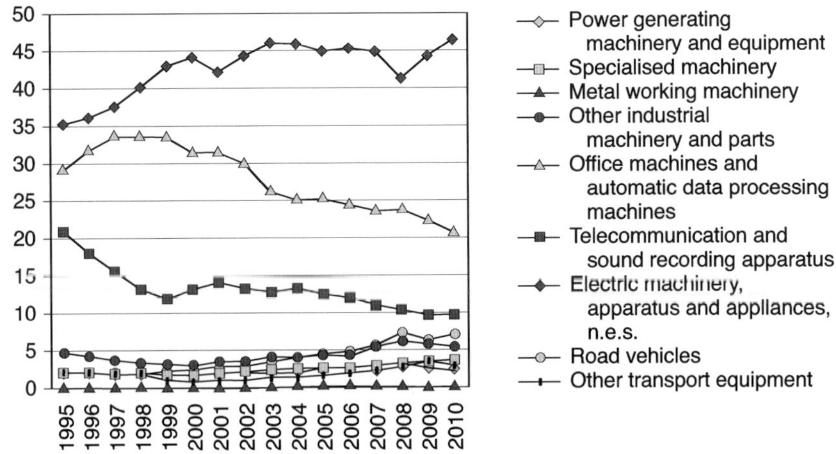

Figure 9. Percentage Distribution of Intra-ASEAN Exports of Machinery and Transport Equipment, by Product, 1995–2010 (%)

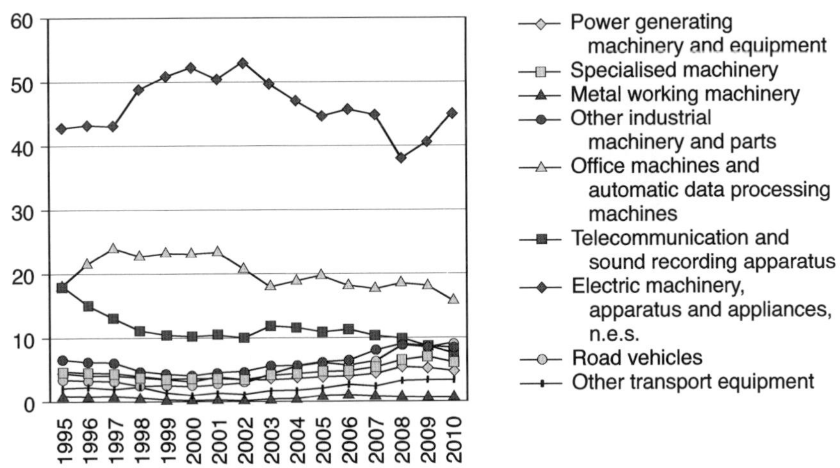

Source: Author's Computations based on data from UNCTADStat

Figure 10. Share of Machinery and Transport Equipment to ASEAN's Total Imports of Manufactured Goods, 1995–2011 (%)

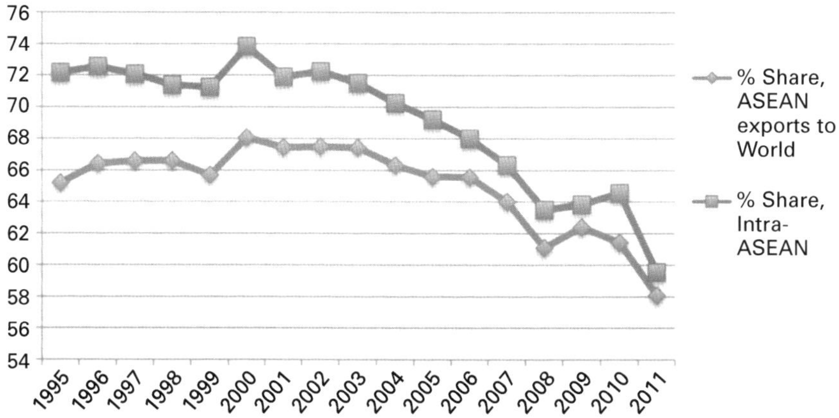

Source: Author's Computations based on data from UNCTADStat

Figure 11. Percentage Distribution of ASEAN's Total Import of Machinery and Transport Equipment, by Product, 1995–2011 (%)

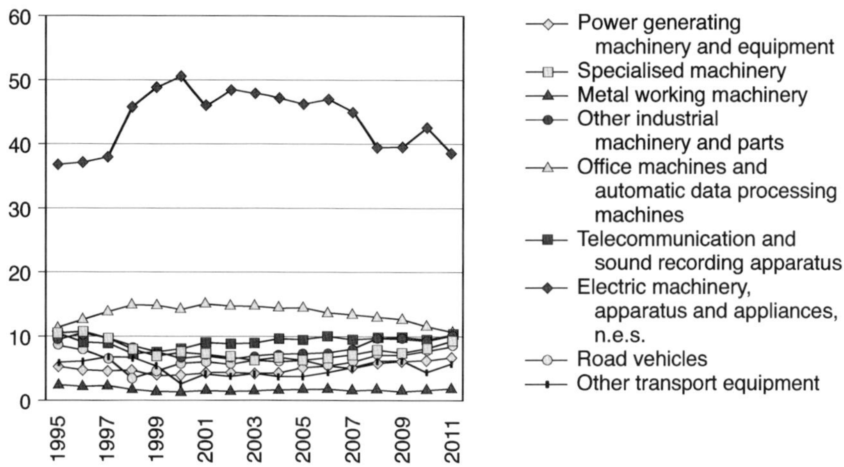

Source: Author's Computations based on data from UNCTADstat

Figure 12. Percentage Distribution of Intra-ASEAN Imports of Machinery and Transport Equipment, by Product, 1995–2011 (%)

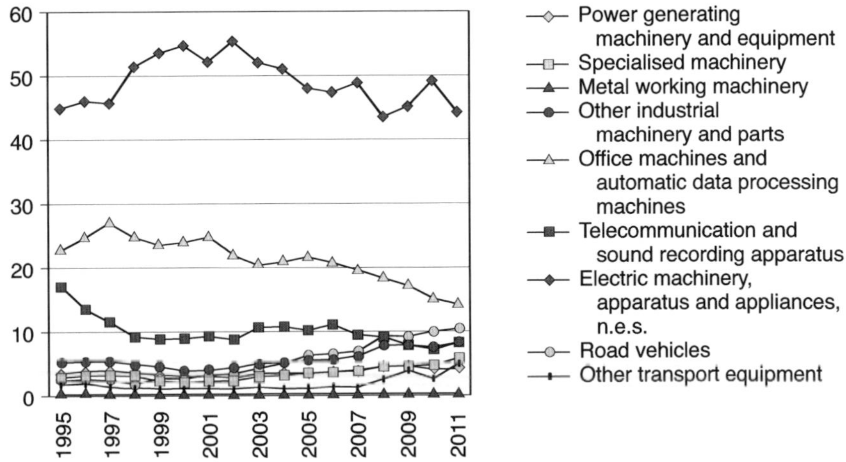

Source: Author's Computations based on data from UNCTADStat

Figure 13. ASEAN Trade with China, Japan, South Korea and India, 2005–2011

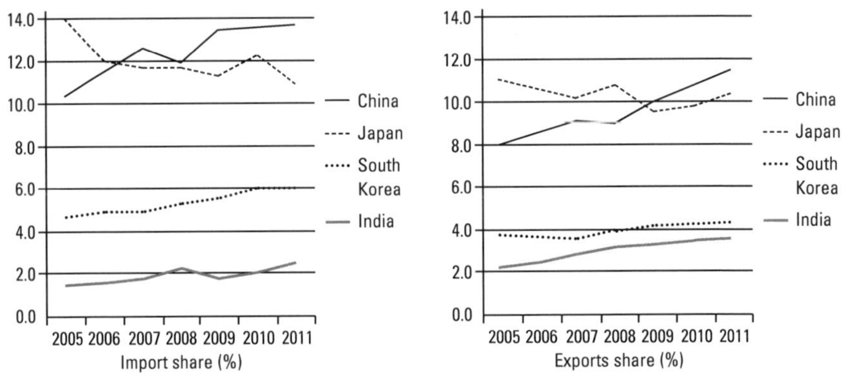

Source: ASB-ARIC Database (Downloaded 22 December 2012)

to assess the actual investment climate of ASEAN member economies show that while the investment climate has improved, restrictions on FDI still exist and the degree of restrictions/openness varies across countries and sectors.[18]

---

[18] Urata and Ando, ibid, evaluated the restrictiveness of FDI regimes by examining legal documents related to FDI of the ASEAN member economies and constructed scores indicating

The ACIA by itself does not guarantee FDI inflows. Initiatives at the regional level, such as the ACIA, will be helpful in attracting FDI but country-specifications on improving the investment climate are still paramount. The experience of the ASEAN-5 in successfully attracting FDI and then later, sustaining their participation as hosts to the global production networks since the 1990s proves that domestic policies matter. At best, the ACIA can serve as a supplement to domestic policies.

This section of the paper attempts to identify policy-related issues which are considered to continue to restrict FDI inflows to the region.

Global competitiveness. Along with the uncertainty of global economic recovery is the volatility of capital flows, including FDI. Competition for FDI is therefore expected to become fierce as developing countries continue to struggle in an increasingly unpredictable global landscape.[19] Amidst this environment, the challenge facing the ASEAN member economies is how to strengthen their position and remain competitive in the international production chain. The Global Competitiveness Index (GCI) 2012–13, which measures the microeconomic and macroeconomic foundations of national competitiveness, bears important lessons for the ASEAN.[20] Singapore remained second place from its previous position; Malaysia and Indonesia dropped four places; Vietnam dropped ten places; Thailand improved one place while the Philippines advanced by ten places, one of the countries that registered the most improvements in 2012 (Table 8). In general, the biggest shortcomings of the ASEAN economies, except of course for Singapore, are in the areas of institutions, infrastructure, technological readiness and innovations (Figure 14).

Achieving a free flow of investment by 2015 for AEC, thus, necessitates improvements on the competitiveness of the ASEAN, especially the weaker

---

restrictiveness in the following areas: market access, national treatment, screening and appraisal, board of directors composition, movement of investors and performance requirements. They also used the information obtained from a survey of Japanese firms operating in ASEAN member economies to assess actual investment climate.

19 UNESCAP, 2012.

20 The *Global Competitiveness Index (GCI)*, prepared annually by the World Economic Forum since 2005, is a 'comprehensive tool that measures the microeconomic and macroeconomic foundations of national competitiveness' rated on a scale between 1 (worst) and 7 (best) (X Sala-I-Martin et al, 'The Global Competitiveness Index 2012–2013: Strengthening Recovery by Raising Productivity' in *The Global Competitiveness Report 2012–2013* (Geneva: The World Economic Forum, 2013). Competitiveness is defined as 'the set of institutions, policies, and factors that determine the level of productivity of a country' (Sala-I-Martin, idem). GCI is composed of 12 pillars namely: institutions, infrastructure, macroeconomic environment, health & primary education, higher education & training, goods market efficiency, labour market efficiency, financial market development, technological readiness, market size, business sophistication and innovation.

Table 8. Global Competitiveness Index Ranking, ASEAN Countries, China, South Korea and India, 2012-2013 & 2011-2012

Countries	2011–2012 (out of 140 countries)	2012–2013 (out of 144 countries)
Brunei	28	28
Cambodia	97	85
Indonesia	46	50
Malaysia	21	25
Philippines	75	65
Singapore	2	2
Thailand	39	38
Vietnam	65	75
China	26	29
South Korea	24	19
India	56	59

Source: Global Competitiveness Index, World Economic Forum.

member economies. There is a need to continue with domestic reforms especially with institutions and regulatory frameworks for managing incoming investments and capital and channelling them into projects that contribute towards sustainable and inclusive economic growth.

Infrastructure and logistics support. The sustained growth of FDI in the region and the participation of the ASEAN member economies in regional/global production sharing hinges largely on logistics performance that makes easy and less costly the vertical and horizontal operations of these networks in the region. Such measures may include anything from institutional and regulatory reform to transport and telecommunication infrastructures, trade procedures, logistics services and customs and port efficiency that would allow goods to move freely and with less cost from the border to consumers in the domestic market (which may include household, firms, and government). These country-specific factors are key considerations by multinational companies when they invest across borders.[21]

Based on the 2012 Logistic Performance Index (LPI), there is a wide gap in the trade facilitation measures and logistics infrastructure among the ASEAN member economies[22] (Table 9 and Figure 15). Singapore ranked

[21] J-F Arvis, M Alina Mustra, L Ojala, B Shepherd and D Saslavsky, *Connecting to Compete 2012, Trade Logistics in the Global Economy,* (Washington DC: The World Bank, 2012).

[22] The *Logistics Performance Index (LPI)* is a multi-dimensional assessment of logistics performance, rated on a scale between one (worst) and five (best). The index consists of both qualitative

Figure 14. Global Competitiveness Index, 2012

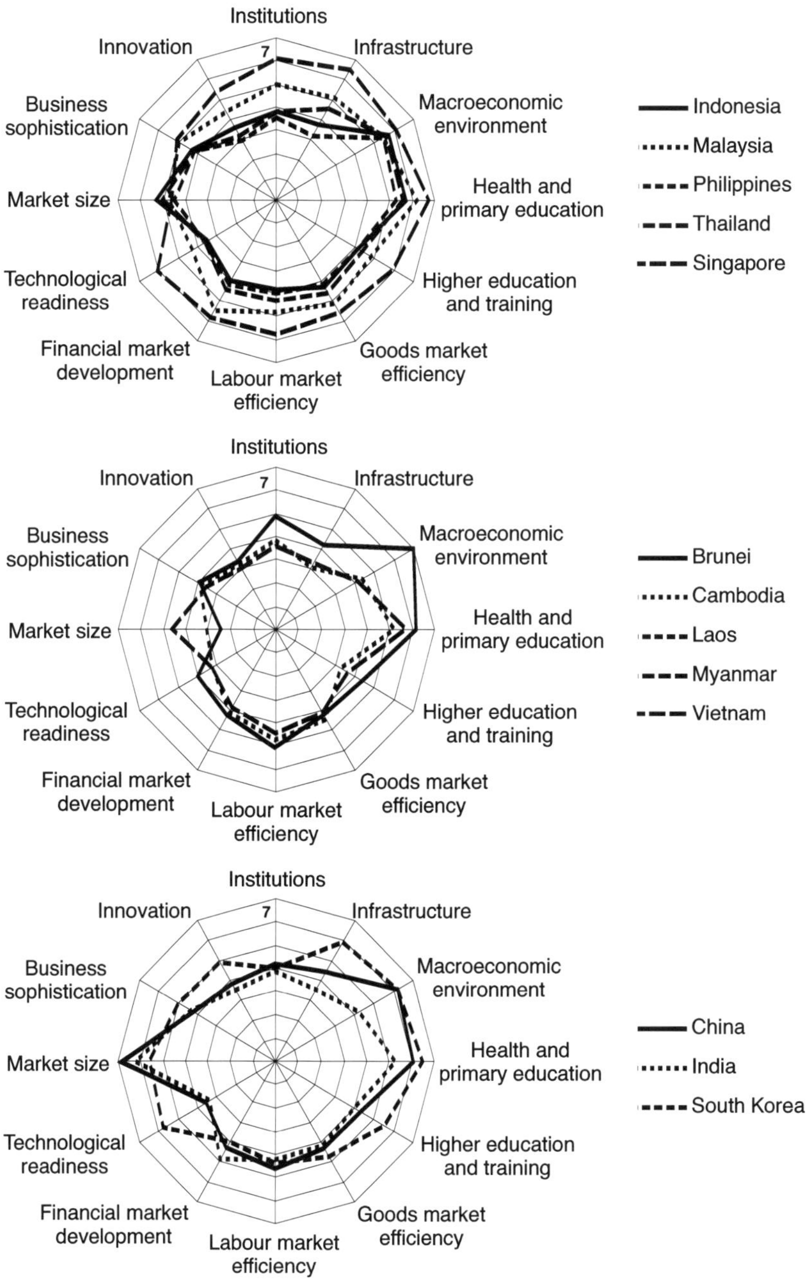

Source: The Global Competitiveness Report 2012-2013 (World Economic Forum)

Table 9. Logistic Performance Index Ranking, ASEAN Countries, China, South Korea and India, 2010 & 2012

	2010		2012	
Countries	Rank	% of highest performer	Rank	% of highest performer
Brunei			–	–
Cambodia	129	44.0	101	50
Indonesia	75	56.5	59	62.2
Lao PDR	118	47	109	48
Malaysia	29	78.4	29	79.8
Myanmar	133	42.7	129	43.8
Philippines	44	68.8	52	64.8
Singapore	2	99.2	1	100.0
Thailand	35	73.6	38	69.6
Vietnam	53	63.1	53	64.1
China			26	80.5
South Korea	23	84.7	21	86.2
India	47	67.9	46	66.4

Note: Rank out of 155 countries

Source: Trade Logistics in the Global Economy 2012.

first among 155 countries in 2012, one step higher from its second position in 2011. Except for the Philippines and Thailand, all member economies registered improvements on their ranks from 2010.

Nonetheless, while all member economies registered substantial improvements in the time and cost for completing trade procedures, logistics disparities persist (Table 10). The performance of individual economies pales in comparison with Singapore which is consistently a logistics top performer. The time for completing trade procedures in Singapore is only 28 per cent of the average of the region; and the cost of completing trade procedures is only 57 per cent of the average of the region.

Infrastructure bottlenecks, as shown by the low scores (Figure 15), particularly for the less developed member economies (CLMV), risk fragmentation

---

and quantitative measures that indicate the logistics 'friendliness' of the countries in which these global operators operate and with which they trade. It has six components: (i) efficiency of the customs clearance process; (ii) quality of trade and transport-related infrastructures; (iii) ease of arranging competitively priced shipments; (iv) competence and quality of logistics services; (v) ability to track and trace consignments; and (v) frequency with which shipments reach the consignee within the scheduled or expected time.

Figure 15. Scorecard, Logistics Performance Index, 2012

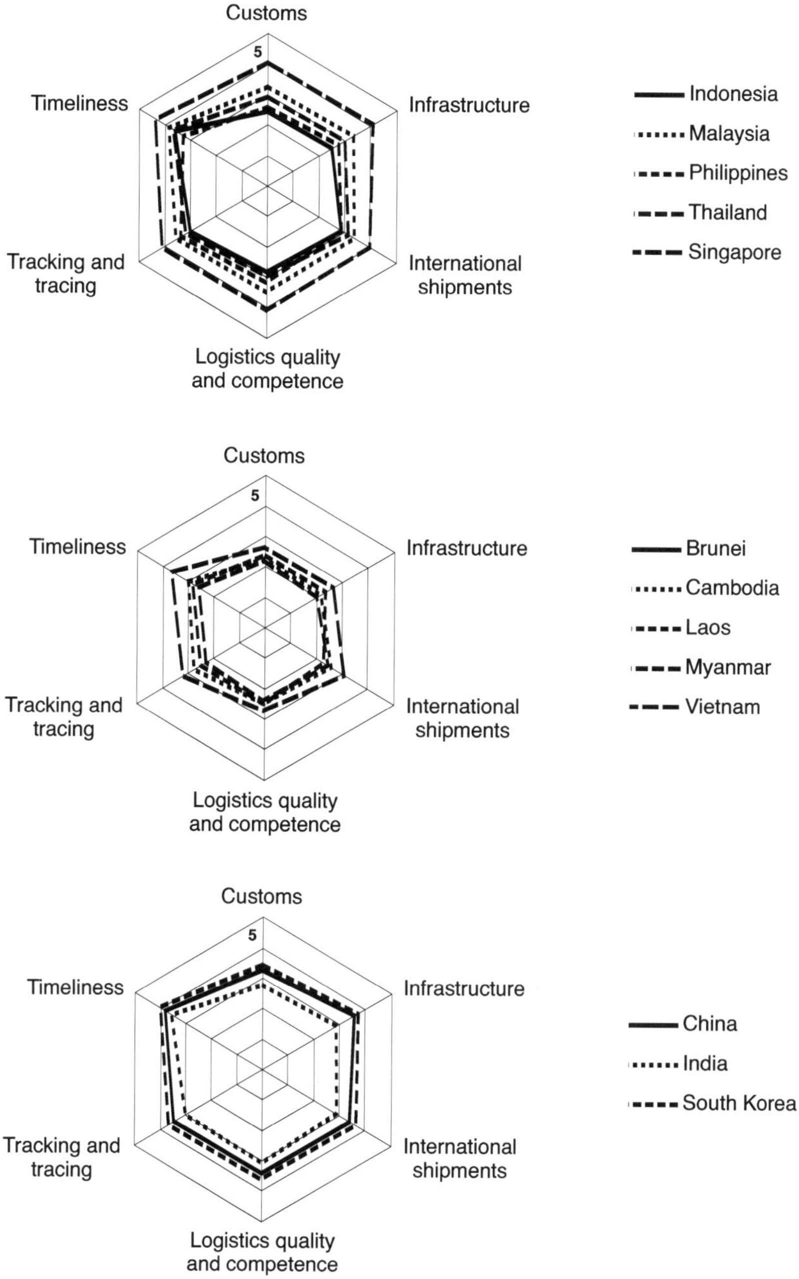

Source: Trade Logistics in the Global Economy 2012

Table 10. Trade facilitation indicators, ASEAN & North-East Asia, 2008 & 2012

	Time for completing trade Procedures(days)			Cost of completing trade procedures (2000 constant United States dollar)			Import–export Facilitation bias 2010	
Countries	2008	2012	% Change	2008	2012	% Change	Time basis	Cost basis
South East Asia	22	18	–21.1	656	619	–5.5	1	1
Brunei Darussalam	23	17			562		0.8	1.1
Cambodia	41	24	–41.5	685	653	–4.7	1.2	1.2
Indonesia	23	20	–11.1	535	515	–3.9	1.4	1
Lao PDR	38	26	–31.6	1601	1683	5.1	1	1
Malaysia	12	10	–17.1	356	337	–5.1	0.7	1
Myanmar								
Philippines	18	15	–17.1	667	491	–27.4	0.9	1.1
Singapore	5	5	0.0	341	353	3.7	0.8	1
Thailand	16	14	–12.9	610	527	–13.6	0.9	1.3
Vietnam	24	21	–10.6	459	477	4.1	1	1
North-East Asia								
China	23	23	0.0	357	472	32.1	1.1	1.1
Hong Kong, China	6	5	–9.1	457	450	–1.5	1	1
Republic of Korea	11	7	–33.3	648	537	–17.2	1	1

Source: APTIR 2012

of the ASEAN, instead of becoming an integrated investment area. They not only limit the ability of multinational companies to operate efficiently beyond borders but also limit the absorptive capacity of the domestic economy to benefit from FDI.

Alignment of domestic policies. The ACIA requires the ASEAN member economies to realign their domestic policies with regional commitments; some of which will require amendments and changes to existing domestic legislation. The alignment is necessary in order to reduce, if not eliminate, the long reservation lists which are prescribed by member economies' constitution or their domestic laws, policies and regulations.

Harmonization of investment treaties. While the ACIA terminated the AIA and IGA, it does not override existing ASEAN bilateral and regional investment treaties. As these investment treaties vary in scope and benefits, too many overlaps and inconsistencies remain. To avoid the noodle bowl effect, it is time to revisit the investment treaties and consolidate and harmonize.

6. SUMMARY AND CONCLUSION

The ASEAN member economies have made substantial progress in improving the investment climate in the region by consolidating the AIA and IGA into one single comprehensive agreement, the ACIA. The challenge now is enforcement of the agreement and for each member economy to honour its commitment to the agreement.

Nonetheless, much of FDI depends on country-specific characteristics. To attain the goal of the free flow of investment, the ASEAN economies should continue addressing domestic policy reforms that promote efficiency and innovation. As competition for FDI becomes fierce, the ASEAN should ensure the quality of its policy environment and the associated regulatory reforms to attract investment. Only an enabling environment that addresses the supply-side capacity constraints (institutions, infrastructures, logistics, regulatory environment, governance, etc) will take the region towards achieving its full potential of becoming an integrated investment area by 2015.

Appendix Table 1. ASEAN Inward FDI, by Member Economies, 2000–2010 (In US$ million)

	2000	2001	2002	2003	2004	2005	2006	2007	2008	2009	2010
A. Intra-ASEAN											
Brunei Darussalam	10.62	10.60	21.23	35.96	19.07	19.58	9.76	62.13	0.91	3.06	89.52
Cambodia	–	37.21	8.52	19.88	31.92	129.18	155.54	271.24	240.93	174.00	348.99
Indonesia	–232.55	–221.29	1,296.61	383.42	204.25	883.32	1,353.90	1,108.19	3,397.97	1,380.07	5,904.44
Lao PDR	13.72	3.06	2.92	2.98	7.75	6.68	10.56	100.41	47.67	57.33	135.38
Malaysia	258.12	79.99	0.02	251.12	980.17	720.92	461.55	3,780.12	1,645.51	–60.20	525.63
Myanmar (1)	74.02	67.36	25.11	24.28	9.31	38.35	71.01	93.51	103.46	67.80	171.70
Philippines	125.40	198.98	87.44	175.10	71.11	3.45	705.41	–705.08	307.78	–4.90	40.22
Singapore (2)	12.30	413.30	1,034.30	777.20	1,261.50	1,143.10	1,065.60	1,366.80	771.20	2,791.10	4,569.00
Thailand	389.03	1,710.70	1,408.29	1,060.42	688.69	1,101.33	4,626.50	2,489.39	508.43	1,463.19	1,236.93
Viet Nam	202.39	241.49	200.43	100.40	242.87	164.72	182.04	546.32	2,705.00	428.72	1,300.88
Total Intra-ASEAN	853.05	2,541.39	4,084.88	2,830.77	3,516.63	4,210.64	8,641.87	9,113.02	9,728.86	6,300.19	14,322.70
B. Extra-ASEAN											
Brunei Darussalam	538.99	515.83	1,014.30	3,262.11	186.54	269.90	424.27	198.04	329.15	368.31	535.87
Cambodia	148.50	112.16	136.58	64.11	99.47	252.04	327.70	596.05	574.25	365.02	433.57
Indonesia	–4,317.43	–2,757.22	–1,151.72	–979.51	1,690.25	7,452.66	3,559.95	5,820.13	5,920.15	3,496.70	7,866.43
Lao PDR	20.29	20.85	22.46	16.52	9.17	21.05	176.85	223.10	180.08	261.29	197.21
Malaysia	3,529.51	473.96	3,203.35	2,222.04	3,643.71	3,342.66	5,610.85	4,758.32	5,602.89	1,465.29	8,630.25
Myanmar (1)	133.98	124.65	166.29	266.95	241.82	197.50	356.77	621.31	872.10	895.50	278.50
Philippines	2,114.22	–3.98	1,454.56	315.72	616.69	1,850.55	2,215.58	3,621.08	1,236.22	1,967.91	1,257.78
Singapore (2)	14,739.90	16,888.50	7,227.80	15,754.50	22,841.60	16,156.60	35,324.30	44,167.80	9,941.00	21,215.00	44,182.60
Thailand	2,961.22	3,350.30	1,926.70	4,174.55	5,173.31	6,946.75	4,833.13	8,840.81	8,031.04	3,390.26	7,874.62
Viet Nam	1,086.31	1,058.78	999.68	1,349.74	1,367.23	1,856.09	2,217.96	6,192.69	6,874.00	7,171.28	6,699.12
Total Extra-ASEAN	–20,955.48	19,783.82	15,000.00	26,446.73	35,869.80	38,345.80	55,047.35	75,039.33	39,560.88	40,596.55	77,955.94

C. Intra- and Extra-ASEAN											
Brunei Darussalam	549.61	526.43	1,035.53	3,298.07	205.61	289.48	434.03	260.17	330.06	371.38	625.39
Cambodia	148.50	149.37	145.11	83.99	131.38	381.22	483.24	867.29	815.18	539.02	782.55
Indonesia	–4,549.98	–2,978.51	144.89	–596.09	1,894.50	8,335.98	4,913.85	6,928.32	9,318.12	4,876.77	13,770.87
Lao PDR	34.00	23.90	25.38	19.51	16.92	27.73	187.40	323.51	227.76	318.62	332.59
Malaysia	3,787.63	553.95	3,203.37	2,473.16	4,623.89	4,063.58	6,072.40	8,538.44	7,248.39	1,405.09	9,155.88
Myanmar (1)	208.00	192.01	191.40	291.23	251.13	235.85	427.79	714.82	975.56	963.30	450.20
Philippines	2,239.62	195.00	1,542.00	490.81	687.80	1,854.00	2,920.99	2,916.00	1,544.00	1,963.01	1,298.00
Singapore (2)	14,752.20	17,301.80	8,262.10	16,531.70	24,103.10	17,299.70	36,389.90	45,534.60	10,712.20	24,006.10	48,751.60
Thailand	3,350.25	5,061.00	3,334.99	5,234.97	5,862.00	8,048.08	9,459.63	11,330.20	8,539.47	4,853.45	9,111.55
Viet Nam	1,288.70	1,300.27	1,200.11	1,450.14	1,610.10	2,020.81	2,400.00	6,739.01	9,579.00	7,600.00	8,000.00
Total Inward FDIASEAN	21,808.53	22,325.21	19,084.88	29,277.49	39,386.43	42,556.44	63,689.23	84,152.35	49,289.74	46,896.74	92,278.64

Source: ASEAN Secretariat – ASEAN FDI Database as of 30 September 2012
Data is compiled from submission of ASEAN Central Banks and National Statistical Offices through the ASEAN Working Group on Foreign Direct Investment Statistics.

Notes:
* Net FDI = Equity + Net Inter-company Loans + Reinvested Earnings.
Unless otherwise indicated, the figures include equity and inter-company loans.
(1) Myanmar's fiscal year starts on 1st April and ends on 31st March of the following calendar year. Data for 2011 is not available.
(2) Singapore's data for 2011 excludes inter-company loans as geographical and industry breakdown are presently not available. Inter-company loans with intra-/extra-ASEAN breakdown for 2011 shown are estimated by the ASEAN Secretariat.

Appendix Table 2. Intra-ASEAN FDI Flows by Economic Sector, 2000–2010 (in US$ million)

Sectors	2000	2001	2002	2003	2004	2005	2006	2007	2008	2009	2010
Agriculture, Fishery and Forestry	22.25	24.95	175.07	78.87	105.14	29.61	63.34	2,103.34	297.33	101.26	373.55
Mining and Quarrying	–121.06	943.21	144.96	191.42	44.00	37.51	–70.09	718.32	768.15	304.51	608.40
Manufacturing	373.18	450.60	521.05	–33.12	558.67	1,546.46	1,562.45	2,242.40	3,292.81	871.91	2,801.54
Construction	–9.37	39.12	–22.01	119.88	8.46	50.77	186.11	443.97	828.91	136.05	56.58
Trade/Commerce	10.75	213.90	870.59	812.52	449.38	72.67	176.11	–232.57	939.17	–204.03	1,637.23
Financial Intermediation (incl. Insurance)	–27.91	–145.50	1,189.57	377.67	–146.52	654.61	2,826.56	2,426.68	2,348.25	1,546.16	2,889.15
Real Estate	–159.36	447.62	847.85	788.63	1,398.24	627.41	958.45	816.83	1,511.64	3,085.81	3,750.05
Services	144.82	291.91	263.74	160.67	198.91	1,075.24	491.69	866.23	–630.81	294.82	2,202.22
Other Activities	288.99	3.23	27.06	37.65	238.54	–53.80	1,543.67	176.42	205.89	193.29	20.00
Unspecified	330.74	253.63	73.45	271.86	661.64	167.53	903.82	–448.58	167.53	–29.58	–16.03
Total ASEAN	853.05	2,522.68	4,091.33	2,806.05	3,516.45	4,208.00	8,642.10	9,113.03	9,728.86	6,300.19	14,322.69

Source: ASEAN Secretariat – ASEAN FDI Database as of 30 September 2012

Appendix Table 3. Inward FDI flows to ASEAN by Dialogue Partner, 2000–2011 (US$ million)

Source	2000	2001	2002	2003	2004	2005	2006	2007	2008	2009	2010
Intra-ASEAN	853.05	2,541.39	4,084.89	2,831.07	3,516.63	4,210.64	8,641.87	9,113.02	9,728.86	6,300.19	14,322.70
Australia	–365.19	–148.99	90.01	207.09	588.21	257.03	569.25	2,170.27	1,042.38	992.98	2,584.94
Canada	–776.25	–65.48	271.28	–480.24	991.61	682.71	364.55	408.72	636.73	720.30	1,393.04
China	–142.58	140.36	–94.54	659.23	742.96	615.62	1,938.46	2,069.15	1,208.35	1,852.55	2,784.64
European Union 27	13,003.61	7,201.18	4,241.86	9,601.38	11,434.83	11,722.32	15,808.19	21,902.05	8,871.74	8,063.15	17,012.07
India	81.01	28.59	132.71	118.91	79.81	471.45	–96.10	2,615.45	1,400.82	616.40	3,351.51
Japan	551.39	2,394.90	3,767.38	3,023.77	5,764.78	6,581.74	10,758.68	8,723.45	4,335.53	3,789.91	10,756.38
New Zealand	43.12	15.22	82.77	–76.18	–22.83	594.97	–144.39	113.95	–106.12	98.89	3.43
Pakistan	4.47	8.78	–1.05	1.85	4.64	4.00	8.63	19.83	6.64	14.29	30.02
Republic of Korea	–49.47	–224.64	212.57	579.10	887.65	528.72	1,290.26	2,444.92	1,550.81	1,794.02	3,764.23
Russian Federation	0.00	0.00	0.00	0.00	0.00	0.00	1.23	30.98	81.27	139.76	60.28
USA	7,489.81	5,340.60	238.27	1,211.64	4,343.82	3,262.60	2,971.36	10,391.64	3,259.14	5,704.28	12,771.58
Total from Dialogue Partners	20,692.96	17,231.92	13,026.17	17,677.62	28,332.11	28,931.81	42,111.99	60,003.44	32,016.16	30,086.71	68,834.80
Non Dialogue Partners	1,115.57	5,093.29	6,058.71	11,599.88	11,054.32	13,624.63	21,577.24	24,148.92	17,273.58	16,810.03	23,443.84
ASEAN TOTAL	21,808.53	22,325.21	19,084.88	29,277.49	39,386.43	42,556.44	63,689.23	84,152.35	49,289.74	46,896.74	92,278.64

Source: ASEAN Secretariat – ASEAN FDI Database as of 30 September 2012
Data is compiled from submission of ASEAN Central Banks and National Statistical Offices through the ASEAN Working Group on Foreign Direct Investment Statistics.

Notes:
* Net FDI = Equity + Net Inter-company Loans + Reinvested Earnings.
Singapore's data for 2011 excludes inter-company loans as geographical and industry breakdown are presently not available. Inter-company loans with intra-/extra-ASEAN breakdown for 2011 shown are estimated by the ASEAN Secretariat.

REFERENCES

ASEAN Secretariat, *ASEAN Investment Report 2011*, (ASEAN Secretariat, Jakarta, 2011).

The Pattern of Intra-ASEAN Trade in the Priority Goods Sector, REPSF Project No. 03/006e (2004) <http://www.ausaid.gov.au/publications/pdf/priority_goods_sector.pdf>.

ERIA, *Mid-term Review of the Implementation of AEC Blueprint: Executive Summary* (ERIA, Jakarta, October 2012).

HG Rammal and R Zurbruegg, 'The Impact Of Regulatory Quality On Intra-Foreign Direct Investment Flows In The ASEAN Markets' (2006) 15 *International Business Review,* 401–414.

K Schwab, *The Global Competitiveness Report 2012–2013* (Geneva: World Economic Forum, 2012).

UN–ESCAP, Asia–Pacific Trade and Investment Report 2011 (New York: United Nations Publications, 2011).

UN–ESCAP, Asia–Pacific Trade and Investment Report 2012, (New York: United Nations Publications, 2011).

5

The Regulation of Investment in the TPP—Towards a Defining International Agreement for the Asia–Pacific Region

*Julien Chaisse**

1. INTRODUCTION

The Trans-Pacific Partnership (TPP) has been repeatedly presented as a 21st century trade pact to change Preferential Trade Agreements (PTAs)[1] and the problems associated with them by making them more useful in spreading liberalization globally, ie by '*multilateralizing regionalism*'.[2] The TPP's potential for successfully achieving such a goal is partly due to the nature of the partners (ie their diversity and geographical spread linking both sides of the

* Associate Professor, Faculty of Law, Centre for Financial Regulation and Economic Development (CeFRED), The Chinese University of Hong Kong, julien.chaisse@cuhk.edu.hk. The research draws on a series of interviews with medium and high ranking government/trade officials from several TPP negotiating countries. Interviews were conducted on the condition of anonymity. The author would also like to sincerely thank Roberto Echandi, Deborah Elms, Patrick Low, Bryan Mercurio, Karl Sauvant and other participants at the 2013 Asian WTO Research Network (AWRN) annual conference for their helpful comments.

[1] This chapter employs the term PTA (instead of the rather misleading FTA or RTA acronyms) which encompasses many different kinds of bilateral and regional trade agreements and underscores their common denominator which is to establish preferences for the signatories over others in trade relations. See S Lester and B Mercurio (eds), *Bilateral and Regional Trade Agreements—Commentary and Analysis* (Cambridge University Press, 2009) 4–5.

[2] Richard Baldwin has argued that since the 'spaghetti bowl's inefficiencies are increasingly magnified by unbundling and the rich–poor asymmetry, the world must find a solution. Since regionalism is here to stay, the solution must work with existing regionalism, not against it. The solution must multilateralise regionalism.' See R Baldwin 'Multilateralising Regionalism: Spaghetti Bowls as Building Blocs on the Path to Global Free Trade' (2012) 29 *The World Economy* 11 1451–1518.

Pacific),[3] and partly due to the intended nature of the deal in achieving an all-new type of PTA design. In the opinion of leading authors, the definition of 'high-quality, 21st century agreement'[4] means that such an agreement should combine three key features. Firstly, such an agreement should have a comprehensive scope. Secondly, it should have a substantial depth that includes cooperation and integration components between its members. Thirdly, it must contain a set of shared values, ideology or norms between the participants.[5]

The TPP is important for the future of trade and investment regulation; this is because it may represent the first concrete effort to sort out some of the negative effects (ie stumbling blocks) created by overlapping trade and investment agreements in the Asia–Pacific region. Having said that, the evolution of the TPP could either strengthen or fracture current trading regimes. The specific architecture of the agreement,[6] including the economic issues of the negotiating chapters, are critical factors for realizing high-quality outcomes.

The present chapter focuses on the investment part of the negotiations which is one of the 26 chapters under negotiation. Although a focus on one sector provides only a partial view and understanding of the overall negotiations, it is worth emphasizing that the TPP is a vital test from the perspective of innovations in investment rule-making for two main reasons. Firstly, the TPP will essentially draw on US rule-making and investment litigation practices[7] rather than on the existing Asian PTAs; this is because being one of the dominant parties in the negotiation process the US pushes the TPP as a model agreement for the region. It also implies that the US-inspired

---

[3] Currently, the TPP countries are Australia, Brunei, Canada, Chile, Japan, Mexico, New Zealand, Malaysia, Peru, Singapore, the United States, and Vietnam. Japan's TPP membership is expected to take effect by July 2013 at the earliest. In an announcement on April 20, 2013, TPP ministers stressed that the process of formalising Japan's entry will be conducted 'in a manner that allows the negotiations to continue expeditiously toward conclusion.' Joint Statement of TPP Ministers, Trans-Pacific Partnership Ministers Chart Path Forward on Key Issues and Confirm Next Steps on Japan's Entry, 20 April 2013 <http://www.ustr.gov/about-us/press-office/press-releases/2013/april/joint-statement-tpp-ministers>.

[4] See CL Lim, DK Elms and P Low (2012) 'What is "high-quality, twenty-first century" anyway?', in CL Lim, D Elms and P Low (eds) *The Trans-Pacific Partnership (TPP)—A Quest for Twenty-first Century Trade Agreement*, (Cambridge University Press, 2012) 3–18; MK Lewis 'The Trans-Pacific Partnership: New Paradigm Or Wolf In Sheep's Clothing?' 34 *BC Int'l & Comp. L. Rev.* (2011) 27–52.

[5] See DK Elms and CL Lim 'An overview and snapshot of the TPP negotiations' in Lim et al (n 4) 21–44.

[6] For example, how will the TPP relate to existing PTAs between TPP negotiating parties, such as the US–Australia, US–Singapore or Singapore–Australia PTAs?

[7] The US already played a decisive role in the path-breaking North American Free Trade Agreement (NAFTA) of 1994, whose Chapter 11 (Investment) embedded a full set of investment disciplines within the ambit of trade architecture for the very first time.

investment rule-making is about to achieve a global status.[8] Secondly, the TPP must be understood in the context of US investment rule-making and more broadly US foreign policy.[9] In this connection, the Transatlantic Trade and Investment Partnership (TPIP)[10] obviously aims to do the same for EU–US relations. One of the significant ramifications will be to establish the US as the key link between the giant TPP and TPIP new blocs. Such a double-headed approach is not only decisive to continuing US leadership but also it will isolate the main emerging economies (Brazil, Russia, India, and above all China) if they decide not to join and agree on the agenda set by the US.

This chapter seeks to contribute to the study of the international law of foreign investment in Asia and the Pacific region by analyzing the likely impact of the TPP on the existing legal frameworks. Whether the TPP will strengthen or fracture the investment protection regimes is the key question which also helps to assess the normative quality of the TPP and to understand whether the TPP is a defining international agreement for the Asia–Pacific region.[11] This chapter is structured around four main issues. It starts with an overview of the (ongoing) investment negotiations. The chapter then explores the current state of the draft investment chapter and reviews the

---

[8] The EU itself has decided to shift to pre-establishment rights and enhanced investment proection. See J Chaisse 'Promises and Pitfalls of the European Union Policy on Foreign Investment' (2012) 15 *Journal of International Economic Law* 1 51–84.

[9] Discussing the new foreign policy team that was assembled by President Obama over the summer 2013, Burke-White analyses the future directions of US policy. He notes that 'Michael Froman, the current deputy national security advisor for international economic affairs, has been a powerful voice within the White House and was nominated in May 2013 to serve as the next US trade representative. Froman's nomination, backed by his close relationship with the president developed while at the White House, suggests that Obama will seek to elevate trade issues on the agenda of the second term. Froman will likely breathe new life into the Transpacific Partnership, the recent proposal for a transatlantic free trade agreement, and other bilateral trade deals'. WW Burke-White 'Obama's Second Term: The Process of Building Global Leadership, Policy Brief' (Series on the Future of US Leadership) Institut Français des Relations Internationales (IFRI), Paris (2013) 7.

[10] In his State of the Union address on 12 February 2013, President Obama announced that the US Administration plans to notify Congress of its intent to launch negotiations of a Transatlantic Trade and Investment Partnership with the European Union (EU). White House, Office of the Press Secretary, Statement from United States President Barack Obama, European Council President Herman Van Rompuy and European Commission President José Manuel Barroso, 13 February 2013.

[11] As analysed by the UNCTAD, the current approach to regionalism leads to a multiplication of treaty layers, making the network of international obligations even more complex and prone to overlap and inconsistency. However, regionalism can also provide an opportunity for rationalisation of the IIA regime. See UNCTAD 'The Rise of Regionalism in International Investment Policymaking: Consolidation or complexity?' International Investment Agreements Issues Note No. 3 (2013) 4.

substance of its key provisions. The subsequent issue is the interplay of the TPP with other investments treaties, mainly through the most favoured nation treatment clause. Finally, the issue of investor-state dispute settlement is discussed, notably in light of the specific approach adopted by Australia and the likely ramifications in the region and beyond in terms of investor-state claims. Finally, the lessons are outlined in the Conclusion section.

2. THE NEGOTIATIONS: STAGES, ACTORS AND ISSUES

Understanding the TPP requires us to first consider what actually has happened during the TPP investment negotiations. The task is not easy because these negotiations are confidential and very few official documents have been (intentionally) released.[12] There is however a fair amount of information that has circulated and which will help to shed light on the negotiations' main steps and issues.

The 2006 initial 'Pacific 4' agreement[13] required parties to commence negotiations on an investment chapter, meaning that negotiations had to start from scratch with the expanded group of TPP countries.[14] Furthermore, although the 2006 P4 agreement did not contain any rules on investment,[15] the parties to the negotiations had already signed several international investment agreements (IIAs)[16] with each other or with third countries, meaning

[12] The 'negotiating member governments have signed a wide ranging confidentiality agreement. [...] Thus, it is not possible to know exactly what each member wishes to have on the negotiating agenda; however, it is clear that countries like the US will not simply be accepting the TPSEP arrangements but rather will be bringing their own agendas into the negotiations. In other words, the negotiating agenda must be fluid and changing with every new entrant. Countries such as Japan will have a considerably different agenda from that of the US and some other countries now in the TPP negotiations. This fluid negotiating agenda is, as suggested above, a radical departure from the norm in international trade negotiations'. See WA Kerr 'Negotiating in Disequilibrium: Can a Trans-Pacific Partnership be Achieved as Potential Partners Proliferate?' (2013) 14 *The Estey Centre Journal of International Law and Trade Policy* 2 1–12.

[13] The P4 agreement, which stands for 'Pacific 4', came into force in 2006 between Brunei Darussalam, Chile, Singapore, and New Zealand. It was the first multi-party free trade agreement linking Asia, the Pacific and the Americas.

[14] On the P4 origins, see Kerr (n 12) 3.

[15] See H Gao 'From the P4 to the TPP: transplantation or transformation?' in Lim et al (n 4) 64–81.

[16] According to the United Nations Conference on Trade and Development (UNCTAD), at the end of 2011 there were 3,190 international investment agreements, of which 2860 were BITs. Investment agreements can also be part of larger agreements, such as the investment chapter of NAFTA, the WTO's Agreement on Trade-Related Investment Measures (TRIMS), and various regional trade agreements. See <http://unctad.org/en/pages/DIAE/International%20Investment%20Agreements%20%28IIA%29/Research-and-Policy-Analysis.aspx>.

that they might view the TPP as a way of expanding and improving on these for the region. Beyond that, the challenges faced by the TPP investment negotiators have been diverse. These challenges arise from a lack of clarity in existing investment rules, from inconsistent treatment in existing PTAs, and from differing understandings of the scope and depth of preferred commitments between TPP member countries. Equally important to the investment negotiators have been some completely new issues which have not been covered in a binding agreement before (for instance, Australia's refusal to agree on investor-state dispute settlement). There has also been the international investment case law which, since March 2010, has seen some major interpretations on key issues such as the most favoured nation treatment and fair and equitable treatment.

The TPP negotiations initially considered different models and approaches to investment regulation, but they quickly adopted the US treaty model to develop the investment chapter. An account of Round 1 to Round 16 representing the TPP negotiations from March 2010 to date is provided in the table below (Table 1); further details are reviewed in the subsequent section.

The First Round of negotiations in Melbourne in March 2010 basically consisted of an exchange of views between the eight members of the Trans-Pacific Partnership which launched discussion on a wide range of issues, including labour, investment, textiles and apparel, e-commerce, competition issues, and trade capacity building. It was only in the Second Round of negotiations that the investment working group was established in San Francisco on 17 June 2010. While the Third Round saw the addition of Malaysia, the work essentially involved discussing approaches to negotiate investment matters. Further discussions resulted in the first exchange of initial offers taking place at the Sixth Round in Singapore in April 2011. Immediately after this Round, the Australian Government released a Trade Policy Statement on 12 April 2011, which, among other things, was opposed to investor-state dispute settlement provisions in future Australian trade agreements.[17]

Since then, the negotiations have featured many exchanges with NGOs invited to be onsite during the rounds, especially in Chicago (Round 8) and Melbourne (Round 11), where a great number of stakeholder groups could share their views with the negotiators. While initial discussions have involved various ideas and treaty models, the US BIT model released in April 2012 by the United States Trade Representative (USTR) gradually emerged as the

[17] Aust. Gov't, Dep't of Foreign Aff. & Trade, Gillard Government Trade Policy Statement: Trading Our Way to More Jobs and Prosperity 14 (April 2011), available at <http://www.dfat.gov.au/publications/trade/trading-our-way-to-more-jobs-and-prosperity.html>.

Table 1. Rounds of TPP negotiations and main investment issues

19th round is scheduled to be held in Bandar Seri Begawan, Brunei on 23–30 August	• For the 12 countries, majority of issues were at an advanced stage. Under investment chapter, dispute settlement seemed to be an outstanding issue.
Round 18—Kota Kinabalu, Malaysia, 15–24 July 2013	• Chief negotiators met. Additional bilateral meetings also took place.
20 April 2013 Japan formally invited to join TPP in July	
Round 17—Lima, Peru, 15–24 May 2013	• Representatives from academia, labour unions, the private sector, and non-governmental organizations from around the world spoke with negotiating teams about priorities.
Round 16—Singapore, 4–13 March 2013	• Minor doubts as for the drafting of the fair and equitable treatment provision and scope of the ISDS clause
Round 15—Auckland, New Zealand, 3–12 December 2012	• Canada and Mexico joined TPP
Round 14—Leesburg, Virginia, 6–15 September 2012	• Several stakeholder groups made presentations directly to delegates from the nine TPP countries
Round 13—San Diego, California, 2–10 July 2012	• While some developing countries expressed concerns as for the ISDS clause, negotiations did not advance
June Leaked draft of the Trans-Pacific Partnership (TPP) investment chapter has been published online by Citizens Trade Campaign	
Round 12—Dallas, Texas, 8–18 May 2012	• Acceleration of negotiations on the investment chapter

Release of BIT US Model

Round 11—Melbourne, Australia, 2–9 March 2012	• Several stakeholder groups made presentations directly to delegates from the nine TPP countries
Round 10—Kuala Lumpur, Malaysia, 5–9 December 2011	• US BIT model clearly appeared as the only model to structure negotiations
Round 9—Lima, Peru, 22–29 October 2011	• Further discussions
Round 8—Chicago, Illinois, 6–15 September 2011	• Several stakeholder groups made presentations directly to delegates from the nine TPP countries
Round 7—Ho Chi Minh City, Vietnam, 15–24 June 2011	• Comments on initial offers
Round 6—Singapore, 24 March–1 April 2011	• TPP teams exchanged initial offers on services and investment
On 12 April 2011 Australian Government released a Trade Policy Statement opposing investor-state dispute settlement provisions in future Australian trade agreements	
Round 5—Santiago, Chile, 14–18 February 2011	• Preliminary discussions on investment
Round 4—Auckland, New Zealand, 6–10 December 2010	• Preliminary discussions on investment
Round 3—Brunei, 4–9 October 2010	• Malaysia joined
Round 2—San Francisco, California, 14–18 June 2010	• Establishment of the investment working group
Round 1—Melbourne, Australia, 15–19 March 2010	• The eight partners began negotiations

Sources: Singapore Ministry of Trade and Industry Overview of Trans-Pacific SEP (http://www.fta.gov.sg/fta_tpfta.asp?hl=12), Office of the United States Trade Representative TPP Website (http://www.ustr.gov/tpp), United States–New Zealand Council–TPP Resources (http://www.usnzcouncil.org/tpp/), New Zealand Ministry of Foreign Affairs and Trade TPP Website (http://www.mfat.govt.nz/Trade-and-Economic-Relations/2-Trade-Relationships-and-Agreements/Trans-Pacific/index.php) and information directly collected by author.

benchmark which would serve as the basis for TPP investment negotiations. It was, however, only inbetween the two US-based rounds of negotiations[18] that the NGO Citizens Trade Campaign released on the web in June 2012 the then-consolidated text of the negotiations;[19] this is the most comprehensive document for helping us to understand and assess the TPP investment negotiations so far. Not surprisingly, at least from the investment perspective, integrating the newest members, Canada and Mexico joined the negotiations in Round 15 (Auckland, New Zealand, 3–12 December 2012), accentuated the perception that the TPP might wish to push forward a NAFTA-related 'codification' on certain issues that have a longer history in NAFTA jurisprudence. In April 2013, the eleven countries formally invited Japan into their ranks, pending the conclusion of their respective domestic procedures.[20] Japan officially joined TPP on 23 July 2013 in the middle of the 18th round of negotiations[21] in Malaysia, while the agreement was still expected to be concluded in the end of 2013.[22]

In the period of negotiations under review (March 2010–October 2013), three key features of TPP regulation on foreign investment have emerged. Firstly, the dynamic character of the negotiations, which have progressed quite regularly while including new countries. Secondly, US leadership, which is obvious in the form but also in the substance of the TPP. While exerting this leadership in a group of 11 countries (half being emerging economies), the US has also isolated the main emerging countries, namely, China, India and Brazil. Thirdly, in light of the previous points, the TPP represents a major PTA which illustrates the regionalization of investment rule-making and probably represents a benchmark for the state of the art of international law of foreign investment.

---

18 After Round 12 (Dallas, Texas, 8–18 May 2012) and before Round 13 (San Diego, California, 2–10 July 2012).

19 Known as the June 2012 leaked draft of the Trans-Pacific Partnership (TPP) investment chapter. The draft of the Trans-Pacific Partnership (TPP) investment chapter was published online by Citizens Trade Campaign <http://www.citizenstrade.org/ctc/wp-content/uploads/2012/06/tppinvestment.pdf>. The leaked chapter indicates in square brackets where aspects of the text have not been agreed. However, references to which countries support particular bracketed text have been removed.

20 Office of the US Trade Representative, 'Obama Administration Notifies Congress of Intent to Include Japan in Trans-Pacific Partnership Negotiations', 24 April 2013 <http://www.ustr.gov/about-us/press-office/press-releases/2013/april/congressional-notification-japan-tpp>.

21 Before formally joining the TPP talks, Japan had had to await the conclusion of the 90-day US consultation period, which began back in April when the US Administration advised Congress of its intention to include Japan in the negotiations. See W Cooper and M Manyin 'Japan Joins the Trans-Pacific Partnership: What Are the Implications?' Congressional Research Service, Washington DC: Report for Congress (2013) 3.

22 Idem.

3. MAPPING THE SUBSTANTIVE INVESTMENT PROVISIONS: TPP AS A NAFTA-RELATED 'CODIFICATION' AND BEYOND

In terms of substance, investment treaty practice shows that virtually all treaties regulating foreign investment matters cover the following nine topics: (1) definitions and scope of application; (2) investment promotion and conditions for the entry of foreign investments and investors; (3) general standards for the treatment of foreign investors and investments; (4) issues of monetary transfers; (5) expropriation (direct or indirect); (6) operational and other conditions; (7) losses from armed conflict or internal disorder; (8) treaty exceptions, modifications, and terminations; and (9) dispute settlement.

These diverse provisions are important to reassure foreign investors that they will be able to reap the benefits of their investment; furthermore, no trend denies such an approach, although evidence on the extent to which investment decisions are influenced by investment treaties is mixed.[23] As shown by the June 2012 leaked draft of the TPP investment chapter, the TPP negotiations have developed against this background (Table 2).

In order to review the TPP key investment provisions, I will address the key provisions by focusing on the specific definition given to the provision in the TPP, its meaning, and lessons that can be drawn from the TPP drafting. The conclusion is that the TPP is largely a NAFTA-related 'codification', as evidenced by the conditions for the entry of foreign investments and investors as well as by the general standards for the treatment of foreign investors and investments.[24] The TPP negotiators have opted for the pre-establishment rights (3.1), while the US influence can also be read in the definition of national treatment (3.2), the minimum standard of treatment (3.3), full protection and security (3.4), and the wording of the provision on indirect expropriation (3.5). In a last sub-paragraph I will also briefly review other provisions (3.6).

---

[23] The extent to which BITs actually attract increased flows of foreign direct investment is disputed. According to Salacuse and Sullivan, entering a BIT with the United States would nearly double a country's FDI inflows. However, entering BITs with other OECD countries had no significant effect on FDI. See JW Salacuse and NP Sullivan, 'Do BITs Really Work? An Evaluation of Bilateral Investment Treaties and Their Grand Bargain' (2005) 46 *Harv. Int'l L.J.* 67 105–111. Another important study concludes that there is 'little evidence that BITs have stimulated additional investment'. M Hallward-Driemeier, 'Do Bilateral Investment Treaties Attract FDI? Only a Bit ... and They Could Bite' (2003) 22 (World Bank Dev. Research Grp, Research Working Paper No. 3121), available at <http://elibrary.worldbank.org/content/workingpaper/10.1596/1813-9450-3121>.

[24] For a detailed analysis of US investment treaties, see K Halverson Cross 'Converging Trends in Investment Treaty Practice', (2013) 38 *N.C.J. Int'l L. & Com. Reg.* 151.

Table 2. TPP rule-making innovations at a glance

TPP Draft provision	Issue of interest
Art. 12(2) Definitions (with Annex 12.K)	NAFTA excludes sovereign debt from coverage of Chapter 11. The TPP includes sovereign long-term debt as a 'form that an investment may take'. Similar to 2012 USA Model BIT
Art. 12(3) Scope and coverage	Art. 12.3(2b) makes clear that the application of the substantive obligations of the BIT to a state enterprise or other person when it exercises any regulatory, administrative, or other governmental authority delegated to it by that Party. Similar to 2012 USA Model BIT (Art. 2.2)
Art. 12(3)bis relation other chapters	Does not apply to measures adopted or maintained by a Party to the extent they are covered by the chapter on financial services
Art. 12(4) national treatment	Comparator is 'in like circumstances'. Similar to NAFTA
Art. 12(5) Most favoured nation treatment	Comparator is 'in like circumstances'. Similar to NAFTA. However, exception on ISDS
Art. 12(6) Minimum standard of treatment	Embodies NAFTA Interpretation regarding the international minimum standard. Similar to 2012 US Model BITs and similar provisions of recent US investment agreements
Art. 12(6)bis Treatment in case of Armed conflict or civil strife	Complemented by Annex 12-B.
Art. 12(7) Performance requirements	Expanded coverage that includes conduct by a host State to preference local technology against 'technology of the Party', which is defined as including technology owned, or held under exclusive licence, by an investor of the other Party. Similar to 2012 USA Model BIT (Art. 8)
Art. 12(12) Expropriation	Complemented by Annex 12-C. Embodies NAFTA Interpretation regarding the international minimum standard. Similar to 2012 US Model BITs and similar provisions of recent US investment agreements
Art. 12(14) Denial of benefits	Similar to ACIA
Art. 12(15) Investment and environment, labour	Encompass a duty to enforce local environmental laws. Addresses environmental and labour obligations in a manner quite different from NAFTA which only contains exhortatory language similar to US free trade agreements

Table 2: Elaboration by the author

3.1. Establishment in the context of investment protection

Among the key issues to tackle in the TPP investment chapter is the degree of liberalization of rules governing the entry of foreign investment. To what extent can the TPP be a driver (or consolidator) of market opening and pro-competitive regulatory reforms in host regimes? In general terms, Asian investments agreements, like the majority of BITs, do not provide entry rights to foreign investors into their territory. Rather, most BITs throughout the world provide only a best-endeavour provision in regard to the admission of the foreign investments. In sharp contrast, the text of the TPP Most-Favoured Nation (MFN) and National Treatment (NT) provisions encompasses pre-establishment rights.

Article 12.4 of the June 2012 leaked draft of the TPP investment chapter defined the NT as follows:

> 1. Each Party shall accord to investors of another Party treatment no less favourable than that it accords, in like circumstances, to its own investors *with respect to the establishment, acquisition, expansion, management, conduct, operation, and sale or other disposition of investments in its territory*.
> 2. Each Party shall accord to covered investments treatment no less favourable than that it accords, in like circumstances, to investments in its territory of its own investors *with respect to the establishment, acquisition, expansion, management, conduct, operation, and sale or other disposition of investments in its territory*.

Article 12.5 of the June 2012 leaked draft of the TPP investment chapter defined the MFN as follows:

> 1. Each Party shall accord to investors of another Party treatment no less favourable than that it accords, in like circumstances, to investors of any other Party or of any non-Party *with respect to the establishment, acquisition, expansion, management, conduct, operation, and sale or other disposition of investments in its territory*.
> 2. Each Party shall accord to covered investments treatment no less favourable than that it accords, in like circumstances, to investments in its territory of investors of any other Party or of any non-Party *with respect to the establishment, acquisition, expansion, management, conduct, operation, and sale or other disposition of investments in its territory*.

The combined reading of Article 12.4 on the national treatment and Article 12.5 on most-favoured-nation treatment indicates that TPP investors of one party will receive treatment no less favourable with regard to investing in the territory of the other party than domestic investors (NT) and investors of any other third country (MFN). These provisions offer pre-establishment non-discrimination guarantee in the admission of investors and their investments.

The use of this approach was traditionally limited to US BITs and later to Canada (essentially post-NAFTA). However, during the last decade other nations, such as Japan, have also adopted this method. Equally important is the increasing use of pre-establishment clauses in Asian PTAs (such as Singapore–USA (2003) and Australia–USA (2004); Singapore–Panama PTA (2006); Japan–Mexico EPA (2007) and Japan–Chile EPA (2007); Taiwan (ROC)–El Salvador–Honduras PTA (2007); and Japan–Switzerland PTA (2009).

Liberalization, in the context of FDI, involves the elimination of restrictions on the entry of foreign companies. TPP countries are negotiating on a 'negative list' basis, which presumes comprehensive coverage but allows countries to negotiate specific exceptions to commitments in specific service sectors. Of course, Articles 12.14 and 12.15 should be complemented by the schedules of commitments to clarify the scope of liberalization. However, these TPP negative lists, subject to the highest level of confidentiality, are still under negotiation. Though it is impossible to anticipate the level of liberalization that TPP countries will reach at this stage, it is certainly an important aspect of current negotiations; this explains why some other aspects (such as the treatment of SOEs, dispute settlement rules, and enhancement of investment standards) of investment regulation have become so important and crucial in the current negotiations.

3.2. National treatment

The principle of national treatment prohibits discrimination on the grounds of nationality[25] and, more generally any discrimination between investors and investments produced domestically and those from other countries.[26] Together with the most favoured nation (MFN) obligation, it operationalizes the fundamental principle of non-discrimination in investment law.[27] Article

[25] *Champion Trading Company and Ameritrade International, Inc. v Arab Republic of Egypt*, ICSID Case No. ARB/02/9, Award, 27 October 2006, paras 128 and 156.

[26] In *Occidental Exploration v Ecuador* the Final Award stated that the purpose of national treatment is to protect investors as compared to local producers, and this cannot be done by exclusively addressing the sector in which the particular activity is undertaken. *Occidental Exploration and Production Company* v *Republic of Ecuador*, LCIA Case No. UN3467, Final Award, 1 July 2004, para 173.

[27] The scope and practical relevance of NT is to a large extent dependent on the reading of the term 'like circumstances'. Its definition essentially sets the benchmark for national regulatory freedom to treat certain imported products differently from domestically produced ones. Indeed, '[o]ften the definition of national treatment is qualified by the inclusion of the provision that it

12.4 of the June 2012 leaked draft of the TPP investment chapter defines NT as follows (*See Annex 2*):

> 1. Each Party shall accord to investors of another Party treatment no less favourable than that it accords, *in like circumstances*, to its own investors with respect to the establishment, acquisition, expansion, management, conduct, operation, and sale or other disposition of investments in its territory.
> 2. Each Party shall accord to covered investments treatment no less favourable than that it accords, *in like circumstances*, to investments in its territory of its own investors with respect to the establishment, acquisition, expansion, management, conduct, operation, and sale or other disposition of investments in its territory.

Such a provision is substantially equivalent to NAFTA Article 1102 which requires that each party treats foreign investors 'no less favourably that it treats its own investors and investments, in like circumstances, with respect to such matters as the establishment, acquisition, operation and sale of investments'. As a result, TPP Article 12.14 requires that a violation must be based on some form of discrimination, where foreign investors are discriminated against on the basis of their nationality. In practice, arbitral tribunals analyse national treatment by determining whether the parties involved were in like situations, and by comparing the treatment being received by foreign investments with the treatment received by local investors.[28]

More precisely, the NAFTA tribunal in *Pope & Talbot v Canada*[29] articulated in 2001 a lucid and compelling analysis of the application of NT which has been (implicitly) observed by every subsequent NAFTA tribunal to date and which has informed the wording of TPP Article 12.14. The *Pope & Talbot* test consists of a three-pronged analysis (the so-called case-law-developed 'non-discrimination test') that requires the investor to make out a prima facie claim that it has received less favourable treatment than any of its domestic competitors. The

---

only applies in 'like circumstances' or 'similar circumstances. As the situations of foreign and domestic investors are often not identical, this language obviously leaves room open for interpretation.' J Chaisse and P Gugler (eds) *Expansion Of Trade And FDI In Asia: Strategic And Policy Challenges* (Routledge 2009) 127.

[28] For instance, the *Bayindir v Pakistan* Award holds that the tribunal must first assess whether the investor was in a 'similar situation' to that of other investors; if that requirement is met the tribunal must further inquire whether the investor was granted less favourable treatment than other investors. See *Bayindir Insaat Turizm Ticaret Ve Sanayi A.S. v Islamic Republic of Pakistan*, ICSID Case No. ARB/03/29, Award, 27 August 2009, para 390. Also, *BG v Argentina* Award states that a measure that breaches national or MFN treatment would be unavoidably 'discriminatory' for the purposes of the BIT standard. See *BG Group Plc. v Republic of Argentina*, UNCITRAL, Final Award, 24 December 2007, paras 355–356.

[29] *Pope Talbot* Final Merits Award 2001, at paras 31–81, and para 78 in particular.

prima facie claim requires: (a) the identification of appropriate comparators; (b) determining the result of the treatment received; and (c) establishing of a reasonable nexus between the disputed treatment and a rational policy objective (the respondent must subsequently demonstrate that such treatment is reasonable and justifiable in the circumstances).

(a) Likeness of the comparators

In cases where the treatment in question is particular to a certain industry, the source of comparison will naturally be between investors operating within that industry (rather than all investors in the territory). The basis for any comparison rests upon the likeness of the comparators. Logically, the *Pope & Talbot* Tribunal concluded that, 'as a first step, the treatment accorded to a foreign owned investment protected by Article 1102(2) should be compared with that accorded to domestic investments in the same business or economic sector'. The *ADF* Tribunal determined that comparison under Article 1102(2) should be made between steel products held by the investor (a steel fabricator) and steel products held by domestic investors, *with respect to their potential use in a highway project*.[30] By necessary implication, the tribunal's comparison focused on firms operating in the steel fabrication business as its 'universe' of comparable investors under Article 1102(1).

(b) Test of 'treatment no less favourable'

Investors and their investments are entitled to the best level of treatment available to any other domestic investor or investment operating in like circumstances. These comparisons are not limited to an evaluation of whether the treatment being received is substantially similar. Rather, the focus is on the result of treatment being received. As the *Myers* Tribunal noted: 'Intent is important, but protectionist intent is not necessarily decisive on its own. The existence of an intent to favor nationals over non-nationals would not give rise to a breach of [Article 1102] if the measures in question were to produce no adverse effect on the non-national complainant. The word "treatment" suggests that practical impact is required to produce a breach of Article 1102, not merely a motive or intent that is a violation of Chapter 11.'[31] The test of 'treatment no less favourable' therefore does not call for a global comparison of treatment received, on the whole, by groups of domestic or foreign investors or investments. It is particular to the experience of the claimant. It does not matter if every other foreign investor is receiving treatment which is effectively identical to that which is provided to

---

[30] *ADF Group Inc. v United States of America*, ICSID Case No. ARB(AF)/00/1, Award, 9 January 2003, para 197, 155.

[31] *S D Myers: v Canada*, Award on Merits, 10 April 2001, 122 ILR (2002) 352, para 254.

all domestic investors. It does not matter if there are other domestic investors who are also receiving less favourable treatment. The comparison is between the treatment being received by the claimant and the best treatment being received by a domestic investor operating in like circumstances.[32]

(c) 'Like circumstances exception'

Once a prima facie breach of NT (or MFN) has been proved by the claimant, the analysis turns to the question of whether the difference in treatment could be rationally explained as justifiable in the circumstances. In each NAFTA case in which a prima facie claim of non-discrimination has been made out, the tribunals turned to the respondent to justify its actions—regardless of whether they were discriminatory on their face[33] or discriminatory in result or application (such as in *Feldman*,[34] *Myers*[35] and *Pope & Talbot*[36]). Also, as an important lesson of NAFTA practice, to safeguard the liberalizing objectives of the treaty, the 'like circumstances exception' must be construed narrowly.

It is also important to stress that national treatment operates differently in trade and investment contexts. In this regard, arbitral tribunals have repeatedly highlighted the different purposes of national treatment in the trade and investment context and the difference between the terms 'in like situations' under BITs and 'like products' in the WTO.[37]

---

[32] It is also unnecessary to prove that the reason for any difference in treatment received by an investor or its investment was due to its nationality (ie, it not being domestic). As the *Feldman* Tribunal has explained: 'It is clear that the concept of national treatment as embodied in [the] NAFTA and similar agreements is designed to prevent discrimination on the basis of nationality, or "by reason of nationality" ... However, it is not self-evident, as the Respondent argues, that any departure from national treatment must be explicitly shown to be a result of the investor's nationality. There is no such language in Article 1102. Rather, Article 1102 by its terms suggests that it is sufficient to afford less favorable treatment to the foreign investor than to domestic investors in like circumstances.' *Marvin Roy Feldman Karpa v United Mexican States*, ICSID Case No. ARB(AF)/99/1, Award, 16 December 2002, 181.

[33] Such as in *US—Trucking*. Under NAFTA, Mexican and USA carriers were authorized to cross the border. But for many years the US refused to allow Mexican trucks full access, citing concerns of their ability to meet US safety and environmental standards. See K Alexander and B Soukup 'Obama's First Trade War: The US–Mexico Cross-Border Trucking Dispute and the Implications of Strategic Cross-Sector Retaliation on US Compliance under NAFTA' (2010) 28 *Berkeley Journal of International Law* 2 313. In 2011, US and Mexico signed a specific arrangement to allow their trucks to use each other's roads, after a 17-year dispute. E Williamson 'US, Mexico Agree to Settle Truck Feud' The Wall Street Journal, 4 March 2011.

[34] *Feldman* (n 32).

[35] *S D Myer* (n 31).

[36] *Pope Talbot* (n 29).

[37] See *Occidental Exploration* (n 26), paras 175–176. Later in 2009, the *Bayindir v Pakistan* Award considered that the treaty clause must be interpreted in an autonomous manner, independently from trade law considerations. See *Bayindir Insaat Turizm* (n 28), paras 389 and 402.

3.3. *Minimum standard of treatment*

The definition of fair and equitable treatment may also be challenging as some TPP countries BITs do take into account the full range of international law sources, including general principles and modern treaties and other conventional obligations to give FET an extended scope of application. Some BITs equate FET to a mere minimum standard of treatment.

Art. 12.6 of the June 2012 leaked draft of the TPP investment chapter (*see Annex 3*) defined FET as follows:

> 1. Each party shall accord to covered investments treatment *in accordance with customary international law, including fair and equitable treatment* and full protection and security.
> 2. For greater certainty, paragraph 1 prescribes the applicable rules of customary international law minimum standard of treatment of aliens as the minimum general standard of treatment to be afforded to covered investments. The concept of 'fair and equitable treatment' and 'full protection and security' *do not require treatment in addition to or beyond that which is required by that standard, and do not create additional substantive rights*. The obligations in paragraph 1 to provide:
>   a. "fair and equitable treatment" includes the obligation not to deny justice in criminal, civil, or administrative adjudicatory proceedings in accordance with the principle of due process embodied in the principal legal systems of the world; and
>   b. [...)
> 3. A determination that there has been a breach of another provision of this Agreement, or of a separate international agreement, does not establish that there has been a breach of this Article.

Such wording echoes typical US treaty practice, as illustrated by the USA–Uruguay BIT which links the FET standard with customary law but makes clear that the former is a component of the latter (as in the TPP, FET is part of customary international law).[38] To avoid any misinterpretation, that same treaty continues: '[f]or greater certainty' the foregoing provision '*prescribes the customary international law minimum standard of treatment of aliens* ... . The concepts of "FET" and "full protection and security" do not require treatment in addition to or beyond that which is required by that standard, and *do not create additional substantive rights*,' which is a similar approach to that found in the TPP Article 12.6. Although there has been

[38] 'Each Party shall accord to covered investments treatment in accordance with customary international law, including FET and full protection and security.' For a commentary on US treaties, see Halverson Cross (n 24) 192.

considerable debate over the drafting and interpretation of FET provisions,[39] it seems that tribunals, in fact, have avoided grand theories about the meaning of the FET standard. Some authors, like Ioana Tudor, have endorsed such an approach, saying that 'FET has only one content which is operating at different thresholds, depending on the context'.[40]

Most commonly, any theoretical discussion is limited to a list of examples of the kinds of behaviour that violate the standard.[41] Illustrative is the NAFTA award in *Waste Management v Mexico*, where the tribunal held that FET is violated by conduct that is 'arbitrary, grossly unfair, unjust or idiosyncratic, is discriminatory and exposes the claimant to sectional or racial prejudice, or involves a lack of due process leading to an outcome which offends judicial propriety—as might be the case with a manifest failure of natural justice in judicial proceedings or a complete lack of transparency and candor in an administrative process. In applying this standard it is relevant that the treatment is in breach of representations made by the host State which was reasonably relied on by the claimant.'[42]

In substance, the protection granted under TPP Article 12.6 relates to an investor's investment decision and on the expectation that he will be treated, in the future, fairly and equitably. In order to violate FET, a disputed measure must treat the investor in an unjust manner. For instance, the *Alpha*

---

[39] In *Total v Argentina* the tribunal noted that the undertaking of the host country to provide fair and equitable treatment to the investors of the other party and their investments is a standard feature in BITs, although the exact language of such undertakings is not uniform, and the generality of the fair and equitable treatment standard distinguishes it from specific obligations undertaken by the parties to a BIT. See *Total S.A. v Argentine Republic*, ICSID Case No. ARB/04/01, Decision on Liability, 27 December 2010, para. 106.

[40] See I Tudor, *The FET Standard in the International Law of Foreign Investment* (Oxford University Press 2008) 154.

The FET standard is expressed in different ways. Some treaties contain a bare reference to FET; others link FET to international law or to customary international law. Still others include the standard in a clause that also contains prohibitions against arbitrary and discriminatory acts and/or a 'non-impairment' obligation. In this regard, the *Sempra v Argentina* Tribunal noted that fair and equitable treatment is not a clear and precise standard and that it has evolved by case-by-case determinations, *Sempra Energy International v Argentine Republic*, ICSID Case No. ARB/02/16, Award, 28 September 2007, para 296. Recently, the *El Paso v Argentina* Tribunal, citing the CMS Annulment Decision, agrees that there is variation in the practice of arbitral tribunals in relation to the fair and equitable standard. *El Paso Energy International Company v Argentine Republic*, ICSID Case No. ARB/03/15, Award, 31 October 2011, para 338.

[41] *Mondev v United States* observed that the minimum standard of treatment applies to a wide range of factual situations, whether in peace or in civil strife, and to conduct by a wide range of State organs and agencies, *Mondev International Ltd. v United States of America*, ICSID Case No. ARB(AF)/99/2, Award, 11 October 2002, para 95.

[42] *Waste Mgmt., Inc. v United Mexican States, ICSID Case No. ARB(AF)/00/3, Award, para 98 (30 April 2004)*

Projecktholding v Ukraine tribunal considered that the principle of fair and equitable treatment includes the obligation to avoid arbitrary government action, regardless of whether there is any discriminatory element involved.[43] The *Roussalis v Romania* tribunal referred to an earlier award in *Rumeli Telekom v Kazakhstan* and found that conduct that is arbitrary, grossly unfair, unjust, idiosyncratic, discriminatory or lacking in due process will breach the fair and equitable treatment standard.[44] More recently, the tribunal in *SAUR v Argentina* summarized earlier case law and found that fair and equitable treatment is closely linked to the prohibition on arbitrariness and discrimination.[45]

The minimum standard of treatment has been frequently invoked under the NAFTA but only found to have been violated in four cases, namely *Metalclad*,[46] *S.D. Myers*,[47] *Pope & Talbot*,[48] and *Cargill.*[49] Although claims of FET breach have rarely succeeded in the NAFTA context, FET has been at issue in other BIT cases—including a range of Argentinean cases and those involving Eastern European states. That being said, this relatively modest role under NAFTA could increase in the context of the TPP and in the scenario of disputes involving developing countries of important relevance for TPP developing countries is the NAFTA Award in *Glamis Gold v United States*. The tribunal found that the customary international law minimum standard of treatment is a minimum standard meant to serve as a level below which conduct is not accepted by the international community, and the standard is not meant to vary from state to state or from investor to investor.[50] This means that unlike the national treatment standard, which is a relative standard, fair and equitable treatment is not dynamic; it cannot vary between nations and thus the protection afforded will have a minimum.[51] Transposed into the context of the TPP, the NAFTA definitions and practice show that the potential of litigation under Article 12.6 is very high.

---

[43] *Alpha Projektholding GmbH v Ukraine*, ICSID Case No. ARB/07/16, Award, 8 November 2010, para 420.

[44] *Spyridon Roussalis v Romania*, ICSID Case No. ARB/06/1, Award, 7 December 2011, para 314.

[45] *SAUR International S.A. v Argentine Republic*, ICSID Case No. ARB/04/4, Decision on Jurisdiction and Liability, 6 June 2012, paras 485–488.

[46] *Metalclad Corporation v United Mexican States*, ICSID Case No. ARB(AF)/97/1, Award, 30 August 2000, paras 97–101.

[47] *S.D. Myers, Inc. v Government of Canada*, UNCITRAL, Partial Award, 13 November 2000, paras 267–268.

[48] *Pope & Talbot Inc. v Government of Canada*, UNCITRAL, Award on the Merits of Phase 2, 10 April 2001, para 181; see also *Pope & Talbot v Canada* Award on Damages, UN/0020/20, para 69.

[49] *Cargill, Incorporated v United Mexican States*, ICSID Case No. ARB(AF)/05/2, Award, 18 September 2009, paras 297–305.

[50] *Glamis Gold, Ltd v The United States of America*, UNCITRAL, Award, 8 June 2009, para 615.

[51] The gist of the tribunal's interpretation of FET is that any changes in the meaning of the standard should be supported by evidence of the evolution in customary international law ie through evolved state practice and opinio juris.

3.4. Full protection and security

One of the key substantive provisions commonly included in investment treaty texts is the obligation to provide 'full protection and security'. However, different variants are also found, such as 'full protection and full security', 'constant protection and security', 'protection and security', or 'physical protection and security' which have not much impacted the way the standard is applied.[52] Article 12.6 of the June 2012 leaked draft of the TPP investment chapter (*See Annex 3*) defined the full protection and security standard as follows:

> 1. Each party shall accord to covered investments treatment in accordance with customary international law, including fair and equitable treatment and full protection and security.
> 2. For greater certainty, paragraph 1 prescribes the applicable rules of customary international law minimum standard of treatment of aliens as the minimum general standard of treatment to be afforded to covered investments. The concept of "fair and equitable treatment" and "full protection and security" do not require treatment in addition to or beyond that which is required by that standard, and do not create additional substantive rights. The obligations in paragraph 1 to provide:
>   a. [...)
>   b. "full protection and security" requires each Party to provide the level of police protection required under customary international law.
> 3. A determination that there has been a breach of another provision of this Agreement, or of a separate international agreement, does not establish that there has been a breach of this Article.

There are no relevant NAFTA cases to shed light on the application of the full protection and security standard in the TPP. Under the CAFTA (another NAFTA-like treaty), however, the *Railroad Development v Guatemala* Award recently noted that 'full protection and security' is a core component of the minimum standard of treatment under the CAFTA.[53] In order to better predict the application of the provision, it is necessary to look at the jurisprudence under BITs.

The extent of the protection was detailed in the *Saluka v Czech Republic* Award which noted that the 'full protection and security' standard applies

---

[52] The *Parkerings v Lithuania* Award found that it is generally accepted that the variation of language between the formulation 'protection' and 'full protection and security' does not make a significant difference in the level of protection a host state is to provide, *Parkerings-Compagniet AS v Republic of Lithuania*, ICSID Case No. ARB/05/8, Award, 11 September 2007, para 354.

[53] *Railroad Development Corporation v Republic of Guatemala*, ICSID Case No. ARB/07/23, Award, 29 June 2012, para 238.

essentially when the foreign investment has been affected by civil strife and physical violence.[54] It is clear that tribunals are in agreement that the standard applies at least in situations where actions of third parties involving either physical violence or the disregard of legal rights occur, and it requires that the state exercise due diligence to prevent harm to the investor, it being understood that the standard does not grant the investor 'insurance against all and every risk', as noted recently in the *Vannessa Ventures v Venezuela* Award.[55]

International law has interpreted this standard of due diligence to require that the Host State exercise a modified objective standard of diligence, viz., the standard of diligence due by a Host State in the circumstances and with the resources of the State in question.[56] This extension has been endorsed by subsequent tribunals.[57] More recently, the scope of the full protection and security concept has been extended to include providing a legal framework that offers legal protection to investors—including both substantive provisions to protect investments and appropriate procedures that enable investors to vindicate their rights.[58] In the context of the TPP, this offers a rich canvass which TPP claimants may prepare their claims.

3.5. Indirect expropriation

Recent practice in IIAs in which some key TPP countries have been involved (such as US, Singapore, Chile, Australia, and Peru) clearly shows that TPP

---

[54] *Saluka Investments BV (the Netherlands) v Czech Republic*, UNCITRAL, Partial Award, 17 March 2006, para 483. Technically, it was *Asian Agricultural Products Limited v Sri Lanka*, Final Award on Merits and Damages, 21 June 1990 (ICSID Case No ARB/87/3) (1991) 30 ILM 577 where the FPS standard was discussed first.

[55] *Vannessa Ventures Ltd. v Bolivarian Republic of Venezuela*, ICSID Case No. ARB(AF)/04/6, Award, 16 January 2013, para 223.

[56] *Pantechniki v Albania* Award, citing Newcombe and Paradell, *Law and Practice of Investment Treaties*. See *Parkerings-Compagniet AS v Republic of Lithuania*, ICSID Case No. ARB/05/8, Award, 11 September 2007, paras 81–84.

[57] For instance, *Paushok v Mongolia* notes that the 'legal protection' clause has been raised in a number of BIT cases and it has sometimes been interpreted as a stand-alone clause, aiming at the physical protection of persons or assets against illegal actions by third parties; in the case before the tribunal the treaty provides clearly for 'full legal protection to investments of investors of the other Contracting Party' and there is therefore no reason to limit the protection guaranteed to mere physical protection. *Sergei Paushok, CJSC Golden East Company and CJSC Vostokneftegaz Company v Government of Mongolia*, UNCITRAL, Award on Jurisdiction and Liability, 28 April 2011, para. 326. See also *Reinhard Unglaube v Costa Rica* and *Marion Unglaube v Costa Rica* Award accepted that 'full protection' may, in appropriate circumstances, extend beyond the traditional standard focused on physical security. *Reinhard Hans Unglaube v Republic of Costa Rica*, ICSID Case No. ARB/09/20, Award, 16 May 2012, para 281.

[58] *Frontier Petroleum Services Ltd v Czech Republic*, UNCITRAL, Final Award, 12 November 2010, para 263.

negotiations will address the important definition of expropriation (*see Annex 4*). There are however significant discrepancies in TPP countries' practices; some IIAs will cover both direct and indirect expropriation, whereas some will not address indirect expropriation. It is not a matter of national investment policies because some TPP countries (such as New Zealand, Singapore, and China)[59] do not always cover indirect expropriation in their IIAs. The choice is important because if indirect expropriation is covered by a treaty, it means that the IIA grants a protection to foreign investors who may be faced with serious alterations of the investment climate which they could not have reasonably anticipated. There is however no clear definition of indirect expropriation. Despite a number of decisions by international tribunals, the line between the concept of indirect expropriation and governmental regulatory measures not requiring compensation has not been clearly articulated and it depends on the specific facts and circumstances of the case.[60] In recent years, a new generation of US and Canadian investment agreements, including the investment chapters of FTAs, have introduced specific language[61] and established criteria to assist tribunals in determining whether an indirect expropriation requiring compensation has occurred. One can also note reservations in US FTAs with Singapore, Chile, Australia, and Peru.

Article 12.12 of the June 2012 leaked draft of the TPP investment chapter is modeled on NAFTA Article 1110 and defines expropriation as follows:

> 1. No Party may expropriate or nationalize a covered investment either directly or indirectly through measures equivalent to expropriation or nationalization ('expropriation') except:
> (a) for a public purpose;
> (b) in a non-discriminatory manner;
> (c) on payment of prompt, adequate, and effective compensation in accordance with paragraphs 2 through 4; and
> (d) in accordance with due process
> [subsequent paragraphs specifying valuation of expropriations and form and procedure of payment].

The jurisprudence of the past decade has demonstrated that cases of indirect expropriation fall short of the actual physical taking of property but that

[59] There is no expropriation protection in the NZ–Singapore CEP; a limited expropriation clause is included in the more recent NZ–China FTA (2008).

[60] See A Van Aaken, 'International investment law between commitment and flexibility: a contract theory analysis', (2009) 12 *Journal of International Economic Law* 507, 510–512.

[61] See, for a discussion, RD Edsall, 'Indirect expropriation under NAFTA and DR–CAFTA: potential inconsistencies in the treatment of state public welfare regulations' 86 *Boston University Law Review* (2006) 931, 953–961.

result rather in the effective loss of management, use, or control, or a significant depreciation of the value of the assets of a foreign investor.[62] In certain cases indirect expropriation can be classified as regulatory takings, which are 'those takings of property that fall within the police powers of a State, or otherwise arise from State measures like those pertaining to the regulation of the environment, health, morals, culture, or economy of a host country'.[63] The issue of regulatory takings is a particular point of concern from the perspective of tobacco control, as well as other sensitive areas of public policy.[64] Despite a number of decisions by tribunals, the line between the concept of indirect expropriation and governmental regulatory measures not requiring compensation has not been clearly articulated. The determination of indirect expropriation very much depends on the specific facts and circumstances of the case.[65] That said, it appears that there are three main criteria that arbitrators are likely to consider in evaluating a measure, as recently summarized in the *Burlington Resources v Ecuador* Decision on Liability. This decision clarifies the criteria to apply and notes that the following requirements must be met in order to find an indirect expropriation: (i) a substantial deprivation of the value of the whole investment (ie the degree of interference with the property right including interference with the investor's reasonable investment-backed expectations); (ii) a permanent measure (ie, the duration of the measure); and (iii) a measure not justified under the police power doctrine (which basically is a review of the measure's purpose).[66]

---

[62] As stated by *Gemplus* Arbitral Tribunal, 'an indirect expropriation occurs if the state deliberately deprives the investor of the ability to use its investment in any meaningful way'. See *Gemplus, S.A., SLP, S.A. and Gemplus Industrial, S.A. de C.V. v United Mexican States*, ICSID Case No. ARB(AF)/04/3 & ARB(AF)/04/4, Award, 16 June 2010, Part VIII, Para 23.

[63] United Nations Conference on Trade and Development, *Taking of Property*, 12, U.N. Doc. UNCTAD/ITE/IIT/15 (2000) (UNCTAD).

[64] See J Chaisse 'Exploring the Confines of International Investment and Domestic Health Protections—General exceptions clause as a forced perspective' (2013) 39(2/3) *American Journal of Law & Medicine* 332–361.

[65] Of course, although there are some variations 'in the way some arbitral tribunals have distinguished legitimate non-compensable regulations having an effect on the economic value of foreign investments and indirect expropriation requiring compensation, examination reveals that, in broad terms, they have identified the following criteria which look very similar to the ones laid out by the recent agreements: (i) the degree of interference with the property right; (ii) the character of governmental measures, ie, the purpose and the context of the governmental measure; and (iii) the interference of the measure with reasonable and investment-backed expectations.' C Yannaca-Small, 'Indirect Expropriation and the Right to Regulate in International Investment Law', in *International Investment Law: A Changing Landscape* (OECD 2005) 43, 54 available at <http://browse.oecdbookshop.org/oecd/pdfs/product/2005141e.pdf>; see also Van Aaken (n 60) 510–12.

[66] See *Burlington Resources Inc. v Republic of Ecuador*, ICSID Case No. ARB/08/5, Decision on Liability, 14 December 2012, para 471.

The TTP Annex 12-C complements Article 12.12 by making clear that: 'Article 12.12(1) is intended to reflect customary international law concerning the obligation of States with respect to expropriation.' It goes further to clarify the application of the provision in cases of indirect expropriation, following the 2012 US Model BIT. In the NAFTA context, *S.D. Myers v Canada* found that the term 'expropriation' in Article 1110 must be interpreted in light of the whole body of state practice, treaties and judicial interpretations of that term.[67] *Glamis Gold v United States* found that the inclusion in Article 1110 of the term 'expropriation' incorporates by reference the customary international law regarding that subject.[68] In *Merrill & Ring v Canada*, the Tribunal observed that while international law recognizes that contractual rights are capable of being expropriated, the protection of contractual rights has been understood within certain limits. This explains the exclusion under NAFTA Article 1139(i) and (j) of claims to money under commercial contracts and other commercial arrangements from the definition of investment.[69]

3.6. Other TPP provisions

In addition to the foregoing 'core' issues, a number of other issues raised in the negotiation of the TPP investment chapter deserve brief mention.

3.6.1. Performance requirements

Performance requirements are generally used by Host States to influence the behaviour of investors.[70] Most investment treaties prohibit imposing or enforcing certain performance requirements, such as export requirements and domestic content rules, in connection with the establishment, acquisition, expansion, management, conduct or operation of investments.[71] They also prohibit 'using the specified performance requirements as conditions attached to advantages such as subsidies, including tax incentives'.[72]

---

[67] *S.D. Myers, Inc. v Government of Canada*, UNCITRAL, Partial Award, 13 November 2000, para 280.

[68] *Glamis Gold, Ltd. v The United States of America*, UNCITRAL, Award, 8 June 2009, para 354.

[69] *Merrill & Ring Forestry L. P. v Government of Canada*, UNCITRAL, ICSID Administrated, Award, 31 March 2010, paras 139–140.

[70] Two types of performance requirements have been identified: mandatory performance requirements and other performance requirements which are based on conditions that an investor must meet to secure a government subsidy or incentive. See Y-S Lee, 'Foreign Direct Investment and Regional Trade Liberalization: A Viable Answer for Economic Development?' (2005) 39 (4) *Journal of World Trade* 707.

[71] See for instance, Malaysia–EU PTA art 12.6; Australia–Singapore FTA art 5.

[72] Idem.

TPP Article 12.7:1 expands the usual performance requirements provision found in US IIAs to include conduct by a Host State to prefer local technology against 'technology of the Party'. This 'technology of the Party' is defined as including technology owned, or held under exclusive licence, by an investor of the other Party (TPP Footnote No 13). According to the draft, 'Neither Party may, in connection with the establishment, acquisition, expansion, management, conduct, operation, or sale or other disposition of an investment of an investor of a Party *or of a non-Party* in its territory, impose or enforce any requirement, or enforce any commitment or undertaking'. The Host State thus will not be entitled to establish a requirement for the purchase, use or other preference in its territory of technology that will afford protection to its own investors or investments or to technology of its nationals on the basis of their nationality. In line with the US Model BIT of 2012, the TPP seeks to eradicate all performance requirements in TPP economies with perhaps a specific focus on Vietnam and Cambodia. This can be explained by the US seeking to ensure that these requirements are embraced in the text with the aim of subsequently imposing them on China, should the latter join the TPP.

3.6.2. *Compulsory licensing*

In accordance with Articles 8 and 40 of the Agreement on Trade-Related Aspects of Intellectual Property Rights (TRIPS), as reaffirmed by the Declaration on the TRIPS Agreement and Public Health[73], governments can take steps to prevent patent owners from abusing their rights, by 'unreasonably' restraining trade or hampering the international transfer of technology. In practice, public authorities can authorize a third party to manufacture a patented product or to use the patented process without the patent owner's consent. Most developed countries and developing countries provide for compulsory licensing concession in their domestic legislation. Recourse to compulsory licensing is permitted by virtue of Article 31 of TRIPS which addresses 'other uses without authorization of the right holder'. Article 31 aims to strike a balance between the concern to promote access to medicines and provide protection/incentive for R&D in the pharmaceutical field. Counter-intuitively, the highest number of compulsory licenses has been issued in the US and not in a developing country. The objective is to create a more competitive environment without ignoring the rights of the patent owner, who ought to be adequately compensated whatever the circumstances.

[73] 'Each member has the right to grant compulsory licences and the freedom to determine the grounds upon which such licences are granted', *WTO, Doha Ministerial Conference 2001, Declaration on the TRIPS Agreement and Public Health*, 14 November 2001, WT/MIN(01)/DEC/2, para 5 b.

Under TRIPS, it is possible to issue a compulsory license under certain conditions which ensure that the legitimate interests of the patent owner have been protected.[74] In particular, an attempt should have been made to obtain a voluntary license from the right holder on reasonable commercial terms (Article 31.b).[75] However, this article provides for making the voluntary license redundant in case of a national emergency, circumstances of extreme urgency, public non-commercial use (or government use) or anti-competitive practices. The compulsory licensing is of particular importance for developing countries that are subject to epidemics such as HIV/AIDS. Their objective is to improve patients' access to drugs.[76] Thus, certain countries see this as a means to stymie the negative effects of patents on prices and availability of medicines, insofar as it makes it possible to reduce prices of drugs protected by a patent in force and to obtain technology.

Against this background, the compulsory licensing exceptions in the TPP Investment Chapter have been subject to intense negotiations. They crystallize the concerns of many developing countries and, in particular, of Malaysia. Article 12.7 1(f) prohibits a TPP Party from imposing or enforcing any investment-related requirement or enforcing any investment-related commitment or undertaking 'to transfer a particular technology, a production process or other proprietary knowledge to a person in its territory.' Should the provision be accepted, it will impact significantly the right to issue compulsory or government use licenses.

3.6.3. Capital controls

The US traditionally outlaws the use of capital controls in its trade and investment treaties. However, following the global financial crisis, the IMF has

---

[74] Article 31 of the Agreement sets out to determine, as accurately as possible, a framework for the CL regime. The list of conditions for the use of CL consists particularly of the following points: authorization to use without the patent owner's consent should be reviewed based on the circumstances peculiar to this problem; a voluntary license should have been requested from the patent owner, at reasonable commercial conditions and within a reasonable period of time (except in times of national emergencies or other circumstances of extreme urgency or in cases of public non-commercial use purposes); the CL's scope and the duration should be limited to the purpose for which it was authorized; its use should be non-exclusive; the use is authorized mainly for replenishment of the domestic market of the member state that granted this license; the right holder shall be paid adequate remuneration in the circumstances of each case, taking into account the economic value of the authorization and the remunerations are likely to be revised. For a detailed discussion on the grant of compulsory licenses for patents trademarks and copyrights.

[75] A VL means that the patent holder has given his consent to a local company to copy the concerned drug, against royalty payments, which shall be marketed only in the internal market.

[76] For a discussion on the IIAs and access to medicine, see RC Bernieri, 'Intellectual Property Rights in Bilateral Investment Treaties and Access to Medicines: The Case of Latin America' (2006) 9 *The Journal of World Intellectual Property* 5 548–572.

reversed its opposition to the use of capital controls accepting that capital controls are an essential part of the toolkit for developing nations wishing to achieve stability. In January 2011, a letter to the Obama administration signed by over 250 economists, including Joseph Stiglitz, noted that past US IIAs 'strictly limit the ability of our trading partners to deploy capital controls'. A February 2012 letter signed by over a hundred prominent economists, including Jagdish Bhagwati, demanded that the parties be allowed to use capital control in the TPP. The TPP June text requires that governments: 'shall permit all transfers relating to a covered investment to be made freely and without delay into and out of its territory' (Article 12.11). This forbids countries from using capital controls or financial transaction taxes and reflects US treaty practice, even if the latter has been subjected to fierce criticism from civil society.

3.6.4. *Sovereign debt*

The NAFTA excludes sovereign long-term debt from coverage of Chapter 11. In sharp contrast, and in the light of the recent *Abaclat* decision,[77] one aspect worth highlighting is the TPP language concerning sovereign debt. The definition of investment in 12.2 includes the following clarification: 'Forms that an investment may take include ... (c) bonds, debentures ... and loans [*but does not include a debt instrument of a Party or state enterprise*].' Annex 12.K, however, may be said to implicitly recognize sovereign debt to constitute an investment: '[N]o award may be made in favor of a claimant for a claim ... with respect to default or non-payment of debt issued by a Party unless the claimant meets its burden proving that such default or non-payment constitutes an uncompensated expropriation.' Annex 12.K also narrows the types of available sovereign debt claims and when they may be advanced. It restricts claims arising in connection with negotiated restructurings,[78] and requires that an investor wait 270 days before advancing a claim arising out of a sovereign debt.[79]

4. THE INTERPLAY BETWEEN TPP AND OTHER INTERNATIONAL INVESTMENT AGREEMENTS

Investment agreements enshrine a series of obligations of the parties aimed at ensuring a stable and favourable business environment for foreign

---

[77] J Chaisse 'Greek Bonds, Collective Action Clauses and Investment Treaty Commitments' in CL Lim and B Mercurio (eds) *International Economic Law after the Crisis: a tale of fragmented disciplines*, (Cambridge University Press, forthcoming 2014).

[78] Annex 12.K para 2.

[79] Annex 12.K para 3.

investors. These obligations stipulate treatment that domestic authorities in Host States should mete out to foreign investors and their investments. TPP will provide for additional protections for foreign investors in TPP countries which are already bound by other IIAs. This section analyses the interplay between the TPP and the other IIAs concluded by TPP countries. To do so, it first provides a map of the current IIAs applicable to TPP countries (4.1). Two categories of treaties are reviewed: treaties involving a TPP country, and those treaties concluded between at least two TPP countries. The analysis then turns to the MFN provision in the TPP agreement which will play a pivotal role in its future application and define its interplay with other IIAs.

4.1. Mapping TPP countries investment treaty commitments

The current system of international law of foreign investment has become increasingly dependent upon international treaties. Bilateral investment treaties (BITs) have gradually become the core of the current framework for FDI. More than 2,850 bilateral agreements have been concluded since the early 1960s, most of them in the 1990s. Regional and plurilateral agreements are also popular means of formalizing international rules on investment. Regional and plurilateral agreements comprise, by definition, a limited number of countries which have increased the importance of preferential trade agreements (PTAs) in terms of investment regulation, in particular for a country like the US.[80]

The original agreement between Brunei, Chile, New Zealand, and Singapore was signed on 3 June 2005, and entered into force on 28 May 2006 without directly addressing investment protection. However, each of these signatories was already bound by some investment treaties with third countries. The same is true for the seven additional countries that subsequently joined negotiations (Australia, Canada, Malaysia, Mexico, Peru, US, and Vietnam). As a result, all of the TPP negotiating partners come to the table with pre-existing investment treaty commitments (Table 3).

The TPP partners are already bound with third countries by 458 investment treaties. Out of them, a great proportion are classical BITs since one can count 387 bilateral pacts. This represents slightly less than 20 per cent of all existing BITs globally.

A closer look at the statistics helps to identify which TPP partners have been the most active in investment rule-making. Not surprisingly, Malaysia (70), Chile (68), Vietnam (59), USA (53), and Singapore (53) lead the race with more than 50 investment agreements each. On the other hand, Brunei

[80] See JJ Schott and J Muir 'US PTAs: what's been done and what it means for the TPP negotiations' in Lim et al (n 4) 45–63.

Table 3. TTP partners existing investment treaty practice (by increasing number)

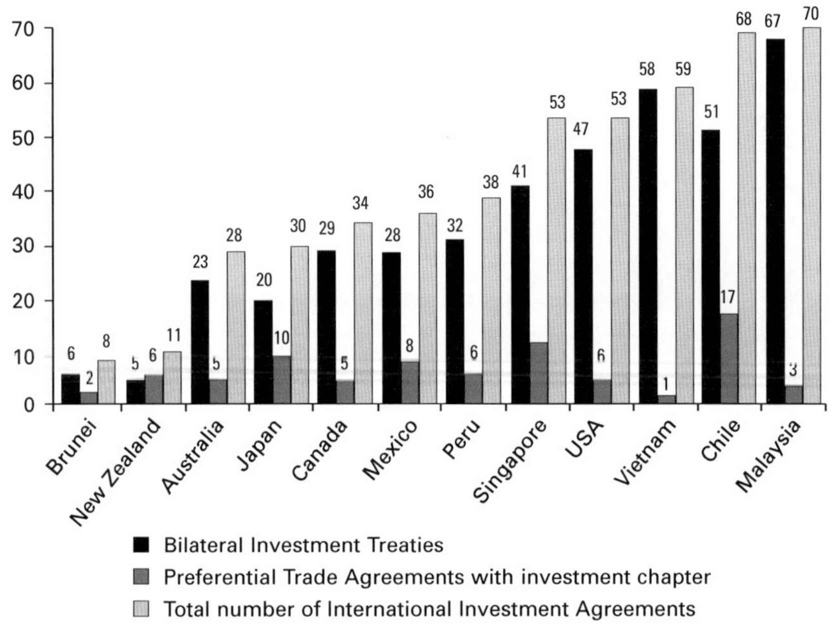

Source: Compiled by the author on the basis of the Organization of American States' Foreign Trade Information System (SICE website); United Nations Conference on Trade and Development (UNCTAD) Database of Investment Agreements and national Ministries of Foreign Affairs public information.

(8) and New Zealand (11) seem to be newcomers in this field as they have concluded only a few IIAs. A third category is comprised of Canada (34) and Mexico (36) which have concluded a rather average number of IIAs compared to other TPP partners and more generally. Canada and Mexico, however, are parties to the NAFTA which is a major treaty both from an economic point of view and in terms of the number of arbitrations brought under its investment chapter.

It is important to take a closer look at these agreements by excluding treaties concluded with non-TPP countries and focusing on the investment pacts which have been concluded between TPP countries. In doing so, one can see the specific network of treaty commitments that bind many TPP countries (and hence constitute the TPP noodle bowl of investment treaties) but which can also favour interplay between them and the TPP. Table 4 summarizes the overlapping of international investment agreements between at least two TPP countries.

Table 4. Overlapping international investment agreements between at least two TPP countries (date of entry into force)

	Australia	Brunei	Canada	Chile	Japan	Malaysia	Mexico	New Zealand	Peru	Singapore	USA	Vietnam
Australia		AANZFTA (2010)		Australia–Chile BIT (1999) Australia–Chile FTA Chapter 10 (2009)		AANZFTA (2010)	Australia–Mexico BIT 2007	Australia–New Zealand Protocol on Investment (signed Feb 2010, not in force) AANZFTA (2010)	Australia–Peru BIT (1997)	AANZFTA (2010) SAFTA Chapter 8 (2011)	AusFTA (2005)	Australia–Vietnam BIT 1991 AANZFTA (2010)
Brunei	AANZFTA (2010)				Brunei Darussalam–Japan FTA (2008)	ACIA (2012) AANZFTA (2010)		AANZFTA (2010)		AANZFTA (2010) ACIA (2012)		AANZFTA (2010) ACIA (2012)
Canada							NAFTA (1995)		Canada–Peru BIT 2007	Canada–Singapore BIT 1971	NAFTA (1995)	
Chile	Australia–Chile BIT (1999) Australia–Chile FTA Chapter 10 (2009)				Chile–Japan FTA (2007)	Chile–Malaysia BIT (1995)		Chile–New Zealand (signed 1999)	Chile–Peru BIT (2001) Chile Peru FTA Chapter 11 (2009)		Chile–US FTA chapter 10 (2004)	Chile–Vietnam BIT (signed 1999)
Japan		Brunei Darussalam–Japan FTA (2008)		Chile–Japan FTA (2007)		Japan–Malaysia FTA (2006)	Japan–Mexico FTA (2005)		Japan–Peru BIT (2009)	Japan–Singapore FTA (2002)		Japan–Vietnam BIT (2004)

(continued overleaf)

Table 4 ***continued***

	Australia	Brunei	Canada	Chile	Japan	Malaysia	Mexico	New Zealand	Peru	Singapore	USA	Vietnam
Malaysia	AANZFTA (2010)	AANZFTA (2010) ACIA (2012)		Chile–Malaysia BIT (1995)	Japan–Malaysia FTA (2006)			AANZFTA (2010) MNZFTA signed 2009	Malaysia–Peru BIT (1995)	AANZFTA (2010) ACIA (2012)		AANZFTA (2010) Malaysia–Vietnam BIT (1992) ACIA (2012)
Mexico	Australia–Mexico BIT (2007)		NAFTA (1995)		Japan–Mexico FTA (2005)					Mexico–Singapore BIT (2011)	NAFTA (1995)	
New Zealand	Australia–New Zealand Protocol on Investment (signed Feb 2010, not in force) AANZFTA (2010)	AANZFTA (2010)		Chile–New Zealand (signed 1999)		MNZFTA signed 2009 AANZFTA (2010)				AANZFTA (2010)		AANZFTA (2010)
Peru				Chile–Peru BIT 2001 Chile–Peru FTA Chapter 11 (2009)	Japan–Peru BIT (2009)					Singapore–Peru BIT (signed 2003) Peru–Singapore FTA (2009)	US–Peru FTA Chapter 10 (2009)	

Singapore	AANZFTA (2010) SAFTA Chapter 8 (2011)	AANZFTA (2010)	Singapore–Canada BIT (1971)		Japan–Singapore (2002)	AANZFTA (2010) FTA	Singapore–Mexico (2011)	AANZFTA (2010) BIT	Singapore–Peru BIT (signed 2003) Peru–Singapore FTA (2009)		USSFTA Chapter 10 (2004)	Singapore–Vietnam BIT (1992) AANZFTA (2010)
USA	AusFTA (2005)		NAFTA (1995)	Chile–US FTA chapter 10 (2004)			NAFTA (1995)		US–PeruFTA Chapter 10 (2009)	USSFTA Chapter 10 (2004)		
Vietnam	Australia–Vietnam BIT (1991) AANZFTA (2010)	AANZFTA (2010) ACIA (2012)		Chile–Vietnam BIT (signed 1999)	Japan–Vietnam BIT (2004)	Malaysia–Vietnam BIT (1992) AANZFTA (2010) ACIA (2012)		AANZFTA (2010)		Singapore–Vietnam BIT (1992) AANZFTA (2010) ACIA (2012)		

Note:
ACIA: ASEAN Comprehensive on Investment Agreement, 1 March 2012
ACiFTA: Australia Chile Free Trade Agreement, 6 March 2009
AUSFTA: Australia United States Free Trade Agreement, 1 January 2005
MNZFTA: Malaysia–New Zealand Free Trade Agreement, 1 August 2010
NAFTA: North American Free Trade Agreement 1 January 1994
Peru Chile Free Trade Agreement, 1 March 2009
PeSFTA: Peru Singapore Free Trade Agreement, 1 August 2009
PTPA: United States Peru Trade Promotion Agreement, 1 February 2009
SAFTA: Singapore Australia Free Trade Agreement, 28 July 2003
United States–Chile Free Trade Agreement, 1 January 2004
USSFTA: United States Singapore Free Trade Agreement, 1 January 2004

Sources: Compiled by the author on the basis of the Organization of American States' Foreign Trade Information System (SICE website); United Nations Conference on Trade and Development (UNCTAD) Database of Investment Agreements and national Ministries of Foreign Affairs public information.

The TPP noodle bowl encompasses 17 intra-TPP BITS and 16 intra-TPP PTAs providing for varying scopes of investment protection. This total of 33 intra-TPP IIAs compared to the 488 IIAs concluded by TPP countries with any third country shows that almost 7 percent of existing TPP countries IIAs may overlap with the TPP investment chapter.

From the quantitative point of view, Brunei, Canada, Japan, Peru, Mexico and the US are the countries that benefit the most from the investment negotiations since the TPP fills a gap in the geographical coverage of their IIAs. These States, however, have dissimilar interests as only Canada and the US truly have an interest in protecting their exported capital to developing countries. Japan is in a unique position because it already has a dense network of IIAs in Asia, although but TPP will provide the missing link to the four key developed economies: Australia, Canada, New Zealand and the US. Finally, Australia and Singapore are already bound with 9 of the 12 TPP countries. The TPP will therefore only provide new investment protection for Australians in Canada and for Singaporeans in Chile. This may mean that Australia and Singapore have only a limited interest in the TPP investment negotiations, with North American investors being the principal drivers.

4.2. Who is the most favoured nation to each TPP partner?

The most favoured nation (MFN) principle guarantees to protected investors and investments treatment no less favourable than that received by the investors or investments of any third state. The principle allows investors covered by one IIA to claim equal benefits to those granted to investors from other countries, irrespective of whether those benefits are derived from other IIAs or the regulatory practice of the host country. While traditionally regarded as a standard clause without major implications, the MFN principle has gained attention in light of the application of this provision by arbitral panels.[81] The *Impregilo v Argentina* tribunal majority noted that the issues remain controversial and that the 'predominating jurisprudence which has developed is in no way universally accepted'.[82]

The TPP draft investment chapter includes a MFN clause in Art. 12.5, which is worded similarly to many existing US treaties (Table 5).

---

[81] *Tza Yap Sum v Peru* recognizes the need to analyse the specific wording of each provision of a treaty in accordance with established rules of international law; an *a priori* decision is not appropriate, ie it is not possible to decide in general that MFN clauses are efficacious in some sorts of situations whereas they are not in others; each MFN clause is a world in itself, which demands an individualized interpretation to determine its scope of application. See *Tza Yap Shum v Republic of Peru*, ICSID Case No. ARB/07/6, Decision on Jurisdiction and Competence, 19 June 2009, paras 196–198.

[82] See *Impregilo S.p.A. v Argentine Republic*, ICSID Case No. ARB/07/17, Award, 21 June 2011, para 107.

Three aspects of the TPP MFN are key in this regard.

- Firstly, whether the obligation applies to investments already established in the country, or whether it applies also to the ability of the investor to claim access to the host country (so-called pre-establishment rights). The TPP MFN expressly extends the coverage of the MFN obligation to pre-establishments rights.
- Secondly, the language which allows the comparison between the treatment of investors from different countries may add specific conditions. The TPP MFN uses the phrase 'in like circumstances', which is typical of US and Canadian treaties and is well-known in NAFTA case law.[83] While some other US BITs, like the one with Honduras, refer instead to 'like situations',[84] most IIAs generally include a reference to 'like circumstances'.
- Thirdly, whether issues pertaining to investor-state dispute settlement procedures are covered by the MFN principle.[85] The TPP MFN clearly excludes such coverage in its third paragraph, which is a welcome choice in light of the lack of consistency in jurisprudence on this issue.[86] MFN clauses in post-2004 US investment agreements do not permit a 'Maffezini-type' result. The US–Peru Trade Promotion Agreement illustrates the MFN language, and 'Maffezini exclusion', used by the US in a number of its recent investment agreements—in

---

[83] *Parkerings v Lithuania* found that for investors to be in like circumstances, three conditions must be met: the investor must be a foreign investor; they must be in the same economic or business sector; and the two investors must be treated differently. See *Parkerings-Compagniet AS v Republic of Lithuania*, ICSID Case No. ARB/05/8, Award, 11 September 2007 para 371.

[84] US–Honduras BIT, art II.1.

[85] Following to the arbitral decision in the *Maffezini* case, much attention has been drawn to the debate of whether provisions relating to the disputes settlement procedures enshrined in one IIA can be 'imported" into another IIA by virtue of the MFN clause. The question posed by the *Maffezini* decision ultimately addresses the general scope of the MFN principle and how the provision is crafted in each individual agreement. This leads us to the last section of this chapter dealing with the TPP investor-state dispute mechanism.

[86] At least, until the remarkable clarification provided by Professor Stern in her dissenting Opinion in *Impregilo v Argentina* in which she agrees with the idea that substantive questions and procedural questions are of a different legal nature, which means that the ejusdem generis principle prevents the two from being equated. *Impregilo S.p.A. v Argentine Republic*, ICSID Case No. ARB/07/17, Concurring and Dissenting Opinion of Professor Brigitte Stern, 21 June 2011, para 28–29 and 37–38. This seems to initiate a new case law as illustrated by the *ICS Inspection v Argentina* Award on Jurisdiction which holds that the MFN clause must be in itself a manifestation of consent to the arbitration of investment disputes according to the rules that the MFN provision might attract from other comparator treaties; should it not be found to operate in a jurisdictional manner, that is to act independently as a substitute for the consent found in the basic treaty's dispute resolution clause, it cannot have the effect advocated by the claimant. *ICS Inspection and Control Services Limited (United Kingdom) v Argentine Republic*, PCA Case No. 2010-9, Award on Jurisdiction, 10 February 2012 para 278.

Table 5. Scope of MFN provisions in US–foreign investment agreements

North American Free Trade Agreement (1994) Article 1103	US–Peru (2004) Article 10.4	Australia–US FTA (2005) Article 11.4
1. Each Party shall accord to investors of another Party treatment no less favorable than that it accords, in like circumstances, to investors of any other Party or of a non-Party with respect to the establishment, acquisition, expansion, management, conduct, operation, and sale or other disposition of investments. 2. Each Party shall accord to investments of investors of another Party treatment no less favourable than that it accords, in like circumstances, to investments of investors of any other Party or of a non-Party with respect to the establishment, acquisition, expansion, management, conduct, operation, and sale or other disposition of investments.	1. Each Party shall accord to investors of another Party treatment no less favorable than that it accords, in like circumstances, to investors of any other Party or of any non-Party with respect to the establishment, acquisition, expansion, management, conduct, operation, and sale or other disposition of investments in its territory. 2. Each Party shall accord to covered investments treatment no less favorable than that it accords, in like circumstances, to investments in its territory of investors of any other Party or of any non-Party with respect to the establishment, acquisition, expansion, management, conduct, operation, and sale or other disposition of investments.*2 **Footnote No.2 For greater certainty, treatment "with respect to the establishment, acquisition, expansion, management, conduct, operation, and sale or other disposition of investments" referred to in paragraphs 1 and 2 of Article 10.4 does not encompass dispute resolution mechanisms, such as those in Section B, that are provided for in international investment treaties or trade agreements.*	1. Each Party shall accord to investors of the other Party treatment no less favourable than that it accords, in like circumstances, to investors of any non-Party with respect to the establishment, acquisition, expansion, management, conduct, operation, and sale or other disposition of investments in its territory. 2. Each Party shall accord to covered investments treatment no less favourable than that it accords, in like circumstances, to investments in its territory of investors of any non-Party with respect to the establishment, acquisition, expansion, management, conduct, operation, and sale or other disposition of investments. *(in which there is no ISDS)*

Dominican Republic–Central America Free Trade Agreement (2009) Article 10.4	U.S. Model Bilateral Investment Treaty (April 2012) Article 4	TPP Draft (June 2012) **Article 12.5**
1. Each Party shall accord to investors of another Party treatment no less favorable than that it accords, in like circumstances, to investors of any other Party or of any non-Party with respect to the establishment, acquisition, expansion, management, conduct, operation, and sale or other disposition of investments in its territory. 2. Each Party shall accord to covered investments treatment no less favorable than that it accords, in like circumstances, to investments in its territory of investors of any other Party or of any non-Party with respect to the establishment, acquisition, expansion, management, conduct, operation, and sale or other disposition of investments.	1. Each Party shall accord to investors of the other Party treatment no less favorable than that it accords, in like circumstances, to investors of any non-Party with respect to the establishment, acquisition, expansion, management, conduct, operation, and sale or other disposition of investments in its territory. 2. Each Party shall accord to covered investments treatment no less favorable than that it accords, in like circumstances, to investments in its territory of investors of any non-Party with respect to the establishment, acquisition, expansion, management, conduct, operation, and sale or other disposition of investments.	1. Each Party shall accord to investors of another Party treatment no less favourable than that it accords, **in like circumstances**, to investors of any other Party or of any non-Party with respect to the establishment, acquisition, expansion, management, conduct, operation, and sale or other disposition of investments in its territory. 2. Each Party shall accord to covered investments treatment no less favourable than that it accords, **in like circumstances**, to investments in its territory of investors of any other Party or of any non-Party with respect to the establishment, acquisition, expansion, management, conduct, operation, and sale or other disposition of investments. 3. **For greater certainty, the treatment referred to in this Article does not encompass international dispute resolution procedures or mechanisms such as those included in Section B**

Source: elaboration by the author

addition, to the typically precise scope language in the MFN text, note specifically footnote 2. One can speculate that the source of the text in TPP proposed Article 12.5.3 is the language found in footnote 2.

The future importance of the TPP MFN can be analyzed in light of the practice of MFN under the NAFTA. In all NAFTA cases, except the annulled *Pope Talbot* award, the importation of more favoured treatment requested by claimants was dismissed. In the most recent decision, the *Chemtura v Canada* Tribunal dismissed an attempt to use NAFTA's MFN clause to import allegedly more favourable standards of fair and equitable treatment from other treaties concluded by the respondent.[87] However, the TPP MFN seems to differ from the NAFTA in respect of two parameters.

- First, the NAFTA MFN puts emphasis on 'like circumstances' and the covered investment activities. NAFTA Contracting Parties also made reservations and exceptions to the MFN application in Article 1108.[88] The Tribunal in *ADF v United States* found the *Maffezini v Spain* approach to MFN treatment to be of no assistance to the claimant because of the operation of these exceptions.[89] In addition to these reservations, the NAFTA Free Trade Commission (FTC)[90] formulated an interpretation note that has restrained several tribunals from taking action in favor of investors seeking to import treatment standards.[91]
- Second, the great number of existing IIAs concluded by TPP countries may favour a different application of the MFN standard compared to that endorsed under the NAFTA. While the NAFTA parties had negotiated around 100 IIAs, the TPP countries now have 458 signed agreements which are subject to the TPP MFN

Besides the exclusion of ISDS from its application, the TPP MFN provision does not offer any specific conditions or carve out provisions.[92] The scope

[87] *Crompton (Chemtura) Corp. v Government of Canada*, Award, 2 August 2010, para 235–236.

[88] The NAFTA parties made reservations to their obligation under Art. 1103 in two ways. First, the text of NAFTA contains expressly agreed general exceptions. Secondly, Schedule to Annexes of NAFTA lists excluded areas and treatment.

[89] *ADF* Award (n 30) para 197.

[90] See NAFTA Art. 1131 2: An interpretation by the Commission of a provision of this Agreement shall be binding on a Tribunal established under this Section.

[91] The interpretation note of certain Chapter 11 Provisions issued in 2001 has been taken into account by investment tribunals. See Statement on NAFTA Article 1105 and the Availability of Arbitration Documents, 31 July 2001.

[92] Basically, the scope of the TPP investment chapter (Basic treaty) is the sole limitation arising from the *ejusdem generis* principle. *Daimler v Argentina* Award noted that the International

of the TPP MFN commitment is rather broad in order not to dilute the advances made in negotiations which the partners may conduct with third countries.[93] This drafting is in line with the US 2012 Model BIT, which left MFN commitments broadly intact compared to the 2004 version.[94] Such broad coverage includes standards of treatment found in other IIAs. For instance, the tribunal in *MTD v Chile* applied an MFN provision to accord an investment the fair and equitable treatment protection of other BITs.[95] The *Impregilo v Argentina* Award examined the claimant's contention that the requirement of 'full protection and security' in the Argentina–US BIT was applicable through the MFN clause in the Argentina–Italy BIT.[96] Also, the *White Industries v India* Final Award held that the BIT's MFN clause, as a substantive provision, enabled the invocation of an 'effective means of asserting claims' provision contained in another of the respondent's BITs.[97] Finally, the *EDF v Argentina* Award found that the applicable treaty's MFN clause permited recourse to the 'umbrella clauses' of third country treaties.[98]

The rather broad scope and potential of the TPP MFN makes it looks like a provision designed for a framework (or perhaps multilateral?) agreement which can attract better substantive provisions. This magnetism might help

---

Law Commission has characterized the ejusdem generis rule as one that is 'generally recognized and affirmed by the jurisprudence of international tribunals and national courts and by diplomatic practice'. *Daimler Financial Services AG v Argentine Republic*, ICSID Case No. ARB/05/1, Award, 22 August 2012, para 211.

[93] One can first observe that the MFN provisions already existing in older IIAs will bring to them the benefits of the TPP new chapter. Indeed, the commitments by TPP countries may have to extend MFN, for instance, to Thailand (except dispute settlement), and to China (except dispute settlement and obligations specific to existing FTA partners).

[94] See M Kantor 'Little Has Changed in the New US Model Bilateral Investment Treaty ICSID Review' (Fall 2012) 27(2): 335–378.

[95] *MTD Equity Sdn. Bhd. and MTD Chile S.A. v Republic of Chile*, ICSID Case No. ARB/01/7, Award, 25 May 2004, paras 104 and 197. This was latter confirmed by *Bayindir v Pakistan* Award applies an MFN clause to import the fair and equitable treatment standard from another treaty entered into after the treaty in question (*Bayindir* (n 28) paras 153–160) and *ATA v Jordan* applies an MFN clause to import a fair and equitable treatment and treatment no less favourable than that required by international law clause (*ATA Construction, Industrial and Trading Company v Hashemite Kingdom of Jordan*, ICSID Case No. ARB/08/2, Award, 18 May 2010, footnote 16).

[96] However, the tribunal considers that having found a breach of the FET standard, it was unnecessary to examine whether there had also been a failure to ensure full protection and security. *Impregilo S.p.A. v Argentine Republic*, ICSID Case No. ARB/07/17, Award, 21 June 2011, para 334.

[97] *White Industries Australia Limited v The Republic of India*, UNCITRAL, Final Award, 30 November 2011, para 11.2.

[98] In doing so, the tribunal notes that it takes no position on the debate over the interaction of MFN clauses with jurisdictional and procedural requirements. *EDF International S.A., SAUR International S.A. and León Participaciones Argentinas S.A. v Argentine Republic*, ICSID Case No. ARB/03/23, Award, 11 June 2012, paras 930–936.

to establish the TPP as a framework regime, relegating bilateral agreements to a peripheral role. This should not be surprising. The principle of MFN treatment in the TPP is of paramount importance to the international investment regime. Non-existent in customary international law,[99] the principle constitutes the very foundation of treaty-based international investment regulation. The MFN clause has the potential to play a particularly important part in dispute settlement: the greater the number of IIAs concluded by a state, the greater possibilities for the invocation of MFN. Malaysia, Chile and Vietnam are, in this regard, the TPP countries which should pay great attention to the wording and scope of the TPP MFN clause because the three have already granted rights to a great number of investors and investments under third party IIAs.

5. THE INVESTOR-STATE DISPUTE SETTLEMENT MECHANISM

The last decade has witnessed a dramatic surge of investment disputes between foreign investors and host country governments. Arbitral panels have been charged with the task of applying the rules of IIAs in specific cases, a task which is not often straightforward, given the broad and sometimes ambiguous terms of these arrangements. This phenomenon of investment litigation has brought about a number of decisions from different arbitral *fora*, contributing to the formation of international investment law elucidating the meaning of its key provisions. The cumulative number of treaty-based cases had risen to more than 400 by 2013, with more than 200 brought before the International Centre for Settlement of Investment Disputes (ICSID). This section introduces the specific TPP investment chapter section devoted to Investor-to-State dispute resolution (5.1), and then it turns to the reservation on the said mechanism introduced by Australia (5.2).

5.1. TPP Section B Investor-to-State Dispute Resolution

In principle, foreign investors may choose to initiate legal proceedings at domestic courts of the host country. Alternatively, they may initiate international arbitration proceedings which can be more favourable to them because the practice and international tribunals are not subject to domestic political

[99] In *Asian Agricultural Products v Sri Lanka* the Dissenting Opinion of Samuel K.B. Asante, citing various publicists, noted that most favoured nation treatment does not derive from customary law. See *Asian Agricultural Products Limited v Democratic Socialist Republic of Sri Lanka*, ICSID Case No. ARB/87/3, Dissenting Opinion of Samuel K B Asante, 27 June 1990 para 40.

Table 6. Investor-State Dispute Settlement

Art. 12(16)bis Scope
Art. 12(17) Consultation and negotiation
Art. 12(19) Submission of a claim to arbitration
Art. 12(19) Consent of each party to arbitration
Art. 12(20) Conditions and limitation on consent of each party
Art. 12(21) Selection of arbitrators
Art. 12(22) Conduct of the arbitration
Art. 12(22)bis Proposal on Amicus curiae submissions
Art. 12(23) Transparency of arbitral proceedings
Art. 12(24) Governing law
Art. 12(25) Interpretation of annexes
Art. 12(26) Expert reports
Art. 12(27) Consolidation
Art. 12(28) Awards
Art. 12(29) Service of documents

pressure. Should TPP investors face discrimination in a State with a weak legal system, initiating international arbitration proceedings would be subject to TPP Articles 12.16 to 12.29, which are summarized in Table 5.

TPP Section B Investor-to-State Dispute Resolution is relatively typical in its structure and drafting. Comments will be limited to four procedurally important issues relating to: (1) the procedural requirements prior to filing the arbitration claim; (2) the clause to avoid multiple proceedings on the same matter; (3) the choice of the venue for the arbitration of TPP disputes; and (4) some transparency related issues.

A number of IIAs require the foreign investor to fulfill certain procedural requirements prior to filing the arbitration claim. The most usual procedural restrictions pertain to waiting periods and the exhaustion of local remedies. TPP Article 12.18 requires a six-month waiting period. These types of requirements are commonly found in BITs. Prior to the launch of arbitration, foreign investors must hold negotiations with the host country's authorities with a view to reaching an amicable settlement. Should these negotiations fail to bring the parties to a commonly agreed solution within a six-month period, the investor may bring the claim to international arbitration.

International arbitration is the process by which neutral arbitrators settle disputes concerning bilateral IIAs between sovereign states and foreign investors. In order to avoid multiple proceedings on the same matter, however, the TPP, like many IIAs, establishes that once a dispute has been brought to one forum—or, in some cases, a decision has been reached—the dispute may not be pursued in another venue (TPP Article 12.18(4)).

As most IIAs, Article 12.18 of the TPP draft further allows the foreign investor to choose the venue for the arbitration. Ad hoc arbitration allows the parties to agree on the procedural rules to the dispute, although states commonly rely on the established UNCITRAL arbitration rules. The parties may also resort to organizations that provide a venue and have developed their own arbitral procedures. The ICSID, which was established in 1967 under the umbrella of the World Bank, specialises in investor-state disputes, and it has received the most attention, totalling well over half the investor state claims brought hitherto. The TPP features more than one option for international arbitration. It allows resort to ICSID, to ad hoc arbitration under UNCITRAL rules, and to the Kuala Lumpur Regional Center for Arbitration or 'any other arbitration institution'.[100]

Finally, since 2004, the US Model BIT has contained provisions mandating publication of documents and open hearings which is adopted in the TPP Article 12.23. In the same vein, since 2004, the US Model BIT has also made explicit the authority of the tribunal to take amicus curiae submissions, and this has been embraced in TPP Article 12.22:3. However, what is especially innovative is that the TPP adds further provisions requiring the State Parties (1) to consult with each other regularly as to transparency matters (TPP Article 12.23:2) and (2) to include transparency procedures in any future appellate mechanism for investment arbitration (TPP Article 12.23:10).

5.2. *Scaling down investor-state enforcement in trade agreements?*

A key factor in the evolution of international investment law over the last decade has been the increased number of investor-state disputes which might be a matter of great controversy between TPP countries. On April 12, 2011 the Australian Government released a Trade Policy Statement opposing investor-state dispute settlement provisions in future Australian trade agreements.

Public Citizen, the Sierra Club, Friends of the Earth, and other organizations have called for a different trade agreement model that would protect the environment, workers' rights, and the general public interest. This new model would necessitate eliminating or dramatically scaling down the 'investor-state enforcement' provisions of trade agreements which corporations can use to sue Host States. While investor-state dispute settlement is advocated by the US Business Coalition for the TPP, there is also resistance; for example, from New Zealand environmental groups.

Similarly, some treaty instruments already take a very conservative stance on investor-state arbitration. For example, the Australia–US FTA does not contain an investor-state dispute settlement clause, although other

[100] TPP art 12.18(3). Although not expressly mentioned, arbitration in the Stockholm Chamber of Commerce and the International Chamber of Commerce is covered by this provision.

Australian PTAs—eg, the Singapore–Australia FTA—do contain such a clause. At present, Australia has also opposed investor-state dispute settlement provisions in the TPP and the question which arises here is how far that view will influence the other TPP parties. Thus far Australia has been seeking to persuade all the TPP members to do away with ISDS in the investment chapter. The reason for doing so, according to Australia, is that ISDS is not an important factor to secure FDI into TPP countries, and they confirm this through an independent study.[101] This is a key issue for the developing State members of the TPP to seriously consider and retain a prominent role in the negotiations until the August 2013 round of negotiations,[102] further research and evidence to confirm or rebut Australia's stance would be useful. New Zealand's position appears to be softening. Much of the debate regarding the ISDS provisions of the Korea–US FTA is viewed as more an outgrowth of political posturing prior to the parliamentary and presidential elections that are looming next year rather than a legal or economic argument. But the developments in Korea will have potentially lasting effects throughout the Asia–Pacific region and beyond (especially in the context of Japan joining TPP negotiations).

The potential use of investment arbitration to challenge tobacco regulations has also become a source of controversy in the negotiations on the TPP after Philip Morris instigated arbitral proceedings against Australia over its plain packaging laws.[103] Beyond tobacco regulations, there are many laws in TPP countries that could lead to litigation: current examples of laws currently being considered include tighter regulations of onshore and offshore mining exploration, stopping foreign sales of taonga, banning the sale of the kind of toxic financial products that fuelled the financial crisis, restrictions on the sale of strategic assets to foreign firms, a tax on "hot" money flowing into and out of the country.

It seems that Australia's change in policy did not affect other TPP countries. It is more likely to be that the multiplication of investment disputes, combined with some questionable awards, has gradually led some governments to question the benefit of arbitration. Besides, one wonders what the alternative to ISDS should be. ISDS aimed to take these cases out of the (arbitrary) political realm of diplomatic protection on the one hand, and out

---

[101] Department of Foreign Affairs and Trade (DFAT) 'Gillard Government Trade Policy Statement: Trading our way to more jobs and prosperity' (2011) <http://www.dfat.gov.au/publications/trade/trading-our-way-to-more-jobs-and-prosperity.html#investor-state>.

[102] Notably during the 19th round held in Bandar Seri Begawan, Brunei on 23–30 August. See above Section 1. See also W Cooper and M Manyin 'Japan Joins the Trans-Pacific Partnership: What Are the Implications?' Congressional Research Service, Washington DC: Report for Congress (2013) 3.

[103] <http://www.iisd.org/itn/2011/07/12/philip-morris-v-uruguay-will-investor-state-arbitration-send-restrictions-on-tobacco-marketing-up-in-smoke/>.

of (non-neutral) domestic courts on the other. Although the ISDS process has shortcomings and the substantive rules it applies need refinement, I would prefer it to be improved rather than abandoned. Caught between the alternative options of embracing state-to-state dispute settlement and establishing an innovative international mediation framework, States seem to prefer simply to avoid including investor-state dispute provisions in new IIAs. Such a trend may also postpone the need to clarify many of the key provisions found in IIAs.

There are different levels of consensus to investor-state dispute settlement under the existing investment agreements between the TPP negotiating parties, rendering this aspect of TPP negotiations very challenging. As a result, TPP negotiators will have to consider various technical questions relating to investor-state arbitration. For example, can TPP countries innovate with regard to access and procedures of investment arbitration in a manner that preserves Host State policies while safeguarding the legitimate interests of investors? What filtering mechanisms can be devised to guard against frivolous investor-state lawsuits? To what extent do recent IIAs reveal a desire to circumscribe the scope of what is actionable under IIAs, particularly as regards investor-to-state dispute settlement?

It should not be concluded that the TPP will not include investor-state arbitration provisions. Rather, Australian negotiators may 'seek to exclude investor-state dispute settlement in the TPP insofar as it applies to Australia but without rejecting its application among other treaty partners'.[104] There is a precedent for this in a plurilateral structure with the exchange letters between Australia and New Zealand accompanying the 2010 ASEAN–Australia–New Zealand Free Trade Agreement.[105] As New Zealand and four ASEAN Members are also parties to the TPP negotiations (Brunei, Malaysia, Singapore, and Vietnam), the inclusion of investor-state dispute settlement in the TPP which would only apply to a selected number of parties is a hypothesis to be seriously taken into consideration. Time will tell how much Australia's new policy towards ISDS can affect the outcome of TPP negotiations and perhaps, more importantly, how much the TPP treatment of ISDS will affect the approaches taken in the near future by other countries.

Last but not least, it is important to recall that Article 12.5 of the June 2012 leaked draft of the TPP investment chapter defined the MFN, as

---

[104] K Juergen 'The Australian Trade Policy Statement on Investor-State Dispute Settlement', *American Society of International Law (ASIL) Insights* (2011) 15, 22, 4.

[105] See Exchange of letters between the Hon. Tim Groser, Minister of Trade, New Zealand and the Hon. Simon Crean, Minister of Trade, Australia (27 February 2009) (confirming an agreement that Chapter 11 (Investment) of the ASEAN–Australia–New Zealand Free Trade Area 'shall not create any rights or obligations between New Zealand and Australia'), available at <http://www.dfat.gov.au/fta/aanzfta/index.html#FullText>.

follows: '3. For greater certainty, the treatment referred to in this Article does not encompass international dispute resolution procedures or mechanisms such as those included in Section B.' This kind of provision is now found in many treaties but it clearly means that TPP investors will not be able to import ISDS provisions from third party treaties.

6. CONCLUSION

The ability of foreign investors to bring their disputes before independent arbitrators provides an extra guarantee that domestic authorities will live up to their international obligations, thus ensuring a favourable and stable investment climate in the host country. One of the key features of investment protection therefore consists in allowing foreign investors to challenge the host government's actions before an international arbitral court. Investment treaty arbitration is the process by which neutral arbitrators settle disputes concerning bilateral treaty agreements between sovereign States and foreign investors. However, Australia is opposed to such a mechanism while the US has never lost a NAFTA Chapter 11 dispute. It obviously points litigation in the direction of the TPP emerging countries, namely, Chile, Malaysia, Mexico, Peru, and Vietnam. The litigation potential is especially high for these states.

The June 2012 leaked draft of the TPP investment chapter resembles in large measure the more recent US IIAs rather than the 1994 text of NAFTA Chapter 11. In a nutshell, the TPP investment chapter does not offer major innovations in terms of treaty drafting. However, the TPP crystallizes most recent innovations since 2001 in terms of NAFTA interpreting notes and also reflects developments in arbitral case law.

The normative quality and geographic scope of the TPP, however, places the agreement among the most detailed and important investment treaties. In this light, it is possible to return to the question raised in the beginning of this chapter whether the TPP will strengthen or fracture current investment treaty regimes. If the TPP negotiations proceed successfully, then as a broad preferential trade agreement the TPP will presumably supersede NAFTA and other existing IIAs identified in Table 4 (where there is overlap). Interestingly, the TPP may be read as a strengthening or a de facto renegotiation of NAFTA and many other agreements such as the 2010 AANZ FTA. The TPP is even more clearly a strengthening of investment disciplines for some developing countries such as Vietnam or Malaysia which have not hitherto been bound to the US through bilateral or multilateral arrangements but only customary international law.

Last but not least, the TPP membership is open to new members willing to sign up to its terms under the sole condition that the country is accepted by the current TPP members.[106] The absence of geographic or economic conditions gives the TPP a significant attractiveness. Japan officially joined TPP negotiations in July 2013. The list of prospective Member States is long and includes such countries as South Korea, Thailand, Taiwan ROC,[107] Philippines, Laos, Colombia, and Costa Rica. Should all these countries join the TPP and ratify, among others, the investment chapter, there is no doubt that we would have an embryonic form of a long-awaited multilateral agreement on investment.

[106] Since the beginning, the US was clearly interested not so much in the relatively small markets of the P4, but rather in using the TPP as a platform to lure in bigger fish from around the Pacific Rim. See Kerr (n 13) 5.

[107] Tawain's President Ma Ying-jeou said his government will work hard to create the conditions for Taiwan to participate in the US-led Trans-Pacific Partnership at an appropriate time. L Shu-hua and Y-F Low 'President pledges to create conditions for Taiwan's TPP access' 2013/03/21.

6

Regional Integration and Foreign Direct Investment in COMESA

*Dirk Willem te Velde and Themba Munalula**

1. INTRODUCTION

The Common Market of Eastern and Southern Africa (COMESA) aims to create a competitive COMESA Common Investment Area (CCIA). The decision to establish the CCIA was proposed in 1998. The ultimate objective of the CCIA is to promote sustainable economic growth in the region through intra-COMESA trade and investment flows as well as by attracting FDI through the region's increased attractiveness to investment.[1] Following negotiations, the COMESA Council of Ministers approved the CCIA Agreement in 2007.[2] Its approval paved the way for the region to acquire greater levels of investment through the creation of an international competitive investment area allowing for the free movement of factors across borders of Member States. Nevertheless as of this writing, the CCIA Agreement has yet to come into force, leaving many of its promises still to be attained.

The key questions that this chapter addresses are: what is the role of regional integration in attracting FDI? How well has COMESA performed in attracting FDI compared to other regional economic communities in Africa (RECs) and how have COMESA's investment provisions facilitated the process? Can COMESA do more to attract FDI?

The structure of the chapter is as follows. Section 2 presents the theoretical and empirical evidence on the link between regional integration and FDI. Section 3 discusses how well COMESA is doing in attracting FDI,

* Head of Programme, Overseas Development Institute, dw.tevelde@odi.org.uk; Head of Statistics, COMESA Secretariat, tmunalula@comesa.int.

[1] Preamble COMESA (2007) Investment Agreement for the COMESA Common Investment Area.

[2] The twelfth Summit of COMESA Authority of Heads of State and Government, held in Nairobi, Kenya, on 22nd and 23rd May 2007.

what investment provisions it has put in place to attract investment and in particular how the rise of the middle class has affected FDI in Africa. Section 4 concludes by discussing what COMESA can do to attract more FDI.

2. THE LINKS BETWEEN REGIONAL INTEGRATION AND FDI—THEORY AND EVIDENCE

Much has been written and said about what attracts investment. This section reviews the literature on FDI attraction and examines the role of regional integration in this context. Generally, there are a host of factors that attract investment and these can be divided into:

i) Host-country economic conditions, including market size and market growth, good quality and appropriate infrastructure and skills, and natural resources;[3]
ii) Host-country policies, institutions, administrative procedures and governance (eg the ease of doing business);[4]
iii) International rules and activities (multilateral, bilateral and regional instruments);[5]
iv) Home-country policies (eg directed credit, investment guarantees etc).[6]

A range of factors is important for different types of investments at varying time periods. It is notable that for low income countries market size is consistently a key basic driver for market seeking FDI; subsequent drivers are skills, customs procedures, infrastructure for efficiency-seeking investment, and the availability of natural resources.[7] The focus of this chapter is to provide an understanding of the role of regional integration (in addition to these other key variables). Beyond the impact of regional integration, there will be other directly identifiable effects stemming from trade and investment rules.

---

[3] J Kubny, F Mölders, P Nunnenkamp, 'Regional Integration and FDI in Emerging Markets', Kiel Working Paper No. 1418, April 2008, 3.

[4] DW te Velde and D Bezemer 'Regional Integration and Foreign Direct Investment in Developing Countries', *Transnational Corporations*, Vol. 15, No. 2 (August 2006), 46.

[5] M Blomstrom and A Kokko 'Regional Integration and Foreign Direct Investment' *NBER Working Papers* 6019, (1997) 13.

[6] Ibid.

[7] te Velde and Bezemer (n 4) 46.

3. REGIONAL INVESTMENT TREATMENT OF STANDARDS AND FDI

Throughout the region there are investment treatment standards which apply to FDI. Standards usually consist of norms on the treatment and protection of investments and investors and guarantees of a favourable investment climate. Although investment disciplines are not as common in regional integration agreements as rules on trade, investment disciplines have begun to be found in a handful of Regional Trade Agreements (RTAs). Some regions rely on aspirational principles without direct legal recourse, other regions include rules backed by investor-state dispute settlement arrangements. The important point to make here is that there may be differences among investment provisions in regional treaties (eg they may vary in their scope, the wording of standards of treatment, the inclusion of performance requirements, and dispute settlement options), and each one of these provisions may have a different effect on the volume of inward FDI.

There are opposing views as to how investment rules (bilateral, regional and multilateral) affect investment decisions.[8] Generally, a predictable investment climate is in the interest of investors, which have historically faced unpredictable investment conditions in host states. It is not clear, however, whether the treaty-based guarantees of a favourable investment climate would lead to *additional* FDI or to an increase in the comfort level of the investor, allowing the latter, for example, to benefit from reduced insurance premium levels. Surveys of investors have confirmed that they seek a predictable investment climate.[9] The predictability of the investment climate may be enhanced if domestic policies are internationalised through incorporation into regional treaties. Internationalisation of investment treatment also serves as a signal in that adopting an RTA signals an intention to liberalize the investment framework, which in turn can be interpreted as a favourable sign by both intra and extra-regional investors.[10] Ultimately, much of the impact of such internationalised investment rules will also depend on the existing state of the investment protection framework in a State or a region. If the treatment of existing investors is already adequate, new (regional) rules lead to a marginal improvement and are unlikely either to influence the generation of new investment or facilitate a better investment climate.[11] Much will also depend on whether regional rules do in fact

---

[8] Ibid 62.

[9] Economist Intelligence Unit 'Into Africa: Institutional Investor Intentions to 2016' (Invest AD 2012) 18.

[10] F Jaumotte 'Foreign Direct Investment and Regional Trade Agreements, The Market Size Effect Revisited', *IMF Working Paper* 04/206, (2004) 4.

[11] McKinsey Global Institute 'Lions on the Move: The Progress and Potential of African Economies' (McKinsey & Company 2010), 15.

serve to liberalize investment by granting market access to investors through pre-establishment guarantees.[12]

4. REGIONAL TRADE RULES AND FDI

The effects of trade rules on investment are more complex. This is because the issue is not one of uncertainty but rather of trade-off between servicing a market via (arm's length) trade or doing so directly in-market through a subsidiary. For example, the elimination of intra-regional tariffs will affect trade vis-à-vis the level of sales by multinational subsidiaries depending on the importance of transport (eg tariff) costs, plant-level and firm-level costs in setting up multinational subsidiaries.[13] Hence, the type and motive of investment plays an important role in understanding how FDI is affected by tariffs and trade.[14] To reflect this, it is important to distinguish between intra-regional and extra-regional FDI as well as between horizontal (market-seeking: subsidiaries selling similar products) and vertical (efficiency and natural resource seeking: subsidiaries exploiting efficiencies or control over inputs) FDI.

Regional tariff preferences can decrease *horizontal* (tariff-jumping), intra-regional FDI because it may become less expensive to serve the partner country by trade rather than to establish a subsidiary, which would incur multiple plant-level costs.[15] On the other hand, however, regional tariff preferences encourage *vertically-motivated* intra-regional FDI.[16] This is because lower trade costs provide incentives to establish both international production networks and establish an efficiency-seeking subsidiary in a partner country that can process imports for re-export.

Extra-regional FDI can also be affected by declining regional tariff preferences in different ways. First, by lowering tariffs amongst parties to the RTA, it may become profitable for an extra-regional investor to avail itself of an effectively larger market (horizontal market-seeking FDI) from one or more locations in the region (export platforms). If individual countries of a region

---

[12] Ibid.

[13] JR Markusen and T Venables 'The Role of Multinational Firms in the Wage-Gap Debate', 5 *Review of International Economics* 4 (1997) 437; SL Brainard 'An Empirical Assessment of the proximity-Concentration Trade-Off Between Multinational Sales and Trade', 87 *American Economic Review* 4 (1997) 525.

[14] R Barrell and DW te Velde 'European Integration and Manufactures Import Demand' *German Economic Review* 3 (2002) 3, 272.

[15] R Adams, PDJ Gali and G McGuire 'The Trade and Investment Effects of Preferential Trading Arrangements: Old and New Evidence', *Productivity Commission Staff Working Paper, Canberra* (2003), 90.

[16] P Dee and J Gali 'The trade and investment effects of preferential trading arrangements', *NBER working paper* 10160 (2003).

are previously served by trade, this may then raise inward FDI (export platforms or beachhead locations).[17] However, if the Member States of a regional arrangement were already served through sales of a multinational subsidiary, concentration of production may occur in one or a few countries in the region, with ambiguous or negative effects for the volume of extra-regional FDI in each country. The combination of lower internal tariffs and significant plant-level fixed costs would lead to a consolidation of several plants in several members of the region into one or a few plants, used by the parent to serve the region as a whole. This may also induce FDI inflows to the most cost-efficient location (usually nearest to the largest market), possibly at the cost of FDI to other members in the same region.[18] Secondly, the effects of regional trade preferences for extra-regional vertical (or efficiency-seeking) FDI are likely to be small, though lower regional preferences may lower costs and raise efficiency in a vertically motivated subsidiary when it uses inputs from more than one country in the region (eg regional enterprises in ASEAN or the Andean Community).[19]

There are various effects of regional tariff preferences on inward FDI. However, in the context of developing country regions, where most inward FDI is inter-regional (even though South Africa is an important investor in Southern African Development Community (SADC)), the market size argument would be the most important and, apart from other factors, regional tariff preferences would tend to raise inward FDI. It must be noted, however, that the strength of this argument depends on the difference between tariffs applied regionally and tariffs applied to others on a Most Favoured Nation (MFN) basis. Indeed, the market size gained as a result of regional integration should be *corrected* for initial MFN rates, as this will indicate the maximum scope of the market size gained. Hence, the higher the MFN rate and the larger the market size, the more likely it is that market-seeking investors will respond.[20] Accounting for this, regions in Africa such as COMESA and SADC have as much additional market size to offer as the Andean region, for example, not because of their similar market size but because of similar regional market size *corrected* for MFN tariffs.[21] This could lead to additional FDI.[22]

Rules of origin constitute another trade rule that can affect location decisions. The effects of rules of origin (RoO) on investment can vary depending

---

[17] WJ Ethier 'Regionalism in a multilateral world'106 *Journal of Political Economy* (2003), 1231.

[18] DJ Feils and M Rahman 'The Impact of Regional Integration on Insider and Outsider FDI' 51 *Management International Review* (2011) 55.

[19] Association of Southeast Asian Nations.

[20] Jaumotte (n 10) 6.

[21] Compare population sizes the Andean Community, COMESA and SADC.

[22] Into Africa: Institutional Investor Intentions to 2016 (n 9) 10.

on the type of investment as well as the interaction with regional tariff preferences. The RoO can encourage the use of intra-regional inputs instead of extra-regional inputs, even if the latter are more efficient. However, a stricter and more costly RoO would stifle intra-regional trade favouring extra-regional imports (which are likely to face the MFN tariff). The larger the difference between MFN tariffs and regional tariffs, the greater the incentive to comply with the RoO by importing regionally using the appropriate certificates.[23]

Non-tariff barriers (NTBs) to trade, including voluntary export restraints, can also affect investment. For example, the threat of imposing EU quotas and using anti-dumping legislation against Japanese exports motivated the Japanese to set up operations inside the EU. Barrell and Pain found that after controlling relative labour costs and market size, Japanese investment flows to EC countries over 1980–91 were significantly influenced by anti-dumping activities taken in the EC.[24]

On balance, RTAs should lead to increased extra-regional FDI, but there are more ambiguous results for intra-regional FDI. Among other things, the ambiguity of the effects of trade rules stems from the fact that multinational enterprises are motivated by exploiting firm-specific assets (eg firm-specific fixed costs) and hence seek to enjoy economies of scale and scope, in addition to simply jumping trade barriers.[25]

5. OTHER REGIONAL INITIATIVES AND FDI AND DYNAMIC EFFECTS

Some argue that a region can do much more in order to promote investment than design and implement trade and investment rules.[26] They can, for example, put in place the regional infrastructures (legal, institutional etc.) to deal with investment issues at a regional level. Or they can design other rules such as free movement of people (eg CARICOM).[27] Further, regions can also decide to harmonize fiscal and monetary policies.[28]

---

[23] A Estevadeordal and K Suominen, 'Rules of Origin: A World Map', Paper presented at the seminar 'Regional Trade Agreements in Comparative Perspective: Latin America and the Caribbean and Asia Pacific (2003) 10.

[24] R Barrell and N Pain 'Trade restraints and Japanese direct investment flows' 43 *European Economic Review* (1999) 31.

[25] Feils and Rahman (n 18) 54.

[26] Brainard (n 13) 522.

[27] Revised Treaty of Chaguaramas Establishing the Caribbean Community Including the CARICOM Single market and Economy (2001).

[28] For instance the Euro area (within the EU), the UEMOA and SACU (within SADC) have common currencies. This should reduce intra-regional exchange rate variability and cross-border

Some regional initiatives such as in the Andean, ASEAN, and MERCOSUR regions envisage cooperation schemes which aim to establish regional enterprises by promoting joint ventures. By way of example, the ASEAN Industrial Cooperation scheme (AICO Scheme) seeks to promote joint manufacturing industrial activities between ASEAN-based companies.[29] The ASEAN secretariat also has various activities in the area of investment facilitation, by providing information through portals, databases, publications and statistics.[30]

Some have argued that important effects of RTAs on FDI are dynamic, with competition creating a more efficient industry and growth, which in turn can affect FDI.[31] Blomstrom and Kokko have concluded that regional integration leads to efficiency gains and higher growth and thus further FDI. FDI can operate as a catalyst through spillovers in terms of technology transfer and the promotion of other linkages with local firms.[32] This can generate long-lasting effects on growth and productivity in the host state as opposed to a one-off effect based on a more efficient allocation of resources. Schiff and Wang have shown that imports from NAFTA countries have raised productivity in Mexico, while other imports from outside the NAFTA region have had no discernible effects.[33] Elsewhere te Velde has examined evidence for the productivity enhancing effects of regional integration at the firm level for countries such as Benin, Malawi and South Africa.[34]

6. EMPIRICAL EVIDENCE

Empirical studies on the impact of RTAs on FDI tend to suggest that RTAs encourage extra-regional FDI flows and, for some regions, intra-regional FDI, although it is not always clear whether this influence should be linked

transaction costs, which are amongst the factors contributing to investment. Because the EU and SADC are incomplete currency areas, there should be implications for which parts of the region are influenced.

29 Preamble, Basic Agreement on the ASEAN Industrial Cooperation Scheme.

30 Association of South East Asian Nations Secretariat (ASEAN) Compendium of Investment Policies & Measures in ASEAN Countries (ASEAN Secretariat, 1998); ASEAN, Handbook of Investment Agreements in ASEAN (ASEAN Secretariat, 1998).

31 JP Neary 'Foreign Direct Investment and the Single Market' *CEPR and University College Dublin Draft Paper* (2001) 9.

32 Blomstrom and Kokko (n 5) 7.

33 M Schiff and Y Wang 'Regional integration and technology diffusion: the case of the North American Free Trade Agreement', *World Bank Policy Research Working Paper* 3132 (World Bank, 2003) 8.

34 te Velde and Bezemer (n 4) 52.

Table 1. Regional trade agreements and FDI, selected econometric studies

Study	Type of study, methodology, data	Findings
Pain and Lansbury (1996)	How has intra- and extra EC FDI by UK and German firms in different sectors changed with the introduction of the Internal Market Programme (IMP)? UK and German outward FDI for seven sectors, 1980/81–92 Sector output, factor costs, currency volatility, corporate finance conditions, non-tariff barriers (1–3 scale), IMP dummy, sector dummies	FDI determinants differ by sectors IMP introduction boosted FDI IMP redirected UK FDI from US to EC
Srinivasan and Mody (1998)	Which factors determine US and Japanese FDI? 35 OECD and non-OECD countries, 1977–92, split out in groups of low-middle, high income countries; and EEC, Latin America, East Asia Market size, labour costs, capital costs, .previous FDI, infrastructure (telephone, electricity), country risk, openness	When split into periods (1977–81; 1982–86; 1987–92), no evidence that IMP increased US and Japanese FDI (but we should bear in mind that IMP was complete only in 1993).
Brenton et al. (1998)	Does European integration increase FDI? Does it divert FDI? Are trade and FDI substitutes or complements? FDI in and outflows, imports, exports for EU and CEE countries Population, distance, trade/FDI agreement dummies, host country economic freedom dummies, CEE dummies, host country EU membership dummy, FDI residual in trade regression	Single European Act (1992) and Iberian enlargement led to more FDI but no observed FDI diversion.

Levy, Stein and Daude (2002)	How do RTAs affect the location of FDI? FDI from 20 OECD countries to 60 OECD/non-OECD countries, 1982–98 RTA membership, extended market host, extended market source, capital/worker ratio, distance, market size, bilateral trade, inflation, trade/GDP, privatization, investment, environment, common border, common language	RTA membership doubles FDI stocks on average FDI increases upon joining a FTA with: more trade/GDP (openness) more similar capital/worker ratios better investment environment larger market.
Dee and Gali (2003)	Gravity model of trade and investment between pairs of countries from 1988–1997. Uses a large panel of OECD data on stocks of outward FDI.	Study suggests that FDI responds significantly to the non-trade provisions of preferential trade agreements (PTAs). Further, for most of those agreements where non-trade provisions have affected FDI, the result has been net investment creation rather than diversion.
Adam et al. (2003)	Version of the gravity model to analyse whether certain RTAs are associated with net investment creation or diversion	Study finds that non-trade provisions significantly impact investment flows. It finds evidence of net investment creation in response to the 'new age' non-trade provisions of PTAs.
Jaumotte (2004)	Sample of 71 developing countries during the period 1980–99	Confirms the increasing attraction of regions for FDI. FDI diverted from non-RTA countries to RTA countries. For the Maghreb region it was estimated that the increased market size would stimulate the increase in FDI stocks by 62% for Algeria, 85% for Morocco and 165% for Tunisia.

(*continued overleaf*)

Table 1 ***continued***

Study	Type of study, methodology, data	Findings
Te Velde and Bezemer (2006)	The real stock of UK and US FDI in developing countries, covering 68 (UK) and 97 (US) developing countries from 1980–2001.	Regions with more investment provisions provide United States and UK investors with positive signals about how countries will treat their investors (coefficient on the variable measuring regional investment provisions is positive and significant). While membership of a regional group can lead to further extra regional FDI inflows, the type of regional grouping matters for attracting FDI—ie whether or not RTA include certain trade and investment provisions. Moreover, the position of countries within a regional grouping also matters—smaller countries and countries located further away from the largest country in the region benefit less from being part of a regional grouping than larger countries and those close to the core of the region.
OECD (2006)	Analysis of the economic consequences of investment provisions in RTAs by creating an index of the extensiveness of investment provisions in RTAs and then using that index in a gravity model framework of trade and investment. Uses data on bilateral outward FDI flows for the period from 1990–2004.	Analysis suggests that investment provisions in RTAs are positively associated with both trade and investment flows. Moreover, the coefficients indicate that they matter more for FDI flows than trade flows. This dual positive effect indicates that investment may be more efficiency-seeking than market-seeking, thus acting more as a complement to, rather than a substitute for, trade in the context of RTAs.
Medvedev (2006)	A panel of 143 countries over 1980–2003.	FDI benefits of RTAs increase with the size of regional partners; the effects increase in North–South partnerships as those provide for deep integration
Feils and Rahman (2011)	OECD bilateral data for 24 OECD countries covering 1980–2003.	Regional integration leads to an increase in inward FDI. Common economic area membership is associated with greater FDI flows, with the larger members gaining more.

to trade or investment disciplines.[35] Empirical evidence has also been deployed to show that different countries within a region experience different effects.[36] This difference reflects not only variations in the relative size of the industrial sectors among Member States, but also the degree to which economic integration, directly or indirectly, increases the locational advantage of a country relative to other Member States.[37] Finally, the strength of investment provisions also matter.[38]

A number of studies have offered more details on the relevance of different types of regional investment provisions. Dee and Gali have suggested that FDI responds significantly to the non-trade provisions of RTAs.[39] Te Velde and Bezemer have found that membership in a regional arrangement (including African, Caribbean and Pacific Group of States (ACP) and non-ACP regions) as such is not significantly related to inward FDI.[40] However, crucially when a country is a member of a regional arrangement with an RTA with detailed trade and investment provisions (eg describing treatment of foreign firms, large trade preferences), this will help to attract more inward FDI to the region.[41] Since ACP regions (eg COMESA, ECOWAS) are at an earlier stage of implementing investment provisions compared to other regions (eg NAFTA and MERCOSUR), the costs of non-integration in terms of attracting FDI can be considerable for such regions.

3. BENCHMARKING COMESA FDI PERFORMANCE WITH OTHER REGIONAL ECONOMIC COMMUNITIES IN AFRICA

This section offers a comparative analysis of COMESA FDI performance with other RECs in Africa. There has been a notable rise in inward stock of FDI (roughly defined as the accumulation of FDI inflows) across African regions. For some regions, such as SADC, COMESA and ECOWAS, the FDI stock has been increasing markedly since the mid-1980s. Importantly,

---

[35] N Pain and M Lansbury 'The Impact of the Internal Market on the Evaluation of European Direct Investment', London NIESR, mimeo (1996); Blomstrom and Kokko (n 5); P Brenton, F Di Mauro, M Luecke 'Economic Integration and FDI: An Empirical Analysis of Foreign Direct Investment in the EU and in Central and Eastern Europe', Kiel Working Paper no. 890 (1998); YE Levy, E Stein, C Daude 'Regional Integration and the Location of FDI', IADB Draft (2002); Jaumotte (n 10); Feils and Rahman (n 18) 43.

[36] Brenton et al (n 35) 14.

[37] Ibid, 18.

[38] Ibid, 20.

[39] Dee and Gali (n 16) 9.

[40] te Velde and Bezemer (n 4) 64.

[41] Ibid.

Figure 1. Inward FDI Stock in various African regions over 1981–2011)

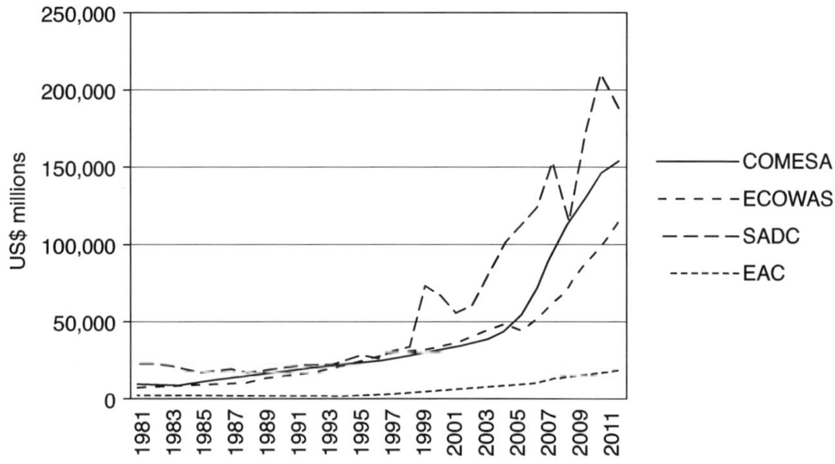

Source: UNCTAD

the inward FDI stock for COMESA has seen the highest increase (of 380 per cent) among all the RECs since 2000. This is followed by EAC (277 per cent) and ECOWAS (238 per cent).

When expressed as a per cent of GDP (figure 3), inward FDI stock for COMESA is impressive, with COMESA's ratio increased by 14 percentage points between 2000 and 2011 (the highest of the RECs in figure 2).

The inward stock of FDI in COMESA countries before and after the launch of the FTA in 2000 is also worth comparing (figure 3). The purpose is to collate the average stock of inward FDI before and after the conclusion of the COMESA FTA which marks the commencement of effective economic integration. Generally, the analysis shows that on average there has been an increase in the intensity of inward FDI stock in 2000–11 compared to 1988–99 for most COMESA countries.

The analysis of the relative performance of COMESA compared to other regional blocs within Africa is clearer when the growth rate of inward FDI stocks is considered over the same periods of 1988–1999 and 2000–2011 (figure 4). COMESA and SADC had the highest percentage point improvement in average growth rates of FDI intensity (ie 13 percentage points increases each) between the two decades.

The foregoing analysis notwithstanding, what remains an issue is whether the FDI potential of the COMESA region has been fully exploited. As is evident from UNCTAD indices on inward FDI potential, COMESA countries are exploiting less than a maximum of 22 per cent of their inward

Figure 2. Inward FDI stock for COMESA and Other African RECs, 2000–2011 (as % of GDP)

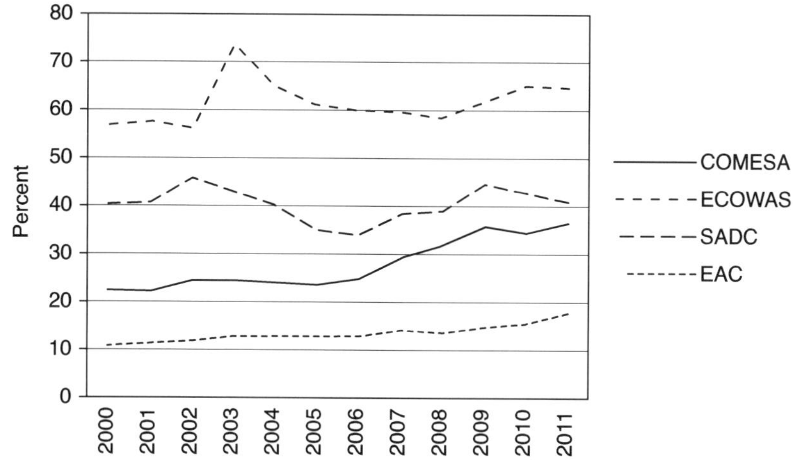

Source: UNCTAD

Figure 3. Average Inward FDI Stock for COMESA Countries across Time Episodes (as % of GDP)

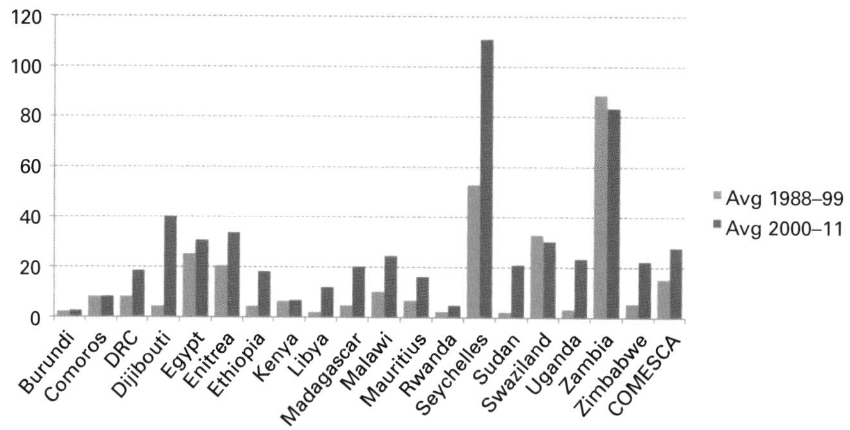

Source: UNCTAD

Figure 4. Growth (%) in Inward Stock of FDI for COMESA and Other African Regions

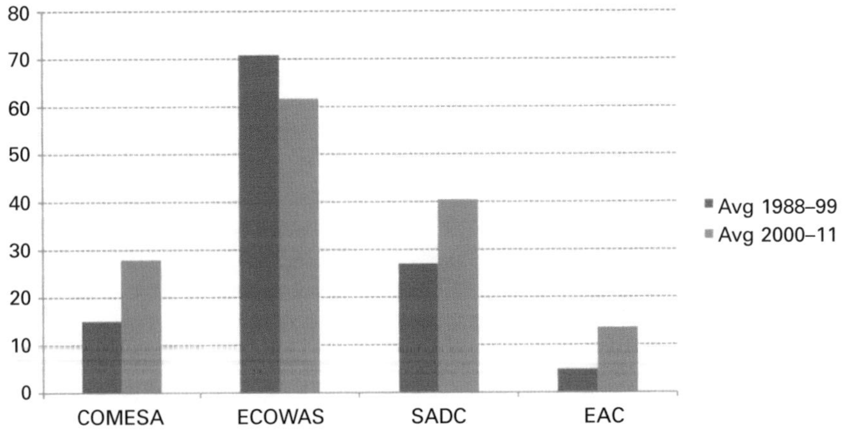

Source: UNCTAD

FDI potential.[42] Libya has led the COMESA group with 22 per cent of exploited potential followed by Egypt (17 per cent), Kenya, Zambia and Uganda with 11 per cent respectively. Clearly, this data implies that there is room for further exploitation of the FDI potential in the region. The ensuing sections will discuss the policy issues and opportunities in the COMESA market.

4. INVESTMENT-RELATED PROVISIONS IN COMESA

The COMESA regional integration initiative includes several provisions relevant for investment. Using the distinction identified in section 2, the analysis here distinguishes between trade, investment and other provisions.

Existing Trade Provisions:

a. The COMESA FTA Agreement. The FTA established in November 2000, allows for goods qualifying under the COMESA rules of origin to be traded free of the payment of import duties (for participating countries).

[42] UNCTAD, 'World Investment Report 2011: Non-Equity Modes of International Production and Development' BOPCOM—11/22, 44.

b. Trade facilitation regimes such as the COMESA Regional Customs Transit Guarantee (RCTG) Scheme and Yellow Card. The RCTG was developed under the auspices of the Protocol on Transit Trade and Transit Facilities (Annex I of the COMESA Treaty). This customs transit regime was designed to facilitate the movement of goods in transit under customs seals by providing adequate security of guarantee to the transit countries to recover their duties and taxes, should the goods in transit be illegally used within the transit countries. The COMESA Yellow card is a Third Party Liabilities Motor Vehicle Insurance Scheme[43] which is valid in all the participating states. It facilitates cross-border movement of vehicles between COMESA Member States.
c. The COMESA Customs Union. The Customs Union is in transition period to allow for country preparation in advance its full implementation.[44] The 2012 Extraordinary Council of Ministers reviewed and decided that the transition period be extended to June 2014.[45]

Investment Provisions:
The CCIA Agreement Part 1 details objectives, features, issues on transparency, general obligations, institutional arrangements, implementing programmes and action plans, as well as rules on modifications of schedules, annexes and action plans. The other three parts of the agreement establish rights and obligations of Member States and COMESA investors, provisions on dispute settlement, a part on final provisions detailing how the CCIA agreement relates to other existing agreements, adoption of protocols, additional membership, withdrawal and renewal of membership, and ratification of the agreement.

The key investment provisions in the CCIA Agreement include the following:

a. The COMESA treaty guarantees fair and equitable treatment of COMESA investors, albeit in such a way which requires that host state development conditions be taken into account in applying the standard.[46]

---

[43] COMESA/EAC/SADC 3rd party Motor Vehicle Insurance Scheme, available at: <http://www.trademarksa.org/sites/default/files/publications/Meeting%20Report%20%7C%20Tripartite%20Steering%20Commitee%20%7C%20Harmonisation%20of%20Third%20Party%20Motor%20Vehicle%20Insurance.pdf>

[44] COMESA (2012) Report of the Twenty Eight Meeting of the Trade and Customs Committee 18–20 July 2012, Lusaka, Zambia, COMESA.

[45] COMESA (2012) Report of the Fourth Extra Ordinary Meeting of the Council of Ministers 04–05 October 2012 Lusaka, Zambia, COMESA.

[46] Art 14, COMESA (2007) Investment Agreement for the COMESA Common Investment Area.

b. The COMESA treaty further ensures the free transfer of funds across borders of Member States.[47]
c. Unlike many other regional investment arrangements, the CCIA goes a further step by allowing investors the free movement of capital, labour and goods and services across borders of Member States.[48]
d. The CCIA Agreement contains national treatment commitments extending to any COMESA investor and its investments in other COMESA member states.[49] An exception is made for investments that fall within the rubric of sensitive activities and are thus excluded from the national treatment provision.[50]
e. The COMESA agreement also provides for most favoured nation treatment which commands that no COMESA investor or their investments be granted treatment less favourable than that given in similar circumstances to investors and investments of any third country in the Host COMESA State.[51]
f. The CCIA Agreement further makes provision for protection of COMESA investors and their investments from expropriation or nationalization by Member States in their territory, except where such expropriation or nationalisation is in the public interest, on a non-discriminatory basis, in accordance with due process of law, and accompanied by the payment of compensation.[52] The treaty further guarantees compensation to COMESA investors for losses due to war or civil conflict, or any form of political instability, provided that the Member State offers such compensation and restitution to their own investors.[53]
g. The CCIA Agreement makes provision for dispute settlement, which encompasses both State-State and investor-State resolution mechanisms, offering recourse to competent national courts, the COMESA Court of Justice or international arbitration.[54]
h. Finally, the CCIA Agreement also stipulates general obligations of Member States to promote transparency through the publication of information related to investment rules and regulations.[55]

---

47 Art 15, ibid.
48 Arts 15 and 16, ibid.
49 Art 3(b)(i), ibid.
50 Art 17, ibid.
51 Art 19, ibid.
52 Art 20, ibid.
53 Art 21, ibid.
54 Art 27, ibid.
55 Art 5, ibid.

Other existing investment-related provisions:

a. The COMESA Adjustment Facility (CAF) provides support to countries making the relevant fiscal, economic and social adjustments required to implement regional integration commitments. This includes revenue loss arising from the implementation of trade liberalisation. The COMESA Fund Protocol governs the operation of the CAF.[56]
b. The COMESA Regional Payment and Settlement System (REPSS), which came in to effect on 3 October 2012, was established to facilitate efficient cross border payments for COMESA Member States.[57] REPSS is built on open standards and is also accessible to non-Member States.

As specified in the CCIA Agreement, the institutions within COMESA responsible for the administration of the agreement include the CCIA Committee, comprised of ministers responsible for investment in each Member States, and the Coordinating Committee on Investment (CCI), involving senior officials from ministries in Member States responsible for investment. Other institutions involved in the CCIA are the COMESA secretariat and the COMESA Regional Integration Agency (RIA). There are a further eight COMESA institutions, including African Trade Insurance (ATI), which provides a form of insurance related to investment trade risks; the COMESA clearing house; the COMESA Court of Justice; the Federation of National Associations of Women in Business in COMESA; the Leather and Leather Product Institute; the PTA Bank, providing trade financing facilities to businesses operating in the region; the Regional Investment Agency (RIA), which is the COMESA investment promotion arm; and the PTA Reinsurance company (ZEP-RE).

Key to achieving the full potential of these wide-ranging provisions and institutions is the speed and depth of implementation at the Member State level. Elsewhere, te Velde has provided an overview of investment provisions in different regions and steps taken in these regions to implement their obligations, such as, for example, drafting common investment codes envisaging the application of transparent policies, the harmonization and stabilization of laws, regulations and administrative practises, as well as, laws mandating non-discriminatory treatment among members. However, in COMESA the

56 COMESA (2014) Report of the Thirty Second Meeting of the Council of Ministers, 22–24 February 2014, Kinshasa, Democratic Republic of Congo, 84.

57 Press Release, COMESA's Regional Payment and Settlement System (REPSS) Goes Live: http://www.comesa.int/index.php?option=com_content&view=article&id=395:comesas-regional-payment-and-settlement-system-repss-goes-live&catid=5:latest-news&Itemid=41.

implementation of provisions of this nature has been slowed down by political and institutional inertia. Other regional arrangements, such as the NAFTA, are well ahead, especially in terms of institutional and legal backing.

5. THE RISING AFRICAN MIDDLE CLASS AND ITS IMPLICATIONS FOR COMESA INWARD MARKET SEEKING FDI

Over the past decade Africa has undergone notable transformations that have made the continent a destination of increased FDI.[58] Dramatic improvement in governance—particularly democratic governance including elections, flourishing civil society and media freedom—has been argued by some to have been crucial to investor decisions in Africa.[59] In addition to political transformation, other factors such as economic liberalization and deregulation, a boom in the natural resource sector in several African States, and the reduced level of indebtedness following improved economic performance and debt relief from both bilateral and multilateral creditors have all been crucial factors driving investment into the continent.[60] Hence, in 2012 KMPG concluded '[i]ncreasingly, investors have become aware not only of the risks of investing in Africa, but the risk of not investing in the continent. They have become more focused on where in Africa to invest, as opposed to whether to invest or not.'[61]

Juma suggests that in addition to improving economic growth in the continent, Africa is moving at a faster pace to promote regional economic integration aimed at creating larger continental markets.[62] This includes the move in June 2011 by the tripartite regional blocs of EAC, COMESA and SADC to launch a large free trade area which will encompass countries from Egypt and Libya right down to South Africa and is aimed at bringing together countries with a combined population of 700 million, a combined

---

[58] While several academic studies and IMF reports had already noted a turn-around in Africa's growth prospects in the 2000s, in recent years business consultancies have noted the potential for investment.

[59] M Primorac, IMF Survey Magazine: Countries & Regions Africa Enjoying Newfound Optimism, (2011); Jaumotte (n 10); C Juma, 'Africa's New Engine: Africa Looks to its Middle-Class Consumers to Drive Prosperity. Finance & Development', December 2011: https://www.imf.org/external/pubs/ft/fandd/2011/12/juma.htm; Economist Intelligence Unit, 'Into Africa: Institutional Investor Intentions to 2016' (Abu Dhabi: Invest AD 2012) 8.

[60] Trademark Southern Africa (TMSA) 'Report on the COMESA-EAC-SADC Tripartite North–South Corridor Aid for Trade Programme (Infrastructure)', April 2012; World Trade Organisation (WTO) Trade Policy Review: Zimbabwe, 2011: http://www.wto.org/english/tratop_e/tpr_e/tp352_e.htm;

[61] KPMG 'African Emergence: The Rise of the Phoenix' (South Africa: KPMG Service Proprietary Limited 2012).

[62] Juma (n 60).

GDP of over US$1 trillion and combined exports worth US$154 billion. If realized, this large market is likely to be of significant attraction to both foreign and domestic investors. The study suggests that one result of the economic growth facilitated by these large trade blocs be further expansion of the African middle class.[63]

As a consequence of impressive economic performance, improved political stability and governance, arising middle class, and increasing regional integration in the continent, there has been increased interest from large global investors in investing in Africa. Recent investors that have sought out new markets in Africa include Wal-Mart Stores, which recently agreed to pay around $2.4 billion to buy South Africa's Massmart holdings, with South Africa acting as an entry point for investment in the continent.[64] In 2012, Yum Brands Inc announced plans to double its KFC outlets in Africa to 1,200 in the next few years.[65] Google Inc and Microsoft Corp have also been jointly making efforts to fund local entrepreneurs with the hope that providing initial capital to African technology firms will eventually lead to local growth and innovation through which these investors may grow their own businesses.[66] In the COMESA area, Nestle SA opened a new factory in the DR Congo.[67] The 2011 COMESA RIA report provides a long list of top investors in COMESA, which includes global giants such as BT, HSBC, Pepsi, Philips, Citibank, Mobil, Nestle, Total, Vodafone, Orange, Fiat, Gap, Benz, HP Invent, Nike, IBM, Hilton, BMW, Petronas, and Coca-Cola.[68]

Africa has grown impressively at a time when advanced economies have been struggling to ensure domestic growth. This has helped reduce poverty levels to such a degree that a substantial chunk of the poor has been lifted into a new middle class of Africans.[69] The growing size of the middle class in the continent is in turn capable of stimulating greater demand for global goods and services.[70] China and India have already shown that the middle class can

---

63 Ibid.

64 Wall-Mart annual report (2012): http://www.walmartstores.com/sites/annual-report/2012/WalMart_AR.pdf.

65 Yum Brands Inc annual report (2012): http://www.yum.com/annualreport/pdf/2012yumAnnReport.pdf.

66 Wall Street Journal 'Google to Fund, Develop Wireless Networks in Emerging Markets' (2013): <http://online.wsj.com/news/articles/SB10001424127887323975004578503350402434918>.

67 Press-release 'Nestle invests CHF 150 million in the Equatorial African Region' (2010): http://www.nestle.com/Media/NewsAndFeatures/Nestle-invests-CHF150-million-in-the-Equatorial-African-Region.

68 COMESA RIA 'OPI Board Approves up to $100 Million for Real Estate Investment Fund for Sub-Saharan Africa' COMESA RIA News 21 June 2012.

69 Juma (n 60).

70 Wall Street Journal 'A New Class of Consumers Grows in Africa: Market on Par with China's and India's'; Africa News, May 2 2011, www.wsj.com.

be a powerful an engine of economic growth, eg through the ability to stimulate domestic demand for non-essential goods, driving consumption expenditures and thereby economic growth, which in turn affects the States' ability to attract market-seeking FDI.[71]

The role of the middle class in stimulating economic growth is well acknowledged in contemporary development thinking. A rising middle class has been shown to be associated with development outcomes such as improved governance, economic growth and poverty reduction.[72] The economic power associated with middle class status tends to inspire people to demand more accountable governments.[73] Moreover, as noted earlier, the rising middle class in Africa is associated with increased consumption expenditure which in turn is associated with poverty reduction and economic growth, thus making it a strong indicator of medium and long-term development in a continent considered to be the world's poorest.[74]

The OECD has recently conducted a comprehensive study of the global middle class.[75] The report includes an estimate of the global middle class including Africa. Using a definition of the middle class as those within daily expenditure between US$10 and US$100 in Personal Purchasing Power (PPP), the OECD estimates Sub-Saharan Africa's middle class at 32 million, which excludes North Africa, consuming US$256 billion annually. The report further projects that the number of middle class Sub-Saharan Africans will increase from 32 million to 57 million by 2020 and to 107 million by 2030. Whilst the share in global consumption remains low, the expected increase in consumer purchasing from US$ 256 billion in 2009 to US$827 billion in 2030 is significant (Table 2).

For its part, the African Development Bank (AfDB) presents a picture of a rising middle class in Africa that is expected stimulate demand for global investment and economic development in general. The AfDB's report provides an in-depth analysis of Africa's growing middle class and its implications for the continent's economy and poverty reduction.[76] From a study of 45 African countries, the report provides evidence to argue that the growing African middle class is crucial to the continent's development efforts through driving the African economy towards more dependency on

---

[71] Ibid.

[72] D Court and L Narasimhan 'Capturing the World's Emerging Middle Class' *McKinsey Quarterly*, July 2010, <http://www.mckinsey.com/insights/consumer_and_retail/capturing_the_worlds_emerging_middle_class>.

[73] African Development Bank 'The Middle of the Pyramid: Dynamics of the Middle Class in Africa. Market Brief', (2011) 3.

[74] Ibid.

[75] H Kharas, 'The Emerging Middle Class in Developing Countries' *OECD Development Centre Working Paper* No. 285 (2011) 65.

[76] 'The Middle of the Pyramid' (n 74) 3.

Table 2. Spending by the Global Middle Class, 2009 to 2030 (millions of 2005 PPP dollars)

	2009		2020		2030	
North America	5602	26%	5863	17%	5837	10%
Europe	8138	38%	10301	29%	11337	20%
Central and South America	1534	7%	2315	7%	3117	6%
Asia Pacific	4952	23%	14798	42%	32596	59%
Sub-Saharan Africa	256	1%	448	1%	827	1%
Middle East and North Africa	796	4%	1321	4%	1966	4%
World	21278	100%	35045	100%	55680	100%

Source: OECD (2010: 28)

domestic demand rather than exports (which has traditionally been in primary commodities) and stimulating the promotion of inclusive growth and faster poverty reduction. The AfDB's conclusion is that the middle class will create demand for global products and hence FDI in Africa.[77] Indeed, according to AfDB estimates, by 2010 the broad category of the middle class across Africa had risen to 34.3 per cent of the population (ie 326 million people) up from 26.2 per cent (or 115 million) in 1980, 27 per cent (157 million) in 1990 and 27.2 per cent (204 million) in 2000. Moreover, the movement of the poor into the middle class outperformed the drop of the rich class into the middle class, suggesting a rising of all boats across Africa, fuelling demand for private sector supplied consumables and bolstering development of the African economy.[78]

The AfDB defines the middle class as those people with per capita daily expenditures of \$2–\$20. That category is split into three sub-categories based upon daily per capita consumption levels:

1. The floating middle class with per capita consumption levels of between \$2 and \$4 per day. This category is viewed by the report to be crucial for policy intervention as it remains just above the poverty level but below the lower middle class and thus remains vulnerable to the potential of slipping back into the category of the poor in the event of external shocks.

[77] Ibid, 5.
[78] Ibid, 14.

2. The lower middle class with daily per capita consumption levels of between \$4 and \$10. This group lives above the subsistence level and therefore are able to save and consume non-essential goods, thus making this group crucial for increased demand of consumables.
3. The upper middle class, with daily per capita consumption levels of \$10–\$20. This group exhibits the greatest stability and the greatest resilience to external shocks.

A rising middle class in the economy is a complement to the traditional reliance of economic growth on agriculture, exports, mineral production and energy. But the growth of the middle class varies significantly across the continent and much of the middle class remains vulnerable.[79]

North Africa has the highest concentration of middle class, though with significant portions represented in the floating middle class.[80] Indeed, in the most populous countries in Africa (Nigeria, Egypt and Ethiopia), the floating class dominates the middle class.[81] The floating middle class is a vulnerable class and can easily be reverted to poverty in the presence of external shocks. AfDB estimates for 2010 show that 21 per cent of the African population fell within the floating middle class, representing about 216 million people. The lower middle class comprised a further 138 million people and is described as a stable class, useful for consumption of non-necessity products that may constitute large portions of future FDI. In the end, therefore, the outlook is positive but optimism must be balanced with caution. On the one hand, the existing high proportion of Africa's poor implies that, should economic conditions continue to improve to lift them out of poverty, there is potential for a bigger middle class and hence for consumption expenditure increases which is likely to increase prospects for FDI. At the same time, much of the African middle class exists in a state of vulnerability to external shocks, such as were seen in the aftermath of the 2008 global financial crisis.[82]

Moreover, although the middle class in Africa is vital for FDI flows, the AfDB report notes other obstacles to middle class development in Africa in practice. In particular, FDI flows are usually associated with areas with more skilled labour such as in China and India, whereas skilled labour remains in limited supply in the case in Africa. Education, and specifically, education designed to prepare workers for skilled positions, remains a challenge in Africa.

---

[79] Ibid.

[80] Ibid, 5.

[81] Ibid, 6

[82] Ibid, 15.

In summary, a rising middle class in Africa has major long-term implications for attracting FDI flows to Africa and COMESA in particular. This conclusion is premised on three principal reasons.

- First, the rise in consumer demand will attract more market-seeking FDI into Africa. By 2020, four groups of industries (consumer, resources, agriculture and infrastructure) could have combined revenue of $2.6 trillion.[83] Of these, the consumer industry is likely to acquire more than half, about $1.4 trillion, up from an estimate of about $860 billion in 2008.[84] The number of Africans with discretionary incomes (which affects global consumer goods and services) will reach 128 million by 2020.[85] These trends will affect the levels and patterns of market seeking FDI to service these consumers (food, drink, retail etc).
- Secondly, the rise in the middle class will attract FDI to niches. By 2030, half of Africa's population will reside in cities thus emphasising the tendencies of urbanisation and consumption patterns associated with that.[86] It is likely, for example, that more specialized medical services will be needed, requiring more FDI in medical and related services.
- Finally, the expanding middle class is expected to transform the region into a better place to do business as it is expected that the African population of working age will reach 1.1 billion by 2040, thus leading to an increased labour force available for manufacturing and services[87]. As a consequence, the economy in the region will be less dependent on agricultural income, and economic fundamentals (skills) for all types of FDI will be further improved.

6. CONCLUSION: FDI AND REGIONAL INTEGRATION—WHAT MORE CAN COMESA DO?

The regional integration process in the COMESA region has progressed gradually over the past decades. The launch of the free trade agreement in 2000 was followed by the negotiations towards the customs union in 2009. The CCIA Agreement has been in place since 2007 (although, as noted, it has not yet come into force). A number of regional institutions, including a

[83] 'Lions on the Move' n 4.

[84] Ibid.

[85] Ibid.

[86] Ibid, 8.

[87] Minister of Commerce and Industry, Republic of Liberia, Speech at LPS Sixth Annual Meeting. 'Impact Investments: Transforming lives through innovative investments that contributes to inclusive growth', 23 September 2013, 3.

COMESA Regional Investment Agency, have also been put in place. A review of the theoretical and empirical literature suggests that deeper regional integration should help to attract FDI, especially from outside the region. So, what more can be done by COMESA to attract FDI?

The fact is that COMESA is already performing well compared to several other African regions. Apart from recent political upheavals in Egypt and Libya, COMESA has attracted more FDI (as a percentage of GDP) than other African regions. Moreover, impressive growth rates and the rise in the middle class in some African countries have put the continent and COMESA into a more positive light for investors. This notwithstanding, there is scope for COMESA Member States to do more to attract FDI into the region. These options are considered below.

1. *Full implementation of existing provisions:* First, with regards to investment protection the signing and ratification of the CCIA Agreement throughout the region would send a positive signal to the investor community.[88] COMESA Member States should not only ratify the CCIA but back this up with effective institutions to ensure implementation at the Member State level. Secondly, insofar as trade provisions are concerned, the expansion of the COMESA FTA would increase the market size and enhance further opportunities for market-seeking FDI. Within the cluster of trade provisions, Member States need to continue upholding treaty provisions and implement Council Decisions on the removal of non-tariff barriers.
2. *Move towards deeper integration:* The evidence clearly suggests that deeper integration is better for attracting investment than narrow integration. There are a range of provisions and actions that can be taken at a regional level, such as co-operation on transport services or regional infrastructure. Progress towards the attainment of a customs union within COMESA, moreover is critical as a signal for further FDI.[89] That the recent COMESA Extraordinary Council of Ministers pronounced itself in favour of this step is a positive sign.[90] Secondly, the current tripartite negotiations among EAC, COMESA and SADC provide a useful framework for achieving deeper integration. Areas for cooperation include road transport infrastructure, rail transport, ports, energy and energy distribution and

[88] The signing parties of the CCIA included Burundi, Comoros, DRC, Djibouti, Egypt, Eritrea, Ethiopia, Kenya, Libya, Madagascar, Malawi, Mauritius, Rwanda, Seychelles, Sudan, Swaziland, Uganda, Zambia and Zimbabwe.

[89] UNCTAD World Investment Report 2013, Chapter III, Global Value Chains: Investment and Trade for Development, 103.

[90] COMESA Report (n 45).

border posts.[91] The Tripartite negotiations have emerged as a critical structure for addressing integration of COMESA, EAC and SADC Member States and in the process a coordinated approach to common areas of integration is developing. The use of the Yellow Card Insurance Scheme by COMESA importers, for instance, will benefit from tripartite level cooperation. At the moment due to non-implementation of the COMESA Yellow Card Insurance Scheme, transport costs in the Beira Corridor are 5–10 per cent higher than in other corridors of the region. With implementation, these additional costs should disappear.[92]

3. *Regional investment negotiations with third countries:* COMESA could more effectively negotiate regional investment arrangements with other African RECs. The Tripartite agreement in particular offers the opportunity to overcome existing obstacles.[93] As noted by COMESA further negotiation through the Tripartite Framework would also obviate the need for countries to continue to sign bilateral investment treaties.[94]
4. *Entrenching the regional strategy for improving the business environment*: The current strategy to improve the investment and business climate in COMESA Member States needs to be entrenched in the entire region. Establishing a country-by-country basis provides the most practicable 'project' approach. This will ensure that the identified areas for improvement in each country are targeted and reforms domesticated within the country itself. Greater emphasis on *in*-country reform is necessary to achieve further improvements in investment climate and enhance the region's attractiveness to FDI as a whole.
5. *Seizing the opportunities of the COMESA middle class*: The middle class that has emerged in Africa and in COMESA particularly suggests a number of interesting opportunities as far as FDI is concerned. Four industries, ie consumer, agriculture, resources and infrastructure, will underpin market-seeking FDI in Africa. In order to maximise the impact of the growing middle class on the flow of FDI into the region, COMESA policy makers need to fully enhance and implement regulatory strategies aimed at improving the business and economic environment to serve this middle class and take steps to ensure that members of the vulnerable middle class do not step back into poverty.

[91] TMSA Report (n 61).
[92] COMESA Report (n 45).
[93] COMESA Investment Report 2011.
[94] Ibid.

7

The Invisible MIT: The Curious Case of the Agreement for the Promotion, Protection and Guarantee of Investments among Member States of the Organisation of the Islamic Conference

*George Burn**

1. INTRODUCTION

The Organisation of the Islamic Conference (the OIC) came into being on 25 September 1969, following a summit in Rabat, Morocco. The first summit was convened to address issues of Islamic solidarity in the immediate aftermath of an arson attack on the al Aqsa Mosque in Jerusalem. It had originally been alleged that Israeli forces were responsible for the arson, but it was later established that it was the act of a non-Israeli person acting alone. Nonetheless, the incident provided the impetus for representatives of Afghanistan, Algeria, Chad, Guinea, Indonesia, Iran, Jordan, Kuwait, Lebanon, Libya, Malaysia, Mali, Mauritania, Morocco, Niger, North Yemen, Pakistan, Palestine, Saudi Arabia, Somalia, South Yemen, Sudan, Tunisia, Turkey, the United Arab Republic (Egypt and Syria) and the Muslim Community of India to meet and discuss ways in which they might collaborate for mutual benefit.

Although the original inspiration for the establishment of the OIC derived from issues of the greatest political and religious sensitivity, the States that were present in Rabat declared that henceforth 'Their Governments shall consult together with a view of promoting between themselves close cooperation and mutual assistance in the economic, scientific, cultural and spiritual

* Partner in Vinson & Elkins RLLP, based in London, gburn@velaw.com. Any views expressed are mine only, and are not to be attributed to Vinson & Elkins RLLP or anyone else.

fields, inspired by the immortal teachings of Islam.'[1] The intention therefore was for the OIC's Member States to collaborate in many fields, including in economic matters.

The membership of the OIC has evolved over time, and today stands at 57, turning it into the second-largest intergovernmental organisation after the United Nations. While the newer Member States are, for the most part, former Soviet Republics, States from Asia beyond the Middle East and from Sub-Saharan Africa, there are two States from South America and one Member from Europe.[2] It is notable that some of the OIC's Member States are not majority Muslim States. The aggregate population of the OIC Member States is around one billion people. Bearing these facts in mind, the OIC is truly a sleeping giant amongst regional international organisations.

The OIC is active in various areas, with standing committees, subsidiary and affiliated bodies, specialised institutions active in areas from social research to broadcasting, agriculture to tourism, and sports to banking. There are eight principal substantive agreements in place amongst OIC Member States that cover trade, tariffs, economic cooperation, civil aviation, telecommunications, meteorology and, the subject matter of this paper, the OIC's Agreement on the Promotion, Protection, and Guarantee of Investments (the Investment Agreement) concluded in Baghdad in 1981. The OIC has a General Secretariat comprising a Secretary-General and supporting staff, which is based in Jeddah in Saudi Arabia. The Secretary-General serves for a term of five years (renewable once) and is elected by the OIC's Council of Foreign Ministers. The current Secretary-General is His Excellency Prof Dr Ekmeleddin Ihsanoglu, from Turkey, who has held the post since 2005. Previous Secretaries-General have come from Malaysia, Egypt, Senegal, Tunisia, Pakistan, Niger and Morocco.

Of the 57 current Member States of the OIC, 34 have signed the Investment Agreement and 27 have ratified it.[3] (The OIC's published records suggest that four Member States have lodged papers confirming ratification but not signature of the Investment Agreement.) It is interesting to note that just one of the six former Soviet Republics that are Members of the OIC, Tajikistan, has signed the Investment Agreement, and none of them (including Tajikistan) has ratified it. Beyond that, the geographical spread of OIC Member States that have ratified the Investment Agreement is fairly consistent with the OIC's overall membership. Some important capital-exporting States (such as Saudi Arabia, Egypt, Turkey, Kuwait, the United Arab Emirates, Qatar and Oman) have ratified it, as have some important capital-importing

---

1 Declaration of the Rabat Islamic Summit Conference, 25 September 1969.

2 Suriname, Guyana and Albania.

3 For details, refer to <http://www.oic-oci.org/english/convenion/Accords_Eng_31_01.pdf>.

countries (including Pakistan, Indonesia, Cameroon and Sudan). It is also significant that States such as Iran, Tunisia, Lebanon, Morocco, Jordan, Syria and Libya have ratified the Investment Agreement. That said, there are some significant absentees from amongst the OIC's membership, even beyond the CIS States. For example, Algeria, Malaysia, Iraq and Nigeria are currently beyond the scope of the Investment Agreement.

The current position on signature and ratification of the Investment Agreement is summarised in the table below.

OIC Member States that have signed or ratified the Investment Agreement
Correct as of 31 January 2012

	OIC Member State	Investment Agreement	
		Signed	Ratified
1.	Afghanistan	✓	
2.	Albania	✓	
3.	Algeria		
4.	Azerbaijan		
5.	Bahrain		
6.	Bangladesh	✓	
7.	Benin		
8.	Brunei-Darussalam		
9.	Burkina-Faso		✓
10.	Cameroon	✓	✓
11.	Chad		
12.	Comoros		
13.	Côte d'Ivoire	✓	
14.	Djibouti	✓	
15.	Egypt		✓
16.	Gabon		✓
17.	Gambia	✓	✓
18.	Guinea	✓	✓
19.	Guinea-Bissau	✓	
20.	Guyana		
21.	Indonesia	✓	✓
22.	Iran	✓	✓
23.	Iraq		
24.	Jordan	✓	✓
25.	Kazakhstan		
26.	Kuwait	✓	✓
27.	Kyrgyz Republic		

(continued overleaf)

	OIC Member State	Investment Agreement	
		Signed	Ratified
28.	Lebanon	✓	✓
29.	Libya	✓	✓
30.	Malaysia	✓	
31.	Maldives		
32.	Mali		✓
33.	Mauritania		
34.	Morocco	✓	✓
35.	Mozambique		
36.	Niger		
37.	Nigeria	✓	
38.	Oman	✓	✓
39.	Pakistan	✓	✓
40.	Palestine	✓	✓
41.	Qatar	✓	✓
42.	Saudi Arabia	✓	✓
43.	Senegal	✓	✓
44.	Sierra Leone	✓	
45.	Somalia	✓	✓
46.	Sudan	✓	✓
47.	Suriname		
48.	Syria[4]	✓	✓
49.	Tajikistan	✓	
50.	Togo		
51.	Tunisia	✓	✓
52.	Turkey	✓	✓
53.	Turkmenistan		
54.	Uganda	✓	✓
55.	United Arab Emirates	✓	✓
56.	Uzbekistan		
57.	Yemen	✓	

The official languages of the OIC being Arabic, English and French, the Investment Agreement was drafted in all three languages and is equally authentic in each of them.[5] While this paper focuses on the English language version, the English text is not grammatically perfect and, in certain respects, that is relevant to the determination of States' obligations and investors'

[4] Membership currently suspended, *per* the Resolutions of the Fourth Extraordinary Islamic Summit Conference, held in Mecca, Saudi Arabia on 14–15 August 2012.

[5] Art 25 of the Investment Agreement.

rights. Reference to all the versions of the Investment Agreement is therefore important.

The objectives of the Investment Agreement are set out in its preamble in the following terms:

> The Governments of the Member States of the Organisation of the Islamic Conference signatory to this Agreement,
>
> In keeping with the objectives of the Organisation of the Islamic Conference as stipulated in its Charter,
>
> In implementation of the provisions of the Agreement for Economic, Technical and Commercial Cooperation among the Member States of the Organisation of the Islamic Conference and particularly the provisions of Article 1 of the said Agreement,
>
> Endeavouring to avail of the economic resources and potentialities available therein and to mobilize and utilize them in the best possible manner, within the framework of close cooperation among Member States,
>
> Convinced that relations among the Islamic States in the field of investment are one of the major areas of economic cooperation among these States through which economic and social development therein can be fostered on the basis of common interest and mutual benefit,
>
> Anxious to provide and develop a favourable climate for investments, in which the economic resources of the Islamic countries could circulate between them so that optimum utilization could be made of these resources in a way that will serve their development and raised the standard of living of their peoples,
>
> Have approved this Agreement,
>
> And have agreed to consider the provisions contained therein as the minimum in dealing with the capitals and investments coming in from the Member States,
>
> And have declared their complete readiness to put the Agreement into effect, in letter and in spirit, and of their sincere wish to extend every effort towards realizing its aims and objectives.

It is notable that the provision and development of a favourable climate for investments is explicitly recognised as a core objective of the Member States that have ratified the Investment Agreement.

The definitions clause of the Investment Agreement is contained in Chapter I and includes the following:

> 2. <u>CONTRACTING PARTIES</u>
>
> The Member States of the Organisation of the Islamic Conference signatories to the Agreement and in respect of which the Agreement has become effective.
>
> 3. <u>HOST STATE</u>
>
> Every contracting party in which the invested capital is present and to which it has become lawfully, or which permits the investor to comply his capital therein.
>
> 4. <u>CAPITAL</u>
>
> All assets (including everything that can be evaluated in monetary terms) owned by a contracting party to this Agreement or by its nationals, whether a natural

person or a corporate body and present in the territories of another contracting party whether these were transferred to or earned in it, and whether these be movable, immovable, in cash, in kind, tangible as well as everything pertaining to these capitals and investments by way of rights or claims and shall include the net profits accruing from such assets and the undivided shares and intangible rights.

5. <u>INVESTMENT</u>

The employment of capital in one of the permissible fields in the territories of a contracting party with a view to achieving a profitable return, or the transfer of capital to a contracting party for the same purpose, in accordance with this Agreement.

6. <u>INVESTOR</u>

The Government of any contracting party or natural corporate person, who is a national of a contracting party and who owns the capital and invests it in the territory of another contracting party. Nationality shall be determined as follows:

(a) <u>Natural Person</u>:
Any individual enjoying the nationality of a contracting party according to the provisions of the nationality law in force therein.

(b) <u>Legal Personality</u>:
Any entity established in accordance with the laws in force in any contracting party and recognized by the law under which its legal personality is established.

The definition of qualifying investors is very broad. An 'Investor' can be (i) the Government of another OIC Member State, (ii) a natural person who has qualifying nationality in an OIC Member State, and (iii) a corporate person incorporated in an OIC Member State, so long as the relevant entity is investing in the territory of another OIC Member State. There is no reference to local subsidiary companies qualifying as investors, but that would appear to be one of the few limitations on the scope of the enterprises that qualify for protection.

Articles 2 to 7 of the Investment Agreement set out various general provisions on the promotion and protection of capital and investments. The Member States that have ratified the Investment Agreement are required to do the following:

<u>Article—2</u>

The contracting parties shall permit the transfer of capitals among them and its utilization therein in the fields permitted for investment in accordance with their laws. The invested capital shall enjoy adequate protection and security and the host state shall give the necessary facilities and incentives to the investors engaged in activities therein.

<u>Article—3</u>

The contracting parties shall endeavour to open up various fields and investment opportunities to the capital on the widest possible scale, in such a way that may suit their economic conditions and on the basis of achieving mutual benefits for the parties to the investment in a way that will foster the social and economic development of the host state in accordance with its set objectives and plans while, at the same time, achieving a profitable investment return for the capital.

Article—4

The contracting parties will endeavour to offer various incentives and facilities for attracting capitals and encouraging its investment in their territories such as commercial, customs, financial, tax and currency incentives, especially during the early years of the investment projects, in accordance with the laws, regulations and priorities of the host state.

Article—5

The contracting parties shall provide the necessary facilities and grant required permits for entry, exit, residence and work for the investor and his family and for all those whose work is permanently or temporarily connected with the investment such as experts, administrators, technicians and labourers in accordance with the laws and regulations of the host state.

Article—6

The host state shall—within the provisions of its regulations and its economic and social policies—encourage the local private sector to cooperate with and participate in investments in the contracting parties.

Article—7

In the case of withdrawal of a contracting party from the Agreement, the rights and obligations arising under the Agreement in the host state towards the investor, which have accrued before the receipt of the notice of withdrawal of the contracting party shall continue and shall not be affected by the withdrawal.

Supplementing these protections is a most-favoured-nation provision in Article 8:

> Article—8
>
> The investors of any contracting party shall enjoy, within the context of economic activity in which they have employed their investments in the territories of another contracting party, a treatment not less favourable than the treatment accorded to investors belonging to another State not party to this Agreement, in the context of that activity and in respect of rights and privileges accorded to those investors.

Article 8(2) spells out certain reservations to the guarantee of most-favoured nation treatment stipulated in Article 8(1). The meaning of the term 'party to this Agreement' as used in Article 8 is not exactly clear. Notably, there is a difference between that formulation and the definition of the term "Contracting Parties" in Article 1(2) which expressly refers to Member States that have ratified the Investment Agreement. The term 'party to this Agreement', by contrast, could be read as extending to those Member States that have signed but not ratified the Investment Agreement. That could be relevant in terms of understanding the scope of the most-favoured nation treatment standard. It should also be noted that the structure of this most-favoured nation provision would exclude from consideration any bilateral investment treaties made by any Investment Agreement Member State, of which there will be many.

One striking feature of the Investment Agreement is that there is no provision setting out a promise by Member States to accord to investors and their investments fair and equitable treatment. In that context, the most-favoured nation assumes a significant position, hence it will likely be invoked to argue that the FET guarantees offered by Member States to investors from other States must also apply to investors protected by the Investment Agreement. Of course, there would be numerous other areas in which the most-favoured nation provision would come into play.

Article 9 of the Investment Agreement sets out investors' obligations to abide by local laws and regulations in force in the Host State. The inclusion of such a provision is, in itself, unusual (but certainly not unprecedented) within the spread of investment protection treaties, the main purpose of such instruments being the regulation of the behaviour of States and their agencies, rather than the behaviour of investors. Article 9 goes on to state that investors must also 'refrain from all acts that may disturb public order or morals or that may be prejudicial to the public interest [and that] [h]e is also to refrain from exercising restrictive practices and from trying to achieve gains through unlawful means.' This is an unusually broad provision: while some investment protection treaties expressly require investor compliance with national laws or mandate admission of the investment in accordance with local procedures (eg, Indonesia's treaty with the United Kingdom), the reference to investors not disturbing public order or morals and so on sets a bar that is both higher and more nebulous. Given the breadth of the formulation, one would expect this provision to feature heavily in respondents' defences to claims. However, the concepts that are wrapped into Article 9 are so vague that one would anticipate that tribunals would understand the provision to have various meanings, or none. The nature of this provision is certainly something that investors seeking to invoke the protection of the OIC Agreement would be well-advised to consider, since it almost invites States to make an Article 9 argument.

Chapter III of the Investment Agreement stipulates various 'Investment Guarantees' to be afforded to investors of contracting parties. These provisions cover expropriation (Article 10), the free transfer of funds (Article 11), disposal of ownership (Article 12), rights to compensation for misconduct by the acts of contracting parties or their subsidiary units (Article 13), rights to treatment that is at least equivalent to that accorded to nationals of the Host State or others in circumstances of international hostilities or civil disturbances (Article 14), and insurance of investments (Article 15).

The wording of the expropriation standard in Article 10 differs from the traditional language used in great many existing investment protection treaties. It states that:

1. The host state shall undertake not to adopt or permit the adoption of any measure—itself or through one of its organs, institutions or local authorities—if such a measure may directly or indirectly affect the ownership of the investor's capital or investment by depriving him totally or partially of his ownership or of all or part of his basic rights or the exercise of his authority on the ownership, possession or utilization of his capital, or of his actual control over the investment, its management, making use out of it, enjoying its utilities, the realization of its benefits or guaranteeing its development and growth.
2. It will, however, be permissible to:—
   (a) Expropriate the investment in the public interest in accordance with the law, without discrimination and on prompt payment of adequate and effective compensation to the investor in accordance with the laws of the host state regulating such compensation, provided that the investor shall have the right to contest the measure of expropriation in the competent court of the host state.
   (b) Adopt preventative measures issued in accordance with an order from a competent legal authority and the execution measures of the decision given by a competent judicial authority.

By any standards, it is clear that the provision is expressed in broad terms, covering as it does the possible direct or indirect impact of a measure, bringing within the scope of the provision those measures that *affect the ownership of the investor's capital or investment* without substantively destroying the investment or denying the investor the ability to use it. By extending protection to the total or partial deprivation of 'basic rights' as well as to the management, use and enjoyment of the investment, the expropriation standard goes well beyond the traditional focus on ownership. The provision setting out what would constitute permissible expropriation is drafted in familiar terms, and is consistent with the Hull formula that requires prompt, adequate and effective compensation. The reference to investors having the right to contest an expropriatory measure in the host State's courts is, given the terms of Articles 16 and 17 (see below), probably best understood to provide investors with a right rather than imposing an obligation to take matters to such courts.

The OIC Investment Agreement is also somewhat unique as it offers protections that are rarely found in other treaty models. For instance, Article 13 stipulates that:

1. The investor shall be entitled to compensation for any damage resulting from any action of a contracting party or one of its public or local authorities or its institutions in the following cases:—
   (a) Violation of any of the rights or guarantees accorded to the investor under this Agreement;
   (b) Breach of any of the international obligations or undertakings imposed on the contracting party and arising under the Agreement for the benefit of

the investor or the non-performance of whatever is necessary for its execution whether the same is intentional or due to negligence;

(c) Non-execution of a judicial decision requiring enforcement directly connected with the investment;

(d) Causing, by other means or an act or omission, damage to the investor in violation of laws in force in the state where the investment exists.

2. The compensation shall be equivalent to the damage suffered by the investor depending on the type of damage and its quantum.
3. The compensation shall be monetary if it is not possible to restore the investment to its state before the damage was sustained.
4. The assessment of monetary compensation shall be concluded within 6 (six) months from the date when the damage was sustained and shall be paid within a year from the date of agreement upon the amount of compensation or from the date when the assessment of the compensation has become final.

This is an interesting provision, guaranteeing compensation in various scenarios, including where a Member State has breached the terms or the Investment Agreement or other international law or local law provisions, including by reason of omission or negligence. Such a provision will offer opportunities for aggrieved investors to challenge a variety of Host State measures in a broad range of circumstances. Importantly, this provision will enable investors to challenge State measures which have traditionally been brought under the fair and equitable treatment standard. As the OIC Investment Agreement omits any references to fair and equitable treatment, Article 13 essentially provides an alternative cause of action to which investors can resort.

Dispute resolution provisions are set out in Articles 16 and 17, which merit close examination, not least given certain drafting errors in them.

Article—16

The host state undertakes to allow the investor the right to resort to its national judicial system to complain against a measure adopted by its authorities against him, or to contest the extent of its conformity with the provisions of the regulations and laws in force in its territory, or to complain against the non-adoption by the host state of a certain measure which is in the interest of the investor, and which the state should have adopted, irrespective of whether the complaint is related, or otherwise, to the implementation of the provisions of the Agreement to the relationship between the investor and the host state.

Provided that if the investor chooses to raise the complaint before the national courts or before an arbitral tribunal then having done so before one of the other two quarters he loses the right of recourse to the other.

Article—17

1. Until an Organ for the settlement of disputes arising under the Agreement is established, disputes that may arise shall be entitled through conciliation or arbitration in accordance with the following rules and procedures:—

1. Conciliation
   a) In case the parties to the dispute agree on conciliation, the agreement shall include a description of the dispute, the claims of the parties to the dispute and the name of the conciliator whom they have chosen. The parties concerned may request the Secretary General to choose the conciliator. The General Secretariat shall forward to the conciliator a copy of the conciliation agreement so that he may assume his duties.
   b) The task of the conciliator shall be confined to bringing the different viewpoints closer and making proposals which may lead to a solution that may be acceptable to the parties concerned. The conciliator shall, within the period assigned for the completion of his task, submit a report thereon to be communicated to the parties concerned. This report shall have no legal authority before a court should the dispute be referred to it.
2. Arbitration
   a) If the two parties to the dispute do not reach an agreement as a result of their resort to conciliation, or if the conciliator is unable to issue his report within the prescribed period, or if the two parties do not accept the solutions proposed therein, then each party has the right to resort to the Arbitration Tribunal for a final decision on the dispute.
   b) The arbitration procedure begins with a notification by the party requesting the arbitration to the other party to the dispute, clearly explaining the nature of the dispute and the name of the arbitrator he has appointed. The other party must, within sixty days from the date on which such notification was given, inform the party requesting arbitration of the name of the arbitrator appointed by him. The two arbitrators are to choose, within sixty days from the date on which the last of them was appointed arbitrator, an umpire who shall have a casting vote in case of equality of votes. If the second party does not appoint an arbitrator, or if the two arbitrators do not agree on the appointment of an Umpire within the prescribed time, either party may request the Secretary General to complete the composition of the Arbitration Tribunal.
   c) The Arbitration Tribunal shall hold its first meeting at the time and place specified by the Umpire. Thereafter the Tribunal will decide on the venue and time of its meetings as well as other matters pertaining to its functions.
   d) The decisions of the Arbitration Tribunal shall be final and cannot be contested. They are binding on both parties who must respect and implement them. They shall have the force of judicial decisions. The contracting parties are under an obligation to implement them in their territory, no matter whether it be a party to the dispute or not and irrespective of whether the investor against whom the decision was passed is one of its nationals or residents or not, as if it were a final and enforceable decision of its national courts.

It should be noted that there are two sub-articles enumerated in Article 17(1), which gives rise to some minor difficulties, in addition to a number of substantive questions arising from the text of Articles 16 and 17. These questions include the following:

- Does the text of Articles 16 and 17 establish that the OIC Member States consented to arbitration of disputes with protected investors?
- Given that the text of the first paragraph of Article 16 refers only to the right to take matters to national courts, are investors' dispute settlement options restricted to litigation in national courts?
- What is the 'Organ for the settlement of disputes arising under the Agreement' referred to in the first Article 17(1), has it been established and, if it has, what would that mean for investors' dispute settlement rights?
- Given the potentially contradictory wording of provisions in Article 17(1), Article 17(1)(a) and Article 17(2)(a), are investors obliged to pursue disputes through conciliation before they invoke arbitration?
- What role does the OIC's Secretary General have in the process, and what happens if he or she fails or refuses to appoint an arbitrator when requested?
- With regard to recognition and enforcement as addressed in Article 17(2)(d), what is 'the decision [that] was passed'? Is it the original decision that prompted the complaint by the investor, or is it the decision of arbitrators?

2. HAVE OIC MEMBER STATES CONSENTED TO ARBITRATION OF DISPUTES WITH PROTECTED INVESTORS?

The drafting of the Investment Agreement is imperfect, in particular in its English version, there is no wording clearly stating that investors may invoke arbitration as a means of enforcing their substantive rights. Article 17(1) goes some way towards addressing the point by stipulating that 'disputes that may arise shall be entitled through conciliation or arbitration in accordance with the following rules and procedures'. Clearly, something went wrong with the drafting of this part of the Investment Agreement since the provision, when read in its entirety, does not make sense; how can a dispute be entitled to do anything? In any event, what it is supposedly entitled to do is missing. Fortunately, the French language version has been drafted more carefully. It provides that:

> En attendant la création d'un organisme le règlement des litiges résultant de cet Accord, les litiges qui pourraient de présenter seront règlès [sic] par conciliation ou par voie d'arbitrage conformément aux règles suivantes [...].

That translates into English roughly as follows:

> Pending the creation of a dispute settlement organ under this Agreement, any dispute which may arise will be resolved by conciliation or arbitration in accordance with the following rules [...].

This strongly suggests that the OIC Member States did indeed consent to arbitration of disputes with investors, and that such investors can bring direct arbitration under the Investment Agreement.[6] An offer to arbitrate disputes is set out in Article 17 (albeit in defective terms in the English language version) and, with the ratification of the Investment Agreement, that offer is made by the OIC Member States to all qualifying investors. That, it is submitted, is consistent with the objective of the Investment Agreement 'to provide and develop a favourable climate for investments, in which the economic resources of the Islamic countries could circulate between them so that optimum utilization could be made of these resources in a way that will serve their development and raise the standard of living of their peoples.' Affording investors opportunities to enforce their rights in a manner that is reliable, neutral and direct is a vital component of a favourable climate for investments.[7] The necessity to take all such disputes to national courts, with no choice and no recourse to independent arbitration, will always be less attractive for investors. The purpose of the Investment Agreement is to facilitate investment flows between and amongst OIC Member States, as part of the project of mutual development and economic solidarity. Ensuring that foreign investors have an effective device for the enforcement of substantive rights is of fundamental importance to the success of investment treaties, of which the Investment Agreement is one (albeit unusual) example.

Debates may arise as to whether the arbitral process envisaged by Articles 16 and 17 is intended to be limited to disputes amongst the OIC Member States themselves, and should not be read as extending to investors the right to initiate arbitration directly against Host States. Anecdotally, that would appear to have been the working assumption in the OIC Secretariat. However, the text of Articles 16 and 17 renders this argument unconvincing. Article 17 is a standalone provision on ad hoc arbitration. The provision consistently refers to 'parties to the dispute' (without, however, defining the term) whereas throughout the rest of the Investment Agreement the terms 'contracting parties' and 'host state' are used. Clearly, had the OIC Member States intended the arbitral procedure in Article 17 to be limited to state-to-state disputes, they would have used the appropriate

---

[6] The Arabic version of the same text in the Investment Agreement apparently bears out the reading of the French language version, but since I do not read or speak Arabic, I will not comment further on it.

[7] Preamble of the Investment Agreement.

language in Article 17 and referred to 'contracting parties', not 'parties to the dispute'. Furthermore, the definition of the term 'Investor' in Article 6 expressly draws the distinction between 'the Government of any contracting party' or 'natural [or] corporate person'. Article 16 anticipates that Host States will allow any one of the types of investor referred to in Article 6 to choose between litigation and arbitration as the means to pursue complaints.

Although the text of the Investment Agreement is marred by imperfections, the drafting and the intent underlying its dispute settlement provisions are clear: arbitration under the Investment Agreement is not limited to claims or complaints brought by States against other States, and investors are entitled to institute arbitration directly against Member States.

3. ARE INVESTORS' RIGHTS RESTRICTED TO THE RIGHT TO PURSUE MATTERS IN HOST STATE COURTS?

The first paragraph of Article 16 refers only to the right to take matters to national courts, which might be read as suggesting that investors' options are limited to pursuing grievances under the Investment Agreement only in local courts. That interpretation could be said to be fortified by the (defective) English text of the first Article 17(1) and perhaps even by Article 10(2)(a) stating that 'the investor shall have the right to contest the measure of expropriation in the competent court of the host state'. However, the second paragraph of Article 16 expressly stipulates a fork in the road choice for the investor: 'if the investor chooses to raise the complaint before the national courts or before an arbitral tribunal then having done so before one of the other two quarters he loses the right of recourse to the other.' Even without analyzing Article 17(1) to understand the true meaning obscured by the errors in the English version of the text, it is submitted that the fork in the road provision in Article 16 puts beyond doubt that investors have a choice of forum: they can choose to take their disputes either to national courts or to arbitration.

4. WHAT IS THE 'ORGAN FOR THE SETTLEMENT OF DISPUTES ARISING UNDER THE AGREEMENT', HAS IT BEEN ESTABLISHED, AND WHAT WOULD BE THE EFFECT IF IT HAS?

The 'organ for the settlement of disputes arising under the Agreement' is a term that is not explained or defined in the Investment Agreement. This is a matter of great significance for understanding investors' rights under the Investment Agreement as the opening phrase of Article 17 is the only limitation on investors' ability to initiate conciliation or arbitration proceedings.

In order to uncover the meaning of the reference to 'organ for the settlement of disputes', one must look at other OIC documents, in particular the Charter of the OIC[8] (the OIC Charter). Article 5 of the OIC Charter lists the organs of the OIC, which would include an International Islamic Court of Justice. Article 14 of the OIC Charter provides that 'The International Islamic Court of Justice established in Kuwait in 1987 shall, upon the entry into force of its Statute, be the principal judicial organ of the Organisation'. A number of questions arise from this text:

(i) The use of the past tense ('established') suggests that the International Islamic Court of Justice is in existence, and yet there is no sign of such a Court; there is no website (nor reference on the OIC website), there is no postal address, fax number or telephone number, there is no court building, there is no secretariat or judiciary, there is no case law. So, has it been established or not?

(ii) The text of the OIC Charter anticipates that the Statute of the International Islamic Court of Justice has not yet (at least as of 2008) entered into force, and yet a Draft Statute was approved in January 1987.[9] Article 49 of the Draft Statute states that it will not come into force unless ratified by a two-third majority of the Member States.

(iii) There is nothing in the OIC Charter or in the Draft Statute approved in 1987 explicitly stating whether the International Islamic Court of Justice is intended to be the 'Organ for the settlement of disputes arising under the Agreement' referred to in Article 17(1) of the Investment Agreement.

(iv) There is nothing in the OIC Charter explicitly stating whether the International Islamic Court of Justice is intended to deal with State-to-State disputes, or whether it would also have jurisdiction to deal with disputes brought directly by investors against States. However, Article 21 of the Draft Statute expressly states that the jurisdiction of the International Islamic Court of Justice will (if and when it becomes operational) be limited to State-to-State disputes.

(v) The Draft Statute provides that the International Islamic Court of Justice shall be composed of seven judges; however, judges have not been elected and a registrar has not been appointed.

---

[8] Signed with the establishment of the OIC on 25 September 1969 and amended on 14 March 2008.

[9] OIC Resolution No. 13/5-P (IS), adopted by the Fifth Islamic Summit Conference, held in Kuwait on 26–29 January 1987.

(vi) A note on the Investment Agreement stipulates that 'the setting up of a dispute settlement organ will surely enhance the degree of confidence to guarantee the investment promotion and better capital movement'.[10] The note confirmed that the International Islamic Court of Justice did not constitute the organ for the settlement of disputes as referred to in Article 17, and confirmed that such organ does not exist.

The picture is a confusing one, but it is beyond debate that the International Islamic Court of Justice, if it has been established at all, has been established only in name. For this reason alone, it cannot be considered as the 'organ for the settlement of disputes arising under the Agreement' as leaving investors to enforce their rights before a non-operational, functionally non-existent court would contradict the substantive and procedural protections the Member States sought to provide to each other's investors, and would frustrate other objectives set out in the Preamble to the Investment Agreement.

Assuming that the Draft Statute approved in 1987 is adopted if and when the International Islamic Court of Justice commences its work, it is clear that the International Islamic Court of Justice will not be competent to deal with investor-State disputes. At present, there is nothing to suggest that the OIC has plans for the establishment of such a court.

5. ARE INVESTORS OBLIGED TO PURSUE DISPUTES THROUGH CONCILIATION BEFORE THEY INVOKE ARBITRATION?

A literal reading of Article 17(2)(a) seems to suggest that the unsuccessful completion of a conciliation process is a prerequisite to arbitration under the Investment Agreement. There is no reference to circumstances where the disputing parties will not have embarked on conciliation at all. Thus, the text appears to have been drafted on the assumption that there would have been a prior process of conciliation in respect of the dispute:

> If the two parties to the dispute do not reach an agreement as a result of their resort to conciliation, or if the conciliator is unable to issue his report within the prescribed period, or if the two parties do not accept

[10] Note on the Agreement on Investment Promotion, Protection and Guarantee, which was concluded between the OIC member states and presented by The Islamic Centre for Development of Trade to the 25th Session of the Standing Committee for Economic and Commercial Co-operation of the OIC (COMCEC) in Istanbul–Republic of Turkey on 5–7 November 2009.

the solutions proposed therein, then each party has the right to resort to the Arbitration Tribunal for a final decision on the dispute.

There is certainly room for an argument that conciliation is a prerequisite to the investor's recourse to arbitration. However, such an argument contradicts the choices the investor is expressly afforded under the Investment Agreement, including the right to pursue the dispute in national courts (Article 16 and Article 10(2)(a)), resort to conciliation (Article 17(1)) or arbitration (the first Article 17(1) and second paragraph of Article 16). If read as a whole and in conjunction with other provisions of the Investment Agreement, Article 17 appears to offer resort to conciliation as an option in the hands of the investor, not an obligation. While the Agreement's silence as to circumstances where there is no conciliation process is unfortunate, the only way to make sense of the text in its entirety and to give effect to all of it is to read the reference to conciliation as being non-binding and not being a prerequisite to arbitration.

6. WHAT ROLE DOES THE OIC'S SECRETARY GENERAL HAVE IN THE PROCESS?

The Secretary General's role in respect of arbitration brought under the Investment Agreement is clear: where the process for the constitution of a tribunal fails for some reason, the Secretary General is meant to fill the gap by appointing an arbitrator or umpire. However, assumptions in this regard ought not to be made; the Secretariat in Jeddah (and therefore one assumes also the Secretary General) have proceeded to date in ignorance of the possibility of investor-State arbitration being brought under the Investment Agreement. Under the Investment Agreement, the Secretary General does not have any role beyond the appointment of an arbitrator or umpire (where such a need arises by reason of a failure to appoint an arbitrator by the State or an umpire by the two party-appointed arbitrators). So, unlike under the ICSID Arbitration Rules, the Secretary General has no power to screen requests for arbitration. This means that, whatever the Secretary General and the OIC Secretariat assume to be a tribunal's jurisdiction under the OIC Investment Agreement, they have no power and no right to refuse to do anything other than appoint an arbitrator or umpires when requested to do so. Jurisdiction (including as regards investors' rights to initiate arbitration directly against OIC Member States under the OIC Investment Agreement) is a matter for the tribunal to determine. Therefore, there is a real danger that, where there is a failure of the dispute resolution process set out in Article 17(2), it may be compounded rather than alleviated with a reference to the Secretary General. Given that there has now been one confirmed award on jurisdiction,[11] views at the Secretariat may develop. It is certainly to be hoped that they will; if they do not, there is a very real risk that investors' rights will be frustrated and one of the objectives of the OIC Agreement will not be realised.

7. RECOGNITION AND ENFORCEMENT UNDER ARTICLE 17(2)(D): WHAT IS 'THE DECISION [THAT] WAS PASSED'?

The wording of Article 17(2)(d) provides another example of imperfect drafting in the Investment Agreement:

> The contracting parties are under an obligation to implement [the tribunal's decisions] in their territory, no matter whether it be a party to the dispute or not and irrespective of whether the investor against whom the decision was passed is one of its nationals or residents or not, as if it were a final and enforceable decision of its national courts.

There is a degree of ambiguity as regards what exactly is 'the decision [that] was passed'. There are at least two ways the term can be read: either the decision in question is the original decision of the Host State that gave rise to the investor's complaint (eg the decision to expropriate an investment), or it is a decision against the investor from within the arbitration itself, that is to say a positive ruling on a counterclaim made against the investor by the respondent-State.

There is no reference to counterclaims in the Investment Agreement, their admissibility in investor-State arbitration remaining a matter of considerable debate. Instead, all claims are assumed to be brought by the investor against the Host State. The phrase in Article 17(2)(d) is therefore significant, particularly given that its ambiguity could be exploited to the advantage of respondent-States. However, such a reading would appear to be unsupported by the wording of the Agreement: had Article 17(2)(d) been drafted on the basis that there would be counterclaims against an investor, one would surely expect provisions considerably less oblique than this. Had it been the shared intent of the OIC Member States to provide for enforceability of awards against investors, the wording of the Agreement would be expected to support such interpretation.

More importantly, a reading of the whole of Article 17(2)(d) strongly suggests that the relevant provision refers back to the State's original decision

---

[11] *Al Warraq v Republic of Indonesia*, dated 21 June 2012. The Tribunal comprises Bernardo Cremades (President, Spain), Fali Nariman SC (India) and Michael Hwang SC (Singapore).

breaching investor rights. The purpose of the provision is to regulate the enforcement and recognition of arbitrators' decisions, making clear that they are to be binding as if they were final judgments of national courts and without any recourse against them being possible, whether by way of review, appeal or any other post-award process. Thus, the provision does not aim to address issues of admissibility or arbitral procedure (these matters are addressed in Articles 17(2)(a)–(c). As Article 17(2)(d) deals with post-arbitration matters, it is most doubtful that it can be read as also extending to issues outside the scope of the post-arbitration phase.

8. CONCLUSION

It is remarkable that the OIC Investment Agreement has garnered so little attention to date, despite the fact it has been in existence for more than 40 years. Perhaps one cause of its low profile is the fact that the text of the Investment Agreement was not even posted on the OIC website until 2008. Beyond its inclusion in an UNCTAD compendium in 1996,[12] the extent of the Agreement's coverage in legal scholarship seems to have been restricted to the occasional references such as that in a 1987 academic paper on the OIC generally,[13] a 1993 study of multilateral investment treaties by Ibrahim Shihata (then Secretary General of ICSID),[14] an article in the ICSID Review in 1997 written by Antonio R Parra (then Deputy Secretary General of the ICSID),[15] a paper delivered by an Egyptian lawyer, Mohamed Madkour, to a 2011 Arab League conference on investment between Arab countries[16] and a recent article by the respected Tunisian jurist, Walid Ben Hamida.[17]

While the text of the Investment Agreement may be imperfect in various areas, the mere possibility of a multilateral investment treaty ratified by 27

---

12 *Volume II of International Investment Instruments: A Compendium*, published by UINCTAD in 1996.

13 Appendix III of *The Charter of the Islamic Conference and Legal Framework of Economic Co-operation among its Member States*, H Moinduddin (1987). Frank E Vogel reviewed the Moinduddin book (83 *American Journal of International Law* 1).

14 Ibrahim Shihata's study of 25 multilateral instruments entitled *Legal Treatment of Foreign Investment: the World Bank guidelines* (1993).

15 AR Parra, 'Provisions on the Settlement of Investment Disputes in Modern Investment Laws', *Bilateral Investment Treaties and Multilateral Instruments on Investment*, 12 *ICSID Review Foreign Investment Law Journal* 2 (1997). The article includes comments on the consent to arbitration in Article 17.

16 M Madkour *The dispute settlement mechanism under OIC agreement*, a paper submitted to a 2011 Arab League conference on investment between Arab countries.

17 WB Hamida, 'A Fabulous Discovery: The Arbitration Offer under the Organization of Islamic Cooperation Agreement Related to Investment' 30 *Journal of International Arbitration* 6 (2013) 637.

States ought to have made the Investment Agreement the focus of considerable attention before now.

Greater knowledge of, and reliance on, the Investment Agreement will no doubt be aided by the fact that there have been at least one arbitral award confirming a tribunal's jurisdiction to hear claims brought by an investor under the Investment Agreement. In *al Warraq v the Republic of Indonesia*, a panel of arbitrators made a positive ruling on jurisdiction in what appears to be a first investor-state dispute brought under the Investment Agreement. The positive ruling on jurisdiction will give comfort to many who were uncertain whether investors could directly invoke the protections set out in the Investment Agreement. Given the Investment Agreement's provision for ad hoc arbitration, there may have been other such decisions; but anecdotally, the suggestion is that the *al Warraq* case is the first to reach the stage of a tribunal ruling on jurisdiction in respect of investors' right to bring arbitration directly.

With investment flows between countries in the Middle East, South-East Asia, Sub-Saharan Africa and North Africa on the rise, it seems inevitable that the Investment Agreement will be the focus of greater attention in the future. And so it should be: it could play an important role in facilitating investment flows, and in providing investors from OIC Member States with valuable protections. Governments of the Member States could benefit from advertising the promises made in the Investment Agreement, so as to convince more investors to make investments, and investors would do well to bear in mind the protections that have been afforded to them.

8

Regional Investment Treaty Arrangements in the Caribbean: Developments and Implications

*Chantal Ononaiwu**

A. INTRODUCTION

Caribbean countries have entered into bilateral investment treaty arrangements, most frequently as standalone investment agreements but also as investment chapters in free trade agreements. However, they are also parties to or in the process of elaborating investment treaty arrangements at the regional level. This Chapter examines two such arrangements. The first is an investment agreement being developed within the context of a broader effort at regional economic integration among the countries of the Caribbean Community (CARICOM)—the draft CARICOM Investment Code. The second is the much discussed free trade agreement concluded in 2004 between the Dominican Republic, five Central American countries and the United States—the CAFTA-DR.

In addition to exploring the motivations behind these regional investment agreements, the Chapter will examine their key features and compare them to the bilateral investment agreements involving CARICOM countries and the Dominican Republic. Finally, the Chapter will assess the implications of these regional agreements for the investment treaty programme of CARICOM countries and the Dominican Republic and developments in the Caribbean more generally.

* Trade Policy and Legal Specialist, Office of Trade Negotiations, Caribbean Community (CARICOM) Secretariat, chantal.ononaiwu@crnm.org. The views expressed are solely the author's and do not necessarily represent those of the CARICOM Secretariat or its staff.

B. THE DRAFT CARICOM INVESTMENT CODE

1. Background

CARICOM is a regional organisation of fifteen Caribbean countries,[1] which was constituted originally by the 1973 Treaty of Chaguaramas establishing the Caribbean Community and Common Market. Economic integration under the original treaty was deepened by the 2001 Revised Treaty of Chaguaramas establishing the Caribbean Community including the CARICOM Single Market and Economy.[2]

A central aim of the Revised Treaty is the creation of a fully integrated internal market. In addition to the free movement of goods, the free provision of services and the free movement of skilled nationals, the Revised Treaty addresses the right of establishment of CARICOM nationals and the free movement of capital. Community nationals are afforded the right of establishment, which includes the right to create and manage economic enterprises.[3] The removal of restrictions on the right of establishment extends to restrictions on the movement of managerial, technical and supervisory staff of economic enterprises and on establishing agencies, branches and subsidiaries of legal entities established in the Community.[4] The Treaty also prohibits new restrictions and mandates the removal of existing restrictions on the movement of capital payments and current transactions.[5]

At a more general level, non-discrimination is a guiding principle of the Revised Treaty. Any discrimination on the grounds of nationality is prohibited with respect to matters within the scope of application of the Treaty.[6]

---

[1] Antigua and Barbuda, The Bahamas, Barbados, Belize, Dominica, Grenada, Guyana, Haiti, Jamaica, Montserrat, St Kitts and Nevis, St Lucia, St Vincent and the Grenadines, Suriname and Trinidad and Tobago.

[2] The Revised Treaty of Chaguaramas entered into force on 1 January 2006. All Members of CARICOM, except for The Bahamas and Montserrat, are parties to the Revised Treaty <http://www.caricom.org/jsp/community/revised_treaty-text.pdf>.

[3] Art 32 prohibits new restrictions on the right of establishment and art 33 mandates the removal of existing restrictions on that right. Art 32(5) defines a national of a Member State as:

> (i) a natural person who is a citizen of that State or has a connection with that State which entitles him to be regarded as belonging to, a native or a resident of that State; or
>
> (ii) an entity constituted under the laws of that State which has its registered office and central administration and carries on substantial activity within the Community and which is substantially owned and effectively controlled by natural persons who are CARICOM nationals.

[4] Ibid, art 35(c) and (d).

[5] Ibid, arts 39 and 40.

[6] Ibid, art 7.

Further, Members of CARICOM are required, with respect to any rights covered by the Treaty, to accord to each other treatment no less favourable than that accorded to third States.[7]

These treaty guarantees are important to the facilitation of cross-border investments in CARICOM. However, the Revised Treaty contemplates the adoption of a host of other measures to support the realization of the CARICOM Single Market and Economy (CSME). Among the common supportive measures mandated by the Treaty is the formulation of a Community investment policy, including a harmonized system of incentives.[8] The draft CARICOM Investment Code is being developed as part of the process of elaborating the Community's investment policy. It is intended to be an agreement among CARICOM Members that creates a common regime for the protection, promotion and facilitation of investment in CARICOM. A harmonized system of incentives is not a part of the draft Code. However, recommendations have been made for the introduction of a framework agreement for the harmonization of such incentives.

2. *Objectives and Key Features*[9]

The objectives of the draft CARICOM Investment Code include attraction of investment from investors of CARICOM Members and third countries, greater cross-border investment and reinvestment in CARICOM, and transparency and predictability in the treatment of investment in CARICOM.

The CARICOM Investment Code is intended to build on the existing guarantees in the Revised Treaty, such as the right of Community nationals to establish enterprises and the free movement of capital. Given that the Code is intended to address more broadly the treatment of investments of investors of CARICOM Members, the investments within the scope of application of the draft Code extend beyond enterprises. As with standard investment treaties, the draft Code elaborates the obligations of a host Party concerning the treatment of investors of another Party and their investments. These include obligations concerning national treatment, most favoured nation (MFN) treatment, the minimum standard of treatment, performance requirements, the appointment of key personnel, transfers, expropriation and compensation and compensation for losses resulting from war or civil strife. These core protection provisions are important given that they largely do not feature in the Revised Treaty and there are no bilateral investment treaties (BITs) between CARICOM countries.

---

[7] Ibid, art 8.

[8] Ibid, arts 68 and 69.

[9] As the draft text of the Code is not publicly available, its key features will be outlined but its provisions will not be discussed in detail.

The draft Code also elaborates measures to promote and facilitate investment flows as well as measures to ensure that investment supports economic development, in particular those to promote the corporate social responsibility of investors. In addition, it is contemplated that the Code will feature provisions to address the needs of the less developed countries of CARICOM.[10] This accords with the regime under the Revised Treaty granting special and differential treatment for disadvantaged countries, regions and sectors.[11]

Also included in the draft Code are mechanisms for the settlement of disputes between investors and host Parties and disputes between the Parties. In that regard, the draft Code draws on the dispute settlement framework elaborated under the Revised Treaty.[12] This framework provides for a range of mechanisms for the settlement of disputes between Member States, including adjudication before the Caribbean Court of Justice.[13] Significantly, the Revised Treaty also permits private entities to bring disputes with Member States before the Caribbean Court of Justice.[14]

In addition to an intra-regional framework for the protection, promotion and facilitation of investment, CARICOM countries also are developing a template to guide the negotiation of investment provisions in the

[10] Art 4 of the Revised Treaty distinguishes between the Less Developed Countries (LDCs) and More Developed Countries (MDCs) of CARICOM. The LDCs are designated as Belize, Haiti and Members of the Organization of Eastern Caribbean States (OECS), namely, Antigua and Barbuda, Dominica, Grenada, Montserrat, St Kitts and Nevis, St Lucia and St Vincent and the Grenadines. The MDCs are identified as The Bahamas, Barbados, Guyana, Jamaica, Suriname and Trinidad and Tobago.

[11] Chapter Seven of the Revised Treaty establishes a regime for disadvantaged countries, regions and sectors as well as a special regime for the LDCs which aims to assist them towards becoming economically viable and competitive by appropriate interventions of a transitional or temporary nature. The Chapter provides for a range of measures, including technical and financial assistance.

[12] Ibid, Chapter Nine.

[13] Disputes between Member States concerning the interpretation and application of the Revised Treaty may be settled by good offices, mediation, consultations, conciliation, arbitration and adjudication. The Caribbean Court of Justice has compulsory and exclusive jurisdiction under art 211 to determine disputes concerning the interpretation and application of the Revised Treaty.

[14] Art 222 of the Revised Treaty allows natural and legal persons of a Member State, with special leave of the Court, to bring proceedings against Member States where four conditions are satisfied. First, the Treaty intended that a right or benefit conferred on a Member State shall enure to the benefit of such persons directly. Second, the persons have been prejudiced in respect of the enjoyment of that right or benefit. Third, the person's Member State has omitted or declined to espouse the claim before the Court, or expressly agreed that the person may espouse the claim. Finally, the Court has found that the interest of justice requires that the person be allowed to espouse the claim.

Community's external trade agreements. The Revised Treaty requires Member States to coordinate their trade policy with third States and envisages the Community's pursuit of the negotiation of external trade agreements on a joint basis.[15] While the template is intended to be used as a base text for negotiations on investment in a trade agreement, it can also serve as a reference in the negotiation of bilateral investment treaties by individual CARICOM countries.

3. *Comparison with Bilateral Agreements involving CARICOM Countries*

All Members of CARICOM, except The Bahamas, St Kitts and Nevis and Montserrat, have signed bilateral investment treaties.[16] Between two and five BITs each have been concluded by Antigua and Barbuda,[17] Dominica,[18] Grenada,[19] Haiti,[20] St Lucia,[21] St Vincent and the Grenadines[22] and Suriname.[23] At least seven BITs each have been signed by Barbados,[24] Belize,[25] Guyana,[26] Jamaica[27] and Trinidad and Tobago[28]; the latter two countries have each concluded more than ten such agreements.

In addition, investment provisions feature in external trade agreements concluded by CARICOM countries, namely, CARICOM's bilateral trade

---

[15] Ibid, art 80.

[16] The texts of most of these BITs can be accessed from UNCTAD's International Investments Agreements (IIA) database http://unctad.org/en/pages/DIAE/International%20Investment%20Agreements%20(IIA)/IIA-Tools.aspx.

[17] The United Kingdom (1987) and Germany (1998).

[18] Germany (1984) and the United Kingdom (1987).

[19] The United States (1986) and the United Kingdom (1988).

[20] Germany (1973), the United States (1983), France (1984), the United Kingdom (1985) and the Dominican Republic (1999).

[21] The United Kingdom (1983) and Germany (1985).

[22] Germany (1986) and Taiwan (2009).

[23] Indonesia, (1995), Cuba (1999) and the Netherlands (2005).

[24] The United Kingdom (1993), Venezuela (1994), Germany (1994), Italy (1995), Switzerland (1995), Canada (1996), Cuba (1996), China (1998), Mauritius (2004) and Belgium-Luxembourg (2009).

[25] The United Kingdom (1982), Cuba (1998), Taiwan (1999), Austria (2001), El Salvador (2001), the Netherlands (2002) and Italy (2005).

[26] Germany (1989), the United Kingdom (1989), Cuba (1999), China (2003), Switzerland (2005), Korea (2006), Indonesia (2008) and Kuwait (2010).

[27] The United Kingdom (1987), Switzerland (1990), the Netherlands (1991), Germany (1992), France (1993), Italy (1993), Argentina (1994), China (1994), the United States (1994), Cuba (1997), Egypt (1999), Indonesia (1999), Zimbabwe (1999), Nigeria (2002), Spain (2002) and Korea (2003).

[28] France (1993), the United Kingdom (1993), the United States (1994), Canada (1997), Cuba (1999), Spain (1999), China (2002), Korea (2002), Mexico (2006) and India (2007).

agreements with Costa Rica,[29] Cuba[30] and the Dominican Republic,[31] and the Economic Partnership Agreement (EPA) between the CARIFORUM States and the European Union.[32] Investment is also within the scope of the Trade and Development Agreement being negotiated between CARICOM and Canada.[33]

Several key differences exist between the draft CARICOM Investment Code and the existing bilateral investment treaty arrangements involving CARICOM countries. First, the draft CARICOM Investment Code forms part of an intra-regional framework for investment which accords rights of establishment. As mentioned earlier, CARICOM nationals are guaranteed the right of establishment under the Revised Treaty, which aims more broadly to create a single market. In contrast, most of the bilateral investment treaty arrangements do not grant pre-establishment rights. Exceptions are the bilateral investment treaties which some CARICOM countries have concluded with Canada and the United States. Those agreements accord pre-establishment rights, subject to limited reservations.[34] In addition, the CARIFORUM-EU EPA includes scheduled commitments on market access and national treatment with respect to a commercial presence in services and non-services activities.[35]

---

[29] The Agreement was signed on 9 March 2004 and has entered into force between Costa Rica and Barbados (1 August 2006), Guyana (30 April 2006) and Trinidad and Tobago (15 November 2005). Chapter X includes obligations concerning the promotion and protection of investment <http://www.sice.oas.org/trade/crcrcom_e/crcrcomind_e.asp>.

[30] The Agreement was signed on 5 July 2004 and is being provisionally applied between Cuba and Belize, Guyana, Jamaica, St. Kitts and Nevis, St. Vincent and the Grenadines and Trinidad and Tobago. Pursuant to art 17, CARICOM and Canada concluded an Agreement on Reciprocal Promotion and Protection of Investment, which forms an integral part of the trade agreement <http://www.caricom.org/jsp/secretariat/legal_instruments/agreement_caricom_cuba_investments.jsp?menu=secretariat>.

[31] The Agreement was signed on 22 August 1998 and entered into force for Barbados (1 December 2001), the Dominican Republic (5 February 2002), Guyana (6 October 2004), Jamaica (1 December 2001), Trinidad and Tobago (1 December 2001) and Suriname (August 2005). Annex III contains an Agreement on the Reciprocal Promotion and Protection of Investment <http://www.sice.oas.org/Trade/Ccdr/English/Ccdr_in.asp>.

[32] All Members of CARICOM (except Montserrat) and the Domincan Republic are parties to the EPA, which was signed in October 2008 by all countries except Haiti which signed on 11 December 2009. The Agreement has been applied provisionally since 29 December 2008. The investment provisions in Chapter 2 of Title II apply only to measures affecting a commercial presence and are concerned primarily with liberalization, rather than investment protection <http://www.sice.oas.org/Trade/CAR_EU_EPA_e/careu_in_e.ASP>.

[33] CARICOM and Canada launched negotiations in November 2009, after which three other rounds of negotiations have been held to date.

[34] For example, art II of the BITs between the US and Grenada, Jamaica and Trinidad and Tobago, as well as art II of the BITs between Canada and Barbados and Trinidad and Tobago, guarantee national treatment and MFN treatment with respect to the pre-establishment phases, subject to the right to make exceptions.

[35] Arts 67–69 and Annex IV.

Second, in contrast to most of the bilateral agreements, the draft CARICOM Investment Code and the draft template for investment provisions in trade agreements reflect the more recent treaty practice of focusing and clarifying the scope of investor protection, with a view to balancing more effectively investor protection with the Host State's right to regulate in the public interest. In the draft template, this has been done through making key treaty provisions, such as the definition of investment, more focused and specifying further the content of or providing guidance for the interpretation of investor protection obligations.

These elements are virtually absent in the bilateral investment agreements of CARICOM countries, the overwhelming majority of which were concluded more than a decade ago. For example, the bilateral agreements do not specify the characteristics of an investment and typically do not feature any specific exclusions from that definition. In addition, these agreements often do not provide any clarification of the content of fair and equitable treatment[36] or the parameters of what constitutes indirect expropriation. If the draft template is adopted and in fact used by CARICOM countries in future negotiations, careful consideration will need to be given to the terms of any MFN treatment provision that is negotiated as it could result in the incorporation of standards of protection in earlier treaties.

A third important difference is that the draft CARICOM Investment Code contains provisions that aim specifically to ensure that investment supports economic development. These include measures to promote and facilitate investment flows, measures to promote corporate social responsibility of investors and provisions addressing differences in the levels of development of the Parties. Such provisions rarely feature in the existing bilateral investment agreements of CARICOM countries. One exception is the CARIFORUM-EU EPA. This Agreement includes provisions addressing the behaviour of investors and the maintenance of standards. Specifically, the EPA requires the Parties to cooperate and take any necessary domestic measures to ensure that investors are forbidden from and held liable for bribing public officials, act in accordance with core labour standards to which the Parties have subscribed, do not operate and manage their investments in a manner that circumvents the Parties' international environmental and labour obligations, and have in place, where appropriate, local community liaison processes.[37] The Agreement also requires the Parties to ensure that foreign direct investment is not encouraged by lowering domestic environmental, labour or health and safety standards or by relaxing core labour standards or

---

[36] Exceptions are the BITs with France and Canada, which require fair and equitable treatment in accordance with 'principles of international law', and the BITs with the United States, which call for fair and equitable treatment in accordance with "international law".

[37] Art 72.

laws aimed at protecting and promoting cultural diversity.[38] In addition, the EPA features provisions affording special and differential treatment to the CARIFORUM States, such as different MFN treatment obligations for the Parties,[39] and provisions concerning cooperation, including technical assistance, training and capacity building in areas such as enhancing the capacities of CARIFORUM investment promotion agencies.[40]

C. CAFTA-DR

The Dominican Republic is a party to a regional trade agreement with the United States and five Central American countries, namely, Costa Rica, El Salvador, Guatemala, Honduras and Nicaragua.[41] The Central American Dominican Republic Free Trade Agreement (CAFTA-DR) represented a transition from the unilateral trade preference programmes of the Caribbean Basin Initiative to reciprocity in the trading relationship with the United States. The Dominican Republic commenced negotiations with the United States one year after the negotiations with the Central American countries had been launched. Its participation in the FTA was motivated heavily by the desire to secure a more permanent trading arrangement with the United States, the most important market for its exports, and to avoid the loss of a share of that market to the Central American nations, which would have received enhanced preferences for their goods and services.[42]

The Agreement was also regarded by the United States as a means of expanding economic opportunities, integrating markets, advancing regional

---

[38] Art 73. See also art 188 in the Chapter on the Environment and art 193 in the Chapter on Social Aspects.

[39] Art 79. The MFN treatment obligation of the EU extends to more favourable treatment granted to investors and commercial presences of any third country under future economic integration agreements. In contrast, the MFN treatment obligation of the CARIFORUM States applies only to more favourable treatment granted to investors and commercial presences of any 'major trading economy' under future economic integration agreements. The term 'major trading economy' is defined as a developed country, any country accounting for more than 1% of global merchandise trade or any group of countries accounting for more than 1.5% of global merchandise trade. If a CARIFORUM State does in fact grant more favourable treatment, the Parties must enter into consultations and may decide whether the State may deny such treatment.

[40] Art 121.

[41] The Agreement was signed on 5 August 2004 and entered into force for El Salvador and the United States on 1 March 2006, Honduras and Nicaragua on 1 April 2006, Guatemala on 1 July 2006, the Dominican Republic on 1 March 2007 and Costa Rica on 1 January 2009 <http://www.sice.oas.org/Trade/CAFTA/CAFTADR_e/CAFTADRin_e.asp>.

[42] DJ García Rojas 'DR-CAFTA: Understanding the Reasons why the Dominican Republic joined the CAFTA Negotiations' (MA Thesis Naval Postgraduate School Monterey California June 2009) 91–92 <http://www.dtic.mil/dtic/tr/fulltext/u2/a501777.pdf>.

integration, supporting democracy and economic reform in the Central American countries and the Dominican Republic and contributing to greater peace and stability in the region. It was also considered to be an important vehicle for advancing the United States' trade agenda in the Western Hemisphere, as a means of providing momentum to the Free Trade Area of the Americas, and also at the multilateral level in the World Trade Organization (WTO).[43]

The CAFTA-DR features a comprehensive chapter on Investment,[44] which was viewed as important to guaranteeing a secure, predictable legal framework for US investors operating in the Dominican Republic and Central American countries. The FTA is also viewed by the United States as improving transparency and removing barriers to investment in the Dominican Republic and Central American countries.[45] The investment provisions in the Agreement largely were modelled on, or influenced by the United States' experience with, the Investment Chapter of the North American Free Trade Agreement (NAFTA).[46]

1. *Key Features of the Investment Chapter*

(a) *Scope and Coverage*

The Investment Chapter in the CAFTA-DR applies broadly to a Party's measures relating to investors of another Party and covered investments (that is, investments of investors of another Party). Certain obligations, namely, those concerning performance requirements and investment and environment apply to a Party's measures relating to all investments in its territory.[47] A wide range of assets fall within the definition of investment. Every asset that an investor owns or controls, directly or indirectly, is an investment as long as it has the 'characteristics of an investment', including the 'commitment of capital or other resources, the expectation of gain or profit, and the assumption of risk'. A non-exhaustive list of assets that may qualify as an investment is provided, namely, an enterprise; shares, stock and other forms of equity participation in an enterprise; loans and debt instruments; derivatives; turnkey, construction, management, production, concession, revenue-sharing and

---

[43] 'Statement of Why the Dominican Republic–Central America–United States Free Trade Agreement is in the Interests of US Commerce' 2–3, <http://waysandmeans.house.gov/media/pdf/109cong/dr-cafta/caftastatementofbenefits-final-0608053.pdf>.

[44] Chapter Ten.

[45] Statement of Benefits (n 43) 17.

[46] For a comparison of the investment provisions in the NAFTA and CAFTA-DR, see D Gantz 'Settlement of Disputes under the Central America–Dominican Republic–United States Free Trade Agreement' 30 *Boston College International and Comparative Law Review* (2007) 331.

[47] Art 10.1.1.

other similar contracts; intellectual property rights; licences, authorizations, permits and similar rights conferred under domestic law; and other tangible or intangible, movable and immovable property, and related property rights, such as leases, mortgages, liens and pledges.[48]

There are a few specific exclusions from the scope of covered investments. Claims to payment that are immediately due and result from the sale of goods or services are not covered.[49] Licences, authorizations, permits and similar instruments that do not create any rights protected under domestic law are not regarded to have the characteristics of an investment.[50] An order or judgment entered in a judicial or administrative action is similarly excluded.[51] Public debt has not been excluded. However, the rescheduling of the debts of a Central American Party or the Dominican Republic owed to the United States or creditors in general are subject only to the national treatment and MFN treatment obligations.[52] In addition, a United States investor can only subject a claim to arbitration relating to an investment in sovereign debt instruments with a maturity of less than one year if one year has elapsed from the date of the events giving rise to the claim.[53]

An investor of a Party is also defined broadly to be a Party, a State enterprise of a Party, or a national or enterprise of a Party that attempts to make, is making, or has made an investment in another Party. However, a dual national is deemed to be exclusively a national of the State of dominant and effective nationality.[54] In addition, a Party has the discretion to deny the benefits of the Chapter to an enterprise constituted under the laws of another Party if the enterprise has no substantial business activities in any Party other than the denying Party and it is owned or controlled by persons of a third country or the denying Party. A Party may also deny benefits to an enterprise of another Party if it is owned or controlled by persons of a third country and the denying Party does not maintain diplomatic relations with that country or it takes measures with respect to that country that prohibit transactions with the enterprise or that would be violated if the benefits were granted.[55] In *Pac Rim Cayman v El Salvador*, an arbitral tribunal has found that there is no express time-limit in the CAFTA-DR for a Party to elect to deny benefits and upheld a Party's election to deny benefits after the commencement of arbitration.[56]

---

48 See the definition of the term 'investment' in art 10.28.

49 Footnote 9 to art 10.28.

50 Footnote 10 to art 10.28.

51 Footnote 11 to art 10.28

52 Annex 10-A.

53 Annex 10-E.

54 See the definition of the term 'investor of a Party' in art 10.28.

55 Art 10.12.

56 *Pac Rim Cayman LLC v El Salvador*, ICSID Case No ARB/09/12, Decision on Jurisdiction (1 June 2012) [4.83]–[4.90].

The obligations of the Chapter apply not only to measures by the government, but also to a State enterprise or other person when it exercises any governmental authority delegated to it by a Party.[57] In accordance with the principle of non-retroactivity in the law of treaties, the Chapter does not bind any Party in relation to any act or fact that occurred or situation that ceased to exist before the entry into force of the Agreement.[58] Notably, a CAFTA-DR tribunal has found that 'an omission that extends over a period of time and which, to the reasonable understanding of the relevant party, did not seem definitive' should be regarded as a 'continuous act' under international law.[59] As a result, where such a continuous act existed before the entry into force of the Agreement but also existed thereafter, the Chapter could apply to the portion of the continuous act that lasted after the Agreement's entry into force.

The Investment Chapter does not apply to a Party's measures to the extent that they are covered by the Chapter on Financial Services.[60] The Financial Services Chapter[61] applies to a Party's measures relating to financial institutions, investors of the other Party and their investments in financial institutions. That Chapter creates a distinct framework for investments in financial services, by limiting the application of certain investor protection obligations in the Investment Chapter, as well as the claims that can be submitted to investor-State dispute settlement.

(b) Host State Obligations

National treatment, MFN treatment and the minimum standard of treatment

Investment protection obligations are elaborated in Section A of the Chapter. National treatment and MFN treatment must be accorded to investors of the other Party and their investments which are 'in like circumstances' as domestic investors and investments or investors and investments of a non-Party. These non-discrimination obligations apply with respect to both the pre-establishment and post-establishment phases.[62]

Covered investments must be granted the customary international law minimum standard of treatment of aliens, including fair and equitable treatment and full protection and security.[63] The CAFTA-DR features several clarifications which are intended to guide the interpretation of this obligation

57 Art 10.1.2.
58 Art 10.1.3.
59 *Pac Rim* (n 56) [2.92].
60 Art 10.2.3.
61 Chapter Twelve.
62 Arts 10.3 and 10.4.
63 Art 10.5.

and limit the risk of an expansive interpretation by tribunals. First, the concepts of 'fair and equitable treatment' and 'full protection and security' do not require treatment in addition to or beyond that which is required by the customary international law minimum standard of treatment of aliens, and do not create additional substantive rights. Second, the obligation to provide 'fair and equitable treatment' includes the obligation not to deny justice in criminal, civil or administrative adjudicatory proceedings in accordance with the principle of due process embodied in the principal legal systems of the world. The obligation to provide 'full protection and security' requires the provision of the level of police protection required under customary international law. Third, a determination of a breach of another provision of the Agreement or of a separate international agreement, does not establish a breach of the obligation to grant the minimum standard of treatment.

Finally, 'customary international law' is understood by the Parties to result from a general and consistent practice of States that they follow from a sense of legal obligation. The customary international law minimum standard of treatment of aliens is specified to be all customary international law principles that protect the economic rights and interests of aliens.[64] The reference to customary international law may not be effective in reducing the risk of an expansive interpretation of the standard given that this source of law evolves. Indeed, in *Railroad Development Corporation v Guatemala,* an arbitral tribunal under the CAFTA-DR opined that the minimum standard of treatment is 'constantly in a process of development' and presently proscribed 'arbitrary, grossly unfair, unjust or idiosyncratic' conduct. This interpretation of the content of the standard went beyond that advanced by the Parties to the Agreement.[65]

Treatment in cases of strife, expropriation and transfers

The Chapter requires non-discriminatory treatment of investors of another Party and their investments with respect to measures relating to losses arising from armed conflict or civil strife. Restitution or compensation is required if the investor's investment is requisitioned or destroyed by government forces to an extent not required by the necessity of the situation.[66]

The CAFTA-DR prohibits direct or indirect expropriation except where the expropriation is made for a public purpose, in a non-discriminatory

---

[64] Annex 10-B.

[65] ICSID Case No. ARB/07/23, Award (29 June 2012) [218] and [219]. The CAFTA-DR Parties had argued that the customary international law minimum standard of treatment was still represented by the standard set out in the 1927 *Neer* case, namely, conduct amounting to an outrage, bad faith, wilful neglect of duty or insufficiency of action that was egregious.

[66] Art 10.6.

manner, on payment of prompt, adequate and effective compensation and in accordance with due process of law.[67] The Chapter provides guidelines for the payment of compensation[68] and elaborates the Parties' understanding of expropriation,[69] which can guide the interpretation and application of the provision. The Parties specified that the basic obligation concerning expropriation in the Chapter is intended to reflect customary international law.[70] They further clarified that an action or series of actions only constitutes expropriation if it interferes with a property right or property interest in an investment.[71]

Importantly, the Parties set out their shared understanding of 'indirect expropriation'.[72] This is explained as an action or series of actions by a Party that has an effect equivalent to direct expropriation without formal transfer of title or outright seizure. The Chapter also specifies that the determination of what constitutes indirect expropriation requires a case-by-case, fact-based inquiry considering factors such as the economic impact of the government action, the extent to which the government action interferes with distinct, reasonable investment-backed expectations and the character of the government action. In addition, the fact that a Party's actions have an adverse effect on the economic value of an investment does not, of itself, establish an indirect expropriation. Moreover, except in rare circumstances, a Party's non-discriminatory regulatory actions that are designed and applied to protect legitimate public welfare objectives, such as public health, safety, and the environment, do not constitute indirect expropriations. The Chapter also provides that compulsory licensing in a manner consistent with the WTO Agreement on Trade-related Aspects of Intellectual Property Rights (TRIPS Agreement) does not amount to an expropriation.[73] These clarifications seek to safeguard the Host State's ability to regulate in pursuit of important public policy objectives, by ensuring that such regulatory measures are not considered to be expropriations.

The Parties are required to permit all inward and outward transfers relating to a covered investment to be made freely and without delay.[74] Transfers subject to this obligation include contributions to capital; profits, dividends,

---

[67] Art 10.7.1.

[68] Art 10.7.2–4. Payment of compensation must be made without delay, be equivalent to the fair market value of the investment immediately before it was expropriated, and be fully realizable and freely transferable in a freely usable currency or at the market rate of exchange, plus interest at a commercially reasonable rate.

[69] Annex 10-C.

[70] Ibid [1].

[71] Ibid [2].

[72] Ibid [4].

[73] Art 10.7.5.

[74] Art 10.8.1.

capital gains and proceeds from the sale or liquidation of the covered investment; interest, royalty payments, management fees and technical assistance and other fees; payments made under a contract; payments made pursuant to the provisions on compensation for losses and expropriation; and payments arising out of a dispute. Transfers are to be permitted in a freely usable currency at the market rate of exchange at the time of transfer, and returns in kind pursuant to an agreement must be permitted.[75] However, the Chapter does permit certain restrictions on transfers. A Party may prevent transfers through the equitable, non-discriminatory, and good faith application of its laws relating to bankruptcy, insolvency or the protection of the rights of creditors; issuing, trading, or dealing in securities, futures, options or derivatives; criminal or penal offences; financial reporting or recordkeeping necessary to assist law enforcement or financial regulatory authorities; and ensuring compliance with orders of judgments in judicial or administrative proceedings.[76]

Performance requirements and appointment of senior management and boards of directors

The CAFTA-DR constrains the use of certain performance requirements in connection with the establishment, acquisition, expansion, management, conduct, operation or disposition of any investment in a Party's territory.[77] The Investment Chapter bars the imposition of requirements to export a given level of goods or services; achieve a given level of domestic content; purchase goods locally; relate import volume or value to exports or foreign exchange inflows associated with the investment; restrict domestic sales based on export volume or value or foreign exchange earnings; transfer technology or exclusively supply certain markets. In addition, the receipt of an advantage may not be conditioned on requirements to achieve a given level of domestic content; purchase goods locally; relate import volume or value to exports or foreign exchange inflows associated with the investment and restrict domestic sales based on export volume or value or foreign exchange earnings.

However, performance requirements are permitted in specified circumstances. The Parties are allowed to condition receipt of an advantage on requirements to locate production, supply a service, train or employ workers, construct or expand particular facilities or carry out research and development, in its territory. Moreover, technology transfer requirements are allowed in instances of compulsory licensing and disclosure of proprietary information consistent with the TRIPS Agreement, or in order to remedy anti-competitive

---

75 Art 10.8.2 and 10.8.3.

76 Art 10.8.4.

77 Art 10.9.

practices. Certain performance requirements may also be permitted exceptionally where necessary to secure compliance with laws and regulations not inconsistent with the Agreement, to protect human, animal or plant life or health, or related to the conservation of living or non-living exhaustible natural resources, provided they are not applied in an arbitrary or unjustifiable manner, and do not constitute a disguised restriction on international trade or investment. Certain prohibited performance requirements also do not apply to qualification requirements with respect to export promotion and foreign aid programmes, procurement, and rules of origin for preferential tariffs or preferential quotas.

The Investment Chapter also governs the use of nationality or residence requirements in connection with senior management and boards of directors. Investors may not be required to appoint to senior management positions persons of any particular nationality. However, investors may be subject to a requirement that a majority of the board of directors be of a particular nationality or residents, provided the requirement does not materially impair the investor's ability to exercise control over its investment.[78]

Investment and environment, labour and corruption

The Chapter affords the Parties the latitude to take appropriate measures to ensure that investment activity is undertaken in a manner sensitive to environmental concerns. However, such measures must be otherwise consistent with the Chapter.[79] Notably, there are provisions in other Chapters of the Agreement which address not only the interface between investment and the environment, but also investment and labour and corruption. The Chapter on Environment imposes an obligation on each Party to 'strive to ensure' that it does not reduce the protections afforded in domestic environmental laws in order to encourage the establishment, acquisition, expansion or retention of investment.[80] A similar obligation concerning the maintenance of domestic labour standards features in the Chapter on Labour.[81] In addition, the Chapter on Transparency requires the Parties to take measures to stem the corruption of local and foreign public officials with respect to matters affecting international trade and investment. In particular, there are obligations to take measures establishing specified acts of bribery or corruption as criminal offences, the commission of which is liable to sanctions, and to endeavour to take measures to protect informants.[82]

---

[78] Art 10.10.

[79] Art 10.11.

[80] Art 17.2.2.

[81] Art 16.2.2.

[82] Art 18.8.

Exceptions and reservations for non-conforming measures

The CAFTA-DR permits reservations for measures that do not conform with certain obligations, namely, those pertaining to national treatment, MFN treatment, performance requirements, and senior management and boards of directors.[83] Reservations may be scheduled in Annex I for existing non-conforming measures that are maintained at the central and regional government level.[84] Existing non-conforming measures at the local government level may be maintained without the need for scheduling. The Agreement features both a standstill and 'ratchet' mechanism, whereby existing non-conforming measures can be changed only in order to increase their conformity with the relevant obligation. Additionally, the Parties may take existing and future non-conforming measures with respect to sectors, subsectors or activities, as set out in their schedules to Annex II.[85] However, such future measures cannot require an investor of the other Party, by reason of its nationality, to dispose of an existing investment.

Moreover, specific exceptions are provided for certain obligations.[86] In respect of intellectual property rights, exceptions are provided for measures that are permitted derogations from the national treatment obligation under the Chapter on Intellectual Property Rights. Additionally, the obligations pertaining to national treatment, MFN treatment and senior management and boards of directors to not apply to procurement, or government subsidies or grants.

The Parties are allowed to prescribe special formalities in connection with covered investments, such as a requirement that investors be residents or that covered investments be legally constituted under domestic law, provided that such formalities do not materially impair the investor protections under the Chapter. The Parties are also permitted to require investors to provide information concerning their investment solely for informational or statistical purposes, subject to the protection of confidential business information.[87]

---

[83] Art 10.13.

[84] The Dominican Republic listed reservations pertaining to a range of sectors, including mining, audio-visual services, broadcasting, newsagency services, distribution services, maritime and air transportation, oil exploitation and exploration services, and fishing.

[85] The Dominican Republic reserved the right to adopt or maintain non-conforming measures with respect to, inter alia, government finances, social services and socially and economically disadvantaged groups.

[86] Art 10.13.4.

[87] Art 10.14.

(c) *Investor-State Dispute Settlement*

Submission of claims to arbitration

In addition to the mechanism for the settlement of disputes between the Parties,[88] CAFTA-DR features a detailed mechanism for investor-state arbitration.[89] The parties to an investment dispute are encouraged to initially seek to resolve the dispute through consultation and negotiation, which may include non-binding third party procedures such as conciliation and mediation.[90] If consultation and negotiations are unsuccessful, the investor (on its own behalf or on behalf of an enterprise it owns or controls) may submit to arbitration a claim that the respondent Party has breached an obligation under Section A and that it (or the enterprise) has suffered loss or damage as a result of that breach. Significantly, investor-state arbitration is also available to enforce certain contractual rights as claims may also be submitted in respect of alleged breaches of an 'investment authorization' or 'investment agreement'.[91]

Arbitration is available under the International Centre for the Settlement of Investment Disputes (ICSID) Convention and the ICSID Arbitration Rules, the ICSID Additional Facility Rules, or under the United Nations Commission on International Trade Law (UNCITRAL) Arbitration Rules.[92] Since the Dominican Republic is not a Party to the ICSID Convention, only the ICSID Additional Facility Rules and the UNCITRAL Arbitration Rules are available in the case of disputes initiated by Dominican investors or against the Dominican Republic.

CAFTA-DR Parties consented in advance to the submission of a claim to arbitration in accordance with the Agreement.[93] However, the Agreement specifies a number of preconditions for an investor's submission of a claim. First, the investor must have delivered to the respondent State notice of its intention to submit the claim to arbitration at least 90 days in advance.[94] Second, at least six months must have elapsed since the events giving rise to the claim.[95] Third, more than three years must not

---

88 Chapter Twenty.

89 Section B.

90 Art 10.15.

91 Art 10.16.1. Art 10.28 defines an 'investment authorization' as an authorization that a Party's foreign investment authority grants to a covered investment or investor of another Party. An 'investment agreement' is defined as a written agreement, which takes effect after the entry into force of the FTA, between a national authority (that is, one at the central government level) and a covered investment or investor of another Party that grants rights with respect to natural resources or assets that a national authority controls and upon which the investment or investor relies in establishing or acquiring a covered investment.

92 Art 10.16.3.

93 Art 10.17.1.

94 Art 10.16.2.

95 Art 10.16.3.

have elapsed since the claimant first acquired, or should have first acquired, knowledge of the alleged breach and knowledge that the claimant (or enterprise) has suffered loss or damage.[96] Fourth, the claimant must consent in writing to arbitration.[97]

Further, the claimant (or enterprise) must waive the right to initiate or continue before any local administrative tribunal or court, or other dispute settlement procedures, any proceeding with respect to the disputed measure. An arbitral tribunal has clarified that this requires the claimant not only to file a formal 'written waiver' but also to materially ensure that no other legal proceedings are initiated or continued.[98] This 'no-u-turn' provision does not extend to actions seeking interim injunctive relief and not involving the payment of monetary damages.[99] For US investors, there is a 'fork in the road' provision which precludes them from submitting a claim to arbitration concerning a breach of an obligation under Section A if they (or an enterprise) have alleged that breach in proceedings before a local court or administrative tribunal.[100] In addition, claims concerning an alleged breach of an investment authorization or investment agreement cannot be submitted to arbitration if the claimant has previously submitted the same alleged breach to an administrative tribunal or court of the respondent state, or to any other binding dispute settlement procedure, for adjudication or resolution.[101]

Conduct of Arbitration

The Investment Chapter contains detailed procedural rules concerning the conduct of arbitration. Generally, the arbitral tribunal is to comprise three arbitrators, one appointed by each disputing Party and the third, who serves as presiding arbitrator, is appointed by agreement of the parties. If the tribunal is not constituted within 75 days of submission of the claim to arbitration, the ICSID Secretary-General, at the request of a disputing Party, appoints any arbitrator or arbitrators not yet appointed.[102] Where the Parties fail to reach agreement on the legal place of arbitration, the tribunal, in accordance with the applicable arbitral rules, determines the place of arbitration, which must be in a country which is Party to the New York Convention on the Recognition and Enforcement of Foreign Arbitral Awards.[103]

---

[96] Art 10.18.1.

[97] Art 10.18.2.

[98] *Commerce Group Corp. and San Sebastian Gold Mines Inc. v El Salvador*, ICSID Case No. ARB/09/17, Jurisdiction Award (14 March 2011) [84].

[99] Arts 10.18.2 and 10.18.13.

[100] Annex 10-E.

[101] Art 10.18.4.

[102] Art 10.19.

[103] Art 10.20.1.

The CAFTA-DR specifies the governing law for arbitral tribunals.[104] In respect of claims concerning the treaty obligations, the tribunal is to apply the Agreement and applicable rules of international law. In relation to claims relating to alleged breaches of an investment agreement or investment authorization, the tribunal is to apply the rules of law specified in the agreement or authorization, or as the disputing Parties may otherwise agree, or if the rules of law have not been specified or otherwise agreed, the law of the respondent State and applicable rules of international law. Importantly, the FTA includes mechanisms that enable the Parties to make important determinations concerning the interpretation of the Agreement. The Free Trade Commission, the main institutional body established under the Agreement, is empowered to adopt an interpretation of a provision of the Agreement.[105] Also, the Commission may be requested to provide an interpretation of the Annexes scheduling reservations for non-conforming measures, where the respondent State has asserted as a defence that the disputed measure is within the scope of the Annex.[106] Any interpretation by the Free Trade Commission is binding on arbitral tribunals, and any decision or award issued by the tribunal must be consistent with that decision.[107]

A tribunal is empowered to appoint experts to report on any factual issue concerning environmental, health, safety or other scientific matters raised by a disputing Party in the proceedings.[108] Tribunals may order interim measures of protection to preserve the rights of a disputing party, or to ensure that the tribunal's jurisdiction is made fully effective, such as orders to preserve evidence in the possession or control of a disputing Party or orders to protect the tribunal's jurisdiction.[109] A respondent State is not allowed to assert as a defence, counterclaim, or right of set-off that the investor has received or will receive compensation for the alleged damages under an insurance contract.[110]

The CAFTA-DR includes provisions concerning preliminary objections and consolidation of claims which seek to promote the efficient conduct of arbitral proceedings. A tribunal is required to address and decide as a preliminary question any objection by the respondent that the claim submitted is not a claim for which an award in favour of the claimant may be made. A preliminary objection must be submitted to the tribunal as soon as possible after the tribunal is constituted and the tribunal must suspend any proceedings on the

---

104 Art 10.22.
105 Art 19.1.3(c).
106 Art 10.23.1.
107 Arts 10.22.3 and 10.23.2.
108 Art 10.24.
109 Art 10.20.8.
110 Art 10.20.7.

merits in order to consider the objection.[111] Where requested by the respondent within 45 days after the tribunal is constituted, the tribunal must decide a jurisdictional objection on an expedited basis.[112] The tribunal is empowered to award to the prevailing Party reasonable costs and attorney's fees incurred, having considered whether the claim or objection was frivolous.[113] The Agreement also allows a disputing Party to seek consolidation of separately submitted claims which have a question of law or fact in common and arise out of the same events or circumstances. Consolidation may be ordered by a specially constituted tribunal if it is satisfied that it is in the interest of fair and efficient resolution of the claims.[114]

The Agreement also contains mechanisms designed to enhance the transparency of arbitral proceedings. A non-disputing Party may make oral and written submissions to the tribunal regarding interpretation of the Agreement.[115] The tribunal is empowered to accept and consider *amicus curiae* submissions from any person or entity that is not a disputing Party.[116] Further, the respondent State is to transmit to the non-disputing Parties and make available to the public certain documents, namely, the notice of intent; notice of arbitration; pleadings, memorials and briefs submitted by a disputing party to the tribunals and any *amicus curiae* submissions or submissions by a non-disputing Party; any available minutes or transcripts of hearings; and orders, awards and decisions of the tribunal.[117] Also, hearings are to be open to the public.[118] However, provision is made for safeguards to protect confidential business information or information that is protected from disclosure under a Party's law.[119]

Awards

CAFTA-DR includes an interim review mechanism, under which a disputing Party may request the tribunal to transmit its proposed decision or award on liability in advance for the comments of the disputing Parties. The tribunal is required to consider any such comments before issuing its decision or award.[120] Final awards against a respondent State are limited to only monetary damages and any applicable interest, and restitution of property, in lieu of which monetary damages and interest may be paid. A tribunal is also

111 Art 10.20.4.
112 Art 10.20.5.
113 Art 10.20.6.
114 Art 10.25.
115 Art 10.20.2.
116 Art 10.20.3.
117 Art 10.2.1.
118 Art 10.2.2.
119 Art 10.2.4.
120 Art 10.20.9.

empowered to award costs and attorney's fees.[121] Tribunals are not authorized to award punitive damages.[122]

Awards are final and binding for the Parties to the dispute.[123] Enforcement of a final award may only be sought if 120 days has elapsed in the case of an award under the ICSID Convention, or 90 days has elapsed in the case of an award under the ICSID Additional Facility Rules or the UNCITRAL Arbitration rules, and no disputing Party has requested revision or annulment under the ICSID Convention or commenced court proceedings to revise, set aside or annul the award under the other two sets of rules. Enforcement may also be sought if any revision or annulment proceedings have been completed, or a court has dismissed or allowed an application to revise, set aside or annul the award and there is no further appeal.[124] Each Party is to provide for the enforcement of an award in its territory. In addition, provision is made for the investor to ask its Home State to request the establishment of an arbitral panel under the State-to-State dispute settlement procedures if the respondent State fails to comply with a final award. The Home State may seek a determination that the failure to comply with the award is inconsistent with the Agreement and a recommendation that the respondent State comply with the final award.[125] This does not prevent the investor from seeking enforcement of the award under the ICSID Convention, the New York Convention or Inter-American Convention on Commercial Arbitration.[126]

A notable innovation of the CAFTA-DR is that it contemplates the establishment of an appellate body or similar mechanism to review awards by tribunals, with a view to providing coherence to the interpretation of the investment provisions in the Agreement.[127] The Free Trade Commission was mandated, within three months of entry into force of the Agreement, to establish a Negotiating Group to develop such a mechanism, taking into account issues such as composition, scope and standard of review, transparency of proceedings, the effect of decisions, relationship to the applicable arbitral rules and domestic laws and international law on enforcement of arbitral awards. The Commission is to provide a draft amendment to the Agreement within one year of establishment. Alternatively, if a separate multilateral agreement establishes an appellate body to review awards of investor-state tribunals, the Parties are to strive to agree to the review by that

[121] Art 10.26.1.
[122] Art 10.26.3.
[123] Art 10.26.4.
[124] Art 10.26.6.
[125] Art 10.26.8.
[126] Art 10.26.10.
[127] Annex 10-F.

body of awards rendered by tribunals under the FTA.[128] These provisions notwithstanding, the Parties have made no progress towards this goal to date.

2. *Comparison with the Dominican Republic's Bilateral Agreements*

The Dominican Republic has concluded sixteen bilateral investment treaties,[129] and investment provisions feature in several of its bilateral trade agreements, namely, its FTAs with Central America[130] and CARICOM[131] and the CARIFORUM-EU Economic Partnership Agreement.[132] Key differences exist between the CAFTA-DR and these bilateral agreements.[133]

One important difference is that most of the Dominican Republic's bilateral agreements, unlike the CAFTA-DR, do not attempt to focus or clarify the scope or content of investor obligations. For example, none of those agreements specifies the characteristics of an investment and most do not feature exclusions from the definition of investment. An exception is the FTA with Central America, which specifically excludes state debt and claims to money arising solely out of commercial contracts.[134] Additionally, the Dominican Republic's bilateral agreements do not provide clarifications of the content of key standards or concepts, such as fair and equitable treatment and indirect expropriation. Exceptions are the BIT with France[135] and the FTAs with CARICOM[136] and Central America,[137] which prescribe that fair and equitable treatment or the minimum standard of treatment must be granted in accordance with international law. Additionally, these agreements do not set out detailed procedural mechanisms for investor-State dispute

128 Art 10.20.10.

129 Spain (1995); Ecuador (1998); Cuba (1999); France (1999); Taiwan (1999); Haiti (1999); Chile (2000); Argentina (2001); Finland (2001); United Kingdom (2002); Morocco (2002); Panama (2003); Switzerland (2004); Italy (2006); the Netherlands (2006); Korea (2006). The texts of some of these agreements are available on UNCTAD's IIA database (n 16).

130 This FTA with Costa Rica, El Salvador, Guatemala, Honduras and Nicaragua was signed on 16 April 1998. It has entered into force for Costa Rica (7 March 2002), El Salvador (4 October 2001), Guatemala (3 October 2001), Honduras (19 December 2001) and Nicaragua (3 September 2002). Chapter IX of the Agreement addresses Investment <http://www.sice.oas.org/trade/camdrep/indice.asp>.

131 See n 30.

132 See n 31.

133 For an overview of the Dominican Republic's investment treaty arrangements, see F Medina Garnes 'Dominican Republic' in JC Hamilton OE García-Bolívar and H Otero (eds) *Latin American Investment Protection: Comparative Perspectives on Laws, Treaties and Disputes for Investors, States and Counsel* (Leiden Martinus Nijhoff 2012) 219–44.

134 See definition of investment in art 9.01.

135 Art 3.

136 Art 9.03.1.

137 Art IV of Annex III.

settlement which address issues such as transparency of arbitral proceedings, preliminary objections, consolidation and appellate review of arbitral awards.

Another difference is that the reach of some of the investment provisions in the CAFTA-DR is greater than that of the Dominican Republic's bilateral investment agreements. For instance, the CAFTA-DR grants pre-establishment rights while most of the bilateral agreements afford protection only to the investments which have been made in accordance with domestic law. One exception, as discussed above, is the CARIFORUM-EU EPA which includes liberalization commitments concerning commercial presences. Also, the CAFTA-DR imposes far more constraints on the use of performance requirements than do the Dominican Republic's bilateral agreements, most of which do not include provisions specifically directed at performance requirements. While the FTAs with CARICOM[138] and Central America[139] feature a specific provision on performance requirements, this provision does not prohibit performance requirements beyond those proscribed by the TRIMS Agreement. Further, the scope of investor-state dispute arbitration under the CAFTA-DR extends expressly to certain contractual rights while such contractual claims are not covered expressly by investor-state dispute settlement under the Dominican Republic's bilateral investment agreements.

In addition, most of the Dominican Republic's bilateral agreements, unlike the CAFTA-DR, do not address the relationship between investment and labour, environment and corruption. One exception is the FTA with Central America, which includes in the Investment Chapter a similar provision as that in the Investment Chapter of CAFTA-DR which safeguards the Parties' ability to address environmental concerns.[140] Another is the CARIFORUM-EU EPA which, as discussed above, features provisions on the maintenance of standards and the behaviour of investors.

D. IMPLICATIONS OF REGIONAL INVESTMENT AGREEMENTS IN THE CARIBBEAN

The CAFTA-DR will likely influence the content of future investment treaties negotiated by the Dominican Republic. The intra-regional investment framework being developed in CARICOM could have a similar impact on the treaty-making programme of CARICOM countries. Moreover, the draft CARICOM Investment Code and the draft CARICOM template for investment provisions in trade agreements can serve to encourage greater policy coherence in the investment agreements concluded by CARICOM countries. The template in particular may also serve to encourage some individual countries to revisit or

[138] Art VII of Annex III.
[139] Art 9.07.
[140] Art 9.15.

re-examine their existing agreements, with a view to enhancing their development dimension and avoiding unforeseen consequences, particularly in investor-State dispute settlement.

By virtue of their influence on the investment treaty programme of participating countries, regional investment treaty arrangements can contribute to greater global convergence in the formulation of certain treaty provisions. In this regard, it is notable that the CARIFORUM-EU EPA mandates the Parties to review, within three years of entry into force of the Agreement and periodically thereafter, the investment legal framework consistent with commitments in international agreements, with a view to the progressive liberalization of investments.[141] In view of the fact that the EU now has exclusive competence over foreign direct investment,[142] it is possible that the operation of this review mechanism could result in the elaboration of investment protection disciplines in the Agreement. The regional investment treaty arrangements involving the Dominican Republic and CARICOM countries may prove to be influential on any further development of the investment rules in the EPA.

The operation of the CAFTA-DR is also likely to contribute to the development of greater capacity in the Dominican Republic to handle investment disputes. The country has already been a party to investor-state arbitration under the Agreement. In 2008, US investors TCW Group and Dominican Energy Holdings submitted a claim under the UNCITRAL Arbitration Rules alleging wrongful conduct on the part of the government in relation to their indirect holdings in the electric distribution company Empresa Distribuidora de Electricidad del Este. The claimants alleged that the Dominican Republic had breached several of its obligations under Chapter Ten of the CAFTA-DR, owing to its failure to pay compensation for tariffs and subsidies and to enforce laws governing the electricity sector, including those criminalizing theft of electricity. The claimants sought over US$600 million, interest and costs.[143] This case, along with parallel cases which were initiated under a BIT and before the International Court of Arbitration,[144] was settled in 2009.[145]

---

141 Art 74.

142 See art 207 of the Treaty on the Functioning of the European Union. The Lisbon Treaty, which entered into force on 1 December 2009, made foreign direct investment the exclusive competence of the EU.

143 *TCW Group and Dominican Energy Holdings v Dominican Republic,* Amended Notice of Arbitration and Statement of Claim, 17 June 2008.

144 *Société Générale in respect of DR Energy Holdings Ltd and Empresa Distribuidora de Electricidad del EsteSA v Dominican Republic* (LCIA Case No. UN 7927), submitted under the France–Dominican Republic BIT; *Empresa Distribuidora de Electricidad del Este SA v Corporación Dominicana de Empresas Eléctricas Estatales, como sucesora de la Corporación Dominicana de Electricidad* (ICC Case No. 15749/JRF).

145 *TCW Group and Dominican Energy Holdings v Dominican Republic*, Consent Award, 16 July 2009.

Later, in 2011, US nationals petitioned unsuccessfully the Office of the United States Trade Representative (USTR) to initiate an investigation under Section 301 of the Trade Act of 1974 into an alleged breach by the Dominican Republic of its obligations under Chapter Ten of the CAFTA-DR, by reason of its denial of compensation for alleged expropriations of their father's property in the early 1960s. In deciding not to initiate the investigation, the USTR indicated that such allegations would be addressed more effectively through investor-state dispute settlement of the Agreement.[146] It is significant that, following its signature of the CAFTA-DR, the Dominican Republic designated a national authority for the management of disputes arising from its free trade and investment agreements.[147]

The availability of the Caribbean Court of Justice as a forum for the settlement of investment disputes could also foster greater recourse to international dispute settlement and contribute to the development in CARICOM of legal expertise and regional jurisprudence in the subject area.

E. CONCLUSION

The draft CARICOM Investment Code and CAFTA-DR differ in important respects from the majority of the bilateral investment agreements which have been concluded by CARICOM countries and the Dominican Republic respectively. These regional investment treaty arrangements are likely to influence future investment treaty negotiations in which these countries engage, including the possible elaboration of investment protection disciplines in their Economic Partnership Agreement with the EU. The operation of these agreements is also likely to result in the development of greater capacity in these countries to manage and resolve investment disputes.

Regional investment treaty arrangements, by virtue of their influence on the future investment treaty programme of the participating countries, can contribute to greater global convergence in the crafting of treaty standards. However, some issues lend themselves to the development of solutions at the regional level, particularly where they are being addressed in the context of a broader initiative at regional economic integration.

---

[146] Federal Register, Vol. 76, No.136, Friday 15 July 2011, at 41857–41858.

[147] Decree No. 610-07 of 23 October 2007, establishing as the National Coordinating Authority the Foreign Trade Directorate in the Ministry of Industry and Commerce.

9

Regionalization Trends and Foreign Investment in South America: The Implications of the ALBA and UNASUR Initiatives

*José Manuel García Represa**

The Bolivarian Alliance for the Peoples of Our America and Union of South American Nations initiatives are the most recent attempts at regional integration in South America. Will they be more relevant to foreign investment than the other regionalization initiatives in the continent—such as the Andean Community of Nations and the Southern Common Market—have hitherto been? This article explains why the ALBA and UNASUR initiatives, especially the latter, are set to be of much greater significance to foreign investment than the prior regional integration initiatives. This prospect considers both the principles underlying the integration within ALBA as well as the potential economic influence of the integrated area under UNASUR. It will further discuss the various ways in which the ALBA and UNASUR initiatives may shape foreign investment in the region, with a particular focus on investment protection and dispute settlement. UNASUR, in particular, is considering the creation of an alternative to the ICSID dispute settlement system. The ultimate success of a credible regional dispute settlement mechanism will depend not only on the governing rules and their perceived balance of interests but also on whether the UNASUR member States pursue their integration efforts and do not stop short of a fully-fledged free trade area.

* Partner, Dechert (Paris) LLP, jose-manuel.garciarepresa@dechert.com. The views expressed herein are personal and by no means characterize the views of Dechert or its clients, including various Latin American States that Dechert is honoured to represent.

I. INTRODUCTION

South America is not an exception to the ongoing regionalization trends witnessed worldwide. Within the last 10 years two important regional agreements have been executed, bringing together the near totality of South American States and a handful of Central American and Caribbean States. These two agreements—the Bolivarian Alliance for the Peoples of Our America (Alianza Bolivariana para los pueblos de nuestra América, formerly the Alternativa bolivariana para las Américas—ALBA—TCP (ALBA)) on the one hand, and the Union of South American Nations (Unión de Naciones Sudamericanas (UNASUR)) on the other—have not replaced other existing regional agreements. ALBA and UNASUR coexist today with regional initiatives such as the Andean Community of Nations (Comunidad Andina de Naciones (CAN)) and the Southern Common Market (Mercado Común del Sur (MERCOSUR)), which came into existence in 1969 and 1991, respectively.

Will the ALBA and UNASUR initiatives be any more relevant to foreign investment than the other existing South American regionalization initiatives have hitherto been? Is there any link between the emergence of the ALBA and UNASUR initiatives and the perceived backlash of South American States against investment arbitration—as illustrated by the denunciation of the Convention on the Settlement of Investment Disputes between States and Nationals of Other States (ICSID Convention)[1] by several Contracting States to these regional initiatives? If there is such link, which is the cause and which the effect? Similarly, is there any causal link between the emergence of these two regional initiatives and the significant contemporaneous increase in the flow of foreign direct investment towards both UNASUR and ALBA Member States—up 229 per cent and 185 per cent, respectively, from 2004 to 2011?[2] This article will try to enlighten the reader as to possible answers to these questions by setting out the factual background of ALBA and

[1] See, eg C Schreuer, 'Part IV Chapter 15: Denunciation of the ICSID Convention and Consent to Arbitration' in M Waibel, A Kaushal, et al. (eds), *The Backlash against Investment Arbitration* (Kluwer Law International 2010) 353–354; and TG Nelson, 'Part V chapter 24: "History Ain't Changed": Why Investor-state Arbitration Will Survive the 'New Revolution' in the same volume, 572.

[2] According to the United Nations Commission on Trade and Development (UNCTAD) <http://unctadstat.unctad.org/TableViewer/tableView.aspx?ReportId=88>. UNCTAD's World Investment Report for 2013, published in mid-2013, notes that 'FDI [foreign direct investment] to Latin America and the Caribbean in 2012 was $244 billion, maintaining the high level reached in 2011. Significant growth in FDI to South America ($144 billion) [up 12%] was offset by a decline in Central America and the Caribbean ($99 billion). The main factors that preserved South America's attractiveness to FDI are its wealth in oil, gas and metal minerals and its rapidly expanding middle class.'

UNASUR (Part II) before underlining their implications for foreign investment in South America, with a particular focus on the resolution of investment disputes (Part III).

II. BACKGROUND TO THE ALBA AND UNASUR INITIATIVES

Contrary to a common misperception, the ALBA and UNASUR initiatives are clearly distinguishable in light of their historical background and development. Accordingly, the background to (A) the ALBA and (B) UNASUR initiatives will be described separately below. This description does not purport to be a comprehensive historical analysis of the genesis of these initiatives and their underlying ideology, but rather a chronological outline of those facts that are most relevant to foreign investment in the region.

A. History and recent developments of the ALBA initiative

ALBA is the brainchild of the late Venezuelan President Hugo Chávez Frías and former Cuban President Fidel Castro.[3] The original idea was proposed by President Chávez in 2001 at the 3rd Summit of Heads of State and/or Government of the States and Territories of the Association of Caribbean States.

President Chávez's proposal was to openly counter the U.S.-sponsored Free Trade Area of the Americas (FTAA), intended to unite the economies of the Americas (including the United States of America and Canada) into a single free trade area.[4] According to commentators, ALBA was 'conceived as a means of forging a unified front against the United States [...] grounded in the notion that globalization cannot be left to the private sector, but must be overseen by the state in order to maximize the welfare of its citizens.'[5] The promoters of ALBA sought to correct the neo-liberal practice of granting access to markets through the elimination of tariffs, which was viewed as predominantly serving the interests of developed nations. Accordingly, ALBA emphasized the need to address the causes thought to prevent integration, namely poverty, inequality, imbalances in international relations, large foreign debt, and the imposition of structural

---

[3] ALBA's future without President Chávez' leadership is beyond the scope of this paper.

[4] See <http://www.ftaa-alca.org/View_e.asp>. This project is now dormant. It is worth noting that the last publicly available draft agreement of the FTAA included a chapter on 'investment' <http://www.ftaa-alca.org/FTAADraft03/ChapterXVII_e.asp>.

[5] LC Baker and A Molina, 'Cuba and the Construction of Alternative Global Trade Systems: Alba and Free Trade in the Americas' 31 *U Pa J Int'l L* (2009–2010) 679, 682.

adjustment policies by the Bretton Woods institutions: the IMF, the World Bank and the WTO.[6]

The ideology underlying the ALBA initiative can be traced back as early as Simón Bolivar's writings at the beginning of the 19th century calling for unity amongst the Latin-American and Caribbean nations.[7] ALBA supporters view *Bolivarianism* as a continuation of the independence movement and neo-liberal policies as a new form of European colonialism or American imperialism. Thus, national sovereignty is considered the highest value in international affairs. But ALBA's ideology also draws from the Marxist-socialist principles of the 20th century, whereby the State stands as the ultimate expression and guardian of the socialist ideal. Accordingly, ALBA seeks to reaffirm the preeminent economic and social role of the State, also considered the central piece in transnational relations and tasked with promoting trade and integration between sister nations of Latin America.

The original proposal was developed in a series of speeches and dialogues among Cuban and Venezuelan representatives during the period 2001–2004.[8] ALBA was not formally created until the signing of the Havana Joint Declaration of 14 December 2004,[9] in which Presidents Castro and Chávez set out the ideological foundations and principles for the integration of Venezuela and Cuba. In the Joint Declaration, the Heads of State of Cuba and Venezuela announced *in extenso*:

> We wish to draw attention to the fact that the Free Trade Area for the Americas (FTAA) is the most blatant expression yet of a hunger to dominate the region and, were it to come into effect, it would mark an intensification of neo-liberalism and create unprecedented levels of dependence and subordination.
>
> [...]
>
> We also find that [...] the proliferation of negotiations to reach free trade agreements like the FTAA have set the foundations which give rise to the scenario of subordination and backwardness plaguing our region today.
>
> Therefore, we resolutely reject the FTAA's content and proposals and we share the conviction that the so called integration on neo-liberal bases the FTAA

[6] Ibid 693.

[7] See S Bolívar, Carta de Jamaica (1815), 16: 'I wish more than anyone else to see the biggest nation in the world emerge in America, not really for its extension and wealth but for its freedom and glory'. (Unofficial translation of: 'Yo deseo más que otro alguno ver formar en América la más grande nación del mundo, menos por su extensión y riquezas que por su libertad y gloria') <http://escritoriodocentes.educ.ar/datos/recursos/libros/carta_de_jamaica.pdf>.

[8] Baker and Molina (n 5), 696 see also <http://www.alba-tcp.org/contenido/conceptualización-de-proyecto-y-empresa-grannacional-en-el-marco-del-alba>.

[9] <http://www.alba-tcp.org/en/contenido/joint-declaration-venezuela-cuba>.

> represents would consolidate the scenario described earlier and would only lead to [...] the denationalization of the region's economies and to total subordination to foreign dictates.
> [...]
> We share the opinion that, in order to achieve the aims mentioned above, the ALBA must be guided by the following cardinal principles and bases:
> 1. *Trade and investment must not be ends in themselves, but tools to achieve fair and sustainable development [...] To achieve our aims, the State must efficiently play the role of regulator and coordinator of economic activity*.
> 2. Special and differential Treatment, which takes into account the level of development of the various countries and the size of their economies, and which guarantees that all nations taking part have access to the benefits deriving from the process of integration.
> [...]
> 9. *Encouraging investment of Latin American capital within Latin America and the Caribbean, with the aim of reducing the dependence of the region's nations on foreign investors*. Steps to achieve this would include creating a Latin-American Investment Fund, a Southern Development Bank, and the Latin-American Mutual Guarantee Company.[10]

ALBA is not, strictly speaking, an international organisation. Consistent with its underlying ideology, it focuses heavily on 'intergovernmentalism' rather than institution building. It operates through yearly summit meetings of the Presidential Counsel (meetings of heads of State), its main political organ, which issues joint declarations establishing policy guidelines. Ministers meet on an ad-hoc basis in what is referred to as Social, Economic, Political and Social Movements Councils. These delegate the execution of specific projects to a series of committees and working groups.

As President Chávez described to the United Nations in 2011, ALBA is presented as 'an avant-garde experiment of progressive and anti-imperialist governments, seeking ways to break the prevailing international order and strengthening the capacity of the people to face, together, the prevailing powers.'[11] This 'experiment' was gradually to move from an ideological stance to an initiative with practical consequences.

The first implementation of ALBA came in the form of a bilateral agreement between Cuba and Venezuela, also concluded on 14 December 2004, in which both contracting States, among other things, 'agree[d] to execute investments of mutual interest in conditions equal to those of

[10] Unofficial translation (emphasis added) <http://www.alba-tcp.org/contenido/declaracion-conjunta-venezuela-cuba-141204>.

[11] President Hugo Chávez's Speech to the United Nations, 12 September 2011, 17 *Law & Bus Rev Am* (2011) 626, 632.

national entities.'[12] These investments would take the form of 'mixed companies, cooperative productions, projects of joint administration and other partnership modalities that they may decide to establish.'[13] Further, '[e]ach and every state investment, together with Venezuelan mixed companies, including private Venezuelan capital in Cuba' would be exempt from taxes on profits in Cuba during the period of return on investment.[14] In addition, '[c]oncerning the investments of Venezuelan state entities in Cuba, the Cuban party eliminates any restriction on the possibility that such investments be fully-owned by Venezuelan State investors.'[15] For its part, Cuban State investments and mixed companies in Venezuela would also be exempt from taxes on profits over the period of return on investment.[16] Finally, Venezuela offered to finance 'productive and infrastructure projects, including in the energy sector, the electrical industry, road paving and other roadways projects, port development, aqueducts and sewage, agro-industrial and in the services sector'[17] and offered '[f]acilities for the establishment of mixed companies with Cuban capital for the processing of raw materials downstream.'[18]

On 29 April 2006, Bolivia was the third State to join ALBA by entering into the Agreement for the Application of ALBA-TCP with Venezuela and Cuba. In particular, this Agreement provides that 'with regards to strategic bi-national or tri-national companies, the parties will do their utmost to guarantee that the host country owns at least 51% of the shares as long as the nature and cost of the investment allow it.'[19] This Agreement includes similar tax exemptions to those described above.

This Agreement was referred to as a Tratado de comercio de los Pueblos (The Peoples' Commerce Treaty or TCP) and, as expressed by the signatories, was to be followed by several other similar agreements. In the Joint Communiqué on the adhesion of Bolivia to ALBA, TCPs were defined as 'exchange instruments based on solidarity and complementarity between the countries, intended to benefit the peoples as opposed to Free Trade Agreements that are aimed at increasing the power and the dominance of transnational companies.'[20] TCPs are therefore markedly different from

---

[12] Agreement between Venezuela and Cuba for the ALBA Application (unofficial translation), <http://www.alba-tcp.org/en/contenido/agreement-between-venezuela-and-cuba-alba-application>.

[13] Id.

[14] Ibid, art 12 2nd (unofficial translation).

[15] Ibid, art 12 6th (unofficial translation).

[16] Ibid, art 13 3rd (unofficial translation).

[17] Ibid, art 13 5th (unofficial translation).

[18] Ibid, art 13 10th (unofficial translation).

[19] Agreement for the Application of ALBA-TCP, art 6. <http://www.alba-tcp.org/en/contenido/agreement-application-alba-tcp>.

[20] See <http://www.alba-tcp.org/en/contenido/joint-communiqué>.

conventional trade agreements; they establish trade measures as a means of tackling specific social concerns, rather than providing for free market access.

After 2006, ALBA increased its membership to include Nicaragua (11 January 2007), Dominica (26 January 2008), Honduras (which acceded on 25 August 2008 and then withdrew in 2010), and Ecuador, Saint Vincent and the Grenadines, and Antigua and Barbuda (24 June 2009). These seven countries acceded to ALBA by subscribing to the principles set out in the Havana Joint Declaration of 14 December 2004[21] without concluding new agreements.

In practice, the ALBA initiative has led to several further agreements among its Member States. Of particular relevance to foreign investment are:[22]

- The promotion of 'grannacionales' projects and companies (Supranational Projects and Companies, as opposed to 'multinational' or 'transnational' projects and companies) between ALBA Member States. Grannacionales projects are action programmes aimed at fulfilling the principles and goals of ALBA, validated by ALBA's Member States, and involving two or more ALBA contracting States. ALBA has so far approved twelve such projects,[23] including in industries such as finance (through the ALBA Bank), telecommunications, transport, mining and energy. The concept of grannacionales companies is somewhat nebulous and appears to encompass any State-owned company (including a company owned by several States)[24] in charge of implementing a grannacional project.[25] This concept suggests that any company operating within the ambit of a grannacional project would therefore have to be State-owned (by one or more ALBA contracting States). Such companies would be allowed, however, to conclude partnerships with privately-owned companies;

---

[21] See eg the accession of Ecuador to ALBA: 'Ecuador [...] declares: 1. Its decision to subscribe to the principles set out in the Joint Declaration, constitutive of the Bolivarian Alternative for the Peoples of Our America, signed on December 14th, 2004 between the President of the Bolivarian Republic of Venezuela and the President of the council of State of the Republic of Cuba, to which the Republic of Bolivia, the Republic of Nicaragua, the Commonwealth of Dominica, the Republic of Honduras and Saint Vincent and the Grenadines have acceded.' <http://www.alba-tcp.org/en/contenido/accession-ecuador-alba>.

[22] In addition to these TPCs, ALBA contracting States have concluded a Food Sovereignty and Cooperation Treaty (23 April 2008); Food Sovereignty and Cooperation Treaty between ALBA and PetroCaribe (2 February 2009), and the Treaty creating the Empresa Grannacional de Alimentos ALBA-PetroCaribe 2 February 2009).

[23] See <http://www.alba-tcp.org/en/contenido/grannational>.

[24] See <http://www.alba-tcp.org/en/contenido/conceptualization-project-and-grannational-enterprise-framework-alba>.

[25] Such as, arguably, a company established in Venezuela that would extract crude oil and export it to Cuba.

- The conclusion of the ALBA Energy Treaty between Venezuela, Cuba, Bolivia and Nicaragua on 29 April 2007. This Energy Treaty provides that the Contracting Parties (i) shall hold shares in the 'ALBA Bloc' on the Orinoco Belt in Venezuela (reportedly to control crude reserves sufficient to guarantee the Parties' supply for the next 25 years) to be operated by a grannacional company named Petroalba; (ii) will finance projects for the joint exploitation of natural gas, the processing necessary for the use of such natural gas and the development of transportation infrastructure; (iii) will seek to move to cleaner power generation (hydroelectric projects, combined cycle plants, etc); (iv) will jointly develop research projects for alternative energy sources (geothermal, solar, wind, etc); and (v) will establish energy-saving programmes.[26] This Agreement further provides for the creation of a grannacional energy company constituted as a corporation of State-owned companies.[27] By January 2013, however, the ALBA Energy Treaty had not yet entered into force as it had only been ratified by Bolivia.[28]
- The conclusion of the Agreement for the Creation of the Economic Space of ALBA-TCP (ECOALBA-TCP) signed on 5 February 2012 by ALBA contracting States. This agreement entered into force in April 2013[29] and contains several provisions relevant to foreign investment—by ALBA

---

26 ALBA Energy Treaty, art II.

27 Id.

28 Art VII of the ALBA Energy Treaty provides that it will 'enter into force on the date of the last notification through which the Parties shall communicate to the depository the fulfillment of their constitutional and legal internal formalities for that purpose and will remain in force for a ten(10)-year period, and it may be automatically extended for consecutive periods of five (5) years, unless one of the Parties notifies the depository in writing and the other Parties through diplomatic channel, its intention to denounce it, at least six (6) months prior to the expiry of the Treaty.'

29 Art 18 of the ECOALBA-TCP provides that '[t]his Agreement will enter into force in five (5) calendar days as of the day following deposit of the second ratification instrument at the People's Ministry for Exterior Relations of the Bolivarian Republic of Venezuela and will last for an indefinite term. For the other signatories, it will enter into force in five (5) calendar days as of the day following deposit of the respective ratification instrument, and in the order in which the ratifications were deposited.' We understand that, as of October 2013, the ECOALBA-TCP has been ratified by Venezuela (see <http://www.asambleanacional.gov.ve/noticia/show/id/790> and <http://www.avn.info.ve/contenido/venezuela-aprob%C3%B3-creaci%C3%B3n-del-acuerdo-econ%C3%B3mico-regional-ecoalba-tcp>, Nicaragua (see <http://legislacion.asamblea.gob.ni/SILEG/Iniciativas.nsf/0/5884958874d83bd206257b4a0056326b/$FILE/Dictamen%20del%20Decreto%20Acuerdo%20ECOALBA.pdf> and <http://www.alba-tcp.org/contenido/ratifican-inclusión-de-nicaragua-en-espacio-económico-alba-tcp-18-de-abril-de-2013>) and Bolivia (see <http://www.alba-tcp.org/contenido/comision-en-bolivia-ratifica-acuerdo-para-la-constitucion-del-espacio-economico-del-alba-t> and <http://www.diputados.bo/index.php/prensa/economia/item/89-comision-ratifica-acuerdo-para-la-constitucion-del-espacio-economico-del-alba-tcp-ecoalba-tcp>). An additional framework agreement for the

Member States or otherwise. In particular, the ECOALBA-TCP sets forth the following principles:

> **Article 2**: For compliance with the purpose of this Agreement, the Parties agree that the ALBA-TCP (ECOALBA) Economic Space will be governed by the following ruling principles:
> [...]
> 6. Recognition of the role of sovereign States in the socio-economic development and regulation of the economy. [...] *The TCP supports the nationalization and recovery of companies and natural resources to which the peoples are entitled*, establishing legal defence mechanisms for the same.
> [...]
> 16. Partners, not bosses. The requirement that foreign investment respects national laws. [...] *[T]he TCP seeks foreign investment that respects the laws of, reinvests the profits in and settles any discussion with the State like any national investor.*
> *Foreign investors may not sue National States or Governments because they develop public interest policies.*
> 24. Differentiated and supportive treatment that takes into account levels of development and objectives, as well as the sizes of the economies of each Party, and that guarantees their access to the benefits arising from ALBA-TCP.
> [...]
> **Article 3**: During the period of creation of the ALBA-TCP (ECOALBA) Economic Space that will cover from the entering into force of this Agreement until two (2) years have elapsed, the *Parties will adopt a Regulatory and Programmatic Regime* that regulates the shared-development economic zone of ALBA-TCP as an alternative and innovative proposal of the region against the already established schemes that regulate international trade *in the following aspects*: [...] the protection of national production in sectors deemed strategic to the Parties (within a comprehensive view and with special emphasis on newly-formed industries) and the *settlement of disputes*.
> **[Transitional] Provision**: Until the regulatory and programmatic regime provided in Article 3 is adopted, *the Parties will accept the bilaterally established trade provisions existing between individual members in force at the time of the signing of this Agreement. However, such provisions will be progressively replaced* as new specific instruments resulting from this Agreement materialize.[30]

implementation of ECOALBA-TCP was entered into between Bolivia, Venezuela, Cuba, and Nicaragua in July 2013, but it has not yet entered into force (<http://www.alba-tcp.org/contenido/cancilleria-boliviana-destaca-acuerdo-por-eco-alba-18-de-julio-de-2013>).

[30] Agreement for the Creation of the Economic Space of ALBA-TCP (ECOALBA-TCP) (emphasis added), <http://www.alba-tcp.org/en/contenido/agreement-creation-economic-space-alba-tcp-ecoalba-tcp>.

B. *History and recent developments of the UNASUR initiative*

UNASUR is an ambitious initiative with the long-term goal of achieving the comprehensive integration of South American States. It is a regional organisation for the political and economic integration of all 12 South American States with the stated goal of promoting integration at the social, cultural, political and infrastructure levels.

Its origins can be traced back to a meeting of Heads of State from Member States of the two existing customs unions in Latin America (MERCOSUR and CAN), together with Chile, Guyana and Suriname convened in 2000 by the then Brazilian President Fernando Henrique Cardozo. The Brasilia Declaration of 1 September 2000 emphasized the need for a common agenda of opportunities and goals for South America based on South American geographical continuity and common values.[31]

This call for action took a more concrete form with the creation of the South American Community of Nations (Comunidad Suramericana de Naciones) by the 2004 Cusco Declaration,[32] which in 2007 became UNASUR. In particular, the 2004 Cusco Declaration called for '[t]he deepening of convergence between MERCOSUR, the Andean Community and Chile through the perfection of the free trade area' and '[t]he physical integration and integration of energy and communications in South America based on the deepening of existing bilateral, regional and sub-regional experiences'.[33] These goals were to be attained on an intergovernmental basis.[34]

Following a series of meetings between high-level civil servants of the participating States, the 12 Heads of State of the UNASUR[35] signed the UNASUR Constitutive Treaty (Tratado Constitutivo) on 23 May 2008.[36] The Treaty entered into force on 11 March 2011, following the ninth ratification by a signatory State in accordance with its Article 26.[37] By 14

---

[31] See Brasilia Declaration of 1 September 2000 <http://www.comunidadandina.org/documentos/dec_int/di1-9-00.htm>.

[32] See <http://www.iirsa.org/admin_iirsa_web/Uploads/Documents/oe_cusco05_declaracion_del_cusco_eng.pdf>.

[33] Id.

[34] The Cusco Declaration provides that '[t]he Ministers of Foreign Affairs will draw up a concrete proposal of courses of action that will consider, among other things, the meetings of Heads of State as the supreme political body and of Foreign Ministers as the executive decision-making body of the process.'

[35] Argentina, Bolivia, Brazil, Chile, Colombia, Ecuador, Guyana, Paraguay, Peru, Suriname, Uruguay, and Venezuela.

[36] <http://www.unasursg.org/index.php?option=com_content&view=article&id=290&Itemid=339>.

[37] Art 26 of the UNASUR Constitutive Treaty provides that it will enter into force 'thirty days after the date of receipt of the 9th instrument of ratification. [...] For the Member state which ratifies the Constitutive Treaty after the deposit of the 9th instrument of ratification, the

December 2011, the 12 signatory States had ratified the UNASUR Constitutive Treaty.

UNASUR is a much more structured initiative than ALBA. Its organs include:

- The Council of Heads of State and Government (Consejo de Jefas y Jefes de Estado y de Gobierno), UNASUR's highest organ. It meets on an annual basis and is entrusted with (i) establishing political lines of action, programmes and projects related to the South American integration process and deciding on their implementation; (ii) convening ministerial meetings and creating ministerial-level councils; (iii) deciding on proposals presented by the Council of Foreign Ministers; and (iv) adopting the policy for relations with third parties.
- The Council of Foreign Ministers (Consejo de Ministras y Ministros de Relaciones Exteriores) is charged with (i) adopting and implementing decisions of the Council of Heads of State and Government; (ii) proposing projects to be discussed by the Council of Heads of State and Government; (iii) coordinating positions on issues that are central to South American integration; (iv) developing and promoting political dialogue for relevant issues; (v) approving the organisation's activity programmes and budget; (vi) approving the financing of UNASUR activities; (vii) implementing policy with third parties; and (viii) creating working groups in accordance with the priorities established by the Council of Heads of State and Government.
- The Council of Delegates (Consejo de Delegadas y Delegados), responsible for (i) implementing decisions of the Council of Foreign Ministers and the Council of Heads of State and Government; (ii) preparing the meetings of the Council of Foreign Ministers, (iii) proposing and drafting resolutions to be debated at the Council of Foreign Ministers; (iv) coordinating UNASUR initiatives with other sub-regional organisations; (v) constituting and coordinating working groups; (vi) coordinating political dialogue on issues of regional and international interest; (vii) promoting dialogue favoring the participation of individuals in the process of South American integration; and (viii) discussing and proposing the organisation's budget to the Council of Foreign Ministers. The Council of Delegates comprises one representative of each Member State and meets biannually in the State that holds the Pro Tempore presidency.
- The Secretariat (La Secretaría General), a permanent organ, headquartered in Quito, Ecuador. The Secretariat is primarily responsible for (i)

Treaty will enter into force 30 days after the date in which that State deposits its instrument of ratification.'

supporting all other organs; (ii) serving as a depositary of treaties concluded within UNASUR; (iii) preparing the budget proposal for the Council of Delegates; (iv) preparing proposals for regulations for the functioning of the Secretariat and submitting them for approval by the relevant organs; and (v) coordinating activities with other organizations in South America and the Caribbean.

- The Pro-Tempore Presidency of UNASUR is held by a Member State for a one-year period, shifting in alphabetical order. Its basic role is to convene and preside over meetings of the UNASUR organs and to represent the organisation and execute agreements with third parties.
- Furthermore, the Constitutive Treaty provides for the creation of a South American Parliament, to be located in Cochabamba, Bolivia, subject to the conclusion of an additional protocol.

The decision-making process within UNASUR, as per Article 6 of the Constitutive Treaty, is voting by consensus, as opposed to majority or unanimity (a mechanism inspired by the WTO).

In relevant part, the UNASUR Constitutive Treaty provides:

> **Article 2 Objective:** The objective of the South American Union of Nations is to build, in a participatory and consensual manner, *an integration and union* among its peoples in the cultural, social, economic and political fields [...] to strengthen democracy and reduce asymmetries *within the framework of strengthening the sovereignty and independence of the States*.
> **Article 3 Specific Objectives:** The South American Union of Nations has the following objectives:
> [...]
> d) *Energy integration* for the integral and sustainable use of the resources of the region, in a spirit of solidarity;
> e) *The development of an infrastructure* for the interconnection of the region and among our peoples, based on sustainable social and economic development criteria;
> f) *Financial integration* through the adoption of mechanisms compatible with the economic and fiscal policies of Member States;[38]

The effectiveness of these objectives will depend, to a large extent, on the will of Member States. While a dispute settlement mechanism for resolving disputes between UNASUR Member States is included in the Constitutive Treaty (Article 21), it remains a non-jurisdictional and non-

[38] UNASUR Constitutive Treaty (emphasis added) (see <http://www.unasursg.org/index.php?option=com_content&view=article&id=290&Itemid=339>). It should be noted that the numbering of the arts of the English version of the UNASUR Constitutive Treaty is inconsistent with that of the Spanish version. Notwithstanding, these two versions are deemed equally authentic pursuant to art 27, last paragraph, of this Treaty.

binding mechanism.[39] Indeed, after a mandatory 60-day consultation period, the Council of Delegates will issue a 'recommendation'. If the Council of Delegates does not reach a solution, the dispute is taken to the Council of Ministers. The UNASUR Treaty does not provide for penalties for non-compliance with recommendations of the Council of Delegates or Council of Ministers. This may render the organization 'toothless' in dealing with rogue members (similarly to APEC). Moreover, the substantive provisions of the Constitutive Treaty quoted above (eg Article 3) set mere goals and do not impose any precise, substantial obligations on the Member States.

The implications of the UNASUR Constitutive Treaty on foreign investment and, more particularly, the proposal within UNASUR to establish a Dispute Settlement Centre for the resolution of foreign investment disputes in South America are further developed below.

III. IMPLICATIONS OF THE ALBA AND UNASUR INITIATIVES FOR FOREIGN INVESTMENT AND, IN PARTICULAR, ON THE RESOLUTION OF INVESTMENT DISPUTES

For ease of reference, we address in turn the implications of the ALBA and UNASUR initiatives for (A) the resolution of investment disputes and (B) inflows of foreign investment in South America. Often a direct correlation has been said to exist between the inflow of foreign investment and the availability of an appropriate mechanism for resolving investment disputes. The recent data, however, suggests otherwise.

A. Implications of the ALBA and UNASUR initiatives for the resolution of investment disputes in South America

As noted above, the ALBA and UNASUR are not cut from the same cloth. They have each taken a distinct approach to the resolution of investment

---

[39] As explained by a commentator familiar with the inner workings of UNASUR: 'For the time being, only the resolution of disputes arising out of the interpretation of the Treaty has been provided for. […] what is clear is that there was no consensus on designing a mechanism similar to that existing in Europe or in the CAN, certainly because of the importance that some prefer bestowing on intergovernmentalism and national sovereignties.' (Unofficial translation of 'Hasta el momento se ha previsto lo conducente a solucionar solamente diferencias provenientes de la intepretación del Tratado. […] Lo claro es que no hubo consenso para idear un mecanismo semejante al existente en Europa o en la CAN, seguramente por la importancia que algunos prefieren otorgar a lo intergobernamental y a las soberanias nacionales.') Diego Cardona Cardona, 'EL ABC de UNASUR: Doce preguntas y respuestas' in La Construcción de la integración suramericana (Revista de la integración, Secretaría de la Comunidad Andina, July 2008, No. 2), 27 <http://www.comunidadandina.org/public/revista_2.htm>.

disputes in South America, though both reflect the need to find a regional alternative to the existing paradigm, incarnated by the International Centre for Settlement of Investment Disputes (ICSID).

(i) Implications of the ALBA initiative for the resolution of investments disputes

One of the principles of ALBA is the '[p]romotion of Latin American capital investments within Latin America and the Caribbean, with the aim of curbing the dependence of the countries of the region on foreign investors.' Bilateral investment Treaties (BITs) and ICSID have gradually been perceived as the legal instruments of this dependence. Yet the implications of the ALBA for the resolution of investment disputes are not all clear. Contrary to a simplistic view that has often portrayed ALBA States as guided by the same ideology and adopting the same anti-imperialistic policies, ALBA's contribution appears rather limited. While it may have inspired certain measures adopted individually by its Member States (such as the denunciation of the ICSID Convention and various BITs), not all States have taken the same steps.

(1) Is the denunciation of the ICSID Convention related to or caused by ALBA? It is well known that ALBA's open hostility towards free market and the institutions promoting it, namely the World Bank, has spilled over to one of its agencies: ICSID. It is a fact that the only three Contracting States to have denounced the ICSID Convention to date are all members of ALBA: Ecuador, Bolivia and Venezuela. But these denunciations, when considered in their proper context, appear to result from the individual circumstances of each State rather than an ALBA-sponsored action.

Criticism of ICSID reached a peak in Bolivia following a 2005 decision by an ICSID tribunal that denied Bolivia's objections to jurisdiction in the *Aguas del Tunari* case[40]. This case had drawn attention from the media and NGOs as it involved the citizen's access to water supply. On 29 April 2007, at the closing of ALBA's 5th summit meeting, Bolivian President Evo Morales Ayma announced that 'ALBA member states decided to jointly withdraw and denounce the ICSID Convention, thus guaranteeing the people's sovereign right to regulate foreign investment it its territory.'[41] Bolivia's position was

[40] *Aguas del Tunari, S.A. v Republic of Bolivia*, ICSID Case No. ARB/02/3, Decision on Respondent's Objections to Jurisdiction dated 21 October 2005.

[41] Unofficial translation of 'los Estados parte del ALBA acordaron retirarse y denunciar de manera conjunta la convención del CIADI, garantizando el derecho soberano de los pueblos a regular la inversión extranjera en su territorio'. 'Nicaragua, Bolivia y Venezuela se retiran de organismo que dirime controversias con transnacionales' (29 April 2007) <http://www.rlp.com.ni/noticias/13069/nicaragua-bolivia-y-venezuela-se-retiran-de-organismo-que-dirime-controversias-con-transnacionales>.

publicly supported at the time by President Chávez. But no such decision was formalized in the ALBA 5th summit's final declaration or in any other official document released by ALBA thereafter. A few days later, on 2 May 2007, Bolivia submitted its written notice of denunciation of the ICSID Convention to the ICSID Secretariat.

The same year, on 4 December 2007, Ecuador (which was not yet a member of ALBA) submitted a letter to the ICSID Secretariat withdrawing its consent to arbitration of disputes relating to natural resources, in accordance with Article 25(4) of the ICSID Convention.[42] It is unclear whether this decision was in any way related to the position expressed by Bolivia at the ALBA 5th summit meeting. Ecuador became a member of ALBA on 24 June 2009 and, shortly thereafter, on 6 July 2009, denounced the ICSID Convention in accordance with its Article 71.[43]

For its part, Venezuela submitted its notice of denunciation of the ICSID Convention under Article 71 on 24 January 2012 (ie almost five years after Bolivia and three years after Ecuador). This denunciation could be considered as concluding a process that began in February 2008, when the Venezuelan National Assembly openly rejected the case brought before ICSID by Exxon Mobil (which the Venezuelan National News Agency reported as 'an action of economic and judicial terrorism carried out by the transnational Exxon Mobil and its accomplices')[44] and requested that Venezuela withdraw from the ICSID system.

Given the time lapse between each of these countries' denunciations of the ICSID Convention, it is unclear whether the purported agreement discussed within ALBA in 2007 to withdraw from the ICSID system had much weight in the decision-making process.

(2) Is the denunciation of various BITs related to or caused by ALBA?

Similarly, ALBA's influence on the denunciation of BITS is also unclear.

Bolivia, for example, became a member of ALBA in April 2006 and in

---

[42] Art 25 para (4) of the ICSID Convention provides that: 'Any Contracting State may, at the time of ratification, acceptance or approval of this Convention or at any time thereafter, notify the Centre of the class or classes of disputes which it would or would not consider submitting to the jurisdiction of the Centre. The Secretary-General shall forthwith transmit such notification to all Contracting States. Such notification shall not constitute the consent required by paragraph (1).'

[43] Art 71 of the ICSID Convention provides that: 'Any Contracting State may denounce this Convention by written notice to the depositary of this Convention. The denunciation shall take effect six months after receipt of such notice.'

[44] Unofficial translation of '[una] acción de terrorismo económico y judicial desarrollada por la Transnacional Exxon Mobil y sus cómplices' 'Parlamento aprobó acuerdo de rechazo a 'terrorismo económico' desatado por Exxon', el universal.com <http://www.eluniversal.com/2008/02/14/pol_ava_parlamento-aprobo-ac_14A1366025.shtml>.

May of that year its Constitutional Court (through judgment 0031/2006 dated 10 May 2006)[45] declared constitutional the laws (Laws 1132, 1593, 1594, 1586, 1535, 1897 and 2360) ratifying the BITs with Argentina, the United Kingdom, the Netherlands, France, Spain and the United States. On 10 June 2011, the Department of State and Office of the United States Trade Representative published a Notice of Termination of the United States-Bolivia BIT indicating that

> [t]he Government of Bolivia [...] delivered to the United States a notice of termination for the bilateral investment treaty between the two countries, a termination that will take effect on June 10, 2012. As of June 10, 2012, the treaty will cease to have effect except that it will continue to apply for another 10 years to covered investments existing at the time of termination (June 10, 2012).[46]

According to press reports, Bolivia intends to renegotiate all of its existing BITs.[47] An important test will arise following December 2013, when the four-year period established by the 2009 Constitution for the Executive to 'denounce and, should it be the case, renegotiate international treaties contrary to the Constitution' will expire.[48]

---

[45] Corte constitucional boliviana, sentencia constitucional 0031/2006 [2006], <http://www.ciac-iacac.org/documentos/2007_3_6_9_17_49_SENTENCIA%200031%20DEL%202006.pdf>. The constitutional challenge had been brought by a former member of Parliament at the end of 2005 (ie before Bolivia became a member of ALBA).

[46] Department of State and Office of The United States Trade Representative, 'Notice of Termination of United States—Bolivia Bilateral Investment Treaty', Public Notice 7893, Federal Register / Vol. 77, No. 100, Notices (23 May 2012) <http://www.gpo.gov/fdsys/pkg/FR-2012-05-23/pdf/2012-12494.pdf>.

[47] 'Bolivia fija 5 ejes para renegociar 22 pactos bilaterales de inversión', América Economía (25 November 2011) ('The new BITs will be entered into using criteria that take into account the protection of the interests of the people; the balance of public and social interest with private property and profit; the formulation of solutions combining the rights of indigenous peoples, social and human rights, the environment and respect for the planet; and investors seeking to contribute to the economic and social development of the region. "Partners not bosses"' Unoficial translation of 'Los nuevos TBI, precisó, serán suscritos bajo criterios que consideren la protección de los intereses de los pueblos; el equilibrio del interés público y social con la propiedad y la ganancia privada; la articulación de soluciones de controversias que combinen derechos indígenas, sociales, humanos, de medio ambiente y de respeto a la tierra; y la búsqueda de inversores que contribuyan al desarrollo económico y social de la región. 'Buscar socios no patrones' <http://www.americaeconomia.com/economia-mercados/comercio/bolivia-fija-5-ejes-para-renegociar-22-pactos-bilaterales-de-inversion>.

[48] Unofficial translation of the Ninth Transitory Provision of the 2009 Bolivian Constitution ('Los tratados internacionales anteriores a la Constitución y que no la contradigan se mantendrán en el ordenamiento jurídico interno, con rango de ley. En el plazo de cuatro años desde la elección del nuevo Órgano Ejecutivo, éste denunciará y, en su caso, renegociará los tratados internacionales que sean contrarios a la Constitución').

Ecuador, for its part, launched a process to denounce various BITs in 2008 (ie before becoming a member of ALBA). According to President Correa's letter to the National Congress requesting the denunciation, the BITs 'contain clauses that are contrary to the [former 1998] Constitution and harmful to the national interest, such as the clause subjecting the Ecuadorian State to international arbitrations for the resolution of disputes relating to such treaties, ignoring the Ecuadorian jurisdiction.'[49] Before the entry into force of the new Ecuadorian Constitution in October 2008,[50] Ecuador had already denounced BITs concluded with nine countries—including some ALBA members—(the Dominican Republic, El Salvador, Nicaragua, Cuba, Guatemala, Honduras, Uruguay, Paraguay and Romania).[51] These countries, however, accounted for a very small fraction of the flow of foreign investment into Ecuador. The year 2010 marked the launch of a second wave of BIT denunciations, involving treaties with 13 countries, including the largest contributors of foreign direct investment in Ecuador (Argentina, Canada, Chile, China, Finland, France, Germany, the Netherlands, Sweden, Switzerland, the United Kingdom, the United States, and a fellow ALBA Member State, Venezuela). By then, the new Constitution and a new Law on the Legislative Branch had entered into force and required the Executive to consult the Constitutional Court and obtain approval from the National Assembly before denouncing a BIT. As of October 2013, of these 13 Ecuadorian BITs only one has been formally denounced (with Finland).[52]

Recently, through Executive Decree 1506 dated 6 May 2013, Ecuador established a study group (the Commission for the Integral Citizens' Audit of the Treaties of Reciprocal Protection of Investments and of the International Arbitral System on the Subject of Investments—CAITISA—

---

[49] Unofficial translation of '[…] contienen cláusulas contrarias a la Constitución y lesivas para los intereses nacionales, como la de someter al Estado ecuatoriano a arbitrajes internacionales para la solución en caso de conflictos relativos a dichos convenios, desconociendo la jurisdicción ecuatoriana.' 'Los Tratados Bilaterales de Inversión (TBIs) del Ecuador: Consecuencias de la Denuncia', <http://www.ecamcham.com/download/cam/TBIs%20DEL%20ECUADOR%20CONSECUENCIAS%20DE%20LA%20DENUNCIA%20RJ.pdf>.

[50] At that time, the Executive could denounce BITs without the intervention of the Constitutional Court or the Legislative Branch.

[51] Although several publications state that Ecuador also denounced its BIT with Costa Rica, in fact this BIT never entered into force.

[52] The denunciation of four BITs has been approved by the National Assembly, but President Correa has not notified the countries involved (France, Germany, Switzerland, and the United Kingdom). The National Assembly has denied the President's request to denounce four other BITs (with Chile, China, the Netherlands, and Venezuela) and the process for denouncing the remaining four BITs (Argentina, Canada, Switzerland, and the United States) is reportedly still pending before the Constitutional Court and the National Assembly.

formed by four representatives of the State, four experts and four representatives of social movements) to perform a comprehensive citizens' audit ('auditoría integral ciudadana') of investment arbitration within eight months. The Commission's various tasks include evaluating and examining a very wide number of issues relating to investment arbitration in general, and to specific investment awards in particular. Press reports of early October 2013 indicate that the Commission will audit 26 Ecuadorian BITs.

As for Venezuela's stance vis-à-vis BITs, the only reported action dates back to 2008, when it notified the Netherlands that Venezuela did not intend to extend the BIT beyond its expiration date (one year later) and, instead, wanted to renegotiate the text of a new BIT. Though very little information has leaked on the process, it appears that the Netherlands and Venezuela are still negotiating. Some press reports suggest that Venezuela intends to renegotiate all of its existing BITs, but no material steps in this direction seem to have been taken yet.[53]

(3) *Will ALBA create its own dispute resolution mechanism for investment disputes?*

The creation of a regional centre for the resolution of disputes has been on the agenda of ALBA since, at least, 2009. A proposal to create ALBA's own dispute resolution mechanism was approved at the 2nd meeting of ALBA's Council for Economic Complementation in Cochabamba, Bolivia, on 16 October 2009. In turn, the declaration that resulted from the 7th ALBA summit of October 2009 'instructed [a working group dedicated to this issue] to take further its work in order to be able to make concrete proposals in Caracas, Venezuela, within a period not exceeding 30 days.'[54] It is uncertain whether this working group ever made such proposals.

The fact that in 2010, as further described below, Ecuador sponsored a proposal to establish a regional dispute resolution centre within the framework of UNASUR suggests that the ALBA initiative has migrated into a larger forum. Yet in 2012 the ECOALBA-TCP provided for the adoption of a regulatory framework that would include a mechanism for the settlement of disputes (within two years of its entry into force).[55]

---

53 See, for example, <http://www.eluniversal.com/2008/05/01/eco_art_venezuela-denuncia-t_01A1549161> and <http://focus.ie.edu/es/el-verdadero-alcance-del-%C3%B3rdago-de-ch%C3%A1vez>.

54 7th ALBA Summit, Joint Declaration of Cochabamba (17 October 2009), point 21 (unofficial translation of 'instruyen continuar profundizando en su trabajo para estar en capacidad de realizar propuestas concretas al respecto en un plazo no mayor de 30 días, en la ciudad de Caracas, Venezuela.') <http://www.alba-tcp.org/contenido/declaracion-conjunta-vii-cumbre>.

55 See 5 February 2012 Agreement for the Creation of the Economic Space of ALBA-TCP (ECOALBA-TCP), art 3: '[d]uring the period of creation of the ALBA-TCP (ECOALBA) Economic Space that will cover from the entering into force of this Agreement until two (2)

In April 2013, the final declaration of the 1st Ministerial Conference of Latin-American States Affected by the Interests of Transnational Companies (Conferencia Ministerial de Estados Latinoamericanos Afectados por Intereses de Transnacionales) announced the creation of an Executive Committee of the Conference entrusted with 'designing and implementing political and legal actions for supporting States in defending against claims by transnational companies.' The Executive Committee will also 'coordinate joint defense efforts through teams of international experts and lawyers' and will 'develop public relations campaigns to counter those of transnational companies.'[56]

The final declaration of the 1st Ministerial Conference of Latin-American States Affected by the Interests of Transnational Companies also confirms that the ALBA Member States 'support UNASUR's project to set up its own arbitration court for commercial and investment cases, as an alternative to the current arbitral systems'[57] and even foresees that the UNASUR arbitration centre will be ready before the end of 2013 and will be approved by the UNASUR Member States by mid-2014.

More recently, ALBA's 12th summit meeting held in Guayaquil, Ecuador on 30 July 2013 saw the adoption of a Special Resolution on Arbitration and Transnational Companies in which the ALBA Member States agreed to:

> Coordinate effective actions to consolidate new arbitration bodies that contribute to the strengthening of an appropriate legal framework to ensure fair and balanced process for investors and States.

---

years have elapsed, the Parties will adopt a Regulatory and Programmatic Regime that regulates the shared-development economic zone of ALBA-TCP [...] in the following aspects: [...] the settlement of disputes' (see <http://www.alba-tcp.org/en/contenido/agreement-creation-economic-space-alba-tcp-ecoalba-tcp>.

56 Unofficial translation from ALBA-TCP's press release dated 23 April 2013 ('en la declaración final del encuentro se resolvió constituir un Comité Ejecutivo de la Conferencia, el cual se encargará de "diseñar y ejecutar acciones de apoyo mutuo en los ámbitos político y jurídico", para ayudar a los países de la región que se vean inmersos en controversias arbitrales con transnacionales. Igualmente, el Comité deberá "coordinar la defensa conjunta de acciones jurídicas a través de equipos legales internacionales de expertos y abogados profesionales", así como "diseñar estrategias de comunicación, como contrapeso a las campañas globales emprendidas por las compañías transnacionales') <http://www.alba-tcp.org/contenido/alba-crea-mecanismo-de-defensa-legal-ante-arbitraje-de-transnacionales-23-de-abril-de-2013>.

57 Unofficial translation from ALBA-TCP's press release dated 23 April 2013 ('En la resolución también se apoya el proyecto de la Unión de Naciones Suramericanas (Unasur) para constituir su propia corte de arbitraje para casos de comercio e inversiones, como una alternativa a los actuales sistemas arbitrales. Dicho tribunal de Unasur estará listo para finales de este mismo año—según las previsiones del ente—y el proyecto debería ser aprobado en la reunión de cancilleres prevista para julio próximo') <http://www.alba-tcp.org/contenido/alba-crea-mecanismo-de-defensa-legal-ante-arbitraje-de-transnacionales-23-de-abril-de-2013>.

> Reaffirm and continue with the implementation of the agreements generated in the framework of the First Ministerial Conference of Latin American and Caribbean Affected by Transnational Interests, held in the city of Guayaquil on April, 22nd, 2013, such as: i) Create an International Observatory funded by contributions from the States. ii) Establish the Executive Committee of the Conference, among others [...][58]

The next Ministerial Conference of Latin-American States Affected by the Interests of Transnational Companies is scheduled to take place in November 2013 in Caracas, Venezuela. In the meantime, UNASUR continues with its ambitious project of setting up a new investor-State dispute resolution mechanism.

(ii) UNASUR's project to create an investor-State dispute resolution mechanism

The most salient contribution of UNASUR to date for the resolution of investment disputes is the project of a UNASUR Investment Arbitration Centre (the Centre). Ecuador has taken a leading role in advancing this project since its inception. The first reported reference to the creation of an arbitration centre within UNASUR was made by the Ecuadorian Foreign Minister (Fander Falconí) shortly before the Ecuadorian term of the rotating Presidency of UNASUR in 2009. At the thirty-ninth Session of the General Assembly of the Organization of American States, Minister Falconí stated:

> In Ecuador's case, foreign investment's legal protection is set forth by international agreements that we have ratified, by the protective laws in force and by the constitutional rule equating the rights of nationals and foreigners; even further, the Constitution of the Republic is the first in the world to raise the principle of legal certainty to the category of constitutional right.
>
> With this legal structure, domestic or foreign investors can take legal action at any time if they consider that their constitutional right to this legal certainty has been infringed, without it being necessary to wait until an investment dispute arises. We cannot allow any investor, whatever its

---

[58] Unofficial translation of: 'Coordinar acciones efectivas para consolidar nuevas instancias de arbitraje que coadyuven al fortalecimiento de un marco jurídico adecuado que garantice procesos justos y equilibrados para los inversionistas y para los Estados. Reafirmar y continuar con la puesta en marcha de los acuerdos generados en el marco de la I Conferencia Ministerial de Estados Latinoamericanos y del Caribe afectados por Intereses Transnacionales, realizada en la ciudad de Guayaquil, el 22 de abril de 2013, tales como: i) Crear un Observatorio Internacional financiado con aportaciones de los Estados. ii) Constituir el Comité Ejecutivo de la Conferencia, entre otros') <http://www.alba-tcp.org/contenido/resolucion-especial-sobre-arbitraje-y-transnacionales>.

> importance, to have a greater legal status than a State. As a result, it is necessary to denounce the International Convention on the Settlement of Investment Disputes between States and Nationals of Other States which established the International Centre for Settlement of Investment Disputes (ICSID), a private arbitral entity attached to the World Bank which subordinates States.
>
> To proceed in this way does not imply leaving foreign investment unprotected; it involves perfecting an alternative vision of international arbitration in which equity between the parties prevails, instead of the superiority of one of them. *To this effect the creation of a Centre for Legal Advice on Investment-related Issues is being agreed within the Union of South American Nations (UNASUR). This would certainly be the first step towards the establishment of a regional arbitral jurisdiction as an alternative to the ICSID and other international arbitration bodies.*[59]

Following this declaration, Ecuador submitted the project to the 4th Cartagena Summit Meeting of Heads of South American Judiciary Powers of 28 August 2009. The proposal was then elevated to the Council of Heads of

---

59 Unofficial translation of: 'En el caso ecuatoriano, la protección jurídica a la inversión extranjera está dada por los convenios internacionales que hemos ratificado, por las leyes de protección vigentes y por la norma constitucional que equipara los derechos de nacionales y extranjeros; más aún, la Constitución de la República es la primera en el mundo en elevar el principio de seguridad jurídica a la categoría de derecho constitucional. Con esta estructura jurídica, el inversionista nacional o extranjero puede demandar, en cualquier momento, si considera que su derecho constitucional a esta seguridad jurídica ha sido vulnerado, sin tener que esperar a que se produzca una diferencia relativa en materia de inversión. No podemos permitir que un inversionista cualquiera, por importante que sea, tenga un estatus jurídico superior al de un Estado. En consecuencia, es necesario denunciar el Convenio Internacional sobre Arreglo de Diferencias Relativas a Inversiones entre Estados y Nacionales de Otros Estados, que origina el Centro Internacional de Arreglo de Diferencias Relativas a Inversiones (CIADI), instancia arbitral privada del Banco Mundial, al que deben subordinarse los Estados. Proceder de esta manera no implica desproteger a la inversión extranjera; implica perfeccionar una visión alternativa del arbitraje internacional en la que prevalezca la equidad para las partes y no la superioridad de una de ellas. *Para esto, en el seno de la Unión Sudamericana de Naciones (UNASUR) ya se está consensuando la creación de un Centro de Asesoramiento Jurídico para el Arreglo de Diferencias Relativas en Materia de Inversiones. Esto sería, sin duda, el primer paso hacia el establecimiento de una jurisdicción arbitral, regional, alternativa al CIADI y a los otros organismos de arbitraje internacional*' (emphasis added). Minutes of the thirty-ninth Session of the General Assembly of the Organization of American States, 2–3 June 2009, 56 (emphasis added) <http://www.oas.org/consejo/GENERAL%20 ASSEMBLY/actas.asp>. See also, 'Ecuador propondrá un nuevo sistema de arbitraje durante su presidencia en la Unasur' (Terra, 8 July 2009): 'We denounced ICSID and BITs (Bilateral Investment Treaties) and we would like rules in the context of UNASUR to strengthen the mechanisms for the treatment of foreign direct investment'. (Unofficial translation of 'Hemos denunciado al CIADI y a los TBI (Tratados Bilaterales de Inversión) y quisiéramos una normatividad en el contexto de Unasur para fortalecer los mecanismos de tratamiento de inversión extranjera directa') <http://www.terra.com.mx/articulo.aspx?articuloid=845136>.

State and Government of UNASUR at the 4th Summit Meeting in Georgetown, Guyana, on 26 November 2010, where the foreign ministers agreed to set up a working group to 'consider the proposal put forward by the Republic of Ecuador regarding the following issues: Dispute Settlement Centre; Centre for Legal Advice on Investment-related Issues and Code of Conduct for the Members of the Arbitration Tribunals.'[60] Ecuador's proposal was discussed again at the 5th and 6th Summit Meetings of Heads of South American Judiciary Powers, respectively in Cuenca, Ecuador and Brasilia, Brazil, in 2012. Both meetings recommended further studies on and analysis of Ecuador's proposal, which is still under discussion.

UNASUR has recently communicated on the status of this initiative in the final declaration of the Council of Heads of State and Government at the 7th Summit Meeting in Paramaribo (on 30 August 2013): 'the High Level Experts' Working Group on Resolution of Disputes in investment matters has made significant progress, [this Council] instructs that this work be completed as soon as possible, preferably before the end of the year, for the potential establishment of an Investment Dispute Settlement Centre.'[61] Officials have even publicly stated that the project is 80 per cent ready and that a final text should be approved in October 2013 and submitted to the Heads of State for approval at the next UNASUR summit meeting.[62]

Reports indicate, however, that some disagreements amongst UNASUR nations are still unresolved. In particular, Brazil's traditional refusal to submit to international arbitration, further described below, caused UNASUR to propose expanding the scope of the UNASUR Centre to provide for mediation in addition to arbitration. For its part, Bolivia's constitutional provision preventing the Plurinational State from submitting to international arbitration in relation to hydrocarbons is still an obstacle for Bolivia's acceptance of the UNASUR Centre.[63]

[60] UNASUR, Georgetown Declaration (21 November 2010), para 21 <http://www.guyanachronicleonline.com/site/index.php?option=com_content&view=article&id=21734:the-georgetown-declaration&catid=2:news&Itemid=2>.

[61] Unofficial translation of 'En vista de que los trabajos del Grupo de Trabajo de Expertos de Alto Nivel para la Solución de Controversias en materia de inversiones registra importantes avances, instruye a que se culmine este trabajo a la mayor brevedad posible, preferentemente antes de fin de año, para el eventual establecimiento de un Centro de Solución de Controversias en materia de inversiones' <http://www.unasursg.org/uploads/46/7f/467f20df2089365674121e39649b4e5f/Declaraci%C3%B3n-de-Paramaribo.pdf>.

[62] See, for example, press release dated 12 September 2013 reporting statements by Ecuador's Deputy Minister of Foreign Affairs <http://www.eluniverso.com/noticias/2013/09/12/nota/1431871/centro-arbitraje-unasur-promovera-tambien-mediacion-facilitacion>.

[63] Art 366 of the 2009 Bolivian Constitution provides that every foreign company that conducts activities in the hydrocarbons production chain in name and representation of the State will submit to the sovereignty of the State, and to the laws and authority of the State. No foreign court case or foreign jurisdiction will be recognized, and foreign investors may not invoke any

While the scope of the UNASUR Centre remains uncertain, several South American States have leveled against the existing investor-State dispute settlement mechanisms. In particular, the Draft Rules seek to emphasize (i) national sovereignty, (ii) the need for speedy resolution of disputes, and (iii) the need for increased transparency.

(1) The emphasis placed on national sovereignty

The Draft Rules incorporate many of the region's traditional concerns over the preservation of national sovereignty. For example:

- After providing that the Centre's jurisdiction ratione materiae would extend to 'all disputes related to investments [...] when the Parties have decided, through a treaty or contract, that legal disputes arising out of its interpretation or execution will be submitted to [the Centre]' (Article 2), the Draft Rules go on to exclude, unless otherwise agreed by the host State, disputes concerning public development policies in matters of health, education, taxation, natural resources, and the environment, 'among others;'
- Similarly, the Draft Rules provide that under no circumstance would the 'legitimacy' of an internal law of a Member State be subject to arbitration (Article 2);
- Whenever the dispute involves challenging an administrative act, the investor has to exhaust all local remedies (including before the Administration and the Administrative courts) before resorting to international arbitration;
- Investors are required to notify their Home State before resorting to arbitration and procure their State's authorization as a condition for the admissibility of a claim. However, no mention is made as to how much time States have to grant such authorization or how a lack of response by the Home State should be interpreted; and
- Finally, recognition and enforcement of awards can be denied if the losing party establishes that 'in accordance with the Constitution or the laws of the State affected by the award, the object of the dispute cannot be arbitrated or the award is contrary to the State's public policy [ordre public].'

---

exceptional situation for international arbitration, nor appeal to diplomatic claims. Unofficial translation of 'Todas las empresas extranjeras que realicen actividades en la cadena productiva hidrocarburífera en nombre y representación del Estado estarán sometidas a la soberanía del Estado. No se reconocerá en ningún caso tribunal ni jurisdicción extranjera y no podrán invocar situación excepcional alguna de arbitraje internacional, ni recurrir a reclamaciones diplomáticas.'

(2) The need for speedy resolution of disputes

Contrary to a general belief, States do not always seek to delay the final resolution of investment disputes. Very often delay (and the corresponding increase in costs) is a major source of concern for States. To tackle this concern, the Draft Rules include very tight deadlines and even provide for the mandatory joinder of proceedings in some cases. Some of these short deadlines seem unrealistic and will most probably be extended in the final version of the rules. For example:

- The Draft Rules provide that arbitral tribunals would be comprised of three members and that each party would designate one arbitrator (and one substitute) within 15 days from the submission of a request for arbitration to the Centre. The same period applies to the appointment of the presiding arbitrator. If the parties fail to make the required appointments within the specified time limit, the Centre's secretariat would make the appointment by drawing from a list of 13 arbitrators, previously recommended by UNASUR's Member States (of these, at least 7 must be specialists in public law or investment law);
- To challenge the appointment of an arbitrator, parties would have to do so within ten days following the appointment or within five days from gaining knowledge of the circumstances on which the challenge is based. One interesting feature is the reference to a code of conduct for arbitrators (an arbitrator could be challenged whenever the 'circumstances give rise to justifiable doubts as to an arbitrator's impartiality, independence or compliance with the Code of Conduct');
- Once constituted, the arbitral tribunal would have 120 days (extendable by a maximum of 30 days) to render its award. Any requests for extension of the original 120-day period would have to be justified to the Centre and the Parties, with an indication of the date on which the award is to be rendered. Thereafter, Parties would have 15 days from the rendering of an award to request clarification or revision;
- For annulment requests (provided in very similar circumstances to those envisaged in the ICSID Convention[64]), the deadline would be 180 days from the notification of the award. The Centre's secretariat would constitute ad-hoc tribunals to address each annulment request. Interestingly, the Draft Rules also include an appeal mechanism (for the review only of issues of law) before a permanent appellate body comprising eight magistrates, from which three will be designated to hear a case. No mention is

64 The grounds for annulment are as follows: (a) the Tribunal was not properly constituted; (b) the Tribunal has manifestly exceeded its powers; (c) there was corruption on the part of a member of the Tribunal; (d) there has been a serious departure from a fundamental rule of procedure; or (e) the award has failed to state the reasons on which it is based (art 52(1) of the ICSID Convention; art 13(2) of the Draft Rules).

made as to the procedure for the nomination of this appellate body, other than that it would include renowned investment arbitration practitioners;

- The Draft Rules also include a deadline for compliance with awards: in principle, awards should be complied with immediately; where this is impossible, the parties would have 15 days to agree on a deadline for compliance, which cannot exceed 90 days from notification of the award (180 days if the State demonstrates that immediate compliance can cause social unrest or serious economic damage to strategic sectors of its economy); and
- The Draft Rules provide that 'in order to avoid contradictory awards and decisions, the Arbitral Tribunal must join two or more proceedings involving common issues of fact or law relating to the same State measure or matter.' It remains to be seen how this mandatory joinder would operate in practice.

(3) The need for transparency

The final articles of the Draft Rules provide that hearings as well as all documents related to the arbitral proceedings would be public and that amicus curiae briefs would be allowed. The latter is subject to strict limitations, however (amicus curiae briefs must be submitted within 10 days after the tribunal is constituted; must not exceed 15 pages including annexes; etc).

The only exceptions to the principle of transparency are made in respect of (i) matters or documents that involve issues of national security or defense and (ii) cases where the tribunal issues confidentiality orders covering certain types of information (eg to protect commercial or trade secrets).

(iii) Will UNASUR's Centre constitute a credible alternative to the ICSID dispute settlement mechanism?

There is a clear political will to advance in the establishment of UNASUR's Centre, but it will only be a credible alternative to the ICSID system if foreign investors are willing to consent to arbitration under the Centre's jurisdiction.

Consent remains the cornerstone of any international dispute settlement mechanism. Disputes would only be submitted to the Centre for resolution if both Parties (ie the Host State and the foreign investor) have previously consented to it. The ICSID dispute settlement system has risen to prominence partly because the States' consent to arbitrate is found in hundreds of BITs[65] providing for the resolution of disputes through arbitration under the

---

[65] Or, to a lesser extent, through their enactment of investment laws providing for the resolution of investment disputes through ICSID arbitration or consent expressed on an ad-hoc basis.

auspices of ICSID. For the Centre to become widely used, BITs, investment laws or contracts would have to include the Parties' consent to submit to the Centre's jurisdiction. Of course Parties to a dispute could consent on an ad-hoc basis, but it is hardly the case in practice when a dispute has already arisen. It is reasonable to assume that consent to the UNASUR Centre's jurisdiction will be part of BITs to be entered into between UNASUR Member States. The challenge remains whether non-UNASUR Member States, and particularly capital-exporting countries, will accept such a forum. The current BIT negotiations and new model BITs from the region will be the first test for the credibility of UNASUR's projected Centre.

As regards the ratione materiae jurisdiction of the Centre, however, an overly narrow scope (such as the one provided by the Draft Rules) will operate as a disincentive to foreign investors and capital exporting countries and could prevent the Centre from becoming a real alternative to ICSID. In particular, Article 2 of the Draft Rules would exclude from the jurisdiction of the Centre (unless otherwise agreed by the host State) disputes concerning public development policies in matters of health, education, taxation, natural resources, and the environment, 'among others.' In providing for an open-ended list of policies excluded from the jurisdiction of the Centre ('among others'), the Draft Rules create legal uncertainty as to the Centre's jurisdiction. These exclusions, if they were to remain in the final version of the Draft Rules may arguably drive capital-exporting countries away from the Centre. In the same vein, by providing that under no circumstances will the 'legitimacy' of an internal law be subject to arbitration, UNASUR would be sending the wrong message and could be perceived as attempting to rewrite international law (according to which States may not invoke compliance with internal laws to avoid their international law obligations).[66]

In sum, for the projected UNASUR Centre to become a credible alternative to ICSID, some changes to Draft Rules will certainly be required.

---

[66] See UN International Law Commission, Draft articles on Responsibility of States for Internationally Wrongful Acts, with commentaries (2001), art 3: 'The characterization of an act of a State as internationally wrongful is governed by international law. Such characterization is not affected by the characterization of the same act as lawful by internal law.' And commentary: 'a State cannot, by pleading that its conduct conforms to the provisions of its internal law, escape the characterization of that conduct as wrongful by international law. An act of a State must be characterized as internationally wrongful if it constitutes a breach of an international obligation, even if the act does not contravene the State's internal law—even if, under that law, the State was actually bound to act in that way.'; See also, Vienna Convention on the Law of Treaties 1969, art 27: 'A party may not invoke the provisions of its internal law as justification for its failure to perform a treaty.'

B. Implications of the ALBA and UNASUR initiatives for inflows of foreign investment in South America

To assess the impact of the ALBA and UNASUR initiatives on inflows of foreign investment to their Member States one must first define what 'foreign' investment is in this context. In particular, the implications of ALBA and UNASUR are likely to be very different depending on whether or not 'foreign' investment includes the flow of capital between Member States.

It could be assumed that the 14 December 2004 bilateral agreement between Cuba and Venezuela and the 29 April 2006 Agreement for the Application of ALBA-TCP between these two countries and Bolivia, which contain extensive tax exemptions, would have a significant impact on intra-ALBA investment flows. Unfortunately, the data on foreign direct investment inflows to these countries is scarce and allows only for a partial test of this assumption. Unverified sources indicate that, for instance, several mixed State-owned companies involving Venezuelan capital have been created in Cuba, Bolivia, and recently Ecuador. However, the (incomplete) available data on foreign direct investment flows between ALBA Member States fails to show any correlation between accession to ALBA and foreign direct investment flows within the area. Interestingly, the data shows a correlation between the election of the current Presidents of Nicaragua (Daniel Ortega) and Ecuador (Rafael Correa) and a surge in direct foreign investment inflows originating in Venezuela since 2007. This trend, however, can be interpreted as resulting from the common ideological visions of these Governments, rather than as a direct consequence of ALBA initiatives.

Nevertheless, the increase in intraregional investment flows within ALBA Member States may be occurring at the expense of 'foreign' investment inflows (ie flows from outside the ALBA Member States). For example, the denunciation of the ICSID Convention and various BITs could have a depressing effect on inward foreign investment flows, as foreign investors may not be convinced by the affirmations that their investments remain protected by the Host States' domestic legislation and national courts. On the other hand, this concern is belied by the Brazilian example and ignores that (i) most BITs contain a survival clause providing that their protections will continue to apply to existing investments for several years after the BIT is denounced (usually ten or fifteen years)[67] and (ii) foreign investors may

[67] See, eg Agreement between the Government of the United Kingdom of Great Britain and Northern Ireland and the Government of the Republic of Ecuador (1994), art 14: 'This Agreement shall remain in force for a period of ten years. Thereafter it shall continue in force until the expiration of twelve months from the date on which either Contracting Party shall have given written notice of termination to the other. Provided that in respect of investments made whilst the Agreement is in force, its provisions shall continue in effect with respect to

structure their investments so as to benefit from the protection of BITs still in force.

Indeed, Brazil is not party to the ICSID Convention, has never ratified a single investment treaty, traditionally does not consent to international arbitration in State contracts and yet remains the greatest pole of attraction for foreign direct investment in South America.[68] This example is often put forward to demonstrate that denunciation of the ICSID Convention and BITs may have little (if any) influence on foreign investment inflows. The available data does not show a direct correlation between the denunciation of the ICSID Convention and/or BITs and the level of inward foreign investment. For instance, Ecuador (which denounced the ICSID Convention in 2009 and several BITs) has seen its net foreign direct investment inflows more than double between 2009 and 2011 (to US$ 641 million from US$ 306 million).[69]

In sum, it is difficult to predict the impact that ALBA has and will have on foreign investment originating from outside the ALBA area, especially because ALBA is still in the process of defining itself and is perceived as being tied to the fate of President Chávez. One may argue that the concept of companies grannacionales, coupled with the emphasis on recovering (through nationalization) the companies and natural resources of ALBA Members 'to which the people are entitled'[70], limits the foreign investors' access to key sectors of the economy (including the energy and infrastructure sectors).

Finally, even if the UNASUR initiative has yet to mature into a fully-fledged integration process, it is already very promising as far as foreign investment (whether interpreted as intra-Member States or not) is concerned. The 2004 Cusco Declaration calls for '[t]he deepening of convergence between MERCOSUR, the Andean Community and Chile through the perfection of the free trade area' and '[t]he physical integration

---

such investments for a period of fifteen years after the date of termination and without prejudice to the application thereafter of the rules of general international law.'

[68] In 2011 Brazil attracted USD 66,660 million of net FDI. The second most important pole of attraction for FDI in South America (thus excluding Mexico) is Chile, which attracted USD 17,299 million of net FDI in 2011. See ECLAC, Foreign Direct Investment in Latin America and the Caribbean (2011), 71. In 2012, Brazil again received the largest share of FDI flowing into South America (38%). See ECLAC, Foreign Direct Investment in Latin America and the Caribbean (2012), 10.

[69] See ECLAC, Foreign Direct Investment in Latin America and the Caribbean (2012), 23 Table I.3. It shall be noted, however, that such flows plummeted between 2008 and 2009 (to USD 306 million from USD 1,058 million the year before) in the context of the global slowdown (all other Latin American countries suffered a similar drop in net foreign direct investment inflows). Inward FDI into Ecuador in 2012 was slightly lower than 2011, at USD 587 million.

[70] Agreement for the Creation of the Economic Space of ALBA-TCP (ECOALBA-TCP) of 5 February 2012, art 2(6).

and integration of energy and communications in South America based on the deepening of existing bilateral, regional and sub-regional experiences'.[71] Similarly, the preamble to the UNASUR Constitutive Treaty provides that '[…] South American integration should be achieved through an innovative process, which would include the progress achieved so far by the MERCOSUR and CAN processes, as well as the experiences of Chile, Guyana and Suriname, and which goes beyond the convergence among them.' Should this integration process develop into a free trade area (and further into a common market) it will most certainly boost the economic attractiveness of each one of its Member States as they become platforms for penetrating a market of over 380 million consumers.

[71] Id.

10

The Evolving US Position on International Investment Protection and Its Impact on the US Position in the Trans-Pacific Partnership Negotiations

*James E. Mendenhall**

Evolving political attitudes in the US over the past 15 years toward the protection of foreign investment and the role of international law have had a dramatic effect on US investment agreements, including US bilateral investment treaties (BITs) and the investment chapters of US free trade agreements (FTAs). The US position has also had a deep impact on non-US bilateral investment treaties and free trade agreements, and will strongly influence the investment provisions that will be incorporated into the Trans-Pacific Partnership (TPP) agreement.

The change in US investment policy came about largely due to the fact that investment disciplines have been increasingly linked with trade disciplines. As a result, investment disciplines have been drawn into the broader controversy over globalization and, given the structure of the US system of government as discussed below, subjected to more intense scrutiny by the US Congress. While the turmoil has calmed in recent years, it may return as the US embarks on intense trade negotiations with countries in the Asia–Pacific region, Europe, and elsewhere.

Part I below briefly examines the evolution of the US model bilateral investment treaty prior to 2000. Part II examines the political environment that led to significant changes in the US model investment text used in US FTAs and BITs after 2000. Part III examines how the new US investment

* Partner, International Trade and Dispute Resolution group, Sidley Austin LLP, jmendenhall@sidley.com. The opinions expressed in this paper are entirely his own and do not necessarily reflect the views of Sidley Austin LLP or its clients.

policy has influenced the BITs of other countries that are participating in the TPP negotiations and how the TPP debate may reignite the debate over US investment policy.[1]

I. EARLY US BITS

The United States was a latecomer when it comes to negotiating BITs. As is well known, the first ever BIT was negotiated between Germany and Pakistan in 1959. The United States did not negotiate its first BIT until over 20 years later, when it signed a BIT with Panama in 1982.[2]

The first several generations of US BITs were not dramatically different from those of other countries. The US–Panama BIT, for example, guarantees a fairly standard suite of protections, including a guarantee of most-favored nation (MFN) treatment (Article II(1)) and national treatment (Article II(1)); the right to be compensated for expropriation of an investment (Article IV); the right to 'be accorded fair and equitable treatment' (Article II(2)); the right to 'enjoy full protection and security' (Article II(2)); the right to treatment 'in accordance with applicable national laws and international law' (Article II(2)); the guarantee that '[n]either Party shall in any way impair by arbitrary and discriminatory measures the management, operation, maintenance, use, enjoyment, acquisition, expansion or disposal of investments made by nationals or companies of the other Party' (Article II(2)); and a guarantee that '[e]ach Party shall observe any obligations it may have entered into with regard to investments of nationals or companies of the other Party' (Article II(2)). The United States–Panama BIT also provides for investor-state arbitration (Article VII). Over the next decade, the United States proceeded to negotiate several more BITs, including those with Senegal, the Democratic Republic of Congo, Morocco, Turkey, Bangladesh, Cameroon and others, which generally followed this same approach.

During the first several years of the US BIT programme, the US developed various model BIT texts, including in 1982, 1983, 1984, 1987, 1991, 1992 and 1994.[3] These BITs differed from each other in certain respects, but

[1] Much of this discussion is based on my personal experience participating in the formulation of the US model investment chapter used in certain FTAs from 2001–2007, the drafting of the 2004 US model BIT, and the negotiation of US legislation permitting 'fast track' approval of trade agreements during the early 2000s.

[2] Treaty Between the Government of the United States of America and the Government of the Republic of Panama Concerning the Treatment and Protection of Investments, at. art X(1), 27 October 1982, S Treaty Doc No 99-14 (1986).

[3] A comprehensive review of the evolution of US model BITs is provided in K Vandevelde, *US International Investment Agreements* (OUP 2009).

they were fairly similar and, on the whole, were in line with the BITs negotiated and signed by other countries around the world.

Things began to change with the North American Free Trade Agreement (the NAFTA), which entered into force on 1 January 1994.[4] The NAFTA was a comprehensive trade and investment agreement among the US, Mexico and Canada, and covered tariffs, trade in services, intellectual property, and other matters. Chapter 11 of the NAFTA covered investment and effectively replicated the protections that were typically found in BITs. It was the first time that investment disciplines were incorporated into a US trade agreement rather than a BIT.

At least in appearance, Chapter 11 differed in several important ways from contemporaneous US BITs. Whereas, for example, the US–Moldova BIT[5] signed in 1993 contains a single article on investor-state dispute settlement, covering about a page and a half of text, Chapter 11 of the NAFTA contains 24 articles on the arbitration process covering 11 pages of text. The NAFTA also includes four annexes of exceptions and reservations to the MFN and national treatment obligations, and certain other substantive obligations of the investment chapter, covering 197 pages.

Despite these differences from past investment agreements, the provisions in Chapter 11 of the NAFTA with respect to expropriation, MFN and national treatment, fair and equitable treatment and other substantive protections were cast in essentially the same terms as those of the preceding (and several subsequent) US BITs. However, Article 1131(2) of the NAFTA allowed the NAFTA Free Trade Commission (comprised of cabinet-level representatives from each of the three NAFTA Parties) to issue '[a]n interpretation ... of a provision of this Agreement [that] shall be binding on [an investor-state arbitration] Tribunal ... .' As we shall see, that provision was later used to interpret the fair and equitable treatment obligation in a manner that many believe significantly diverged from past practice.

The textual differences between the NAFTA and other BITs negotiated around the same time were not, however, what truly set the NAFTA apart. The conclusion of the NAFTA was a watershed event in US investment policy because of the nature and relationship of the Parties themselves. US BITs before and after the NAFTA were negotiated with smaller, developing countries, and the flow of capital primarily ran from the US to the BIT

[4] 32 *ILM* 289, 605 (1993). The text of the NAFTA is available at http://www.nafta-sec-alena.org/en/view.aspx?x=343.

[5] Treaty Between the United States of America and the Republic of Moldova Concerning the Encouragement and Reciprocal Protection of Investment, with Annex, Protocol and Exchange of Letters, 21 April 1993, S Treaty Doc No 103-14 (1993) http://2001-2009.state.gov/documents/organization/43578.pdf.

partner. The possibility that the US would be subject to challenge through investor-state arbitration was remote. The NAFTA Parties were different, and the risk profile for the US was different. The NAFTA involved three large countries, two of which were developed economies, with extensive two- and three-way investment flows. As a result, for the first time, the US faced a real risk of being challenged in investor-state arbitration, which would prove to have significant political consequences.

The NAFTA was a controversial agreement, and was made a significant issue in the 1992 presidential campaign, especially by independent candidate Ross Perot, who campaigned on the theme that the NAFTA would create a 'giant sucking sound' to the south as Mexico siphoned jobs from the US economy. Soon after the NAFTA entered into force, the controversy over Chapter 11 in particular was heightened by the fact that several of the first NAFTA cases involved sensitive issues, including challenges to environmental regulations. In January 1997, a US investor claimed that Mexico had breached the NAFTA by refusing to issue permits for a waste disposal facility, ostensibly to allow the creation of an environmental preserve (*Metalclad v. Mexico*). In April 1997, a US investor asserted that a Canadian ban on the import and inter-provincial trade of a certain gasoline additive breached Chapter 11 (*Ethyl v. Canada*). In December 1999, a Canadian investor challenged California's ban of another gasoline additive (*Methanex v. United States*). In addition, in October 1988, a Canadian investor challenged the actions of a Mississippi court (*Loewen v. United States*), raising questions about whether Chapter 11 would be used to appeal (or 'second guess', as some would have it) US court decisions.

While these cases were proceeding, a much broader political controversy over trade and investment agreements was brewing. The US and many of its trading partners hoped to launch a new round of World Trade Organization negotiations at the WTO Ministerial conference in Seattle in November–December 1999. These hopes were dashed when the conference collapsed amid rioting in the streets. It quickly became clear that the 'business as usual' approach to trade would no longer work. If there were going to be any significant new trade initiatives in the near future, something would have to be done to calm the waters.

II. THE NEW INVESTMENT POLICY

The Office of the US Trade Representative (USTR) is the lead agency within the Administration charged with negotiating and enforcing trade agreements. With respect to the negotiation of BITs, USTR shares competency with the US State Department. However, as discussed below, once investment became embedded in trade agreements, as was the case with the

NAFTA, USTR assumed a much more prominent role in the formulation of US investment policy.

After President George W. Bush entered office in January 2001, he appointed an extraordinarily ambitious and energetic US Trade Representative, Ambassador Robert Zoellick. Less than two years after the collapse of the Seattle WTO Ministerial, Ambassador Zoellick brought with him big plans for an aggressive trade agenda, including launching a new round of WTO negotiations and embarking on a series of new free trade agreement negotiations.

Trade was the overarching focus of the agenda, not BITs and not investment protection more broadly. However, by virtue of the fact that the NAFTA incorporated investment protections, trade and investment were now inextricably linked. Indeed, the changes that were to come in US investment policy were a direct result of the fact that investment protection was now fully at play in the larger trade debate. In practical terms, this meant that the future of US investment policy would be shaped by the needs of the trade agenda.

The changing US approach was eventually reflected in the 2004 US model BIT. However, contrary to a common misperception, the changes did not begin with the development of that text. The shift came a few years earlier and it arose from the trade debates that took place in the first years of the Bush Administration, and, in particular, the haggling between the Bush Administration and the US Congress with respect to the legislation that put in place 'fast track' approval for the FTAs the Administration would soon negotiate. The new US investment policy originated there.

A. Fast Track Authority and the Need for Congressional-Executive Cooperation

When the Bush Administration came to office, the US was a party to only three FTAs—the US–Israel FTA,[6] the United States–Jordan FTA,[7] and the NAFTA (the earlier Canada–US FTA had effectively been superseded by the NAFTA). As with the US BIT programme that began two decades earlier, the US was a laggard in the negotiation of FTAs. As a result, there was a widespread belief that the US had fallen behind Europe and needed to catch up. As Ambassador Zoellick explained,

---

[6] Agreement on the Establishment of a Free Trade Area between the Government of Israel and the Government of the United States of America, 24 *ILM* 653; (1985), http://tcc.export.gov/Trade_Agreements/All_Trade_Agreements/exp_005439.asp.

[7] Agreement between the United States of America and the Hashemite Kingdom of Jordan on the Establishment of a Free Trade Area, 41 *ILM* 63 (2002) http://tcc.export.gov/Trade_Agreements/All_Trade_Agreements/exp_005607.asp

> since the Congressional grant of authority to negotiate trade agreements expired in 1994, 7 years ago, America has fallen behind. Today, the European Union has 27 free trade agreements or special customs agreements around the world, 20 of which were negotiated in the 1990s when we have been caught unable to act, and it is doing 15 more right now. … We have got no one to blame but ourselves for this.[8]

Ambassador Zoellick sought to instill in US trade policy a sense of urgency, arguing that the US needed to lead on trade and it needed to move quickly. In testifying before the Congress, he argued that '[w]e cannot afford to stand still or be mired in partisan division while other nations seize the mantle of leadership of trade from the US. This would be a missed opportunity, indeed, an historic mistake.'[9] At the international level, Ambassador Zoellick sought to create a spirit of competitive liberalization, in which the US would simultaneously pursue trade agreements at the bilateral, regional and multilateral level. By doing so, the international system would be shaken out of its complacency and begin clamoring to liberalize. As Ambassador Zoellick explained, 'if [other countries] are too slow, we will go elsewhere, because our economy is so attractive, the model of our private sector is so appealing, people will come to us if we are ready to deal. For those that will not deal, they are going to be left behind, not us.'[10]

The problem, however, was that the Administration's ambitions would be hamstrung without the cooperation of the Congress. Under the system of checks and balances created by the US Constitution, the President did not have authority to act alone in the negotiation of trade agreements. The Constitution conferred wide authority on the President in the area of foreign affairs, but this authority did not extend to trade. Article II, Section 2, of the US Constitution vests in the President the 'Power, by and with the Advice and Consent of the Senate, to make Treaties.' Presidents used this authority to negotiate investment treaties like BITs, or, decades ago, treaties of friendship,

---

[8] Trade Promotion Authority, Hearings Before the Committee on Finance, United States Senate, S Hrg No 107-171, 107th Cong, 1st Sess, 20–21 June 2001, 76 (testimony of Ambassador Robert B. Zoellick) (TPA Hearing).

[9] Hearing Before the Committee on Finance, United States Senate, on the Nomination of Robert B. Zoellick to be US Trade Representative, S Hrg 107–11, 107th Cong, 1st Sess, 30 January 2001, 13 (testimony of Robert Zoellick) (Zoellick Confirmation Hearing). See also, id. 20–21 ('This is one of those points in history where we have an unparalleled opportunity to shape the international trading order. … All you have to do is read some of these articles and see how Japan and Europe are planning where the international trading system should go. They should not be doing it, we should be leading it. … Frankly, I have said publicly on other occasions, if other countries go ahead with free trade agreements and we do not, I do not blame them, it is our mistake. But we have to get back into this game, and we are certainly in a position to do so').

[10] Zoellick Confirmation Hearing, 42.

commerce and navigation. While the President needed approval of the Senate to ratify treaties, he nevertheless had great autonomy, and, for the most part, BITs were non-controversial and required only limited involvement by the Congress.[11] Trade, however, was different.

The US Constitution gives Congress the authority to regulate trade. Specifically, Article I, Section 8 of the United States Constitution vests in the Congress the right to 'regulate Commerce with foreign Nations' and to 'lay and collect taxes, duties, imposts, and excises.' Consequently, while Presidents had, on occasion, negotiated Treaties of Friendship, Commerce and Navigation that included an obligation to grant MFN treatment with respect to tariffs,[12] the President could not proclaim changes to tariff rates without congressional approval.

For a long time, the Congress regulated tariffs with little or no Presidential involvement. The cooperation between the President and the Congress with respect to trade began in earnest, however, after the disastrous trade wars that resulted from the 'Smoot-Hawley' Tariff Act of 1930, which are often cited as a key contributing factor to the Great Depression. In the wake of these events, Congress began to delegate to the President the authority to negotiate reciprocal trade agreements.[13] These trade agreements were not formal treaties but Congressional-Executive agreements. The President would negotiate the agreements, and then bring them back to Congress for approval. In approving the agreements, the Congress would also adopt implementing legislation that would, among other things, allow the President to proclaim modifications to tariff rates.

---

[11] The Congress, through the Senate, could, of course, leverage its authority to ratify treaties to exert influence on the President, and it has done so in the past. See eg the discussion between the US Administration and the Congress clarifying the scope of the national security exception in BITs after the ICJ decision in *Military and Paramilitary Activities in and Against Nicaragua* (*Nicaragua v. US*), Judgment, 1986 ICJ 14 (June 27) described in WW Burke White & A von Staden, 'Investment Protection in Extraordinary Times: The Interpretation and Application of Nonprecluded Measures Provisions in Bilateral Investment Treaties' 48 *Va J Int'l Law* 307, 352–53, 383–86 (2008).

[12] See eg Article XIV(1) of the US–Japan Treaty of Friendship, Commerce, and Navigation, Protocol, and Exchange of Notes of August 29, 1953, 4 UST 2063; TIAS 2863; 206 UNTS 143 ('Each Party shall accord most-favored-nation treatment to products of the other Party, from whatever place and by whatever type of carrier arriving, and to products destined for exportation to the territories of such other Party, by whatever route and by whatever type of carrier, with respect to customs duties and charges of any kind imposed on or in connection with importation or exportation or imposed on the international transfer of payments for imports or exports, and with respect to the method of levying such duties and charges, and with respect to all rules and formalities in connection with importation and exportation').

[13] JF Hornbeck and WH Cooper 'Trade Promotion Authority (TPA) and the Role of Congress in Trade Policy', 9 August 2012 2–3.

The difficulty with that approach, however, was that it was unpredictable. The President would negotiate the agreements, but the Congress (comprised of 535 individuals, whose opinions were often deeply divided) had the authority to approve or disapprove them. This division of authority presented obvious risks. If the Congress were unhappy with an agreement, it might, for example, demand that the President return to the negotiating table to reopen the negotiations, leading to frustration among trading partners who believed that they had already cut a deal and might already have been trying to ratify the agreement through their own domestic legal system.

In order to resolve this problem, a new approach, known as 'fast track' approval, was developed. 'Fast track' procedures would allow the President to negotiate trade agreements and bring them back to the Congress for an up-or-down vote. The Congress could either approve or reject the agreements, but it could not amend them. Fast track authority would give US negotiating partners confidence that the carefully negotiated deals they struck with the President would stick and not unravel once they were presented to the Congress for approval.[14] While the Congress might reject an agreement, the Congress and the President generally cooperated to make sure that did not happen. The two branches would engage in extensive consultations in advance and would coordinate on the timing and content of any legislation the President might submit to approve and implement the deals.

Fast track legislation, also known as trade promotion authority or 'TPA', was first adopted in the Trade Act of 1974 and was extended multiple times through 1994. Fast track legislation was crafted to strike a balance between Presidential and Congressional authority. While the Congress would grant the President the authority to negotiate trade agreements, it would not do so unconditionally. In order to qualify for fast track treatment, a trade agreement had to meet certain negotiating objectives that were set forth in the legislation itself. As summarized by the Congressional Research Service:

---

[14] As succinctly explained by the Congressional Research Service:

> For more than 30 years, Congress has granted the President TPA/fast track authority, agreeing to consider trade agreement implementing legislation expeditiously and to vote on it without amendment, provided the President meets certain statutory negotiating objectives and consultation requirements, and the implementing bill contains the necessary and limited qualifying provisions. TPA strikes a delicate balance by clarifying how Congress chooses to exercise its constitutional authority over a particular aspect of trade policy, while presumably giving the President additional negotiating leverage by effectively assuring trade partners that a final agreement will be given timely and unamended consideration by Congress.

Hornbeck and Cooper (n 13) 1.

> Congress, drawing on its constitutional authority and historical precedent, define[s] the objectives that the President is to pursue in trade negotiations. Although the executive branch has some discretion over implementing these goals, they are definitive statements of US trade policy that the Administration is expected to honor, if it expects trade agreement implementing legislation to be considered under expedited rules. For this reason, trade negotiating objectives stand at the center of the congressional debate on TPA.[15]

However, one implication of this approach was that, as the scope of trade agreements grew, so did the need for Executive-Congressional cooperation. So, when investment was added to the mix during the negotiation of the NAFTA, and to a lesser extent during the Uruguay Round WTO negotiations, investment policy became much more tied to the broader trade context and to the desires of the US Congress.

Still, this dynamic did not immediately result in any dramatic shifts of policy. Indeed, prior to 2001, the 'fast track' negotiating objectives with respect to investment were relatively simple and general. For example, the Omnibus Trade and Competitiveness Act of 1988 provided:

> (11) Foreign direct investment
>
> (A) The principal negotiating objectives of the United States regarding foreign direct investment are—
>
> (i) to reduce or to eliminate artificial or trade-distorting barriers to foreign direct investment, to expand the principle of national treatment, and to reduce unreasonable barriers to establishment; and
>
> (ii) to develop internationally agreed rules, including dispute settlement procedures, which—
>
> (I) will help ensure a free flow of foreign direct investment, and
>
> (II) will reduce or eliminate the trade distortive effects of certain trade-related investment measures.
>
> (B) In pursuing the negotiating objectives described in subparagraph (A), United States negotiators shall take into account legitimate United States domestic objectives including, but not limited to, the protection of legitimate health or safety, essential security, environmental, consumer or employment opportunity interests and the law and regulations related thereto.[16]

---

15 Ibid, 10.

16 19 USC section 2901(b)(1).

Fast track legislation expired in 1994, and attempts to renew fast track authority in the late 1990s failed.[17]

B. Setting the Groundwork for Trade Promotion Authority

Renewal of fast track authority was a top trade priority of the new Bush Administration. Ambassador Zoellick summed up his approach as follows:

> In the absence of [TPA], other countries have been moving forward with trade agreements while America has stalled. …
>
> In considering this grant of trade promotion authority, I also urge you to give the President more leverage by broadening our options. I want to be able to tell my counterparts that we are willing to negotiate if they are serious about eliminating barriers, and also make clear that America will look elsewhere if they delay, that the United States will move forward and it is up to them to decide to join us or be left behind.[18]

What ensued was a long negotiation between the Administration and the Congress about what the fast track legislation would contain. As with previous fast track legislation, the new law would include negotiating objectives that would set forth Congressional expectations for what future trade agreements should accomplish in order to qualify for fast track approval.

The US experience under the NAFTA would play a very significant role in the formulation of the negotiating objectives. As a result of the debate over Chapter 11 of the NAFTA, concerns were being expressed that the NAFTA model went too far, that it was too much of an infringement on sovereignty and chilled legitimate regulation. As explained in the Senate report that accompanied the fast track legislation that was eventually adopted:

> The growing number of investor-state disputes has caused concern among certain interest groups. In particular, some environmental groups see investor-state dispute settlement provisions as having a potentially chilling effect on the adoption of environmental laws and regulations.
>
> It is argued that arbitral tribunals may interpret the concept of what constitutes a compensable 'expropriation' for purposes of an investment agreement more broadly than courts of the United States have interpreted

---

[17] See Hornbeck and Cooper (n 13) 6 ('In 1997, both the Senate Finance and the House Ways and Means Committees reported out legislation to renew fast track. House Republican leaders pulled it before a floor vote at the request of the Clinton Administration because it lacked sufficient support in the House. In September 1998, the House voted on fast track authority legislation, but the bill failed to pass (180–243)').

[18] Zoellick Confirmation Hearing (n 9) 13.

> what constitutes a compensable 'taking' for purposes of the Constitution of the United States. Thus, a Canadian or Mexican investor might be able to seek compensation for loss of value flowing from a US (or state or local) government measure, whereas a similarly situated US investor would not. ...
>
> Some environmental groups point to the obligation to accord fair and equitable treatment to foreign investments as having a similar impact.[19]

If the Administration was going to build a strong relationship with Congress to pave the way for fast track negotiating authority, it needed to allay these concerns, and it did so by tackling the criticism of the NAFTA head on. Soon after taking office, the new Administration entered into the negotiation of a binding interpretation of the NAFTA investment provisions that was intended to clarify certain substantive investment obligations and, in the process, reduce the exposure of the three NAFTA governments to what some believed were non-meritorious arbitration claims.

On 31 July 2001, the three NAFTA parties reached agreement on two principles.[20] First, in an attempt to demystify the process and improve transparency, '[e]ach Party agree[d] to make available to the public in a timely manner all documents submitted to, or issued by, a Chapter Eleven tribunal, subject to redaction of [confidential information] ...'.

Second, the parties issued a binding interpretation under Article 1131(2) of the NAFTA with respect to Article 1105 (Minimum Standard of Treatment). Article 1105 contained the obligation to guarantee investors fair and equitable treatment and full protection and security. Critics argued that those obligations were too broad and allowed arbitrators to base decisions on personal whim. To address this concern, the binding interpretation sought to anchor the scope of the obligation in customary international law, stating as follows:

> Article 1105(1) prescribes the customary international law minimum standard of treatment of aliens as the minimum standard of treatment to be afforded to investments of investors of another Party. The concepts of "fair and equitable treatment" and "full protection and security" do not require treatment in addition to or beyond that which is required by the customary international law minimum standard of treatment of aliens. A determination that there has been a breach of another provision of the NAFTA,

[19] Bipartisan Trade Promotion Authority Act of 2002, 107th Cong, 2nd Sess, Sen Rep 107–139, 28 Feb, 2002 12–13 (TPA Senate Report).

[20] Notes of Interpretation of Certain Chapter 11 Provisions (NAFTA Free Trade Commission, July 31, 2001), http://www.international.gc.ca/trade-agreements-accords-commerciaux/topics-domaines/disp-diff/NAFTA-Interpr.aspx?lang=eng.

> or of a separate international agreement, does not establish that there has been a breach of Article 1105(1).

The NAFTA interpretation was criticized by some for not going far enough and by others for going too far. Indeed, certain critics argued that the interpretation deviated so far from the text of the NAFTA that it amounted to an amendment, not an interpretation.[21] Critics further argued that the clarification failed, in fact, to clarify anything and that the link to customary international law would serve only to confuse the matter.[22] According to Public Citizen: 'a recent July 31, 2001 clarification by the NAFTA governments has attempted to deal with this issue by seeking to narrow the application of Article 1105 to treatment that is required by 'customary' international law. Yet the new interpretation does not define what is meant by 'customary,' providing enormous opportunity for a continuation of the expansive interpretation by the tribunals.'[23]

While certain commentators argued that the interpretation unjustifiably weakened investment principles that the United States had advocated and helped formulate over several decades,[24] they sometimes failed to recognize, or recognized but dismissed, the broader political (as opposed to policy) context. Specifically, the debate over the NAFTA investment provisions was a potential obstacle to the Administration's broader trade agenda. If the Administration was going to persuade the Congress to approve fast track procedures, then it needed to take steps to address Congressional concerns that could frustrate that objective. Certain members of the Congress would clearly use the investment rules as a reason to grandstand in opposition to future agreements and vote against fast track authority. On the other hand, there were few if any members of the Congress who, even if they were strong advocates of investment protection, would vote against fast track authority as a result of the clarification. From a political perspective, the calculation was clear.

---

[21] *In the Matter of Arbitration Under Chapter 11 of the North American Free Trade Agreement, Pope & Talbot Inc v Government of Canada*, Award in Respect of Damages, May 31, 2002, at para. 47 ('were the Tribunal required to make a determination whether the Commission's action is an interpretation or an amendment, it would choose the latter').

[22] See eg S Schwebel, 'The United States 2004 Model Bilateral Investment Treaty: an Exercise in the Regressive Development of International Law,' *Transnational Dispute Settlement*, Vol. 3, Issue 2, April 2006, 4 ('The profound, and startling, deficiency of the 2004 provision is that there is no agreement within the international community on the content of "customary international law" on which the 2004 Model BIT relies').

[23] NAFTA Chapter 11 Investor-to-State Cases: Bankrupting Democracy, http://www.citizen.org/publications/publicationredirect.cfm?ID=7076.

[24] See eg Schwebel (n 22).

The lack of a strong constituency willing to expend political capital in support of investment protections is a recurring problem for the pro-investment community in the US. Most of the business community would, if asked, support strong investment protections. The same is true for many policymakers, commentators, and average citizens. However, for those who are not steeped in the issues, investment protection is often viewed as an abstract 'lawyer's issue'—that is, until such time as a company runs into problems and needs to invoke the rules to protect its valuable investments. As a result (unlike, for example, issues such as the reduction or elimination of tariffs and subsidies, expansion of market access, or the strengthening of intellectual property protection—issues with a potentially immediate and large impact), investment protection is typically not an issue that wins significant votes in the Congress.

I should be quick to note, however, that none of this is to say that the NAFTA clarification was undertaken purely for political reasons. While there was clearly a political element to the negotiation of the clarification, there were some in the Administration, and certainly in the Congress, who believed that a clarification was necessary on policy grounds.

C. *The Formulation of Fast Track Authority*

Returning to the negotiation of fast track authority, it was evident that, at a minimum, the NAFTA clarification would need to be reflected in one form or another in the negotiating objectives of any new legislation. It was also apparent that more would need to be done.

Fast track authority, which had by that time been dubbed 'Trade Promotion Authority' or 'TPA,' was adopted as part of the Trade Act of 2002.[25] The legislation contained a list of 'foreign investment' objectives.[26] The objectives began with a general paragraph or 'chapeau' that set the overall framework for the specific objectives. The chapeau began by:

> [r]ecognizing that United States law on the whole provides a high level of protection for investment, consistent with or greater than the level required by international law, the principal negotiating objectives of the United States regarding foreign investment are to reduce or eliminate artificial or trade-distorting barriers to foreign investment, while ensuring that foreign investors in the United States are not accorded greater substantive rights with respect to investment protections than United States investors in the United States, and to secure for investors important

---

[25] Pub. L. 107–210, 116 Stat. 993, enacted 6 August 6 2002. The fast track procedures are codified at 19 USC sections 3802 et seq.

[26] 19 USC section 3802(b)(3).

> rights comparable to those that would be available under United States legal principles and practice, by [the series of more specific trade objectives that followed].

There are at least two notable aspects of the chapeau, which reflected the broader tug-of-war between those who advocated a change of direction and those who believed the *status quo* was satisfactory.

First, the chapeau directed US negotiators to 'ensur[e] that foreign investors in the United States are not accorded greater substantive rights with respect to investment protection than United States investors in the United States, and to secure for investors important rights comparable to those that would be available under United States legal principles and practice.' Thus, negotiators were directed to align US law and international investment standards such that the international standards would not provide a higher level of protection. The fact that this provision was directed at 'substantive rights,' rather than procedural rights, was significant in explaining that the purpose was not to constrain or eliminate investor-state arbitration, but to refine the substantive protections. (As will be seen, however, the negotiating objectives nevertheless included certain objectives related to investor-state arbitration procedures).

Second, the chapeau asserted that 'United States law on the whole provides a high level of protection for investment, consistent with or greater than the level required by international law.' This sentence had a dual purpose. Along with the 'no greater substantive rights' language described above, it reflected the general desire to create a fair and level playing field. It implied, in other words, that because US standards are high and can be relied upon by foreign investors, the legal protections for US investors abroad should be equally high.

Moreover, by recognizing that 'United States law on the whole provides a high level of protection for investment, consistent with or greater than the level required by international law,' the chapeau sought to resolve a tension inherent in the very idea of aligning the substantive protections under US and international law. This tension arose from the fact that, even if international protections and US law provided a comparable level of protection, they did so in different ways. To align the two sets of principles, it would be necessary to compare, for example, the takings jurisprudence under the 5th Amendment of the US Constitution with the international law principle of expropriation, or to compare the due process standards of the 4th and 14th Amendments of the US Constitution with the standard investment protections guaranteeing investors 'fair and equitable' treatment and 'full protection and security.' Any differences between the two sets of principles would need to be identified and eliminated. However, drafting investment agreement provisions that would both encapsulate US law and reflect international investment standards was extraordinarily difficult. Standards change over time, their application is highly fact-specific, and their interpretation has been elaborated over centuries of jurisprudence. Trying to capture those principles comprehensively in a few lines of treaty text, and then ensure that the principles are aligned, is a near-impossible task.

Asserting that US law provided a level of protection consistent with or higher than international law was an attempt to resolve that problem. In other words, if US law already provided foreign investors with protections that were equal to or greater than the protections that had traditionally been included in investment treaties, then there was no fear that repeating those substantive protections in future trade and investment agreements would give foreign investors 'greater substantive rights with respect to investment protection than United States investors in the United States.' As the Senate report accompanying the TPA legislation stated, 'when the United States agrees to afford foreign investors the protections required by international law, it is not making a commitment that will result in foreign investors having substantially different rights in the United States than those accorded US investors under US law.'[27] This was, of course, an assertion, not an argument.

Following the chapeau was a series of specific investment negotiating objectives that were intended to elaborate on the general principles set forth in the chapeau. Certain of the objectives were not particularly novel or surprising. For example, one objective was to ensure that US investors were not subjected to discriminatory, less favourable treatment.[28] Other objectives, however, clearly diverged from precedent and elaborated on the general directive in the chapeau to provide no greater substantive rights to foreign investors. For example, negotiators were required to 'seek[ ] to establish standards for expropriation and compensation for expropriation, consistent with United States legal principles and practice.'[29] Another directed negotiators to 'seek[ ] to establish standards for fair and equitable treatment consistent with United States legal principles and practice, including the principle of due process.'[30]

Despite the focus on substantive rights in the chapeau, the legislation also contained several specific negotiating objectives focused on the arbitration process. The objectives directed negotiators to:

> Seek[ ] to improve mechanisms used to resolve disputes between an investor and a government through—

[27] TPA Senate Report (n 19) 13.

[28] 19 USC section 3802(b)(3)(A) (identifying as one objective 'reducing or eliminating exceptions to the principle of national treatment').

[29] 19 USC section 3802(b)(3)(D).

[30] 19 USC section 3802(b)(3)(E).

(i) mechanisms to eliminate frivolous claims and to deter the filing of frivolous claims;
(ii) procedures to ensure the efficient selection of arbitrators and the expeditious disposition of claims;
(iii) procedures to enhance opportunities for public input into the formulation of government positions; and
(iv) providing for an appellate body or similar mechanism to provide coherence to the interpretations of investment provisions in trade agreements.[31]

Finally, the negotiating objectives required that negotiators include procedures to enhance the transparency of investor-state proceedings. Among other things, the transparency-related objectives required negotiators to 'ensur[e] the fullest measure of transparency in the dispute settlement mechanism, to the extent consistent with the need to protect information that is classified or business confidential, by ...' publicly releasing requests for dispute settlement, pleadings, and decisions, opening hearings to the public, and allowing amicus submissions from businesses, unions and nongovernmental organizations.[32]

As is evident from this discussion, the negotiating objectives were ambiguous and internally contradictory. On the one hand, the objectives asserted that US law provided greater protection than international investment protections, which might imply that the investment provisions, as they had previously been formulated in US BITs, were fully in line with the objective of ensuring that foreign investors do not receive greater substantive rights than US investors in the US. On the other hand, the objectives (and the broader political context) also clearly contemplated some modification of the traditional treaty formulations so as to ensure alignment between US and international standards. Furthermore, while the chapeau indicated that the focus of the objectives was on clarifying substantive investment obligations, the objectives included a laundry list of necessary procedural changes. It was left to the Administration to untangle the web.

D. Translating the TPA Objectives Into Model Text

Even while the negotiation of the TPA language was proceeding, and in the immediate aftermath of the passage of TPA, the Administration engaged in a protracted inter-agency process to revise the model investment chapter that it would use in future free trade agreement negotiations, including in the first

---

31 19 USC section 3802(b)(3)(G).
32 19 USC section 3802(b)(3)(H).

two FTAs that were being negotiated, ie those with Singapore and Chile. The result was a very significant restructuring of the basic protections.

The extent of the changes was obvious from even the most cursory review of the investment chapters of the Singapore and Chile FTAs.[33] The previous US model BIT had been approximately 10 pages long covering 16 articles,[34] while the investment chapter of the NAFTA was 29 pages covering 39 articles and a few short annexes (excluding annexes on reservations and exceptions). The investment chapter of the Chile FTA included only 27 articles but it ran to 36 pages, and included eight largely substantive annexes, (excluding annexes on reservations and exceptions). The provisions on investor-state arbitration in the previous model BIT were encompassed in a single article. The section of the investment chapter of the Chile FTA that covered dispute settlement now spanned 13 pages and 13 articles. Unlike the previous model BIT or the NAFTA, the new model contained an annex on the meaning of the expropriation provision, a separate annex on the definition of customary international law, and a third annex on the negotiation of an appellate mechanism.

The substantive changes from earlier model BITs and the investment chapter of the NAFTA have been addressed at length in the literature, and I will not repeat that analysis here, except to highlight a few of the more significant points.

As under the NAFTA clarification, the new model FTA text directly linked the fair and equitable treatment standard to customary international law. Further, the new text clarified that the fair and equitable treatment standard 'includes the obligation not to deny justice in criminal, civil, or administrative adjudicatory proceedings in accordance with the principle of due process embodied in the principal legal systems of the world,' which presumably included the common law legal system of the United States.[35] The text also provided that the obligation to ensure full protection and security 'require[d] each Party to provide the level of police protection required under customary international law.'[36]

The annex on expropriation limited expropriation to property rights and property interests, and stated that, in determining whether a measure amounted to an indirect expropriation, three factors must be taken into account. Those three factors were drawn directly from the US Supreme Court

[33] Chapter 15 of the US–Singapore FTA covers investment and is available at http://www.ustr.gov/trade-agreements/free-trade-agreements/singapore-fta/final-text. Chapter 10 of the United States-Chile FTA covers investment and is available at http://www.ustr.gov/trade-agreements/free-trade-agreements/chile-fta/final-text.

[34] The 1994 US model BIT, as revised in 1998, is available at http://unctad.org/sections/dite/iia/docs/Compendium/en/175%20volume%206.pdf.

[35] See eg art 10.4(2)(a) of the US–Chile FTA.

[36] See eg art 10.4(2)(b) of the US–Chile FTA.

case in *Penn Central Transportation Co v New York City*, 98 S.Ct. 2646 (1978), and included the following:

(i) the economic impact of the government action, although the fact that an action or series of actions by a Party has an adverse effect on the economic value of an investment, standing alone, does not establish that an indirect expropriation has occurred;
(ii) the extent to which the government action interferes with distinct, reasonable investment-backed expectations; and
(iii) the character of the government action.[37]

The annex on expropriation also stated, 'except in rare circumstances, nondiscriminatory regulatory actions by a Party that are designed and applied to protect legitimate public welfare objectives, such as public health, safety, and the environment, do not constitute indirect expropriations.'

The annex on customary international law

> confirm[ed] [the Parties'] shared understanding that 'customary international law' … results from a general and consistent practice of States that they follow from a sense of legal obligation. With regard to [the provision covering the "minimum standard of treatment," which included fair and equitable treatment and full protection and security,] the customary international law minimum standard of treatment of aliens refers to all customary international law principles that protect the economic rights and interests of aliens.[38]

On the procedural side, the new model included procedures that reflected US summary judgment standards by allowing a tribunal to 'address and decide as a preliminary question any objection by the respondent that, as a matter of law, a claim submitted is not a claim for which an award in favor of the claimant may be made. …'[39] The text included a provision indicating that, in the event 'a separate multilateral agreement enters into force as between the Parties that establishes an appellate body for purposes of reviewing awards rendered by tribunals constituted pursuant to international trade or investment agreements to hear investment disputes, the Parties shall strive to reach an agreement that would have such appellate body review awards issued by arbitration tribunals established under the investment chapter.'[40] Finally, the

[37] See eg Annex 10-D of the US–Chile FTA.

[38] See eg Annex 10-A of the US–Chile FTA.

[39] See eg Article 10.19(4) of the US–Chile FTA, Cf Rule 56 of the United States Federal Rules of Civil Procedure ('The court shall grant summary judgment if the movant shows that there is no genuine dispute as to any material fact and the movant is entitled to judgment as a matter of law').

[40] See eg art 10.19(1) of the US–Chile FTA.

new model included a separate annex binding the Parties to consider the establishment of a 'bilateral appellate body or similar mechanism.'[41]

E. The 2004 Model BIT

The new model text was used in the Singapore and Chile FTAs and in all of the FTAs the US negotiated between 2001–2007, with minor variations. The one significant deviation is the US–Australia FTA, which includes an investment chapter but does not include investor-state dispute settlement.

When the Administration decided to reactivate its BIT programme a couple of years after the completion of the model FTA text, it needed to decide whether to convert the FTA text to a model BIT text or to stick with its previous model. As explained, BITs, unlike FTAs, are treaties under US law and so are not subject to the same Congressional approval process used for FTAs. As a result, TPA would not apply to a BIT. Under the Constitution, treaties must be approved by two-thirds of the US Senate, and the US House of Representatives would have no involvement. Nevertheless, the Administration decided that it would be incongruous (not to mention impolitic) to use the new model investment provisions in FTAs and the old model BIT for BIT negotiations. A process was then undertaken to transform the model FTA investment chapter into a new model BIT. The result was the 2004 US model BIT.[42]

During the next few years, the Administration remained focused on trade, not BITs. Between 2001 and 2008, the US negotiated FTAs with Singapore, Chile, Australia, Central America and the Dominican Republic, Panama, Paraguay, Colombia, Bahrain, Morocco, Oman, and Korea. Only two US BITs were negotiated between 2001–2010, one with Uruguay and one with Rwanda. Towards the end of the Bush Administration, the US sought to launch BIT negotiations with the so-called BRIC countries (Brazil, Russia, India and China); however, the effort met with little enthusiasm from Brazil and Russia, and discussions with India and China are, at the time of this writing, still in the very early stages.

F. 10 May 2007 Trade Deal

As discussed, the purpose of TPA was to ensure that Congress would be able to take an up or down vote on trade agreements without requiring amendments. As a practical matter, this meant that an agreement would not be

---

[41] See eg Annex 10-H of the US–Chile FTA.

[42] The 2004 US model BIT is available at http://unctad.org/sections/dite/iia/docs/Compendium/en/model_USA.pdf.

presented to the Congress unless the Administration was reasonably certain that the agreement would pass. An elaborate discussion between the Administration and the Congress would, therefore, precede the submission of the agreement. Consultation requirements were built into the TPA legislation itself, and Congress would hold so-called 'mock markups', in which the relevant Congressional committees would hold hearings to review an agreement and express concerns. By the time an agreement was submitted, the process would (hopefully) be greased.

That arrangement started to unravel in the later years of the Bush Administration, as the Administration prepared to submit the FTAs with Korea, Colombia, Panama and Peru to the Congress. A combination of factors made passage of these agreements more complicated than usual. For example, Congress was getting 'trade fatigue,' as it had been called upon to take a number of hard votes on a series of trade agreements over the preceding years. In addition, each of the agreements had their own peculiar sensitivities. The trade agreement with Korea, for example, was viewed as problematic due to concerns about trade in automobiles, beef and other issues. Certain members of Congress had concerns with Colombia due to Colombia's record on protecting labour rights. Finally, a presidential election was looming, which tends to make voting on trade agreements more difficult.

In order to address some of the Congressional concerns that were being raised, the Administration and the Congress hammered out a deal on 10 May 2007 that addressed several issues, including investment. The deal required two additional changes of relevance to this discussion.

First, new preambular language was added to the FTAs. As stated in the USTR press release,[43] the 'preamble provision would recognize that foreign investors in the United States will not be accorded greater substantive rights with respect to investment protections than United States investors in the United States.' In the Colombia FTA, the new preambular language stated that the Parties 'agree that foreign investors are not hereby accorded greater substantive rights with respect to investment protections than domestic investors under domestic law where, as in the United States, protections of investor rights under domestic law equal or exceed those set forth in this Agreement.'[44] In the Korea–US FTA, the Parties '[a]gree[d] that foreign investors are not hereby accorded greater substantive rights with respect to investment protections than domestic investors under domestic law where, as in the United States, protections of investor rights under domestic law equal

---

[43] http://www.ustr.gov/sites/default/files/uploads/factsheets/2007/asset_upload_file127_11319.pdf.

[44] The US–Colombia FTA is available at http://www.ustr.gov/trade-agreements/free-trade-agreements/colombia-fta/final-text.

or exceed those set forth in this Agreement.'[45] (Interestingly, this provision does not appear in the 2012 US model BIT).

The precise effect of these provisions is unclear, although, as with other preambular language, tribunals may take the language into account when interpreting the agreements.[46] An argument could be made, therefore, that a tribunal should, where possible, avoid an interpretation of the agreement that would provide more protection to a foreign investor than it would otherwise be entitled to under US law. What that means in practice remains to be seen.

Second, the 10 May trade deal included a new provision to deal with a controversy that had arisen the year before with respect to port security. In 2006, Dubai Ports World (DPW) acquired Peninsular and Oriental Steam Navigation, which, among other things, provided port services in the United States.[47] Concerns were raised that the access DPW gained to US ports as a result of the acquisition could threaten national security. The US government body charged with reviewing such matters, the Committee on Foreign Investment in the United States, had approved the acquisition, but this did not assuage certain members of the Congress and the public. Due to the political outcry, DPW was forced to divest the assets in question. This controversy fed into the trade debate because US FTAs had traditionally prohibited discrimination with respect to the operation of 'landside aspects of port activities', ie cargo handling and similar services.[48] Concerns were raised that this obligation required the US to open its ports to foreign entities regardless of any national security concerns presented by such entities.

USTR had always argued that the essential security exception included in FTAs would address any concerns about national security.[49] The

---

[45] The Korea–US FTA is available at http://www.ustr.gov/trade-agreements/free-trade-agreements/korus-fta/final-text.

[46] See arts 31(1) and (2) of the Vienna Convention on the Law of Treaties ('1. A treaty shall be interpreted in good faith in accordance with the ordinary meaning to be given to the terms of the treaty in their context and in the light of its object and purpose. 2. The context for the purpose of the interpretation of a treaty shall comprise, in addition to the text, … its preamble and annexes …').

[47] DE Sanger, 'Under Pressure, Dubai Company Drops Port Deal' NY Times, 10 March 2006.

[48] See eg US–Oman FTA, Annex II, US-5–US-7, http://www.ustr.gov/trade-agreements/free-trade-agreements/oman-fta/final-text.

[49] The essential security exception in US FTAs allowed a Party to take measures that 'it considers necessary for the fulfillment of its obligations with respect to the maintenance or restoration of international peace or security, or the protection of its own essential security interests.' See eg art 21.2 of the Dominican Republic–Central America–United States FTA, available at http://www.ustr.gov/trade-agreements/free-trade-agreements/cafta-dr-dominican-republic-central-america-fta/final-text ('Nothing in this Agreement shall be construed: … (b) to preclude a Party from applying measures that it considers necessary for the fulfillment of its obligations with respect to the maintenance or restoration of international peace or security, or

Administration asserted that the essential security exception was self-judging, meaning that, whenever a Party took a measure that it believed was necessary to protect national security, that measure would fall within the scope of the exception. Certain members of Congress disputed this interpretation.[50] As a result, a new provision was added to the pending FTAs.

According to the USTR press release, '[a] new FTA provision would clarify that the agreement's 'essential security' exception, which can be invoked to override any FTA obligation, including on port services, is not subject to challenge.' This change was reflected, for example, in a footnote to Article 23.2 (the essential security exception) of the US–Korea free trade agreement, which states as follows: 'For greater certainty, if a Party invokes Article 23.2 in an arbitral proceeding initiated under Chapter Eleven (Investment) or Chapter Twenty-Two (Institutional Provisions and Dispute Settlement), the tribunal or panel hearing the matter shall find that the exception applies.' As a result of this provision, it became crystal clear that a Party may decide for itself if a measure is necessary to protection national security, and that, once the Party invokes the exception, the measure cannot be challenged in dispute settlement.

G. 2012 Model BIT

When President Barack Obama came to office in 2009, a new process was begun for reviewing the 2004 US model BIT. That review was not completed until April 2012. During that time, extensive discussions took place within the government and with the private sector, including through the work of the Advisory Committee on International Economic Policy, a group of private sector experts established by the State Department. As a result of this work, a new US model BIT was released in 2012.[51] While the new model BIT made a few changes to the 2004 BIT, it did not change the basic substantive protections.

---

the protection of its own essential security interests'). According to USTR, 'Under that article, nothing in an agreement can prevent us from applying measures that we consider necessary for the protection of our essential security interests. This exception is self-judging. The validity of the defense turns on what the USG considers necessary to protect our essential security, not on a tribunal's assessment of our essential security. All the commitments we undertake in a trade agreement are subject to this overarching provision.' Office of the US Trade Representative, Trade Facts: Free Trade Agreements and the Supply of Services at US Ports (2006), http://ustraderep.gov/assets/Document_Library/Fact_Sheets/2006/asset_upload_file655_9595.pdf.

[50] See Letter from Charles Rangel, Benjamin Cardin, Sander Levin, and Xavier Becerra to Susan Schwab (September 14, 2006).

[51] The 2012 US model BIT is available at http://www.ustr.gov/sites/default/files/BIT%20text%20for%20ACIEP%20Meeting.pdf.

The new model BIT has been examined extensively elsewhere, and I will not repeat that analysis here. In summary, however, the new model strengthened the BIT provisions on labour rights[52] and environmental regulation.[53] It also required enhanced provisions on transparency and standard-setting,[54] performance requirements,[55] and state-owned enterprises.[56] Some of these changes, in particular those on performance requirements and state-owned enterprises, were in contemplation of the BIT the United States is, at the time of this writing, seeking to negotiate with China.

No new US BITs or FTAs have been negotiated based on the new model. However, the new model forms the basis of USTR's initial negotiating position in the pending BIT discussions with China and India, and, as discussed in the next section, in the ongoing negotiation of the TPP agreement.

III. THE SPREAD OF THE US MODEL AND THE TRANS-PACIFIC PARTNERSHIP AGREEMENT

As of the time of writing, the US, Australia, Brunei, Canada, Chile, Japan, Malaysia, Mexico, New Zealand, Peru, Singapore and Vietnam are negotiating the TPP agreement. The TPP will be a comprehensive free trade agreement, and is intended to include a chapter on investment. It is likely that the chapter will be strongly influenced by the 2012 US model BIT.

---

52 For example, the 2012 US model BIT requires each Party to 'ensure' that it does not weaken its labour laws in a manner inconsistent with certain core labour rights 'or fail to effectively enforce its labour laws' to attract investment, and 'reaffirms' the Parties' obligations under certain International Labour Organization instruments.

53 For example, the 2012 US model BIT requires each Party to 'ensure' that it does not weaken 'or fail to effectively enforce those laws' to attract investment.

54 For example, the 2012 US model BIT builds on the 2004 US model BIT by imposing due process obligations (advance notice, opportunity to present argumentation, right to appeal) with respect to administrative proceedings, and regulatory transparency (eg advance publication and participation in standard-setting).

55 Subject to certain exceptions, the new BIT prohibits the Parties from imposing or enforcing obligations that give a preference to domestic technology.

56 Like the 2004 US model BIT, the 2012 US model BIT applies to actions taken by a state-owned enterprise 'when it exercises any regulatory, administrative, or other governmental authority delegated to it by that Party.' The 2012 US model BIT then expressly states that the delegation of government authority to a state-owned enterprise can be the result of 'a legislative grant, and a government order, directive or other action transferring to the state enterprise or other person, or authorizing the exercise by the state enterprise or other person of, governmental authority.'

A. Spreading Influence of the US Model within the Region

There are good reasons to believe that the TPP negotiations will not result in a dramatically different text than the 2012 US model BIT, at least with respect to the core substantive investment protections.

First, while the US is only one of several participants in the negotiation, it will, given its economic position, have a very significant influence on the outcome. The starting point for the US is the 2012 US model BIT, and its position on investment seems to have stabilized after the upheaval over the last decade.

Second, many of the TPP participants already have FTAs with the United States that have investment chapters based on the model developed in the US in early 2002, which is very similar to the 2012 US model BIT. This is the case with respect to Chile, Peru, and Singapore. Australia has also agreed to the same basic principles of that text, although, significantly, the US–Australia FTA does not include investor-state dispute settlement. Canada and Mexico are not signatories to recent BITs with the United States, but they are parties to the NAFTA, and, as noted, the three NAFTA parties have already agreed to a clarification of the fair and equitable treatment standard that is similar to standard in the 2012 US model BIT and have agreed to transparency commitment with respect to investor-state arbitration that reflects many of the principles codified in the 2012 US model BIT.

Third, the basic principles formulated by the US in the early 2000s have begun to spread to non-US agreements. Indeed, some of the other TPP participants have adopted FTAs and BITs that have protections similar to those first put forward by the United States in the early 2000s. For example:

- Chapter 11, Article 6(2)(c) of the ASEAN–Australia–New Zealand Free Trade Agreement states that 'the concepts of "fair and equitable treatment" and "full protection and security" do not require treatment in addition to or beyond that which is required under customary international law, and do not create additional substantive rights.'[57]
- Article III(1)(b) of the Canada–Slovak Republic BIT states: 'The concepts of "fair and equitable treatment" and "full protection and security" in subparagraph (a) do not require treatment in addition to or beyond that which is required by the customary international law minimum standard of treatment of aliens.'[58] Annex A of the BIT also includes

[57] The ASEAN–Australia–New Zealand Free Trade Agreement, http://www.asean.fta.govt.nz/preamble/.

[58] The Agreement Between Canada and the Czech Republic for the Promotion and Protection of Investments, http://unctad.org/sections/dite/iia/docs/bits/canada_czech%20republic.pdf.

an annex on expropriation[59] that is similar to the annex used in the 2012 US model BIT.

- Article 5(2) of the Japan–Peru BIT states that 'the concept of "fair and equitable treatment" and "full protection and security" do not require treatment in addition to or beyond that which is required by the customary international law minimum standard of treatment of aliens.'[60] Annex IV of the BIT contains an expropriation annex similar to that used in the 2012 US model BIT.[61]
- The Protocol to the Mexico–Czech Republic BIT states: 'Article 2, paragraph (3) prescribes the customary International Law minimum standard of treatment of aliens as the minimum standard of treatment to be

---

59 The Annex states, for example:

(b) The determination of whether a measure or series of measures of a Contracting Party constitute an indirect expropriation requires a case-by-case, fact-based inquiry that considers, among other factors:
   (i) the economic impact of the measure or series of measures, although the sole fact that a measure or series of measures of a Contracting Party have an adverse effect on the economic value of an investment does not establish that an indirect expropriation has occurred,
   (ii) the extent to which the measure or series of measures interfere with distinct, reasonable, investment-backed expectations, and
   (iii) the character of the measure or series of measures, including their purpose and rationale; and

(c) Except in rare circumstances, such as when a measure or series of measures are so severe in the light of their purpose that they cannot be reasonably viewed as having been adopted and applied in good faith, nondiscriminatory measures of a Contracting Party that are designed and applied to protect legitimate public welfare objectives do not constitute indirect expropriation.

60 The Agreement Between Japan and the Republic of Peru for the Protection, Promotion and Liberalisation of Investment is available at http://unctad.org/sections/dite/iia/docs/bits/japan_peru.pdf.

61 For example, the Annex states:

(b) The determination of whether a measure or series of measures by a Contracting Party, in a specific fact situation, constitutes an indirect expropriation requires a case-by-case, fact-based inquiry that considers, among other factors:
   (i) the economic impact of the measure or series of measures, although the fact that such measure or series of measures has an adverse effect on the economic value of investments, standing alone, does not establish that an indirect expropriation has occurred;
   (ii) the extent to which the measure or series of measures interferes with distinct, reasonable expectations arising out of investments; and
   (iii) the characteristic of the measure or series of measures, including whether such measure or series of measures are non-discriminatory; and

(c) Non-discriminatory measures of a Contracting Party that are designed and applied to protect legitimate public welfare objectives stated in paragraph 1 of Article 19 do not constitute indirect expropriation.

> afforded to investments of investors of another Contracting Party. … The concepts of "fair and equitable treatment" and "full protection and security" do not require treatment in addition to or beyond that which is required by the customary International Law minimum standard of treatment of aliens.'[62]

Whether the US TPP partners will accept other aspects of the 2012 model US text dealing with labour, environment and other issues remains to be seen, however.

B. Next Steps on TPP

At the same time, at least two issues may lead to a change of direction in the TPP. The first is the political context in the US. So far, the US has been negotiating the TPP without fast track authority. As of the time of this writing, however, it is not clear when the Administration and Congress will consider new fast track legislation. Whenever fast track legislation is taken up for debate, it is at least possible that the Congress will demand additional changes to the investment text through new investment negotiating objectives.

It is, however, unclear whether anyone will want to re-ignite the debate. Indeed, as of the time of this writing, at least, there appears to be little appetite for doing so. It helps, of course, that—whether by good governance, skillful advocacy, the availability of better alternatives through local courts, or just plain luck—the US still has not lost an investment dispute under NAFTA or any other investment agreement. If the US were to lose an investment dispute, that might change the political dynamic.

The second issue is Australia's position on investor-state dispute settlement. As noted, at Australia's insistence, the US–Australia FTA does not include investor-state arbitration. Since the conclusion of that agreement, Australia has adopted a general position of excluding investor-state arbitration from its agreements. The change of policy was in part driven by a pending arbitration challenging Australia's new regulation on the plain packaging of cigarettes and by concerns that Australia's price control legislation would be subject to challenge. Using language reminiscent of the language that had been included in the US fast track legislation, the Australian Government stated in April 2011 that:

---

62 The Agreement Between the Czech Republic and the United Mexican States on the Promotion and Reciprocal Protection of Investments, http://unctad.org/sections/dite/iia/docs/bits/czech_mexico.PDF.

> [T]he Government does not support provisions that would confer greater legal rights on foreign businesses than those available to domestic businesses. Nor will the Government support provisions that would constrain the ability of Australian governments to make laws on social, environmental and economic matters in circumstances where those laws do not discriminate between domestic and foreign businesses. The Government has not and will not accept provisions that limit its capacity to put health warnings or plain packaging requirements on tobacco products or its ability to continue the Pharmaceutical Benefits Scheme.[63]

The statement concluded that '[t]he Gillard Government will discontinue th[e] practice' of including investor-state arbitration mechanisms in future trade agreements. 'If Australian businesses are concerned about sovereign risk in Australian trading partner countries, they will need to make their own assessments about whether they want to commit to investing in those countries.'

It would seem unlikely that the other TPP participants, including the US, would allow Australia to dictate the terms of the investment chapter and exclude investor-state arbitration altogether. However, questions remain as to how Australia's opposition to investor-state arbitration will be addressed. It is possible that Australia will, on balance, accept arbitration in exchange for other benefits in the agreement. Alternatively, it may demand a special carve-out from the arbitration provisions and, if it prevails, others may follow suit.

IV. CONCLUSION

The evolution of US investment policy over the last decade is largely a product of the fact that investment and trade are now inextricably linked. Some might argue that the result has diluted investment protection principles and weakened the position of US investors abroad. On the other hand, an argument could be made that, by linking trade and investment, investment protection is much broader than it otherwise might have been. As evidence, one might point to the fact that the US has only entered into two BITs over the past decade, while the US has entered into new trade agreements with investment chapters covering sixteen countries. That number will expand if the TPP is concluded and if the recently launched negotiation of a potential US–EU free trade agreement (known as the 'Transatlantic Trade and Investment Partnership' or 'TTIP') comes to fruition.

---

[63] Gillard Government Trade Policy Statement (April 2011), http://www.dfat.gov.au/publications/trade/trading-our-way-to-more-jobs-and-prosperity.html.

Whichever position one takes in the debate, it is likely that investment protections will continue to evolve as cross-border investment continues to grow and more large and/or developed countries seek to negotiate investment agreements with each other, a trend that presents commercial advantages but also an increased risk of challenge through arbitration, with the attendant political consequences. The possibility of a US BIT with China has already had an impact on the 2012 model BIT, as discussed above. The TTIP may prompt further changes, particularly if the EU advocates an approach similar to that taken by EU Member States in their individual BITs, which by and large do not reflect the types of changes adopted by the United States in the early 2000s.

As the complexity of the agreements and the parties continues to advance, the political debate may deepen once again. In the US, the Congress may reassert itself and call for another period of reflection and re-evaluation, and the President may need to act nimbly in response to political pressures. The only thing that is clear is that the evolutionary process is not over, and likely never will be.

11

Between Regional Harmonization and Global Fragmentation? The Variable Geometry and Geography of Investment Treaty Law Through the Prism of Regulatory Flexibility Provisions

*Mavluda Sattorova**

1. INTRODUCTION

Originally embraced as a means of tackling the historical disagreement about the meaning and scope of international rules on the protection of foreign investment, international investment agreements (IIAs) have often been analysed through the competing prisms of universality and diversity. It has been argued, for instance, that the widespread endorsement of similarly-worded provisions in IIAs—such as the expropriation, non-discrimination, and fair and equitable treatment standards—is nothing but evidence of the universal acceptance of underlying legal principles and of the commonality of interests between states which use IIAs in their foreign investment policies.[1] To quote Schill, 'international investment treaties have, to a significant extent, developed a surprisingly uniform structure, often converging in their wording and endorsing uniform principles of investment protection.'[2] Likewise, Lowenfeld suggested that the growth of IIAs has reached the 'point where one can speak of consensus.'[3] Investment treaty law has thus

* Lecturer in International Economic Law, University of Liverpool, m.sattorova@liverpool.ac.uk.

[1] See S Schill, *The Multilateralization of International Investment Law* (CUP, 2009).

[2] Ibid, 65.

[3] AF Lowenfeld, 'Investment Agreements and International Law' (2003–2004) 42 *Colum J Transnatl L* 123; also SM Schwebel, 'The Reshaping of the International Law of Foreign

been conceptualised as a fairly homogenous and internally coordinated global regime. A lack of uniformity and the ensuing fragmentation have been predominantly viewed as problems that beset the practice of investment arbitration and the interaction between international investment law and other areas of international law.[4] Many scholars have contributed to an ongoing debate over inconsistency in the interpretation and application of investment treaty rules by arbitral tribunals.[5] Much ink has also been spilled on the conflicts between IIAs and general international law as well as between IIAs and WTO agreements, international environmental instruments, and human rights conventions.[6] By contrast, an increasingly fragmented nature of investment treaty practice, which for the purposes of this paper includes the process of formation of IIAs, remains largely unexplored.

This contribution aims to fill this gap in existing scholarship by offering a critical evaluation of a growing disparity and diversification of IIAs and questioning the causes of this disparity. In particular, it will focus on the variable geometry of international investment law with regard to the so-called regulatory flexibility provisions. Through uncovering disparity in investment treaty practice, the paper will elucidate evolving perceptions of the function of IIAs and the extent to which these instruments could and should make room for the pursuit of competing social policy objectives on a national and international level. While a new breed of IIAs mirrors these evolving perceptions, other treaties continue to steadfastly adhere to the minimalist texts and maximalist focus on investment protection that defined the drafting of the first generation IIAs. Does this variance in drafting approaches to regulatory flexibility provisions signify an emergence of a new ideological divide or a mere inertia in adapting treaties to changing realities of the global investment environment? What lies beneath an increasingly fragmented investment treaty practice? In its analysis of theoretical underpinnings and practical implications of the variation and intra-regime fragmentation in investment treaty

---

Investment by Concordant Bilateral Investment Treaties' in S Charnovitz, DP Steger and P Van Den Bossche (eds) *Law in the Service of Human Dignity: Essays in Honour of Florentino Feliciano* (CUP, 2005) 241.

[4] SD Amarasinha and J Kokott, 'Multilateral Investment Rules Revisited' in P Muchlinski, F Ortino, C Schreuer, *The Oxford Handbook of International Investment Law* (OUP 2008) 122; P-M Dupuy, 'Unification Rather than Fragmentation of International Law? The Case of International Investment Law and Human Rights Law' in P-M Dupuy, F Francioni & E-U Petersmann (eds) *Human Rights in International Investment Law and Arbitration* (OUP 2009) 45–62.

[5] See eg OK Fauchald, 'The Legal Reasoning of ICSID Tribunals—An Empirical Analysis' (2008) 19 *EJIL* 301.

[6] See A van Aaken, 'Fragmentation of International Law: The Case of International Investment Protection' *University of St. Gallen Law School Law and Economics Research Paper Series*, Working Paper No. 2008-1.

law, the Chapter will highlight the role of internal political processes in the formation of IIAs, whilst also revisiting the hegemonic critique of investment treaty law and questioning the role of universality and regional diversity in an increasingly multidimensional global economic environment. The overarching aim of this contribution is to elucidate the role played by local and regional preferences, capacities, and idiosyncrasies in the shaping of a multilateral response to the clash between economic liberalisation and the pursuit of socially desirable policies.

2. REGULATORY FLEXIBILITY PROVISIONS AND THE RISE OF INTER-TREATY VARIANCE: BETWEEN THE FIRST GENERATION IIAS AND NEW MODELS

2.1. *Making room for public policy: interpretive statements*

Despite exhibiting a certain degree of variance in their substantive and procedural terms, the first generation IIAs could indeed be regarded as offering 'a surprisingly uniform protection against political risk.'[7] These instruments displayed a considerable measure of homogeneity in terms of their structure, content, and objectives,[8] which is not surprising given their largely shared historical origins in the Abs-Shawcross Convention and the OECD Draft Convention on the Protection of Foreign Property.[9] The arrival of a new generation of IIAs—which departed from the traditional models and introduced variance into a hitherto fairly homogenous body of treaties—was a reaction to the first wave of investor-state arbitrations at the end of the 1990s and the dawn of the new millennium. The awards in these proceedings revealed the impact of broad and open-ended investment protection guarantees (construed in an investor-friendly manner in many arbitral awards) on the exercise of regulatory powers by host governments and ignited an ongoing debate about the design, function and place of IIAs. While questioning the wisdom of delegating so much power to investment tribunals,[10] host states endeavoured to regain some control over the functioning of the regime

[7] Schill (n 1) 65.

[8] Schill (n 1) 364.

[9] See HJ Abs, *Proposals for Improving the Protection of Private Foreign Investments* (Rotterdam, 1958) 35. For a general discussion of the Draft, see G Schwarzenberger, *Foreign Investments and International Law* (Steven & Sons, 1969) 109–134. The Abs-Shawcross Draft can be found in UNCTAD, *International Investment Instruments: A Compendium* (United Nations, 2000) vol. V, 395). For the text of the OECD Convention, see <http://www.oecd.org/investment/internationalinvestmentagreements/39286571.pdf>.

[10] A Roberts, 'Clash of Paradigms: Actors and Analogies Shaping the Investment Treaty System' (2013) 107 *AJIL* 45, 79. See also SA Spears, 'Quest for Policy Space in New-Generation International Investment Agreements' (2010) 13 *JIEL* 1037.

by drafting a new breed of IIAs which clarified the limits of State commitments to foreign investors. This clarification has been achieved through the incorporation of the so-called regulatory flexibility provisions, ranging from interpretive statements to fully-fledged exceptions clauses.

Unlike the new breed, the first generation of IIAs—the early bilateral investment treaties (BITs)—did not provide much room for regulatory flexibility. A selection of early UK IIAs, for instance, features a limited exception clause precluding the application of the national treatment and MFN provisions in the areas covered by customs union, taxation, and similar international agreements.[11] An analogous exception to otherwise non-derogable investment protection guarantees was consistently adopted in US IIAs post-1987.[12] The early generation of IIAs was thus driven predominantly by considerations relating to the protection of investment, providing little to no guidance as to how investment protection was to be balanced against and reconciled with other competing socio-economic policy objectives. It was the subsequent rise of the regulatory state and, perhaps more importantly, the surge in the number of investment arbitration cases at the end of the 1990s and at the dawn of the new millennium that pushed some States to reconsider their IIAs. The first wave of arbitral cases manifested the actual and potential reach of IIAs, including the fact that both developing and developed States could be targeted by claims disputing an almost infinite range of governmental measures under open-ended and far-reaching guarantees against expropriation, discrimination, and unfair and inequitable treatment. Concerns were raised that through exposing Host State conduct to arbitral scrutiny and monetary liability, IIAs fettered sovereign regulatory power and limited States' capacity to pursue competing policies in such areas as public health and safety, environmental protection, labour standards, and human rights. Yet the ways in which States responded to these concerns in their investment treaty policies have been far from uniform.

Some of the new generation IIAs have been redesigned to embrace an evolved notion of investment protection. In contrast with the first generation treaties that remained silent about the interplay between investment

---

[11] See eg art 7 of the 1980 United Kingdom–Bangladesh BIT providing: 'The provisions in this Agreement relative to the grant of treatment less favourable than that accorded to the nationals or companies of either Contracting Party or of any third State shall not be construed so as to oblige one Contracting Party to extend to the nationals or companies of the other the benefit of any treatment, preference or privilege resulting from (1) any existing or future customs union or similar international agreement to which either of the Contracting Parties is or may become a party, or (b) any bilateral international agreement or arrangement relating wholly or mainly to taxation or any domestic legislation relating wholly or mainly to taxation.'

[12] Even prior to the 1987 model draft, the customs union and free trade area exception was included in selected US BITs. See K Vandevelde, 'US Bilateral Investment Treaties: The Second Wave' (1993) 14 *Mich J Intl L* 621, 644–6.

protection and national regulatory flexibility in pursuit of socially desirable policies, the new instruments contain interpretive statements which expressly acknowledge the importance of promoting and protecting investment in a manner that does not undermine the State's promotion of other public goods, such as socially responsible corporate practices, sustainable development, public health, labour, and environmental protection concerns. The United States was among the first to herald regulatory flexibility clauses as a key feature of its new generation IIAs.[13] For instance, the preamble of the US–Uruguay BIT expressly acknowledges the desirability of promoting and protecting investment in a manner consistent with the protection of the environment.[14] In a similar vein, the preamble of the 2004 Canadian Model FIPA contains a reference to the promotion of sustainable development as one of the overarching objectives behind investment promotion and protection.[15]

In contrast with express treaty-based exceptions, interpretive statements—including those contained in treaty preambles—do not explicitly insulate certain areas of governmental decision-making or certain industries and economic sectors from the scope of investment protection guarantees. Instead, such statements aim to clarify the purpose and scope of investment treaty provisions and to ensure that, in deciding investment claims under IIAs, arbitral tribunals take into account, and are more sensitive to, the fact that investment protection is but one of the policies Host States pursue in regulating economic and social affairs within their national boundaries. The fact that such provisions are declaratory in their nature and do not create enforceable obligations for contracting State Parties detracts from their effectiveness. Nonetheless, they provide textual guidance in establishing the object and purpose of a relevant IIA and thus can have a certain bearing on the interpretation of substantive treaty obligations.[16] The lack of references to non-investment policy objectives in the early IIAs has led to situations where the protection of investment was construed as a primary and overriding treaty goal, thus prioritising investor rights over States' duty to regulate.[17] The inclusion of statements in

---

13 In so doing, the United States was building upon its experiences under the North American Free Trade Agreement which had already introduced a number of innovations in its chapter on investment. See eg NAFTA Preamble and art 1114 (Environmental Measures).

14 See the text at <http://unctad.org/sections/dite/iia/docs/bits/US_Uruguay.pdf>.

15 See the text at <http://italaw.com/documents/Canadian2004-FIPA-model-en.pdf>.

16 See the Vienna Convention on the Law of Treaties, art 31 (1969).

17 See eg *SGS Société Générale de Surveillance SA v Philippines*, Decision on Objections to Jurisdiction and Separate Declaration, 29 January 2004 (ICSID Case No ARB/02/6) para 116: 'The object and purpose of the BIT supports an effective interpretation of Article X(2). The BIT is a treaty for the promotion and reciprocal protection of investments. According to the preamble it is intended "to create and maintain favourable conditions for investments by investors of one Contracting Party in the territory of the other". It is legitimate to resolve uncertainties in its interpretation so as to favour the protection of covered investments.'

the preamble on the importance of socially desirable regulation in some of the new generation IIAs is likely to militate against considering investment treaties solely through the prism of investment protection and promotion. By explicitly acknowledging the significance of non-investment policy objectives alongside the creation and maintenance of favourable conditions for investors and investments, the new Canadian and US models (among others) strive to redefine prospectively the limits of investment protection guarantees and to ensure that their effective interpretation does not compromise the pursuit of other economic and social ends on a national and international level.

It is noteworthy, however, that the creation of the new breed of IIAs and in particular the use of regulatory flexibility provisions has been confined to certain countries and regions, pointing to the emergence of something akin to a new form of regionalism. The amended versions of the UK, Germany, and Netherlands IIAs, as well as the recently concluded Swiss IIAs continue to follow the traditional drafting patterns, and do not feature any significant changes of the kind embraced in the US and Canada models.[18] Such variance in the drafting of IIAs of different States can be seen as a 'two-speed' or 'variable geometry' evolution, whereby some treaties increasingly endorse and make room for non-investment values such as environmental protection, public health, and sustainable development, whilst others continue to prioritise investment protection as a dominant and overriding objective. The two-speed development of investment treaty practice can be seen as the rise of a 'New Conservatism' in the sense that some of the erstwhile advocates of strong and unadulterated investment protection guarantees, like the United States and Canada, have come to disagree with the status quo and have proposed new rules as well as amendments to existing norms. The fact that a number of long-standing investment treaty champions still continue to favour the first generation drafting models in their treaty-making practice is reminiscent of the historic opposition by developing States to the customary rules on the protection of foreign investment, with some developed states now standing in the vanguard of contesting and retuning the traditional investment protection maxims. The question is whether this variable geometry is an expression of some form of regionalism both as 'a technique for international law-making'[19] and 'as the pursuit of geographical exceptions to

[18] This conclusion is drawn on the basis of a textual analysis of the Netherlands Model BIT (1997) and the UK Model BIT (2005, with 2006 amendments) (available in Z Douglas, *The International Law of Investment Claims* (Cambridge 2009) 547, 559) as well as of the German Model BIT (2008) <http://www.italaw.com/sites/default/files/archive/ita1025.pdf> and the Switzerland-Syria BIT (2007).

[19] 'Fragmentation of International Law: Difficulties Arising From The Diversification and Expansion of International Law', Report of the Study Group of the International Law Commission, finalized by Martti Koskenniemi (A/CN.4/L.682 13 April 2006) 106.

universal law rules',[20] namely those norms contained in the first generation of IIAs. Before turning to this phenomenon and analysing its underpinnings and policy implications, the next sections will examine the variable geometry of IIAs through the prism of regulatory flexibility provisions incorporated into the substantive treaty obligations.

2.2. *Regulatory flexibility and national treatment*

Some of the more recent IIAs have gone beyond modifying the language of preambles, and revised the wording of substantive obligations so as to reconcile the promotion and protection of investment with the exercise by Host States of their regulatory functions. The national treatment clause in the Investment Agreement for the COMESA Common Investment Area provides an interesting case in point. It offers explicit textual support for the inclusion of policy objectives into the non-discrimination analysis, particularly at the stage of establishing whether national and foreign investors are in like circumstances.[21] This grants Host States freedom to use differentiation as a means of achieving legitimate non-protectionist policy objectives such as the protection of public health, safety and the environment. Unlike its more sparsely-worded counterparts among the first generation IIAs, this model embodies a compromise between contracting State Parties' efforts on the one hand to provide their companies with investment access and protection on equal terms with their competitors in Host States and international competitors, and on the other hand to prevent an unnecessarily restrictive interpretation of the national treatment standard which may result in legitimate policy differentiations being condemned as incompatible under the relevant treaty.

---

[20] Ibid, 108.

[21] Art 17 (2) [National Treatment] reads as follows:

> For greater certainty, references to 'like circumstances' in paragraph 1 of this Article requires an overall examination on a case by case basis of all the circumstances of an investment including, inter alia:
>
> (a) its effects on third persons and the local community;
> (b) its effects on the local, regional or national environment, including the cumulative effects of all investments within a jurisdiction on the environment;
> (c) the sector the investor is in;
> (d) the aim of the measure concerned;
> (e) the regulatory process generally applied in relation to the measure concerned; and
> (f) other factors directly relating to the investment or investor in relation to the measure concerned;
>
> and the examination shall not be limited to or be biased towards any one factor.

(The full text is available at <http://vi.unctad.org/files/wksp/iiawksp08/docs/wednesday/Exercise%20Materials/invagreecomesa.pdf>)

Indeed, differentiation is an important economic and social policy device, especially in such areas as environmental protection, sustainable development, and climate change and mitigation. For instance, investments in green energy may call for preferential tax rates so as to facilitate their competitiveness in a marketplace dominated by conventional energy products with higher carbon footprints. Would such differentiation be challenged and pronounced inconsistent with the national treatment obligation, and therefore wrongful and leading to an obligation to pay damages to an aggrieved investor? A decision on compatibility of green energy incentives with the State's commitments to national treatment would hinge on the wording of the latter, namely the extent to which the relevant provision allows contracting State Parties to make legitimate non-protectionist differentiations. By expressly providing that rational policy distinctions in pursuit of policy objectives in such areas as public health, safety and environmental protection are not to be seen as discriminatory, the COMESA IIA model responds to the lack of uniformity and particularly to the possibility of a broad interpretation of national treatment provisions in the practice of investment arbitration. Among other things, investment tribunals have been far from consistent in their approaches to determining whether a foreign investment and its domestic counterpart are in like circumstances. Some arbitral panels have set disturbing precedent by setting too broad a basis for comparing between local and foreign investments.[22] Whilst many policy measures—in particular those aimed at the protection of public health, safety, and the environment—frequently necessitate differentiation between investments that are greener, healthier, and safer and those that are less so, arbitral tests setting too broad a basis of comparison render such differentiation impossible. This in turn delimits the range of policy solutions which host governments can adopt in the exercise of their decision-making powers in the public interest. It also remains unclear whether tribunals would consider a disputed differentiation to be justifiable by public policy considerations, even where the applicable IIA does not contain express derogations to this effect.[23] By expressly insu-

[22] The broader the range of comparators to choose from, the greater the possibility that a disputed measure might be found to be discriminatory. For example, in *Occidental v Ecuador*, an investor claimed that a refusal to grant VAT refunds to oil companies was in violation of the national treatment standard because companies engaged in the export of other goods, such as flowers and seafood products had been entitled to the refunds. The tribunal held that the 'like circumstances' prerequisite ought not to be confined to companies operating in the same sector but called for comparison between exporters generally. Selecting a domestic comparator from a broader range of exporters was the vehicle by which the tribunal arrived at its finding of discrimination (*Occidental Exploration and Production Company v Ecuador*, Award, 1 July 2004 (LCIA Case No UN 3467) para 173).

[23] Some tribunals have read an implicit derogation into the non-discrimination provisions of IIAs. See *Pope & Talbot Inc v Canada*, Award on the Merits of Phase 2, 10 April 2001 (Ad hoc—

lating legitimate policy measures from the scope of national treatment provisions in their revised IIAs, COMESA States have made an effort to reclaim control over the application of investment treaty protections so as to prevent their expansive interpretation by arbitral tribunals and forestall their constraining effect on national policy-making capacity.

Again, what is noteworthy is the fact that such clarification of the scope of national treatment clauses has been undertaken only in the selected IIAs of the revised and new stock. The 2006 Model IIA of the UK, for example, continues to favour the same wording of the national treatment clause as has been used since the UK first launched its bilateral investment programme in 1974.[24] Likewise, the Netherlands, Switzerland and to a large extent Germany endorse the traditional drafting models, and have not clarified the scope of the national treatment standard. This variance results in an increasingly fragmented treaty landscape, counteracting the creation of uniformity in international investment law, defying the claims of its multilateralization and pointing to new forms of regionalism in the drafting of IIAs.

2.3. *Regulatory flexibility and expropriation*

The regionalisation of investment treaty practice and its variable geometry can also be discerned in existing preferences to the drafting of expropriation clauses. Since the expropriation standard has historically played a leading role in the harnessing of IIAs to challenge regulatory acts of host states, it is unsurprising that the wording of the relevant provisions has been revisited in a number of newer model treaties. The expropriation standard in the first generation BITs was founded upon the Hull formula and reflected an effort by capital-exporting developed States to counter the opposition to the customary international rules from developing states.[25] In the 1960s and 1970s, as the

---

UNCITRAL Arbitration Rules) para 79. See also *GAMI Investments, Incorporated v Mexico*, Final Award, 15 November 2004 (Ad hoc—UNCITRAL Arbitration Rules) para 114 (the measure must be plausibly connected with a legitimate goal of policy); *Saluka Investments BV v Czech Republic*, Partial Award, 17 March 2006 (PCA—UNCITRAL Arbitration Rules) para 307 (any differential treatment of a foreign investor must not be based on unreasonable distinctions and demands, and must be justified by showing that it bears a reasonable relationship to rational policies not motivated by a preference for other investments over the foreign-owned investment).

[24] See, for example, art 3 of the UK Singapore BIT (1975) where the national treatment obligation, subsumed in the MFN clause, does not offer much detail except for requiring the contracting state to subject investors and investments of the other contracting party treatment no less favourable than that which it accords to its own investors and their investments.

[25] See eg the UN GA Resolution No 1803 (14 December 1962) and No 3281 (12 December 1984). For the impact of UN resolutions on the international law of expropriation, see HW Baade, 'Permanent Sovereignty over Natural Wealth and Resources', in RS Miller and RJ Stanger (eds) *Essays on Expropriation* (Ohio University Press, 1967); BH Weston, 'The Charter

UN General Assembly increasingly contested the customary rules on the protection from expropriation, and newly-independent states embarked on large-scale expropriations and nationalisations of property belonging to owners from former colonial nations, capital-exporting states turned to bilateral agreements to ensure that such interference with foreign investment would always be compensated. The first generation IIAs exhibit a remarkable uniformity in their endorsement of the rule that host governments are free to expropriate foreign investment but only if such expropriation is for a public purpose, non-discriminatory, and—importantly—accompanied by the payment of 'prompt, adequate and effective' compensation.[26]

The recent modification of expropriation clauses in some of the new generation IIAs is a response to yet another fundamental shift in the international law on foreign investment, namely further liberalisation of investment markets, the change in the direction of investment flows, the steady rise of indirect, regulatory State interference in economic affairs, and the proliferation of investor claims seeking damages caused therefrom. Already at a time when the first generation IIAs offered little room for distinguishing between compensable expropriation and non-compensable legitimate regulatory action, selected scholars and arbitrators acknowledged the need to exclude the pursuit of certain public policy objectives from the scope of expropriation provisions.[27] The conflict between the protection of property rights and regulatory freedom acquired a new dimension following the vociferous opposition to the Multilateral Agreement on Investment (and its eventual failure).[28] Subsequently, after the first wave of investment arbitrations manifested the extent to which the expropriation clause could encroach upon States' regulatory freedom in such areas as public health and safety and the

of Economic Rights and Duties of States and the Deprivation of Foreign-Owned Wealth' (1981) 75 *AJIL* 437, D Johnson, 'The Effect of the Resolutions of the General Assembly of the UN' (1955) 32 *British Ybk Intl L* 97; R Higgins, 'The Taking of Property by the State: Recent Developments in International Law' (1982) 176 *Recueil des Cours* 259.

26 See examples cited in NJ Calamita, 'The British Bank Nationalizations: An International Law Perspective', 58 *ICLQ* 119 (2009).

27 The doctrinal codification of the international law on state responsibility in the Harvard Draft Convention provides the most influential example of support for the police powers exception. It acknowledged that, subject to procedural and substantive legality conditions, no international wrong results from an uncompensated taking that is carried out as part of the normal operation of the laws or from the pursuit of important public policy objectives ((1961) 55 *AJIL* 515, 554).

28 The NGO community made a significant contribution to the failure of the efforts by the OECD to launch a multilateral agreement on investment (MAI). NGO opposition to the MAI raised awareness of its one-sided nature as a pure investment protection instrument and of its restrictive effect on the ability of states to regulate in the public interest. See P Muchlinski, 'The Rise and Fall of the Multilateral Agreement on Investment: Where Now?' (2000) 33 *Int'l L* 1033, 1049.

protection of the environment,[29] the renewed political sensitivity surrounding the interpretation and application of expropriation clauses forced treaty drafters to clarify the meaning and scope of the relevant provisions in the new and revised treaties. The recent Canadian IIAs, for instance, have responded by delimiting the exposure of contracting State Parties to liability for expropriation through the exclusion of certain categories of governmental action from the scope of the otherwise absolute obligation to compensate:

> Except in rare circumstances, such as when a measure or series of measures are so severe in the light of their purpose that they cannot be reasonably viewed as having been adopted and applied in good faith, non-discriminatory measures of a Contracting Party that are designed and applied to protect legitimate public welfare objectives, such as health, safety and the environment, do not constitute indirect expropriation.[30]

Similar efforts to curb the expansive interpretation of expropriation clauses and to redefine their protective scope can be found in the modifications adopted in US IIAs. Yet again, the clarification of the scope of expropriation provisions has not been uniformly adopted in recent IIAs. Among other investment treaty champions, Germany, the Netherlands, Switzerland, and the UK continue to provide for a categorical and absolute protection against expropriation, with no exception for regulatory measures adopted in pursuit of public policy objectives.[31] Under these models, the task of drawing a line between compensable expropriation and non-compensable regulatory interference remains vested in arbitral tribunals. It should be conceded that even in the absence of clarification in a treaty text, some tribunals may endorse the stance taken by the NAFTA tribunal in *Methanex v United States*[32] and determine that a disputed measure is a lawful exercise of regulatory powers.[33] However, the lack of predictability and consistency in arbitral jurisprudence

[29] See eg *Waste Management Inc v Mexico*, ICSID Case No ARB(AF)/98/2 (Award, 2 June 2000); *Metalclad Corp v Mexico*, ICSID Case No ARB(AF)/97/1 (Award, 30 August 2000).

[30] See Annex A to art VI of the 2009 Canada–Czech Republic BIT.

[31] See eg art 5(1) of the UK Model BIT stating that 'Investments of nationals or companies of either Contracting Party shall not be nationalised, expropriated or subjected to measures having effect equivalent to nationalisation or expropriation (hereinafter referred to as 'expropriation') in the territory of the other Contracting Party except for a public purpose related to the internal needs of that Party on a non-discriminatory basis and against prompt, adequate and effective compensation.' A largely similar provision is contained in the Netherlands and Germany IIAs, with no express mention made of non-expropriatory regulatory interference.

[32] *Methanex Corporation v United States*, Final Award on Jurisdiction and Merits, 3 August 2005 (Ad hoc—UNCITRAL Arbitration Rules) Part IV Chapter D, para 7.

[33] See eg *Saluka Investments BV (The Netherlands) v Czech Republic*, UNCITRAL PCA Trib. (Parital Award, 17 March 2006).

also suggests that the absence of regulatory flexibility provisos in an IIA may well be construed as an express endorsement by contracting states of the expropriation standard in an unmitigated form. Should this happen, legitimate regulation in the public interest may be found expropriatory and the payment of compensation may be required.[34]

Given the role expropriation clauses may play in allocating the cost of regulatory intervention in the public interest, the emerging dichotomy between the new vision heralded by the US model treaties (also embraced among others by Canada and members of COMESA) and the traditional concept of expropriation endorsed by other States is significant in terms of its doctrinal and normative implications. Among other things, the variable geometry and geography of IIAs point to a fundamental shift in the ideological divide that long characterized both the formation and operation of international investment law. It offers yet further evidence of the replacement of the long-standing but increasingly dwindling North–South divide by a more complex ideological disagreement about the place of non-investment interests and policy demands on the investment protection and promotion agenda.

2.4. Regulatory flexibility and other treaty provisions

The emerging but very fragmented recognition of the need to promote non-investment values alongside the promotion and protection of investment can be discerned not only in the key treaty standards on expropriation and non-discrimination but also in clauses dealing with performance requirements and other stand-alone treaty provisions. Under the recent Canadian model IIA, for instance, a measure that requires an investment to use a technology to meet generally applicable health, safety or environmental requirements is not to be regarded as a prohibited performance requirement.[35] The US model too redefines the scope of the otherwise categorical prohibition of performance requirements by incorporating a GATT-like general exception proviso which bars a range of regulatory measures from being regarded as performance requirements. The exception covers environmental regulations, as well as measures that are necessary for the protection of human, animal, or plant life or health, and those related to the conservation of living or non-living exhaustible natural resources.[36] A prominent feature that sets the 2012 US

[34] This outcome can always be supported by the wording of expropriation clause in the first generation IIAs, which require that expropriation is always subject to the payment of compensation.

[35] Art 7(2) (see the full text at <http://italaw.com/documents/Canadian2004-FIPA-model-en.pdf>).

[36] The 2012 US Model BIT, art 8(3)(C) <http://italaw.com/sites/default/files/archive/ita1028.pdf>.

Model IIA apart from both its predecessors and IIAs of other states is that regulatory flexibility or the right-to-regulate provisions have been incorporated in the form of two stand-alone clauses on 'Investment and Environment' and 'Investment and Labour.' Even though the language of these provisions renders them largely declaratory, the fact that the importance of non-investment related concerns has been expressly acknowledged can be seen as evidence of a shift away from the hitherto prevailing practice of prioritising investment protection at the expense of competing public policy objectives. Besides, just like treaty preambles, such declaratory clauses—although not quite carrying the same weight as express exceptions—have the capacity to influence the interpretation of investment protection standards in cases where the exercise by a host government of its regulatory powers in the areas of environmental protection, public health and the like detrimentally affects an investor's undertaking. Ultimately, even given their declaratory nature, the stand-alone provisions on environmental and labour standards facilitate the defragmentation of international investment law, and militate against it being pigeon-holed into a specialist field where the enforcement of private rights can be undertaken in isolation from and immune to the application of international environmental, labour, and human rights instruments. However, such developments in the architecture of IIAs are presently confined to only a few States, with the majority of States remaining silent on, or reluctant to acknowledge, the importance of non-investment interests in their new and revised instruments.

3. WHERE WORLDS COLLIDE: TREATY EXCEPTIONS AS AN UNCOMMON DENOMINATOR

Fragmentation is particularly discernible in existing approaches to public policy derogations, which include non-precluded measures clauses and exceptions. Just like interpretive statements, exceptions did not feature widely in the first generation IIAs.[37] The first wave of investor-State disputes exposed the far-reaching effect of investment treaty protections and the extent to which they could impinge on the regulatory freedom of host governments, particularly in times of economic emergency. This has inevitably cast into sharp relief the importance of providing Host States with a means of defending their measures and precluding unmitigated exposure to monetary claims. General exceptions clauses are traditionally regarded as a device enabling States to pursue specific policy objectives—such as the

[37] Only selected BITs included some form of exception clause other than the commonly used REI, tax customs union exception. See for instance, art 10 of the US–Egypt BIT (1986).

protection of the environment and public health, safeguarding public morals, and preserving public order and security—without incurring liability for a violation of their international obligations. By expressly insulating certain categories of governmental measures from the protective scope of IIAs, treaty exceptions offer a potent means of both defending host state action *ex post* and safeguarding regulatory freedom *ex ante*.

It has been rightly observed that 'exceptions in some cases actually may serve to strengthen the operative provisions of the BIT.'[38] Indeed, the availability of express derogations renders it unnecessary for defendant states to argue for a narrower interpretation of investment protection guarantees and for tribunals to favour such interpretation to balance the investment protection objective with compelling national policy demands. The inclusion of express derogations in a treaty text facilitates drawing a clearer line between what constitutes permissible governmental conduct and what amounts to a treaty violation for which the Host State will be held responsible. Such provisions enhance the overall clarity of investment treaty texts and the predictability of arbitral practice. Express derogations also serve to mitigate criticisms of investment treaty law as a one-sided regime where the protection of investment prevails over other competing policy objectives. The emerging trend towards incorporation of general exceptions in IIAs can therefore be seen as evidence of their gradual recalibration into (bilateral) instruments of economic governance where safeguarding the security of private investment is no longer an absolute and overarching goal of the regime but rather one of its multiple and competing objectives.

The shift towards more flexibility through express treaty derogations, however, has not occurred uniformly across the entire network of IIAs. In contrast with the first generation IIAs that are characterized by a considerable degree of homogeneity so far as the absence of exceptions is concerned, the more recent IIAs exhibit considerable variation in terms of the presence, scope and wording of exceptions contained therein. For the purposes of this paper, the existing landscape of IIAs can be classified into three principal categories. The first category consists of a relatively small number of IIAs that have incorporated a GATT-like comprehensive exception clause.[39] Arguably, this category represents the most progressive and balanced approach to drafting IIAs.

---

[38] KJ Vandevelede, *Bilateral Investment Treaties: History, Policy, and Interpretation* (OUP 2010) 179.

[39] See art 10(1) of the Canada–Peru BIT and art 18 of the Jordan–Singapore BIT. General exceptions also feature in a number of Singapore FTAs with investment chapters, including the 2002 Singapore–Japan New Age Economic Partnership Agreement and the 2003 India–Singapore Comprehensive Economic Cooperation Agreement. For an overview, see A Newcombe, 'General Exceptions in International Investment Agreements' in M-C Cordonier Segger, MW Gehring, A Newcombe (eds), *Sustainable Development in World Investment Law* (Kluwer Law International, 2011) 355.

The second category is exemplified by the recent UK Model BIT which has embraced the idea of regulatory flexibility but in a limited form. In contrast with the earlier UK BITs which contained a fairly limited exception clause dealing with membership in regional economic integration organisations and international agreements on taxation, the new UK model goes a step further and precludes the application of the national treatment and MFN obligations to 'measures which are necessary to protect national security, public security or public order.'[40] The extent to which the incorporation of this type of security exception in IIAs would create regulatory flexibility, in particular by enabling States to act in such areas as the protection of the environment, public health, and sustainable development, remains questionable for a number of reasons.

First of all, the scope of the security exception in the UK model BIT is fairly narrow as it precludes the applicability of national treatment and MFN provisions only. The new German Model BIT has a similar structural problem: the only non-precluded measures that the draft mentions are 'measures that have to be taken for reasons of public security and order.'[41] This exception forms part of the national treatment and MFN clause and, due to its narrow remit, does not insulate the relevant category of governmental measures from the effect of other substantive obligations such as expropriation and fair and equitable treatment, and, in some cases, under the arbitrary and discriminatory measures clause.[42] The fact that claimant-investors can easily circumvent the security exception by invoking alternative standards of treatment in lieu of the national treatment and MFN provisions renders the public security and order exception clause in its current form almost entirely inadequate.

Secondly, compared with the essential security exception in the 2012 US model BIT, the UK version is not self-judging as it refers to 'measures *which are necessary to* …'. This formulation leaves it for arbitral tribunals to decide whether disputed measures were indeed necessary for the protection of security interests.[43] By contrast, the essential security exception in the US model offers a stronger means of protecting States' regulatory freedom as it refers to 'measures that *it* [the State party] *considers necessary* for the fulfilment of its

[40] For the full text, see Douglas (n 18).

[41] Art 3(2) of the German Model BIT <http://www.italaw.com/sites/default/files/archive/ita1025.pdf>.

[42] For a discussion of the interchangeable use of investment treaty standards, see M Sattorova, 'Investment Treaty Breach as Internationally Proscribed Conduct: Shifting Scope, Evolving Objectives, Recalibrated Remedies?' (2012) 4(2) *Trade L & Dev* 315, 347.

[43] On the requirement of necessity and its interpretation in arbitral practice see, among others, a comprehensive account by W Burke-White and A von Staden, 'Investment Protection in Extraordinary Times: The Interpretation and Application of Non-precluded Measures Provisions in Bilateral Investment Treaties' (2008) 48 *Va J Intl L* 307.

obligations with respect to the maintenance or restoration of international peace or security, or the protection of its own essential security interests.'[44] This language enables the Host States to decide on the necessity of security measures, and places such measures by and large outside the purview of arbitral tribunals. The German model features a similar structural issue as its non-precluded measures clause refers to 'measures that *have to be taken*' to safeguard public security and public order. Whilst acknowledging the need to insulate a certain category of governmental decision-making from the effect of investment protection guarantees, this drafting model still constrains regulatory freedom of host states by subjecting their decisions to arbitral review and thus placing control over politically and economically vital matters of public interest in the hands of arbitral tribunals.

Another disadvantage of the UK model IIA is that it limits the scope of the exceptions clause to measures aimed at the protection of public security and order. Compared with comprehensive general exceptions provisions which expressly list a variety of policy objectives, ranging from the preservation of exhaustible resources to the protection of human, animal, and plant life or health, the 'public security and order' clause has a significantly narrower remit. Similarly narrow language features in some of the Indian IIAs which, in addition to being not self-judging, confine the scope of the exceptions clause to situations where essential security interests or circumstances of *extreme emergency* are at stake.[45]

Of course, while the meaning of the terms 'public security' and 'public order' remains imprecise (and is often left to be interpreted by adjudicators), it is in principle possible to construe them flexibly to accommodate a variety of governmental policies. It has been rightly observed that the notion of national security or a State's essential security interests may not remain constant over time.[46] At the time they were first incorporated in the early international commerce and trade agreements the security exceptions may have been conceived with the aim to address 'the immediate political-military conditions that a State deems important for its position in the world'.[47] It is beyond doubt, however, that even a narrow concept of security may change

[44] Above (n 36).

[45] The relevant provision states that 'Notwithstanding paragraph (1) of this Article nothing in this Agreement precludes the host Contracting Party from taking action for the protection of its essential security interests or in circumstances of extreme emergency in accordance with its laws normally and reasonably applied on a non discriminatory basis' (Art 12 of the India–Latvia BIT). See P Ranjan, 'NonPrecluded Measures in Indian International Investment Agreements and India's Regulatory Power as a Host Nation' (2012) 2 *Asian Journal of International Law* 21, 33.

[46] See WJ Moon, 'Essential Security Interests in International Investment Agreements' (2012) 15 *J Int Economic Law* 481, 497.

[47] MJ Hahn, 'Vital Interests and the Law of GATT: An Analysis of GATT's Security Exception' (1991) 12 *Michigan Journal of International Law* 558, 580; also Moon, Ibid.

in keeping with the evolutionary processes that have transformed the entire landscape of international law. The FET standard provides a fitting example of such evolution in the interpretation of core investment protection standards. Many panels have agreed that the threshold of illegality that needs to be shown in order to establish a breach of the FET standard is presently lower than that which was set out in the *Neer* case.[48] The notions of acceptable State behaviour have changed to accommodate higher standards: for an investment treaty breach to be established it is no longer necessary that disputed governmental conduct be egregious and outrageous in its character, and in some cases IIA provisions have been construed as protecting investors against State conduct that displays 'a relatively lower degree of inappropriateness' in comparison with the higher threshold required in establishing a violation of customary international law.[49] When viewed in light of the evolutionary changes in the scope and meaning of investment protection standards, the concept of national security too cannot remain static. 'National' and 'public' security can no longer be confined to political-military and even economic emergency concerns but should arguably also be extended to concerns traditionally falling under the rubrics of 'environment protection' and 'sustainable development'—including the mitigation of climate change and preservation of exhaustible natural resources.[50] The fact that the UN Security Council has recently acknowledged that climate change poses a threat to global security testifies to the changing perceptions of 'security'.[51] Still, notwithstanding the

[48] *LFH Neer v United Mexican States* (1926) AJIL 555 is well known as an early customary international law authority for a high threshold that ought to be satisfied before a breach of the international minimum standard could be established. A number of tribunals, including *Mondev International Ltd v United States*, Award of 11 Oct 2002 (ICSID Case No ARB(AF)/99/2) (2003) 42 ILM 85, para 116, have held that the content of the minimum standard has since evolved and no longer requires showing outrageousness and other extreme forms of illegality in the state behaviour as a pre-condition for establishing a breach of FET.

[49] *Saluka Investments BV v Czech Republic*, Partial Award, 17 March 2006, PCA–UNCITRAL Arbitration Rules, para 293.

[50] See P Muchlinski, 'Balancing Investor Rights and the Right to Regulate. The Issue of National Security' in KP Sauvant (ed) *Yearbook on International Investment Law & Policy 2008–2009* (OUP, 2009) noting that 'depending on how one defines "national security" it could conceivably include any governmental action.'

[51] 'Make No Mistake', Says Secretary-General, 'Climate Change Not Only Exacerbates Threats to Peace and Security, It Is a Threat to International Peace and Security', UN Security Council SC/10332, available at <http://www.un.org/News/Press/docs/2011/sc10332.doc.htm>. The increasing importance of links between renewable energy, energy security and food security can also be garnered from the Report of the Secretary-General at the United Nations General Assembly 'Promotion of new and renewable sources of energy', 17 August 2012 UN Doc A/67/318. It is also noteworthy that already in 1997 the ICJ considered the related notion of ecological damages to fall within the rubric of an essential interest of all states. See *Case concerning the Gabčíkovo-Nagymaros Project* (Hungary v. Slovakia) (1997) ICJ Reports 7, at <http://www.icj-cij.org/docket/files/92/7375.pdf>, para 53.

possibilities of a broad and liberal construction, there are limits beyond which the terms 'public security' and 'public order' cannot be plausibly stretched. These outer limits define the extent to which public security and order exceptions could be utilized in reconciling investment protection with the need for regulatory flexibility.

In a stark contrast with treaties that embrace either comprehensive or more limited forms of exceptions, a significant portion of the more than 3,000 IIAs currently in force, including many new and revised models and recently signed IIAs, contain no general exceptions whatsoever. Some commentators have suggested that general exceptions 'appear in all or most of the BITs concluded by a number of states of importance to international investment flows'.[52] This is not entirely accurate. Long known as strong advocates of IIAs, the Netherlands and Switzerland have a significant share in the existing treaty stock and their treaties contain no exceptions.[53] Moreover, even though a number of German IIAs provide for exceptions, the latter are enshrined in the protocols[54] rather than forming part of the main treaty text. This—along with the fact that general exceptions are absent in the most recent German model—seems to suggest that the right to derogate on specified policy grounds is not considered as a benefit Germany is prepared to offer on a unilateral basis to all of its treaty partners.

The absence of express derogations—even in the limited form—in a large number of IIAs, including recently revised models, is striking. The practice of investment arbitration has amply demonstrated both the bite of investment treaty standards and the importance of providing Host States with the possibilities to derogate from their investment protection commitments in pursuit of other policy objectives. While some States have responded to these concerns by creating a new breed of IIAs, other States continue to steadfastly adhere to the minimalist texts and maximalist focus on investment protection as reflected in the drafting of the first generation IIAs. It is also noteworthy that the IIAs of these States do not contain interpretive references to public goods besides investment protection, such as the importance of the protection of environment and public health, socially responsible investment, and sustainable development. Neither do these treaties include a right-to-regulate provision such as that enshrined in some of the recent Canadian IIAs. Does this variance in drafting approaches to exceptions signify an emergence of a new ideological divide or a mere inertia in adapting treaties to changing realities of the global investment environment? What lies beneath an increasingly fragmented investment treaty practice? What theoretical and practical implications

52 Burke-White & Von Staden (n 43) 318.

53 The UNCTAD BITs database suggests that Switzerland, for example, is among the states with the highest number of BITs.

54 Burke-White & Von Staden (n 43) 326.

is this new form of regionalism likely to have for the functioning and future development of the investment treaty regime?

4. VARIABLE GEOMETRY AND REGIONALISM IN INVESTMENT TREATY PRACTICE: THEORETICAL UNDERPINNINGS AND POLICY IMPLICATIONS

4.1. Regulatory squeeze

The variance in investment treaty practice and the deliberate choice by states not to include any exceptions clauses (or to include such clauses in a very limited form) in some of their new and revised treaties can be explained by reference to the argument which postulates that general exceptions do not enhance regulatory flexibility, especially where general exceptions are framed as a closed list of legitimate policy objectives in pursuit of which states can derogate from their investment protection commitments. The closed list of derogations may have an unintended effect of further squeezing policy space available to States.[55] It has been argued, for instance, that the absence of a GATT-like general exceptions clause in IIAs could in fact be more conducive to a greater regulatory flexibility as tribunals, undeterred by textual formulations in IIAs, might be encouraged to adopt a more deferential approach and allow States to derogate in connection with a potentially unlimited range of policy objectives.[56] Some authors have also argued that arbitral interpretation of policy justifications under IIAs which contain no general exception clauses has been less restrictive than that adopted by WTO panels whose discretion was bound by the narrow frame of reference of GATT Article XX.[57]

Recent arbitral practice, however, casts doubt on whether the absence of derogations in IIAs would encourage tribunals to adopt a more deferential stance in setting the boundaries of regulatory space within which States can operate without exposing their measures to international scrutiny and incurring monetary liability. For instance, in *Continental Casualty v Argentina*, the availability of an express treaty derogation for measures aimed at the maintenance of public order and the protection of essential security interests enabled Argentina to defend its policy decisions adopted in response to the economic

---

[55] Ibid 358.

[56] Ibid.

[57] For instance, while derogations from GATT commitments are usually valid only if *necessary* for the achievement of a certain policy goal, a prima facie breach of investment treaty norm can be justified if shown to be reasonably and rationally *related to* the policy objective at issue. See the awards in *Pope & Talbot* and *GAMI* (n 23); also N DiMascio & J Pauwelyn, 'Non-discrimination in Trade and Investment Treaties: World Apart or Two Sides of the Same Coin' (2008) 102 *AJIL* 48, 77; A Newcombe and L Paradell, *Law and Practice of Investment Treaties: Standards of Treatment* (Kluwer Law International, 2009) 367.

and political crisis in 2001–2002.[58] By contrast, in *Total v Argentina* the applicable BIT did not offer such possibility for derogation, and the respondent government was limited in the range of defences it could invoke in justification of the disputed policy measures.[59] A string of similar claims against Argentina vividly demonstrated the difficulties with relying on the customary international law defence of necessity in an attempt to avoid international responsibility. In matters as important as the exemption of host states from responsibility for economic consequences of national policy measures, the absence of express derogations in the text of an IIA is unlikely to result in tribunals showing more deference to national policy-makers. In fact, a comparative analysis of *Continental Casualty* and *Total* suggests that tribunals are more likely to give weight to policy justifications where the applicable treaty expressly allows them to do so.

The silence of treaties as to policy objectives which may legitimately be invoked in justification of investment treaty breaches—and the lack of regulatory flexibility provisions in general—also may become increasingly problematic as other States begin to include exceptions clauses in their IIAs. The fact that some of the more recent treaties continue to provide no exceptions clause—after a number of IIAs and model treaties have expressly embraced them—might be construed as implicit evidence that the State Parties wish to treat their investment protection commitments as non-derogable. Once exceptions clauses have been included in a number of new and revised IIAs, the absence of such provisions in IIAs that have been signed or drafted during the same period can and is likely to be seen as a deliberate policy choice. A comparative textual analysis of differences in the wording of treaty provisions among various treaties has already been used by arbitral tribunals in clarifying the scope of the FET standard.[60] If a similar approach is adopted in interpreting the absence of justifications in some of the recently revised and new IIAs—and this possibility should not be discounted—the treaties containing no express derogations would entail a greater squeezing effect on national policy-making in the public interest.

---

[58] *Continental Casualty Company v Argentina*, Award, 5 September 2008 (ICSID Case No ARB/03/9) paras 231–3.

[59] Argentina's plea of necessity under customary international law as well as its attempt to invoke art 5 (3) of the Argentine–France BIT were unsuccessful (*Total S.A. v Argentine Republic*, Decision on Liability, 27 December 2010 (ICSID Case No. ARB/04/1) paras 224–230).

[60] For instance, the *Vivendi* tribunal declined to follow some of the previously decided cases and equate FET with the international minimum on the ground that the wording of the applicable treaty did not support such interpretation (*Compañía de Aguas del Aconquija SA and Vivendi Universal SA v Argentina,* Award, 20 August 2007 (ICSID Case No ARB/97/3) para 7.4.7). See also Newcombe and Paradell (n 57) 264 (supporting the view that the interpretation of a specific FET provision depends on the actual text of the treaty in question under principles of treaty interpretation).

4.2. Universalization of the lowest common denominator: a race to the bottom?

Another problematic consequence of the variable geometry and geography of investment treaty practice—is the hindering effect such variation may have upon efforts to embrace non-investment policy objectives in new treaties. To mention one possibility, investors may invoke MFN clauses and resort to corporate structuring and treaty shopping so as to benefit from IIAs that are more-investor friendly and correspondingly less accommodating of environmental protection, sustainable development and other policy objectives.[61] Such forum-shopping and treaty-shopping tactics will greatly detract from efficacy of the treaties that have taken a more progressive stance on reconciling investment protection guarantees with the pursuit of socially desirable policies. As observed earlier, the emergence of distinct centres of regulation-friendly treaty-making could be seen as a form of regionalism in investment treaty law. The fact that some States have moved away from the hitherto universally shared treaty models towards more tailor-made and policy-friendly IIAs could be seen as a means of contesting the old regime by allowing regional practice to take the lead.[62] The regionalism of North American IIAs lies not in their geography but in that they display what Koskenniemi referred to as 'a certain homogeneity based on a convergence of interests, values or political objectives'.[63] This regionalism may represent a first step forward by tackling a global problem to which no multilateral and universally shared solution has yet been offered[64]—such as environmental protection and the promotion of sustainable corporate practices—and can therefore be 'a source of inspiration and influence on the progressive development of international law.'[65] Yet the availability of MFN clauses and treaty shopping would detract from these efforts and hamper the reorientation of the old regime towards a more policy-friendly alternative.

---

[61] The discussion of the MFN clause has so far been framed predominantly in terms of the latter's capacity to entitle investors and investments to 'better' substantive standards from other treaties. However, in the context of new and more policy-friendly IIAs vis-à-vis the old generation IIAs, the availability of 'better' treatment equates to the availability of a regime where investment protection is prioritised at expense of the environment protection, national security and of policy intervention in the public interest.

[62] A-C Martineau, 'The Rhetoric of Fragmentation: Fear and Faith in International Law' (2009) 22 *LJIL* 1, 18.

[63] ILC Report on Fragmentation (n 19) 105.

[64] D Pulkowski, Theoretical Premises of 'Regionalism and the Unity of International Law' (2012) *ESIL Conference Paper Series*, Conference Paper N 16/2012, at 4; available at <http://papers.ssrn.com/sol3/papers.cfm?abstract_id=2193763>).

[65] A de Hoogh, 'Regionalism and the Unity of International Law From a Positivist Perspective' (2012) *ESIL Conference Paper Series*, Conference Paper No. 3/2012, at 3; available at <http://papers.ssrn.com/sol3/papers.cfm?abstract_id=2193745>.

It is interesting that MFN clauses as well as corporate structuring and treaty shopping have been considered to be part of a progressive multilateralization mechanism driven by 'the common interest of States in establishing uniform and universal rules for the protection of foreign investment.'[66] Recent developments, however, render this view less convincing. First, the variable geometry and geography of recent investment treaty practice shows that, beyond the basic consensus on the importance of protecting and promoting investment in facilitating economic growth, States differ in their perceptions of how private rights should be reconciled with the exercise by host governments of their regulatory powers in the wider public interest. The increasingly varied investment treaty landscape displays less commonality of interest between States than that which characterized the first generation of IIAs. Secondly, the emergent (though presently localized) trend towards the incorporation of regulatory flexibility provisions and in particular comprehensive exceptions clauses in some of the new generation IIAs can be viewed as a different form of multilateralization. It appears that multilateral instruments such as GATT have influenced the language of treaty exceptions and thus determined the way in which States have been redesigning their investment treaties. At the same time, despite its origins in the external multilateral legal regime, such influence on investment treaty law has been uneven and confined to a few regional 'reformist' treaty-makers. As noted earlier, only a small number of IIAs follow the GATT's approach to derogations. Ironically, the very devices of multilateralization—MFN provisions, corporate structuring, and treaty shopping—that were allegedly supposed to generate uniformity and facilitate the development of a truly multilateral investment treaty regime[67] are in fact likely to cause fragmentation through encouraging the use of the first generation IIAs by private claimants who prefer the unadulterated strength of protection under traditional treaties to the regulatory flexibility of the new models.

Furthermore, multilateralism arguably 'assumes the existence and legitimacy of interests of an international community beyond the interests of States.'[68] However, the interests of the international community are diverse and not confined to investment protection. It was this diversity of interests and concerns underpinning the contemporary investment environment—and the recognition of the role of national regulation in addressing and reconciling them—that precipitated a failure of the historical attempts to conclude a multilateral agreement on investment.[69] Multilateralization does facilitate overcoming the limits of bilateralism by enabling investors to resort to MFN

---

[66] Schill (n 1) 68.

[67] Ibid.

[68] Ibid, 362.

[69] See above n 28.

provisions and treaty shopping and thus making investment treaty protections universally available. Yet such exercise in private ordering is likely to result in a race to the bottom as far as regulatory flexibility and the creation of policy space for the pursuit of competing public interests are concerned. Until Canada and the US replace all of their IIAs with treaties drafted in accordance with their new (and more policy-friendly) models, investors would be encouraged to take advantage of the first generation treaties through recourse to MFN provisions and corporate structuring. This in turn would defeat the emerging bilateral regional efforts to rebalance investment protection with the pursuit of competing socio-economic policies.

4.3. *Variable geometry and entrenched inequalities of power: revisiting the hegemonic critique of IIAs*

The fact that some States have been reluctant to incorporate regulatory flexibility provisions, including comprehensive general exceptions, in their recent IIAs can be seen as a means of exporting certain normative values aimed at reinforcing power structures which underpin the formation and functioning of international investment law. IIAs have long been considered as instruments of hegemony—even 'prolonged imperialism'[70]—whereby developed States exercised their political and economic power over less developed treaty partners. Reciprocal on their face, IIAs were in fact binding only upon developing States, with investors from developed States acting as beneficiaries of extensive and internationally enforceable investment protection guarantees. Whilst acknowledging that power asymmetries played a considerable part at the time of creation of the investment treaty regime, critics of the hegemonic view have attempted to contest it by advancing two inter-related arguments. First, it has been argued that, although conceived with the purpose of imposing strict investment protection obligations upon developing States, IIAs have been increasingly relevant in ordering investor-State relations between developed States, with the latter becoming a frequent target of investor claims—a destiny that had traditionally been preserved for developing states only.[71] Second, by setting out uniform legal principles on investment protections, IIAs are arguably evolving into a multilateral order which takes away power from States—both developed and developing—and thus presents an alternative model to the hitherto imperial and hegemonic investment treaty law.[72]

As noted earlier, the variable geometry of IIAs and recent developments in the geographic origins and destinations of investment flows tend to detract

[70] Schill (n 1) 62.
[71] Ibid, 363–4.
[72] Ibid, 363.

from the strength of the traditional hegemonic critique of investment treaty law. While it is true that the relevance of the North–South divide has declined, it has been replaced by a different sort of ideological disagreement between States, including between developed countries that were previously known to be on the same side of the divide. The contemporary investment treaty landscape presents a rather complex picture. Even though IIAs can no longer be viewed as instruments of domination by the industrial North over the economically and politically less-developed South, hegemonic behaviour may still offer a conceptual framework for explaining the two-speed evolution of investment treaty practice. Some argue that the new generation of IIAs and their attempt to strike a balance between investment protection and national regulatory flexibility has its roots in the geopolitical shift that has occurred over the last decade or so, in particular the increase in south–south investments, the change in the direction of investment flows, and the use of investment arbitration against developed States.[73] This, in turn, points to what Krisch views as just another form of hegemonic strategy whereby dominant states withdraw from and reshape those international rules which they had earlier advocated but which ceased to serve their interests.[74] Indeed, is it a mere coincidence that developed States which had experience of defending their policy measures in investment arbitration, including Canada and the United States, have incorporated regulatory flexibility provisions in their recent IIAs, whilst other developed States—which have been spared such fate—continue to adhere to the older drafting models? Consider a hypothetical example of a treaty between the UK and the Isle of Growth (a fictitious capital-importing State) which follows traditional drafting patterns: sparsely worded, containing open-ended standards and providing no derogations which both Contracting State Parties might supposedly need to justify their public policy measures. Could the reluctance on the part of the UK to make room for pressing social policy demands in the treaty text be explained by the UK being predominantly focused on ensuring that the treaty safeguards the best protection of British investors in the Isle of Growth and, importantly, being fairly confident that the same treaty will hardly ever be deployed in challenging UK policies by investors from the Isle of Growth (thus rendering general exceptions unnecessary as far as the UK is concerned)? The fact that the US and Canada have embraced regulatory flexibility provisions in their treaties could be regarded not as much as a progressive acknowledgement of the importance of creating space for social policies but merely as a reflection of their dissatisfaction with the emerging reciprocity of IIAs and an attempt to redefine international rules that no longer serve their interests.

---

[73] Spears (n 10) 1043.

[74] N Krisch, 'International Law in Times of Hegemony: Unequal Power and the Shaping of the International Legal Order' (2005) 16 *EJIL* 369.

A recent political science analysis of IIA design by Allee and Peinhardt to a certain extent supports this hegemonic explanation of the variation in investment treaty practice:

> … the home government consistently pursues its universal design preferences, and the resulting treaty typically conforms to its wishes, provided that its relative bargaining power is sufficient. The starting point for this perspective is the long standing emphasis on power politics within international relations … BITs, and the terms within them, are particularly susceptible to global power dynamics. For one, most treaties are signed by pairs of states in which one state is to some degree more powerful than the other.[75]

After empirically testing various theoretical explanations of IIAs design, the study concludes that the so-called 'power and preferences of the home country' approach produces more convincing results in explaining the formation of treaties.

4.4. *Healthy pluralism or perilous exclusion? Variable geometry and the domestic political process*

Although hegemonic behaviour provides a potentially very useful and viable framework for analysing developments in the process of investment treaty-making, it does not quite explain the variation between IIA models of developed States, such as the US and Canada on the one hand and Germany, the UK, and Switzerland on the other. Of interest here is an observation that 'the preferences of *important domestic actors* within the country become integrated into the treaties.'[76] Among such influential actors the authors point to multinational corporations as well as right wing governments who are likely to insist on stronger investment protection clauses.[77] Indeed, the variable geometry and increasingly regionalised patterns of investment treaty-making prompt a question about the role domestic political processes, structures and actors play in shaping international investment rules. Might the abiding loyalty of some investment treaty champions to the traditional sparsely-worded treaty models be seen as evidence of their deliberate failure to adequately respond to the evolving nature of the global economic environment or rather their political incapacity and reluctance to do so? Could the fact that some countries continue to endorse the first generation drafting samples be explained by cost saving behaviour? The cost of the drafting,

---

[75] T Allee and C Peinhardt, 'Evaluating Three Explanations for the Design of Bilateral Investment Treaties' (2014) *World Politics* 47, 62.

[76] Ibid, 72.

[77] Ibid.

negotiation, and conclusion of new IIAs can be a significant factor not only for developing states but also for recession-stricken governments of developed countries. This consideration was put forward to explain similarity between the first generation IIAs of different states.[78] Today it can serve as an explanation for heterogeneity of new models.

Just as the variance between domestic political processes may account for the variable geometry (and geography) of investment treaty practice, the different role for civil society in shaping national treaty models could also be a relevant factor in explaining the emerging fragmentation patterns. In his analysis of the interactions between investment and non-investment obligations, Hirsch has suggested that the interplay between epistemic systems of international law such as the laws of human rights and investment protection could be regarded as an instance of 'social interaction' between discrete communities.[79] Likewise, Koskenniemi has defined fragmentation as the creation of distinct regimes 'that cater for special audiences with special interests and special ethos.'[80] However, the focus of existing scholarship on fragmentation has been largely confined to the perceived reluctance by investment tribunals to apply international norms on human rights. What about the 'socio-cultural distance'[81] between IIA negotiators and those involved in pushing environmental protection, human rights and other social policy agendas? The social interaction (or the lack of it) between discrete communities—or 'special audiences with special interests and ethos'—may be instrumental for advancing our understanding of the processes which lie beneath the increasingly fragmented and regionalised IIAs. Particularly important is the question of how and to what extent domestic political processes that lead to the formation of IIAs accommodate such interaction between different groups with competing agendas. Do Canada, the US and, interestingly, COMESA states provide the necessary platform for the interaction between discrete communities while other states fail to do so? Could it be a varying degree of 'the socio-cultural distance' between those in charge of investment treaty-making and other epistemic communities that leads to the different place allocated to non-investment policy values in IIAs? The related issue is whether the inclusion of regulatory flexibility provisions in new and revised IIAs reflects a progressive acknowledgement of the need to make room for social policy objectives or merely represents an effort to quell civil society opposition.

---

[78] Schill (n 1) 67.

[79] M Hirsch, 'The Interaction between International Investment Law and Human Rights Treaties: A Sociological Perspective' in T Broude & Y Shany (eds) *Multi-Sourced Equivalent Norms in International Law* (Hart Publishing 2011) 219.

[80] Martineau (n 62) 4, citing M Koskenniemi, 'International Law: Constitutionalism, Managerialism and the Ethos of Legal Education' (2007) 1 *European Journal of Legal Studies* 1, 2.

[81] Hirsch (n 79) 219.

Whatever the answer to this question, it seems that in some states the process of formation of investment treaty policies (including the drafting of model IIAs) allows for the non-investment interests and demands to be taken into account to a greater extent than in others.[82] Indeed, the variance in the degree to which regulatory flexibility has been embraced in recent IIAs could be reflecting different socio-cultural values of the involved communities.[83] The question is how social values in the US and Canada differ from those in the UK, and why investment treaties of the latter are characterised by a different set of values for internal and external use (ie in the domestic sphere where the importance of socially desirable regulation is acknowledged, and in the context of drafting IIAs where the UK seems to be reluctant to espouse the pursuit of the same set of policy values).

Closely linked to the place of civil society in the shaping of IIAs is the position of stakeholders other than investors and host states within the emerging architecture of the global investment regime. In their recent political science perspective on government behaviour in signing IIAs, Aisbett and Poulsen question 'whether more participants in the policy-making process reduce the aggregate impact of individual biases.'[84] Could the existing variation in the drafting of treaty models be explained by a more inclusive process in the US and Canada and a relatively limited involvement of stakeholders other than the business community and their lobby in the treaty-making process in the UK, the Netherlands, Germany and Switzerland? It has been observed that the '[i]nvestment treaty system exists somewhere between bilateralism and multilateralism, and between ad hoc and systemic dispute resolution. The risks of this in-between approach are inconsistency and confusion, while the rewards are diversity and dynamism.'[85] The question is whether variable geometry and the ensuing diversity represent 'healthy pluralism' or perilous division.[86] Would a greater involvement of other stakeholders—more participants[87]—in the drafting of model treaties militate against individual biases and lead to a more inclusive and pluralistic investment treaty policy? It appears that, at least at this stage, the diversity and dynamism which flow from the fragmented development of the investment treaty regime are likely to benefit only the party seeking the lowest common denominator in form of

---

[82] See NJ Calamita, 'The Making of Europe's International Investment Policy: Uncertain First Steps' (2012) 39 (3) *Legal Issues of Economic Integration*, 301.

[83] M Hirsch, 'The Sociology of International Investment Law' in Z Douglas, J Pauwelyn, and JE Viñuales (eds), *The Foundations of International Investment Law: Bringing Theory into Practice* (OUP, forthcoming 2014) <http://papers.ssrn.com/sol3/papers.cfm?abstract_id=2322328>.

[84] LN Skovgaard Poulsen and E Aisbett, 'When the Claims Hit: Bilateral Investment Treaties and Bounded Rational Learning' (2013) 65 *World Politics* 273, 303.

[85] Roberts (n 10) 14.

[86] Martineau (n 62) 2.

[87] Skovgaard Poulsen and Aisbett (n 84) 303.

the least policy-friendly IIA. Of all stakeholders, only investors appear to be in a position to gain from the existing variance in treaty practice as it enables them to challenge a broad array of governmental measures under the IIAs that provide little by way of regulatory flexibility safeguards. The divergence of bilateral approaches to regulatory flexibility can also be seen through the prism of a clash between stability and change. However, the multidimensional or cross-policy nature of investment policies means that maintaining stability of investment protection on existing terms, as embodied in the first generation IIAs, would translate into stagnation for other stakeholders—the beneficiaries of policies aimed at the protection of the environment, human rights, public health and safety, and labour rights.

5. CONCLUSION

Regulatory flexibility provisions are just one set of treaty terms that diversifies the new generation of IIAs. Another source of variation between existing models is the provisions relating to transparency of investor-state arbitration and the involvement of third parties in arbitral proceedings. The recent generation IIAs also differ in how they frame the fair and equitable treatment standard, with some models favouring the traditional open-ended formulation and others revealing a somewhat cautious attitude and qualifying its potentially far-reaching effect on regulatory freedom through a combination of drafting techniques. Although not universally endorsed, these additions to the traditionally minimalist treaty texts seem to suggest that there is a growing appreciation of the need to re-orientate investment treaty law towards the regime where investment protection is regarded not as a sole and overriding goal but one among multiple and competing policy objectives. What remains uncertain is whether the fragmentation—variable geometry and geography—that presently characterizes investment treaty practice would hinder this process and result in piecemeal and regionalized reforms. This paper has attempted to uncover some of the doctrinal and normative implications of the variable geometry of IIAs. It has questioned the relevance of the hegemonic critique of IIAs and concluded that, although the traditional North–South divide has receded into the past, it has been superseded by a different sort of ideological divide. The existing variance in investment treaty policies of the erstwhile advocates of strong investment protection can still be explained as an expression of a hegemonic behaviour, prompted in particular by the change in the direction of investment flows and the advent of investor claims against developed States. In its examination of consequences the variable geometry of IIAs may entail, the paper points to the threat of a race to the bottom, where the divergent stances taken by States with regard to regulatory flexibility would mean that investors could, through the use of MFN clauses and treaty shopping, cherry-pick and have resort to least public policy-friendly IIAs. This would enable them to take advantage of the strength of unadulterated investment protection guarantees and thus avoid the effect of the arguably progressive new models. The paper has also considered the role of domestic political process and in particular the role of civil society in the formation of the new generation IIAs, and questioned the extent to which variation in the design of IIAs of different States is rooted in the different role allocated to both civil society groups and other organizations that advance environmental protection, human rights, public health and sustainable development agendas.

Should the variable geometry and fragmented evolution of IIAs be seen as facilitating healthy pluralism and diversity? It has been argued that 'strong concepts of legal unity are not suitable for international law'[88] and that 'regional international law does not jeopardize legal unity by potentially setting out [different] prescriptions'.[89] However, a critical glance at the regulatory flexibility provisions (or their glaring absence) in new and revised IIAs tends to suggest that States which continue to favour the first generation drafting samples are in fact supporting outdated prescriptions that militate against the development of a uniform strategy for addressing the clash between investment protection and the pursuit of public policy objectives in the areas of growing global significance. The emergence of regional approaches to drafting IIAs also brings to the fore the importance of further research, including empirical and interdisciplinary studies, into the factors that shape national and regional investment policies and into the role of disparate epistemic communities in facilitating a more inclusive and pluralistic treaty-making process within the nation States and supranational structures.

[88] Pulkowski (n 64) 8.

[89] Ibid, 9.

Author Biographies

N Jansen Calamita

N Jansen Calamita is Senior Research Fellow and Director of the Investment Treaty Forum at the British Institute of International and Comparative Law. He is also a post-holder in the University of Birmingham School of Law, lecturing in public international law and international dispute settlement. He has previously been a member of the Faculty of Law at the University of Oxford and a visiting fellow of Mansfield College, Oxford and the University of Vienna.

Prior to entering academics, Mr Calamita served in the Office of the Legal Adviser in the US Department of State (International Claims and Investment Disputes Division) and as a member of the UNCITRAL Secretariat. He began his career in private practice in New York. He holds a *Juris Doctor summa cum laude* (Boston) and a Bachelor of Civil Law (Oxford). He continues to counsel governments on matters relating to the law of foreign investment and international dispute resolution issues.

Mr Calamita's research is in general public international law and the international law of investment. His recent publications include *The Principle of Proportionality and Textual Indeterminacy,* Yearbook of International Investment Law and Policy (forthcoming 2014); *Dispute Settlement Transparency in Europe's Evolving Investment Treaty Policy*, Journal of World Investment & Trade (forthcoming 2014); *International Commercial Arbitration in Iraq: Cultural and Legal Reform*, Journal of International Arbitration (forthcoming 2014).

Dr Mavluda Sattorova

Dr Mavluda Sattorova is a lecturer at the University of Liverpool School of Law where she teaches courses in international investment law, international energy law and law of the WTO. Prior to obtaining her PhD and LLM degrees from the University of Birmingham, she completed a PhD in civil law (Tashkent State Institute of Law) and taught at the National University of Uzbekistan. She has published papers on international investment law, its interplay with national agencies and policymaking, and the impact of international investment rules on government behaviour.

Hi-Taek Shin

Professor Hi-Taek Shin is a Professor of Law at Seoul National University School of Law and the director of the Center for International Economic and Business Law at Seoul National University. He teaches courses on the legal aspect of cross-border business transactions and international investment law. He is also serving as the Chairman of the Executive Committee of Seoul International Dispute Resolution Center launched in 2013. He is on the ICSID panel of arbitrators and sits regularly as an arbitrator in international arbitrations.

Prior to joining the law faculty at Seoul National University in 2007, Professor Shin was a partner at Kim & Chang, the leading Korean law firm, where he specialized in foreign direct investment, and resolution of disputes arising from cross-border investment projects.

He is an author of the Korean chapter in C Brown (Ed) *Commentaries on Selected Model Investment Treaties* and *UNCITRAL Arbitration Rules and the Investment Treaty Arbitration* (in Korean, 2013). He was a lecturer at Arbitration Academy in Paris. He received LLM and JSD degrees from Yale Law School and LLB and LLM degrees from Seoul National University.

Hamed El-Kady

Hamed El-Kady specializes in international investment policies and their implications on national development strategies and public policy concerns. He has been working with UNCTAD's Division on Investment and Enterprise (DIAE), in the IIA Section, since 2002.

Mr El-Kady authored several volumes of UNCTAD's Series on International Investment Policies for Development and regularly provides IIA-specific inputs into the *World Investment Report* and other UNCTAD publications (eg the IIA Issues Notes and the IIA Series on Issues in IIAs). Mr. El-Kady was also instrumental in the development of UNCTAD's Investment Policy Framework for Sustainable Development (IPFSD).

Mr El-Kady regularly provides technical assistance to Government officials and policy makers on issues related to IIAs and sustainable development. This includes advisory services on the revision of model BITs and investment chapters in FTAs, as well as ad-hoc advisory services and face-to-face training sessions. He has also coordinated the implementation of over 40 regional and national workshops, seminars and conferences on investment issues world-wide.

Mr El-Kady is a member of UNCTAD's Ad-Hoc Technical Task Force on the Arab States and has published various articles on international trade and investment policies and their development implications. He is a frequent panelist at international conferences on investment policies.

Steve Woolcock

Dr Stephen Woolcock is Associate Research Fellow at the Comparative Regional Integration Studies Programme of the United Nations University (UNU-CRIS) in Bruges. He is also Programme Director for the Masters in

International Political Economy at the London School of Economics, where he teaches international political economy, the political economy of international trade and economic diplomacy. He also heads the LSE's International Trade Policy Unit, which coordinates research on trade topics, runs training programmes for practitioners and organises seminars that bridge the gap between academic research on trade and policy. His previous posts included Senior Research Fellow at the Royal Institute of International Affairs (Chatham House) (1988–94) and Deputy Director for international affairs and the Confederation of British Industry (1985–1988). He has worked as consultant and advisor to a number of international organisations including the EU and national governments.

Myrna S Austria

Dr Myrna S Austria is Full Professor at the School of Economics, De La Salle University. She is also currently the Vice-Chancellor for Academics (VCA) of the same university since 2010. Prior to assuming the post of VCA, she was the Dean of the College of Business & Economics from 2006 to 2010 and the Director for the Center for Business and Economics Research and Development (CBERD) from 2003– to 2006, also of the same university.

She earned both her Masters in Development Economics and Doctor of Philosophy in Economics at The Australian National University in Canberra, Australia. Prior to joining the academe, she was a Senior Research Fellow at the Philippine Institute for Development Studies (the Philippine government think tank) and the Director of the Philippine APEC Study Center Network (PASCN) Secretariat. She was also involved in regional economic planning during her stint with the National Economic and Development Authority.

She has done consultancy work with international development agencies such as the World Bank (WB), Asian Development Bank (ADB), International Development Research Centre (IDRC-Canada), US Agency for International Development (USAID), APEC Business Advisory Council (ABAC), ASEAN Secretariat, Institute for South East Asian Studies (ISEAS).

Her areas of specialization include: trade, investment and industrial policy, development economics, international trade, competition policy, and regional economic integration. She has published journal articles, monographs, books and chapters in books along these areas.

Julien Chaisse

Julien Chaisse is Associate Professor at the Chinese University of Hong Kong (CUHK) and Director of the Center for Financial Regulation and Economic Development (CFRED). Dr Chaisse has authored a broad body of well-regarded and widely-cited articles on topics ranging from the rise of sovereign wealth funds, the regulation of investment in Asia to decision-making challenges facing the WTO. Dr Chaisse has published in the top refereed journals of international economic law, such as the *Journal of International Economic Law*, *Journal of World Trade*, *European Law Journal*, *European*, and *Journal of World Investment and Trade*, as well as in US international law journals (such as Boston, Pennsylvania and Hastings). Dr Chaisse is also the author and editor of books and book chapters published by leading publishers, such as *Oxford University Press*, *Cambridge University Press* and *Routledge*. In recognition of his outstanding scholarly achievements to date, in 2012 Dr Chaisse received the CUHK Research Excellence Award.

Dr Dirk Willem te Velde

Dr Dirk Willem te Velde is Head of Programme of the International Economic Development Group at the Overseas Development Institute which he joined in 2000. He is currently leading the European Report on Development 2014 on Financing for Development, is a research leader of the DFID-ESRC Growth Research Programme, and advised the UK House of Commons Inquiry into the future of development finance. He also led work on Aid for Trade, which culminated in an edited book, launched at the 4th Global Aid for Trade Review in July 2013. He has advised donor agencies (eg DFID, Sida, and the Dutch Ministry of Foreign Affairs), parliaments (eg EU, UK, Cambodia) and multilateral bodies (World Bank, European Commission, UNCTAD, UNDESA, UNIDO, ILO, WTO LDC group) on economic development. He has written and edited several books, more than 25 journal articles and 40 book chapters related to aid, trade, FDI and growth issues. This includes a book on *Regional Integration and Poverty*. He holds a PhD from Birkbeck College, University of London.

Themba Munalula

Themba Munalula is head of statistics at the Common Market for Eastern and Southern Africa (COMESA) which he joined in 2000. Among key statistical projects under his supervision has been the development of member country foreign direct investment (FDI) and foreign affiliates statistics programs. This program, undertaken jointly with UNCTAD, has sought to derive FDI indicators from enterprise surveys in Member countries. A key output from this work are indicators that provide the stock of FDI as well as FDI impact indicators. Another key output from this work has been the launch of the annual COMESA Investment Report Series for which Themba is the lead author. Past series of the investment reports have looked at the COMESA Common Investment Area, FDI and regional integration and the linkage between FDI and development of the small and medium enterprise clusters. He also advises COMESA Member States on other statistical subjects with a direct application to regional integration. He is a member of the International Statistical Institute's Global Capacity Building Committee. Themba holds an MSc from Warwick University in quantitative development economics.

George Burn

George Burn is a lawyer specialising in international arbitration, and he is recognised by the likes of *Chambers* and *Legal 500* as a leading international arbitration practitioner. His practice is evenly divided between commercial arbitration and Investor-State arbitration, and he works as adviser, advocate, counsel and arbitrator. He has appeared in cases in London, Paris, Geneva, Brussels, Stockholm, Dubai, Hong Kong, Washington DC, Singapore and Auckland, and under a variety of arbitral rules, including those of the ICC, LCIA, ICSID, SCC, UNCITRAL, CIArb, LMAA and GAFTA. George's team was "Highly Commended" in the 2013 Legal Business Awards, in recognition of being the first to win an award that confirms jurisdiction for an Investor to bring a claim directly against a State under the Investment Agreement of the Organisation of the Islamic Conference (*Al-Warraq v Republic of Indonesia*).

Chantal Ononaiwu

Dr Chantal Ononaiwu is the Trade Policy and Legal Specialist at the Office of Trade Negotiations, CARICOM Secretariat, where she develops and provides advice on textual proposals pertaining to CARICOM's external trade negotiations; advises on other matters pertaining to external and intra-regional trade; and represents CARICOM in cases before the Caribbean Court of Justice. She has served as CARICOM's Negotiator on Investment, Financial Services and Labour in its external trade negotiations.

Dr Ononaiwu is a lecturer in Public International Trade Law on the MSc in International Trade Policy at the University of the West Indies, Cave Hill, and has lectured Public International Law at the University. Prior to joining the CARICOM Secretariat, she was the Director, Value Proposition Development at Invest Barbados and worked as counsel in the Attorney General's Chambers in Jamaica.

She has published and presented papers in the areas of international trade law, investment law and public international law. Dr Ononaiwu is a Rhodes Scholar and holds a DPhil in Law from the University of Oxford, an LLM from the University of Cambridge and an LLB from the University of the West Indies.

José Manuel Garcia Represa

José Manuel Garcia Represa plays a central role in Dechert's leading Latin American practice. He has been and continues to be a key player, for example, in more than 13 investment treaty arbitrations arising out of Latin

America over the last years, representing both States and investors in a variety of industries, including oil and gas (upstream and midstream), electricity, mining, telecommunications, and civil engineering. On the commercial side, José Manuel is active in cases involving multiple jurisdictions, languages and procedural rules. José Manuel also sits as arbitrator.

He is admitted to the Madrid, Paris and New York Bars, and has lectured on international arbitration worldwide.

Mr García Represa holds law degrees from the Complutense University of Madrid (2000), the Sorbonne University of Paris I (2000, DESS, International Commercial Law, 2001, La Caixa scholar), and Columbia University (LLM, 2003, Fulbright scholar, Parker School Certificate in International Law, 2003).

Mr García Represa is a member of the ICC Institute of World Business Law, the Advisory Board of the Institute for Transnational Arbitration (ITA), the *Club Español del Arbitraje* (CEA), the International Arbitration Institute (IAI—Paris) and the *Asociación Latinoamericana de Arbitraje* (ALARB).

James Mendenhall

James Mendenhall is a partner in the International Trade and Dispute Resolution group in the law firm of Sidley Austin LLP in Washington, D.C., concentrating in international trade policy and litigation, and international arbitration.

From 2005 to January 2007, Mr Mendenhall served as the General Counsel of the Office of the United States Trade Representative (USTR). From 2003 to 2005, Mr Mendenhall served as the Assistant United States Trade Representative (AUSTR) for Services, Investment and Intellectual Property. From 2001–2003, Mr Mendenhall served as USTR's Deputy General Counsel. In that capacity, he handled numerous trade litigation, negotiation and legislative matters.

Prior to joining the US Government, Mr Mendenhall spent nine years in private practice, concentrating in the areas of trade remedies litigation, international arbitration, trade policy and litigation before World Trade Organization panels.